Freedom's Law

FREEDOM'S LAW

THE MORAL READING OF THE AMERICAN CONSTITUTION

Ronald Dworkin

HARVARD UNIVERSITY PRESS
Cambridge, Massachusetts

Library of Congress Cataloging-in-Publication Data

Dworkin, R. M.
Freedom's law : the moral reading of the American Constitution / Ronald Dworkin.
p.   cm.
Includes bibliographical references and index.
ISBN 0-674-31927-3 (cloth)
ISBN 0-674-31928-1 (pbk.)
1. United States—Constitutional law—Moral and ethical aspects.
I. Title.
KF4552.D96   1996
342.73'02—dc20
[347.3022]
95-42193
CIP

For Robert Silvers

Contents

Freedom's Law

Introduction: The Moral Reading and the Majoritarian Premise

Constitutional Confusion

The various chapters of this book were first published separately, over a period of several years, and they discuss a variety of constitutional issues. Most of them were written during bitter constitutional arguments. The book discusses, in fact, almost all of the great constitutional issues of the last two decades, including abortion, affirmative action, pornography, race, homosexuality, euthanasia, and free speech. Some chapters are about particular decisions of the United States Supreme Court, including famous ones like *Roe v. Wade,* in which the Court first recognized a right to abortion, the *Cruzan* case, in which the Court had to consider whether people have a constitutional right to choose death in some circumstances, and *New York Times v. Sullivan,* in which the Court dramatically changed what free speech means in America. Some chapters include more general material. Chapter 3, for example, evaluates the familiar charge that many of the constitutional "rights" that the Supreme Court has identified in recent decades, including the right to abortion, are not actually "enumerated" in the Constitution at all, but were invented by the justices themselves.

The book as a whole has a larger and more general aim. It illustrates a particular way of reading and enforcing a political constitution, which I call the *moral* reading. Most contemporary constitutions declare individual rights against the government in very broad and abstract language, like the First Amendment of the United States Constitution, which provides that Congress shall make no law abridging "the freedom of speech." The moral reading proposes that we all—judges, lawyers, citizens—interpret and apply these abstract clauses on the understanding that they invoke moral principles about political decency and justice. The First Amendment, for example, recognizes a moral principle—that it is wrong for government to censor or control what individual citizens say or publish—and incorporates it into American law. So when some novel or controversial constitutional issue arises—about whether, for instance, the First Amendment permits laws against pornography—people who form an opinion must decide how an abstract moral principle is best understood. They must decide whether the true ground of the moral principle that condemns censorship, in the form in which this principle has been incorporated into American law, extends to the case of pornography.

The moral reading therefore brings political morality into the heart of constitutional law.[1] But political morality is inherently uncertain and controversial, so any system of government that makes such principles part of its law must decide whose interpretation and understanding will be authoritative. In the American system judges—ultimately the justices of the Supreme Court—now have that authority, and the moral reading of the Constitution is therefore said by its critics to give judges absolute power to impose their own moral convictions on the public. I shall shortly try to explain why that crude charge is mistaken. I should make plain first, however, that there is nothing revolutionary about the moral reading in practice. So far as American lawyers and judges follow any coherent strategy of interpreting the Constitution at all, they already use the moral reading, as I hope this book will make plain.

That explains why both scholars and journalists find it reasonably easy to classify judges as "liberal" or "conservative": the best explanation of the differing patterns of their decisions lies in their different understandings of central moral values embedded in the Constitution's text. Judges whose political convictions are conservative will naturally interpret abstract constitutional principles in a conservative way, as they did in the early years of this century, when they wrongly supposed that certain rights over property and contract are fundamental to freedom. Judges whose convictions are more liberal will naturally interpret those principles in a liberal way, as they did in the halcyon days of the Warren Court. The moral reading is not, in itself, either a liberal or a conservative charter or strategy. It is true that in recent decades liberal judges have ruled more statutes or executive orders unconstitutional than conservative judges have. But that is because conservative political principles for the most part either favored or did not strongly condemn the measures that could reasonably be challenged on constitutional grounds in those decades. There have been exceptions to that generalization. Conservatives strongly disapprove, on moral grounds, the affirmative action programs described in Chapter 6, which give certain advantages to minority applicants for universities or jobs, and conservative justices have not hesitated to follow their understanding of what the moral reading required in such cases.[2] That reading helps us to identify and explain not only these large-scale patterns, moreover, but also more fine-grained differences in constitutional interpretation that cut across the conventional liberal-conservative divide. Conservative judges who particularly value freedom of speech, or think it particularly important to democracy, are more likely than other conservatives to extend the First Amendment's protection to acts of political protest, even for causes that they despise, as the Supreme Court's decision protecting flag-burners shows.[3]

So, to repeat, the moral reading is not revolutionary in practice. Lawyers and judges, in their day-to-day work, instinctively treat the Constitution as expressing abstract moral requirements that can only be applied to concrete cases through fresh moral judgments. As I shall argue later in this Introduction, they have no real option but to do so. But it would indeed be revolutionary for a judge openly to recognize the moral reading, or to admit that it is his or her strategy of constitutional interpretation, and even scholars and judges who come close to recognizing it shrink back, and try to find other, usually metaphorical, descriptions of their own practice. There is therefore a striking mismatch between the role the moral reading actually plays in American constitutional life and its reputation. It has inspired all the greatest constitutional decisions of the Supreme Court, and also some of the worst. But it is almost never acknowledged as influential even by constitutional experts, and it is almost never openly endorsed even by judges whose arguments are incomprehensible on any other understanding of their responsibilities. On the contrary, the moral reading is often dismissed as an "extreme" view that no really sensible constitutional scholar would entertain. It is patent that judges' own views about political morality influence their constitutional decisions, and though they might easily explain that influence by insisting that the Constitution demands a moral reading, they never do. Instead, against all evidence, they deny the influence and try to explain their decisions in other—embarrassingly unsatisfactory—ways. They say they are just giving effect to obscure historical "intentions," for example, or just expressing an overall but unexplained constitutional "structure" that is supposedly explicable in nonmoral terms.

This mismatch between role and reputation is easily explained. The moral reading is so thoroughly embedded in constitutional practice, and is so much more attractive, on both legal and political grounds, than the only coherent alternatives that it cannot readily be abandoned, particularly when important constitutional issues are in play. But the moral reading nevertheless seems intellectually and politically discreditable. It seems to erode the crucial distinction between law and morality by making law only a matter of which moral principles happen to appeal to the judges of a particular era. It seems grotesquely to constrict the moral sovereignty of the people themselves—to take out of their hands, and remit to a professional elite, exactly the great and defining issues of political morality that the people have the right and the responsibility to decide for themselves.

That is the source of the paradoxical contrast between mainstream constitutional practice in the United States, which relies heavily on the moral reading of the Constitution, and mainstream constitutional theory, which wholly rejects that reading. The confusion has had serious political costs. Conservative politicians try to convince the public that the great constitutional cases turn not on deep issues of political principle, which they do, but on the simpler question of whether judges should change the Constitution by fiat or leave it alone.[4] For a time this view of the constitutional argument was apparently accepted even by some liberals. They called the Constitution a "living" document and said that it must be "brought up to date" to match new circumstances and sensibilities. They said they took an "active" approach to the Constitution, which seemed to suggest reform, and they accepted John Ely's characterization of their position as a "noninterpretive" one, which seemed to suggest inventing a new document rather than interpreting the old one.[5] In fact, as we shall see, this account of the argument was never accurate. The theoretical debate was never about whether judges should interpret the Constitution or change it—almost no one really thought the latter—but rather about how it should be interpreted. But conservative politicians exploited the simpler description, and they were not effectively answered.

The confusion engulfs the politicians as well, however. They promise to appoint and confirm judges who will respect the proper limits of their authority and leave the Constitution alone, but since this misrepresents the choices judges actually face, the politicians are often disappointed. When Dwight Eisenhower, who denounced what he called judicial activism, retired from office in 1961, he told a reporter that he had made only two big mistakes as President—and that they were both on the Supreme Court. He meant Chief Justice Earl Warren, who had been a Republican politician when Eisenhower appointed him to head the Supreme Court, but who then presided over one of the most "activist" periods in the Court's history, and Justice William Brennan, another politician who had been a state court judge when Eisenhower appointed him, and who became one of the most liberal and explicit practitioners of the moral reading of the Constitution in modern times.

Presidents Ronald Reagan and George Bush were both profound in their outrage at the Supreme Court's "usurpation" of the people's privileges. They said they were determined to appoint judges who would respect rather than defy the people's will. In particular, they (and the platform on which they ran for the presidency) denounced the Court's 1973 *Roe v. Wade* decision protecting abortion rights, and promised that their appointees would reverse it. But (as Chapter 4 explains) when the opportunity to do so came, three of the justices Reagan and Bush had appointed between them voted, surprisingly, not only to retain that decision in force, but to provide a new legal basis for it that more evidently adopted and relied on a moral reading of the Constitution. The expectations of politicians who appoint judges are often defeated in that way, because the politicians fail to appreciate how thoroughly the moral reading, which they say they deplore, is actually embedded in constitutional practice. Its role remains hidden when a judge's own convictions support the legislation whose constitutionality is in doubt—when a justice thinks it morally permissible for the majority to criminalize abortion, for example. But the ubiquity of the moral reading becomes evident when some judge's convictions of principle—identified, tested, and perhaps altered by experience and argument—bend in an opposite direction, because then enforcing the Constitution must mean, for that judge, telling the majority that it cannot have what it wants.

Senate hearings considering Supreme Court nominations tend toward the same confusion. These events are now thoroughly researched and widely reported by the media, and they are often televised. They offer a

superb opportunity for the public to participate in the constitutional process. But the mismatch between actual practice and conventional theory
cheats the occasion of much of its potential value. (The hearings provoked
by President Bush's nomination of Judge Clarence Thomas to the Supreme
Court, discussed in Chapter 15, are a clear example.) Nominees and
legislators all pretend that hard constitutional cases can be decided in a
morally neutral way, by just keeping faith with the "text" of the document, so that it would be inappropriate to ask the nominee any questions
about his or her own political morality. (It is ironic that Justice Thomas, in
the years before his nomination, gave more explicit support to the moral
reading than almost any other well-known constitutional lawyer has; he
insisted, as Chapter 15 explains, that conservatives should embrace that
interpretive strategy and harness it to a conservative morality.) Any endorsement of the moral reading—any sign of weakness for the view that
constitutional clauses are moral principles that must be applied through
the exercise of moral judgment—would be suicidal for the nominee and
embarrassing for his questioners. In recent years, only the hearings that
culminated in the defeat of Robert Bork, discussed in Part III, seriously
explored issues of constitutional principle, and they did so only because
Judge Bork's opinions about constitutional law were so obviously the
product of a radical political morality that his convictions could not be
ignored. In the confirmation proceedings of now Justices Anthony Kennedy, David Souter, Thomas, Ruth Bader Ginsburg, and Stephen Breyer,
however, the old fiction was once again given shameful pride of place.

The most serious result of this confusion, however, lies in the American
public's misunderstanding of the true character and importance of its
constitutional system. As I have argued elsewhere, the American ideal of
government not only under law but under principle as well is the most
important contribution our history has given to political theory. Other
nations and cultures realize this, and the American ideal has increasingly
and self-consciously been adopted and imitated elsewhere. But we cannot
acknowledge our own contribution, or take the pride in it, or care of it,
that we should.

That judgment will appear extravagant, even perverse, to many lawyers
and political scientists. They regard enthusiasm for the moral reading,
within a political structure that gives final interpretive authority to judges,
as elitist, antipopulist, antirepublican and antidemocratic. That view rests,
as we shall see, on a popular but unexamined assumption about the
connection between democracy and majority will, an assumption that

American history has in fact consistently rejected. When we understand democracy better, we see that the moral reading of a political constitution is not antidemocratic but, on the contrary, is practically indispensable to democracy. I do not mean that there is no democracy unless judges have the power to set aside what a majority thinks is right and just. Many institutional arrangements are compatible with the moral reading, including some that do not give judges the power they have in the American structure. But none of these varied arrangements is in principle more democratic than others. Democracy does not insist on judges having the last word, but it does not insist that they must not have it. I am already too far ahead of my argument, however. I must say more about what the moral reading is before I can return to the question of why it has been so seriously misunderstood.

The Moral Reading

The clauses of the American Constitution that protect individuals and minorities from government are found mainly in the so-called Bill of Rights—the first several amendments to the document—and the further amendments added after the Civil War. (I shall sometimes use the phrase "Bill of Rights," inaccurately, to refer to all the provisions of the Constitution that establish individual rights, including the Fourteenth Amendment's protection of citizens' privileges and immunities and its guarantee of due process and equal protection of the laws.) Many of these clauses are drafted in exceedingly abstract moral language. The First Amendment refers to the "right" of free speech, for example, the Fifth Amendment to the process that is "due" to citizens, and the Fourteenth to protection that is "equal." According to the moral reading, these clauses must be understood in the way their language most naturally suggests: they refer to abstract moral principles and incorporate these by reference, as limits on government's power.

There is of course room for disagreement about the right way to restate these abstract moral principles, so as to make their force clearer for us, and to help us to apply them to more concrete political controversies. I favor a particular way of stating the constitutional principles at the most general possible level, and I try to defend that way of conceiving them throughout the book. I believe that the principles set out in the Bill of Rights, taken together, commit the United States to the following political and legal ideals: government must treat all those subject to its dominion as having equal moral and political status; it must attempt, in good faith, to treat them all with equal concern; and it must respect whatever individual freedoms are indispensable to those ends, including but not limited to the freedoms more specifically designated in the document, such as the freedoms of speech and religion. Other lawyers and scholars who also endorse the moral reading might well formulate the constitutional principles, even at a very general level, differently and less expansively than I just have however, and though this introductory chapter is meant to explain and defend the moral reading, not my own interpretations under it, I should say something about how the choice among competing formulations should be made.

Of course the moral reading is not appropriate to everything a constitution contains. The American Constitution includes a great many clauses that are neither particularly abstract nor drafted in the language of moral principle. Article II specifies, for example, that the President must be at least thirty-five years old, and the Third Amendment insists that government may not quarter soldiers in citizens' houses in peacetime. The latter may have been inspired by a moral principle: those who wrote and enacted it might have been anxious to give effect to some principle protecting citizens' rights to privacy, for example. But the Third Amendment is not itself a moral principle: its *content* is not a general principle of privacy. So the first challenge to my own interpretation of the abstract clauses might be put this way. What argument or evidence do I have that the equal protection clause of the Fourteenth Amendment (for example), which declares that no state may deny any person equal protection of the laws, has a moral principle as *its* content though the Third Amendment does not?

This is a question of interpretation or, if you prefer, translation. We must try to find language of our own that best captures, in terms we find clear, the content of what the "framers" intended it to say. (Constitutional scholars use the word "framers" to describe, somewhat ambiguously, the various people who drafted and enacted a constitutional provision.) History is crucial to that project, because we must know something about the circumstances in which a person spoke to have any good idea of what he meant to say in speaking as he did. We find nothing in history, however, to cause us any doubt about what the framers of the Third Amendment meant to say. Given the words they used, we cannot sensibly interpret them as laying down any moral principle at all, even if we believe they were inspired by one. They said what the words they used would normally be used to say: not that privacy must be protected, but that soldiers must not be quartered in houses in peacetime. The same process of reasoning—about what the framers presumably intended to say when they used the words they did—yields an opposite conclusion about the framers of the equal protection clause, however. Most of them no doubt had fairly clear expectations about what legal consequences the Fourteenth Amendment would have. They expected it to end certain of the most egregious Jim Crow practices of the Reconstruction period. They plainly did not expect it to outlaw official racial segregation in school—on the contrary, the Congress that adopted the equal protection clause itself maintained segregation in the District of Columbia school system. But they did not *say* anything about Jim Crow laws or school segregation or homosexuality or gender equality, one way or the other. They said that "equal protection of the laws" is required, which plainly describes a very general principle, not any concrete application of it.

The framers meant, then, to enact a general principle. But which general principle? That further question must be answered by constructing different elaborations of the phrase "equal protection of the laws," each of which we can recognize as a principle of political morality that might have won their respect, and then by asking which of these it makes most sense to attribute to them, given everything else we know. The qualification that each of these possibilities must be recognizable as a political *principle* is absolutely crucial. We cannot capture a statesman's efforts to lay down a general constitutional principle by attributing to him something neither he nor we could recognize as a candidate for that role. But the qualification will typically leave many possibilities open. It was once debated, for example, whether the framers intended to stipulate, in the equal protection clause, only the relatively weak political principle that laws must be enforced in accordance with their terms, so that legal benefits conferred on everyone, including blacks, must not be denied, in practice, to anyone.

History seems decisive that the framers of the Fourteenth Amendment did not mean to lay down only so weak a principle as that one, however, which would have left states free to discriminate against blacks in any way they wished so long as they did so openly. Congressmen of the victorious nation, trying to capture the achievements and lessons of a terrible war, would be very unlikely to settle for anything so limited and insipid, and we should not take them to have done so unless the language leaves no other interpretation plausible. In any case, constitutional interpretation must take into account past legal and political practice as well as what the

framers themselves intended to say, and it has now been settled by unchal-
lengeable precedent that the political principle incorporated in the Fourteenth Amendment is not that very weak one, but something more robust.
Once that is conceded, however, then the principle must be something
much more robust, because the only alternative, as a translation of what
the framers actually *said* in the equal protection clause, is that they declared a principle of quite breathtaking scope and power: the principle that
government must treat everyone as of equal status and with equal concern.

The substantive examples of later chapters give more detail to that
sketchy explanation of the role of history and language in deciding what
the Constitution means. But even this brief discussion has mentioned two
important restraints that sharply limit the latitude the moral reading gives
to individual judges. First, under that reading constitutional interpretation
must begin in what the framers said, and, just as our judgment about what
friends and strangers say relies on specific information about them and the
context in which they speak, so does our understanding of what the
framers said. History is therefore plainly relevant. But only in a particular
way. We turn to history to answer the question of what they intended to
say, not the different question of what *other* intentions they had. We have
no need to decide what they expected to happen, or hoped would happen,
in consequence of their having said what they did, for example; their
purpose, in that sense, is not part of our study. That is a crucial distinction,
as we shall see in Chapter 3 and elsewhere. We are governed by what our
lawmakers said—by the principles they laid down—not by any information we might have about how they themselves would have interpreted
those principles or applied them in concrete cases.

Second, and equally important, constitutional interpretation is disciplined, under the moral reading, by the requirement of constitutional
integrity that is discussed at several points in the book and illustrated in,
for example, Chapter 4.[6] Judges may not read their own convictions into
the Constitution. They may not read the abstract moral clauses as expressing any particular moral judgment, no matter how much that judgment
appeals to them, unless they find it consistent in principle with the structural design of the Constitution as a whole, and also with the dominant
lines of past constitutional interpretation by other judges. They must
regard themselves as partners with other officials, past and future, who
together elaborate a coherent constitutional morality, and they must take
care to see that what they contribute fits with the rest. (I have elsewhere
said that judges are like authors jointly creating a chain novel in which
each writes a chapter that makes sense as part of the story as a whole.)[7]

Even a judge who believes that abstract justice requires economic equality cannot interpret the equal protection clause as making equality of wealth, or collective ownership of productive resources, a constitutional requirement, because that interpretation simply does not fit American history or practice, or the rest of the Constitution.

Nor could a judge plausibly think that the constitutional structure commits any but basic, structural political rights to his care. He might think that a society truly committed to equal concern would award people with handicaps special resources, or would secure convenient access to recreational parks for everyone, or would provide heroic and experimental medical treatment, no matter how expensive or speculative, for anyone whose life might possibly be saved. But it would violate constitutional integrity for a judge to treat these mandates as part of constitutional law. Judges must defer to general, settled understandings about the character of the power the Constitution assigns them. The moral reading asks them to find the best conception of constitutional moral principles—the best understanding of what equal moral status for men and women really requires, for example—that fits the broad story of America's historical record. It does not ask them to follow the whisperings of their own consciences or the traditions of their own class or sect if these cannot be seen as embedded in that record. Of course judges can abuse their power— they can pretend to observe the important restraint of integrity while really ignoring it. But generals and presidents and priests can abuse their powers, too. The moral reading is a strategy for lawyers and judges acting in good faith, which is all any interpretive strategy can be.

I emphasize these constraints of history and integrity, because they show how exaggerated is the common complaint that the moral reading gives judges absolute power to impose their own moral convictions on the rest of us. Macauley was wrong when he said that the American Constitution is all sail and no anchor,[8] and so are the other critics who say that the moral reading turns judges into philosopher-kings. Our constitution is law, and like all law it is anchored in history, practice, and integrity. Most cases at law— even most constitutional cases—are not hard cases. The ordinary craft of a judge dictates an answer and leaves no room for the play of personal moral conviction. Still, we must not exaggerate the drag of that anchor. Very different, even contrary, conceptions of a constitutional principle—of what treating men and women as equals really means, for example—will often fit language, precedent, and practice well enough to pass these tests, and thoughtful judges must then decide on their own which conception does most credit to the nation. So though the familiar complaint that the moral reading gives judges unlimited power is hyperbolic, it contains enough truth to alarm those who believe that such judicial power is inconsistent with a republican form of government. The constitutional sail is a broad one, and many people do fear that it is too big for a democratic boat.

What Is the Alternative?

Constitutional lawyers and scholars have therefore been anxious to find other strategies for constitutional interpretation, strategies that give judges less power. They have explored two different possibilities, and I discuss both later in this book. The first, and most forthright, concedes that the moral reading is right—that the Bill of Rights can only be understood as a set of moral principles. But it denies that judges should have the final authority themselves to conduct the moral reading—that they should have the last word about, for example, whether women have a constitutional right to choose abortion or whether affirmative action treats all races with equal concern. It reserves that interpretive authority to the people. That is by no means a contradictory combination of views. The moral reading, as I said, is a theory about what the Constitution means, not a theory about whose view of what it means must be accepted by the rest of us.

This first alternate offers a way of understanding the arguments of a great American judge, Learned Hand, whom I discuss in Chapter 17. Hand thought that the courts should take final authority to interpret the Constitution only when this is absolutely necessary to the survival of government—only when the courts must be referees between the other departments of government because the alternative would be a chaos of competing claims to jurisdiction. No such necessity compels courts to test legislative acts against the Constitution's moral principles, and Hand therefore thought it wrong for judges to claim that authority. Though his view was once an open possibility, history has long excluded it; practice has now settled that courts do have a responsibility to declare and act on their best understanding of what the Constitution forbids.[9] If Hand's view had been accepted, the Supreme Court could not have decided, as it did in its famous *Brown* decision in 1954, that the equal protection clause outlaws racial segregation in public schools. In 1958 Hand said, with evident regret, that he had to regard the *Brown* decision as wrong, and he would have had to take the same view about later Supreme Court decisions that expanded racial equality, religious independence, and personal freedoms such as the freedom to buy and use contraceptives. These decisions are now almost universally thought not only sound but shining examples of our constitutional structure working at its best.

The first alternative strategy, as I said, accepts the moral reading. The second alternative, which is called the "originalist" or "original intention" strategy, does not. The moral reading insists that the Constitution means what the framers intended to say. Originalism insists that it means what they expected their language to *do,* which as I said is a very different matter. (Though some originalists, including one of the most conservative justices now on the Supreme Court, Antonin Scalia, are unclear about the distinction.)[10] According to originalism, the great clauses of the Bill of Rights should be interpreted not as laying down the abstract moral principles they actually describe, but instead as referring, in a kind of code or disguise, to the framers' own assumptions and expectations about the correct application of those principles. So the equal protection clause is to be understood as commanding not equal status but what the framers themselves thought was equal status, in spite of the fact that, as I said, the framers clearly meant to lay down the former standard not the latter one. The *Brown* decision I just mentioned crisply illustrates the distinction. The Court's decision was plainly required by the moral reading, because it is obvious now that official school segregation is not consistent with equal status and equal concern for all races. But the originalist strategy, consistently applied, would have demanded the opposite conclusion, because, as I said, the authors of the equal protection clause did not believe that school segregation, which they practiced themselves, was a denial of equal status, and did not expect that it would one day be deemed to be so. The moral reading insists that they misunderstood the moral principle that they themselves enacted into law. The originalist strategy would translate that mistake into enduring constitutional law.

That strategy, like the first alternative, would condemn not only the *Brown* decision but many other Supreme Court decisions that are now widely regarded as paradigms of good constitutional interpretation. For that reason, almost no one now embraces the originalist strategy in anything like a pure form. Even Robert Bork, who remains one of its strongest defenders, qualified his support in the Senate hearings following his nomination to the Supreme Court—he conceded that the *Brown* decision was right, and said that even the Court's 1965 decision guaranteeing a right to use contraceptives, which we have no reason to think the authors of any pertinent constitutional clause either expected or would have approved, was right in its result. The originalist strategy is as indefensible in principle as it is unpalatable in result, moreover. It is as illegitimate to substitute a concrete, detailed provision for the abstract language of the equal protection clause as it would be to substitute some abstract principle of privacy for the concrete terms of the Third Amendment, or to treat the clause imposing a minimum age for a President as enacting some general principle of disability for persons under that age.

So though many conservative politicians and judges have endorsed originalism, and some, like Hand, have been tempted to reconsider whether judges should have the last word about what the Constitution requires, there is in fact very little practical support for either of these strategies. Yet the moral reading is almost never explicitly endorsed, and is often explicitly condemned. If neither of the two alternatives I described is actually embraced by those who disparage the moral reading, what alternative do they have in mind? The surprising answer is: none. Constitutional scholars often say that we must avoid the mistakes of both the moral reading, which gives too much power to judges, and of originalism, which makes the contemporary Constitution too much the dead hand of the past. The right method, they say, is something in between which strikes the right balance between protecting essential individual rights and deferring to popular will. But they do not indicate what the right balance is, or even what kind of scale we should use to find it. They say that constitutional interpretation must take both history and the general structure of the Constitution into account as well as moral or political philosophy. But they do not say why history or structure, both of which, as I said, figure in the moral reading, should figure in some further or different way, or what that different way is, or what general goal or standard of constitutional interpretation should guide us in seeking a different interpretive strategy.[11]

So though the call for an intermediate constitutional strategy is often heard, it has not been answered, except in unhelpful metaphors about balance and structure. That is extraordinary, particularly given the enormous and growing literature of American constitutional theory. If it is so hard to produce an alternative to the moral reading, why struggle to do so? One distinguished constitutional lawyer who insists that there must be an interpretive strategy somewhere between originalism and the moral reading recently announced, at a conference, that although he had not discovered it, he would spend the rest of his life looking. Why?

I have already answered that question. Lawyers assume that the disabilities that a constitution imposes on majoritarian political processes are antidemocratic, at least if these disabilities are enforced by judges, and the moral reading seems to exacerbate the insult. If there is no genuine alternative to the moral reading in practice, however, and if efforts to find even a theoretical statement of an acceptable alternative have failed, we would do well to look again at that assumption. I shall argue, as I have already promised, that it is unfounded.

I said earlier that the theoretical argument among constitutional scholars and judges was never really about whether judges should change the Constitution or leave it alone. It was always about how the Constitution should be interpreted. Happily, in spite of the politicians' rhetoric, that is now generally recognized by constitutional scholars, and it is also generally recognized that the question of interpretation turns on a political controversy, because the only substantial objection to the moral reading, which takes the text seriously, is that it offends democracy. So the academic argument is widely thought to be about how far democracy can properly be compromised in order to protect other values, including individual rights. One side declares itself passionate for democracy and anxious to protect it, while the other claims to be more sensitive to the injustices that democracy sometimes produces. In many ways, however, this new view of the debate is as confused as the older one. I shall try to convince you to see the constitutional argument in entirely different terms: as a debate not about how far democracy should yield to other values, but about what democracy, accurately understood, really is.

The Majoritarian Premise

Democracy means government by the people. But what does that mean? No explicit definition of democracy is settled among political theorists or in the dictionary. On the contrary, it is a matter of deep controversy what democracy really is. People disagree about which techniques of representation, which allocation of power among local, state, and national governments, which schedule and pattern of elections, and which other institutional arrangements provide the best available version of democracy. But beneath these familiar arguments over the structures of democracy there lies, I believe, a profound philosophical dispute about democracy's fundamental *value* or *point,* and one abstract issue is crucial to that dispute, though this is not always recognized. Should we accept or reject what I shall call the majoritarian premise?

This is a thesis about the fair *outcomes* of a political process: it insists that political procedures should be designed so that, at least on important matters, the decision that is reached is the decision that a majority or plurality of citizens favors, or would favor if it had adequate information and enough time for reflection. That goal sounds very reasonable, and many people, perhaps without much reflection, have taken it to provide the very essence of democracy. They believe that the complex political arrangements that constitute the democratic process should be aimed at and tested by this goal: that the laws that the complex democratic process enacts and the policies that it pursues should be those, in the end, that the majority of citizens would approve.

The majoritarian premise does not deny that individuals have important moral rights the majority should respect. It is not necessarily tied to some collectivist or utilitarian theory according to which such rights are nonsense. In some political communities, however—in Great Britain, for example—the majoritarian premise has been thought to entail that the community should defer to the majority's view about what these individual rights are, and how they are best respected and enforced. It is sometimes said that Britain has no constitution, but that is a mistake. Britain has an unwritten as well as a written constitution, and part of the former consists in understandings about what laws Parliament should not enact. It is part of the British constitution, for example, that freedom of speech is to be protected. Until very recently, it has seemed natural to British lawyers, however, that no group except a political majority, acting through Parliament, should decide what that requirement means, or whether it should be altered or repealed, so that when Parliament's intention to restrict speech is clear, British courts have no power to invalidate what it has done. That is because the majoritarian premise, and the majoritarian conception of democracy it produces, have been more or less unexamined fixtures of British political morality for over a century.

In the United States, however, most people who assume that the majoritarian premise states the ultimate definition of and justification for democracy nevertheless accept that on some occasions the will of the majority should *not* govern. They agree that the majority should not always be the final judge of when its own power should be limited to protect individual rights, and they accept that at least some of the Supreme Court's decisions that overturned popular legislation, as the *Brown* decision did, were right. The majoritarian premise does not rule out exceptions of that kind, but it does insist that in such cases, even if some derogation from majoritarian government is overall justified, something morally regrettable has happened, a moral cost has been paid. The premise supposes, in other words, that it is *always* unfair when a political majority is not allowed to have its way, so that even when there are strong enough countervailing reasons to justify this, the unfairness remains.

If we reject the majoritarian premise, we need a different, better account of the value and point of democracy. Later I will defend an account— which I call the constitutional conception of democracy—that does reject the majoritarian premise. It denies that it is a defining goal of democracy that collective decisions always or normally be those that a majority or plurality of citizens would favor if fully informed and rational. It takes the defining aim of democracy to be a different one: that collective decisions be made by political institutions whose structure, composition, and practices treat all members of the community, as individuals, with equal concern and respect. This alternate account of the aim of democracy, it is true, demands much the same structure of government as the majoritarian premise does. It requires that day-to-day political decisions be made by officials who have been chosen in popular elections. But the constitutional conception requires these majoritarian procedures out of a concern for the equal status of citizens, and not out of any commitment to the goals of majority rule. So it offers no reason why some nonmajoritarian procedure should not be employed on special occasions when this would better protect or enhance the equal status that it declares to be the essence of democracy, and it does not accept that these exceptions are a cause of moral regret.

The constitutional conception of democracy, in short, takes the following attitude to majoritarian government. Democracy means government subject to conditions—we might call these the "democratic" conditions— of equal status for all citizens. When majoritarian institutions provide and respect the democratic conditions, then the verdicts of these institutions should be accepted by everyone for that reason. But when they do not, or when their provision or respect is defective, there can be no objection, in the name of democracy, to other procedures that protect and respect them better. The democratic conditions plainly include, for example, a requirement that public offices must in principle be open to members of all races and groups on equal terms. If some law provided that only members of one race were eligible for public office, then there would be no moral cost—no matter for moral regret at all—if a court that enjoyed the power to do so under a valid constitution struck down that law as unconstitutional. That would presumably be an occasion on which the majoritarian premise was flouted, but though this is a matter of regret according to the majoritarian conception of democracy, it is not according to the constitutional conception. Of course, it may be controversial what the democratic conditions, in detail, really are, and whether a particular law does offend them. But, according to the constitutional conception, it would beg the question to object to a practice assigning those controversial questions for final decision to a court, on the ground that that practice is undemocratic, because that objection assumes that the laws in question respect the democratic conditions, and that is the very issue in controversy.

I hope it is now clear that the majoritarian premise has had a potent—if often unnoticed—grip on the imagination of American constitutional scholars and lawyers. Only that diagnosis explains the near unanimous view I described: that judicial review compromises democracy, so that the central question of constitutional theory must be whether and when that compromise is justified. That opinion is the child of a majoritarian conception of democracy, and therefore the grandchild of the majoritarian premise. It provokes the pointless search I described, for an interpretive strategy "intermediate" between the moral reading and originalism, and it tempts distinguished theorists into constructing Ptolemaic epicycles trying to reconcile constitutional practice with majoritarian principles.

So a complex issue of political morality—the validity of the majoritarian premise—is in fact at the heart of the long constitutional argument. The argument will remain confused until that issue is identified and addressed. We might pause to notice how influential the majoritarian premise has been in other important political debates, including the pressing national discussion about electoral campaign reform. This discussion has so far been dominated by the assumption that democracy is improved when it better serves the majoritarian premise—when it is designed more securely to produce collective decisions that match majority preferences. The unfortunate Supreme Court decision in *Buckley v. Valeo,* for example, which struck down laws limiting what rich individuals can spend on political campaigning, was based on a theory of free speech that has its origins in that view of democracy.[12] In fact the degeneration of democracy that has been so vivid in recent elections cannot be halted until we develop a more sophisticated view of what democracy means.

In most of the rest of this chapter I shall be evaluating arguments for and against the majoritarian premise. I shall not consider, however, but only mention now, one plainly inadequate argument for it that I fear has had considerable currency. This begins in a fashionable form of moral skepticism which insists that moral values and principles cannot be objectively true, but only represent powerful concatenations of self-interest or taste, or of class or race or gender interest. If so, the argument continues, then judges who claim to have discovered moral truth are deluded, and the only fair political process is one that leaves power to the people. This argument is doubly fallacious. First, since its conclusion, favorable to the majoritarian premise, is itself a moral claim, it contradicts itself. Second, for reasons I have tried to explain elsewhere, the fashionable form of skepticism is incoherent.

In fact the most powerful arguments for the majoritarian premise are themselves arguments of political morality. They can be distinguished and grouped under the three eighteenth-century revolutionary virtues—equality, liberty, and community—and it is these more basic political ideas that we must now explore. If the premise can be sustained, this must be because it is endorsed by the best conception of at least one and perhaps all of these ideals. We must go behind democracy to consider, in the light of these deeper virtues and values, which conception of democracy—the majoritarian conception which is based on the majoritarian premise or the constitutional conception which rejects it—is sounder. But we shall first need another important distinction, and I shall make it now.

We the People

We say that in a democracy government is by the people; we mean that the people collectively do things—elect leaders, for example—that no individual does or can do alone. There are two kinds of collective action, however—statistical and communal—and our view of the majoritarian premise may well turn on which kind of collective action we take democratic government to require.

Collective action is statistical when what the group does is only a matter of some function, rough or specific, of what the individual members of the group do on their own, that is, with no sense of doing something *as* a group. We might say that yesterday the foreign exchange market drove down the price of the dollar. That is certainly a kind of collective action: only the combined action of a large group of bankers and dealers can affect the foreign currency market in any substantial way. But our reference to a collective entity, the currency market, does not point to any actual entity. We could, without changing our meaning, make an overtly statistical claim instead: that the combined effects of individual currency transactions were responsible for the lower price of the dollar at the latest trade.

Collective action is communal, however, when it cannot be reduced just to some statistical function of individual action, when it presupposes a special, distinct, collective *agency*. It is a matter of individuals acting together in a way that merges their separate actions into a further, unified, act that is together *theirs*. The familiar but emotionally powerful example of collective guilt provides a useful illustration. Many Germans (including those born after 1945) feel responsible for what Germany did, not just for what other Germans did. Their sense of responsibility assumes that they are themselves connected to the Nazi terror in some way, because they belong to the nation that committed those crimes. Here is a more pleasant example. An orchestra can play a symphony, though no single musician can, but this is not a case of merely statistical collective action because it is essential to a successful orchestral performance not just that each musician plays some appropriate score, timing his performance as the conductor instructs, but that the musicians play *as* an orchestra, each intending to make a contribution to the performance of the group, and each taking part in a collective responsibility for it. The performance of a football team can be communal collective action in the same way.

I have already distinguished two conceptions of democracy: majoritarian and constitutional. The first accepts and the second rejects the majoritarian premise. The difference between statistical and communal collective action allows us to draw a second distinction, this time between two readings of the idea that democracy is government by "the people." (I shall shortly consider the connection between these two distinctions.) The first reading is a statistical one: that in a democracy political decisions are made in accordance with the votes or wishes of some function—a majority or plurality—of individual citizens. The second is a communal reading: that in a democracy political decisions are taken by a distinct entity—the people *as such*—rather than by any set of individuals one by one. Rousseau's idea of government by general will is an example of a communal rather than a statistical conception of democracy. The statistical reading of government by the people is much more familiar in American political theory. The communal reading sounds mysterious, and may also sound dangerously totalitarian. If so, my reference to Rousseau will not have allayed the suspicion. I shall argue in the next two sections, however, that the supposedly most powerful arguments for the majoritarian premise presuppose the communal reading. They presuppose but betray it.

Does Constitutionalism Undermine Liberty?

The majoritarian premise insists that something of moral importance is lost or compromised whenever a political decision contradicts what the majority of citizens would prefer or judge right if they reflected on the basis of adequate information. We must try to identify that moral cost. What is lost or compromised? Many people think the answer is: equality. I shall consider that apparently natural answer shortly, but I begin with a different suggestion, which is that when constitutional disabling provisions, like those found in the Bill of Rights, limit what a majority can enact, the result is to compromise the community's freedom.[13]

That suggestion plainly appeals to what Isaiah Berlin and others have called positive as distinct from negative liberty, and what Benjamin Constant described as the liberty of the ancients as distinct from that of the moderns. It is the kind of freedom that statesmen and revolutionaries and terrorists and humanitarians have in mind when they insist that freedom must include the right of "self-determination" or the right of the "people" to govern themselves. Since the suggestion that constitutional rights compromise freedom appeals to positive rather than negative liberty, it might be said to pit the two kinds of liberty against each other. Constitutionalism, on this view, protects "negative" liberties, like free speech and "privacy," at the cost of the "positive" freedoms of self-determination.

This means, however, that this argument from liberty we are considering must be based on a communal rather than a statistical reading of government by the "people." On the statistical reading, an individual's control over the collective decisions that affect his life is measured by his power, on his own, to influence the result, and in a large democracy the power of any individual over national decisions is so tiny that constitutional restraints cannot be thought to diminish it enough to count as objectionable for that reason. On the contrary, constraints on majority will might well expand any particular individual's control of his own fate. On the communal reading, however, liberty is a matter not of any relation between government and citizens one by one, but rather of the relation between government and the whole citizenry understood collectively. Positive liberty, so understood, is the state of affairs when "the people" rule their officials, at least in the final analysis, rather than vice versa, and that is the liberty said to be compromised when the majority is prevented from securing its will.

I discuss this defense of the majoritarian premise first because it is emotionally the most powerful. Self-determination is the most potent—

and dangerous—political ideal of our time. People fervently want to be governed by a group not just to which they belong, but with which they identify in some particular way. They want to be governed by members of the same religion or race or nation or linguistic community or historical nation-state rather than by any other group, and they regard a political community that does not satisfy this demand as a tyranny, no matter how otherwise fair and satisfactory it is.

This is partly a matter of narrow self-interest. People think that decisions made by a group most of whose members share their values will be better decisions for them. The great power of the ideal lies deeper, however. It lies in half-articulate convictions about when people are free, because they govern themselves, in spite of the fact that in a statistical sense, as individuals, they are not free, because they must often bend to the will of others. For us moderns, the key to this liberty of the ancients lies in democracy. As John Kenneth Galbraith has said, "When people put their ballots in the boxes, they are, by that act, inoculated against the feeling that the government is not theirs. They then accept, in some measure, that its errors are their errors, its aberrations their aberrations, that any revolt will be against them."[14] We think we are free when we accept a majority's will in place of our own, but not when we bow before the doom of a monarch or the ukase of any aristocracy of blood or faith or skill. It is not difficult to see the judiciary as an aristocracy claiming dominion. Learned Hand described judges who appeal to the moral reading of the Constitution as "a bevy of Platonic guardians," and said he could not bear to be ruled by such a body of elites even if he knew how to select those fit for the task.[15]

But powerful as the idea of democratic self-governance is, it is also deeply mysterious. Why am I *free*—how could I be thought to be governing *myself*—when I must obey what other people decide even if I think it wrong or unwise or unfair to me and my family? What difference can it make how many people must think the decision right and wise and fair if it is not necessary that *I* do? What kind of freedom is that? The answer to these enormously difficult questions begins in the communal conception of collective action. If I am a genuine member of a political community, its act is in some pertinent sense my act, even when I argued and voted against it, just as the victory or defeat of a team of which I am a member is my victory or defeat even if my own individual contribution made no difference either way. On no other assumption can we intelligibly think that as members of a flourishing democracy we are governing ourselves.

That explanation may seem only to deepen the mystery of collective self-government, however, because it appeals to two further ideas that seem dark themselves. What could *genuine* membership in a political community mean? And in what sense *can* a collective act of a group also be the act of each member? These are moral rather than metaphysical or psychological questions: they are not to be answered by counting the ultimate constituents of reality or discovering when people feel responsible for what some group that they belong to does. We must describe some connection between an individual and a group that makes it *fair* to treat him—and *sensible* that he treat himself—as responsible for what it does. Let us bring those ideas together in the concept of moral membership, by which we mean the kind of membership in a political community that engages self-government. If true democracy is government by the people, in the communal sense that provides self-government, then true democracy is based on moral membership.

In this section we are considering the argument that the moral cost incurred when the majoritarian premise is flouted is a cost in liberty. We have now clarified that argument: we must understand it to mean that the people govern themselves when the majoritarian premise is satisfied, and that any compromise of that premise compromises that self-government. But that majoritarianism does not guarantee self-government unless all the members of the community in question are moral members, and the majoritarian premise acknowledges no such qualification. German Jews were not moral members of the political community that tried to exterminate them, though they had votes in the elections that led to Hitler's Chancellorship, and the Holocaust was therefore not part of their self-government, even if a majority of Germans would have approved it. Catholics in Northern Ireland, nationalists in the Caucasus, and separatists in Quebec all believe they are not free because they are not moral members of the right political community. I do not mean that people who deny moral membership in their political community are always right. The test, as I said, is moral not psychological. But they are not wrong just because they have an equal vote with others in some standing majoritarian structure.

When I described the constitutional conception of democracy earlier, as a rival to the majoritarian conception that reflects the majoritarian premise, I said that the constitutional conception presupposes democratic conditions. These are the conditions that must be met before majoritarian decision-making can claim any automatic moral advantage over other procedures for collective decision. We have now identified the same idea through another route. The democratic conditions are the conditions of moral membership in a political community. So we can now state a strong conclusion: not just that positive liberty is not sacrificed whenever and just because the majoritarian premise is ignored, but that positive liberty is enhanced when that premise is rejected outright in favor of the constitutional conception of democracy. If it is true that self-government is possible only within a community that meets the conditions of moral membership, because only then are we entitled to refer to government by "the people" in a powerful communal rather than a barren statistical sense, we need a conception of democracy that insists that no democracy exists unless those conditions are met.

What are the conditions of moral membership, and hence of positive freedom, and hence of democracy on the constitutional conception? I have tried to describe them elsewhere, and will only summarize my conclusions here.[16] There are two kinds of conditions. The first set is *structural:* these conditions describe the character the community as a whole must have if it is to count as a genuine political community. Some of these structural conditions are essentially historical. The political community must be more than nominal: it must have been established by a historical process that has produced generally recognized and stable territorial boundaries. Many sociologists and political scientists and politicians would add further structural conditions to that very limited one: they would insist, for example, that the members of a genuine political community must share a culture as well as a political history: that they must speak a common language, have common values, and so forth. Some might add further psychological conditions: that members of the community must be mainly disposed to trust one another, for example.[17] I shall not consider the interesting issues these suggestions raise here, because our interest lies in the second set of conditions.

These are *relational* conditions: they describe how an individual must be treated by a genuine political community in order that he or she be a moral member of that community. A political community cannot count anyone as a moral member unless it gives that person a *part* in any collective decision, a *stake* in it, and *independence* from it. First, each person must have an opportunity to make a difference in the collective decisions, and the force of his role—the magnitude of the difference he can make—must not be structurally fixed or limited in ways that reflect assumptions about his worth or talent or ability, or the soundness of his convictions or tastes. It is that condition that insists on universal suffrage and effective elections and representation, even though it does not demand that these be the only avenues of collective decision. It also insists, as several of the chapters in Part III argue, on free speech and expression for all opinion, not just on formal political occasions, but in the informal life of the community as well.

It insists, moreover, on interpreting the force of freedom of speech and expression by concentrating on the role of that freedom in the processes of self-government, a role that dictates different answers to several questions—including the question of whether campaign expenditure limits violate that freedom—than a majoritarian conception of democracy would.

Second, the political process of a genuine community must express some bona fide conception of equal concern for the interests of all members, which means that political decisions that affect the distribution of wealth, benefits, and burdens must be consistent with equal concern for all. Moral membership involves reciprocity: a person is not a member unless he is treated as a member by others, which means that they treat the consequences of any collective decision for his life as equally significant a reason for or against that decision as are comparable consequences for the life of anyone else. So the communal conception of democracy explains an intuition many of us share: that a society in which the majority shows contempt for the needs and prospects of some minority is illegitimate as well as unjust.

The third condition—of moral independence—is likely to be more controversial than these first two. I believe it essential, however, in order to capture an aspect of moral membership that the first two conditions may be interpreted to omit. The root idea we are now exploring—that individual freedom is furthered by collective self-government—assumes that the members of a political community can appropriately regard themselves as partners in a joint venture, like members of a football team or orchestra in whose work and fate all share, even when that venture is conducted in ways they do not endorse. That idea is nonsense unless it can be accepted by people with self-respect, and whether it can be depends on which kinds of decisions the collective venture is thought competent to make. An orchestra's conductor can decide, for example, how the orchestra will interpret a particular piece: there must be a decision of that issue binding on all, and the conductor is the only one placed to make it. No musician sacrifices anything essential to his control over his own life, and hence to his self-respect, in accepting that someone else has that responsibility, but it would plainly be otherwise if the conductor tried to dictate not only how a violinist should play under his direction, but what standards of taste the violinist should try to cultivate. No one who accepted responsibility to decide questions of musical judgment for himself could regard himself as a partner in a joint venture that proposed to decide them for him.

That is even more plainly true in the political case, and Part I, which discusses fundamental issues of life, death, and personal responsibility, tries to show why. People who take personal responsibility for deciding what kind of life is valuable for them can nevertheless accept that issues of justice—about how the different and sometimes competing interests of all citizens should be accommodated—must be decided collectively, so that one decision is taken as authoritative for all. There is nothing in that proposition that challenges an individual's own responsibility to decide for himself what life to live given the resources and opportunities that such collective decisions leave to him. So he can treat himself as bound together with others in a joint effort to resolve such questions, even when his views lose. But it would be otherwise if the majority purported to decide what he should think or say about its decisions, or what values or ideals should guide how he votes or the choices he makes with the resources it assigns him. Someone who believes in his own responsibility for the central values of his life cannot yield that responsibility to a group even if he has an equal vote in its deliberations. A genuine political community must therefore be a community of independent moral agents. It must not dictate what its citizens think about matters of political or moral or ethical judgment, but must, on the contrary, provide circumstances that encourage them to arrive at beliefs on these matters through their own reflective and finally individual conviction.

Equality?

Although the argument from liberty is emotionally the most powerful of the arguments that might be made for the majoritarian premise, an argument from equality is more familiar. The dimension of equality in question is presumably political equality, because there is nothing in majoritarianism that could be thought automatically to promote any other form of equality, particularly not economic equality. True, if a society's economic structure is pyramidal, with progressively more people at progressively lower economic levels, then universal suffrage and majoritarian decisions might well push toward greater economic equality. But in the United States, and in other advanced capitalist countries where the profile of distribution is now very different, people in the majority often vote to protect their own wealth against the demands of those worse off than they are.

So the argument that equality is compromised when the majoritarian premise is ignored must appeal to some concept of political equality. But which concept this is depends on which of the two readings of collective action we have in mind. If we take government by "the people" to be only a statistical matter, then the equality in question is the political equality of citizens taken one by one. Such equality was certainly denied before women were permitted to vote, and it was compromised by the electoral system in Victorian Britain, which in effect gave university graduates extra votes. But what metric do we use in making those judgments? What *is* political equality according to the statistical concept of collective political action?

Perhaps surprisingly, we cannot capture political equality if we define it as equality of political *power,* because we have no interpretation of "power" that would make equality of power even an attractive, let alone an attainable, ideal.[18] Suppose we take political power to be a matter of impact, understood in the following way: my political impact, as a citizen of the United States, is a matter of how far my favoring a particular decision, just on its own, increases the antecedent likelihood of that being the collective decision, making no assumptions about what opinion any other citizen has or forms. Impact cannot be equal in a representative democracy: it must inevitably make a greater difference to the antecedent probability of a trade measure being approved that any particular senator favors it than that I do. In any case, impact does not capture any intuitively appealing concept of political power, because impact is insensitive to what is the most important source of unequal political power in modern democracies, which is the inequality of wealth that allows some people vast opportunity to influence public opinion. Ross Perot and I have only one vote each, but he can buy massive television time to persuade others to his opinion, and I cannot buy any.

This might suggest an improved account: that political power is a matter not of impact but of influence, understood as my overall power to affect political decisions, taking into account my power to affect the opinions of others. But equality of influence is plainly an unattractive—as well as unrealizable—goal. We do not want wealth to affect political decisions, but that is because wealth is unequally and unfairly distributed. We certainly do want influence to be unequal in politics for other reasons: we want those with better views, or who can argue more cogently, to have more influence. We could not eliminate differential influence from such sources without savage transformations of our whole society, and these would mean the end, not the triumph, of deliberation in our politics.

We must begin again. Political equality, on the statistical model of collective action, must be defined as a matter not of power but of the kind of *status* I discussed in connection with the conditions of democratic self-government. Male-only suffrage and university votes were inegalitarian because they presupposed that some people were worthier or better fit to participate in collective decisions than others. But mere political authority—the power attached to political office for which all are in principle eligible—carries no such presupposition. That is why the special power of political officials does not destroy true political equality, and it does not matter, for that point, whether or not the officials are directly elected. Many officials who are appointed rather than elected wield great power. An acting ambassador to Iraq can create a Gulf War and the chairman of the Federal Reserve Board can bring the economy to its knees. There is no inegalitarian premise of status—no supposition of first- and second-class citizenship—in the arrangements that produce this power. Nor is there any inegalitarian premise in the parallel arrangements that give certain American judges, appointed and approved by elected officials, authority over constitutional adjudication.

So the statistical reading of collective political action makes little sense of the idea that political equality is compromised whenever majority will is thwarted. And that idea is silly anyway, if we have the statistical reading in mind. In a large, continental democracy, any ordinary citizen's political power is minuscule, on any understanding of what political power is, and the diminution of that individual power traceable to constitutional constraints on majority will is more minuscule still. The egalitarian argument for the majoritarian premise seems initially more promising, however, if we detach it from the statistical reading of collective action and recast it from the perspective of the communal reading. From that perspective, equality is not a matter of any relation among citizens one by one, but rather a relation between the citizenry, understood collectively as "the people," and their governors. Political equality is the state of affairs in which the people rule their officials, in the final analysis, rather than vice versa. This provides a less silly argument for the proposition that judicial review or other compromises of the majoritarian premise damage political equality. It might be said that when judges apply constitutional provisions to strike down legislation that the people, through their representatives, have enacted, the people are no longer in charge.

But this argument is exactly the same as the argument considered in the last section: it appeals, once again, to the ideals of political self-determination. Positive liberty and the sense of equality that we extracted from the communal understanding of "we the people" are the very same virtues. (That is hardly surprising, since liberty and equality are, in general, aspects of the same ideal, not, as is often supposed, rivals.)[19] The objections I described in the last section, which are fatal to any attempt to ground a majoritarian premise in positive liberty, are also decisive against the same argument when it cries equality instead.

Community?

In recent years opponents of the moral reading have begun to appeal to the third revolutionary virtue—community (or fraternity)—rather than to either liberty or equality. They argue that because the moral reading assigns the most fundamental political decisions to an elite legal profession, it weakens the public's sense of community and cheats it of its sense of common adventure. But "community" is used in different senses, to refer to very different emotions or practices or ideals, and it is important to notice which of these is in play in this kind of argument. It is patently true, as philosophers since Aristotle have agreed, that people have an interest in sharing projects, language, entertainment, assumptions, and ambitions with others. A good political community will of course serve that interest,[20] but many people's interest in community will be better served by other, nonpolitical communities such as religious and professional and social groups. The disabling clauses of the American Constitution do not limit or impair people's power to form and share such communities; on the contrary, some constraints, like the First Amendment's protection of association and its prohibition against religious discrimination, enhance that power. The communitarians and others who appeal to community to support the majoritarian premise have something rather different in mind, however. They have in mind not the general benefits of close human relations, which can be secured in many different forms of community, but the special benefits they believe follow, both for people as individuals and for the political society as a whole, when citizens are actively engaged in political activity in a certain spirit.

That is not the spirit recommended by a different tradition of political scientists who regard politics as commerce by other means, an arena where citizens pursue their own advantage through political action groups and special interest politics. Communitarians think that this "interest-group republicanism" is a perversion of the republican ideal. They want people to participate in politics as moral agents promoting not their own partisan interests but rival conceptions of the public good. They suppose that if genuine deliberative democracy of that kind can be realized, not only will collective decisions be better, but citizens will lead better—more virtuous, fulfilled, and satisfying—lives.

Communitarians insist that this goal is jeopardized by judicial review, particularly when judicial review is as expansive as the moral reading invites it to be. But they rely on a dubious though rarely challenged assumption: that public discussion of constitutional justice is of better quality and engages more people in the deliberative way the communitarians favor if these issues are finally decided by legislatures rather than courts. This assumption may be inaccurate for a large number of different reasons. There is plainly no necessary connection between the impact that a majoritarian process gives each potential voter and the influence that voter has over a political decision. Some citizens may have more influence over a judicial decision by their contribution to a public discussion of the issue than they would have over a legislative decision just through their solitary vote. Even more important, there is no necessary connection between a citizen's political impact or influence and the ethical benefit he secures through participating in public discussion or deliberation. The quality of the discussion might be better, and his own contribution more genuinely deliberative and public spirited, in a general public debate preceding or following a judicial decision than in a political battle culminating in a legislative vote or even a referendum.

The interaction between these different phenomena—impact, influence, and ethically valuable public participation—is a complex empirical matter. In some circumstances, as I just suggested, individual citizens may be able to exercise the moral responsibilities of citizenship better when final decisions are removed from ordinary politics and assigned to courts, whose decisions are meant to turn on principle, not on the weight of numbers or the balance of political influence. I discuss the reasons why this may be so in Chapter 17, and so will only summarize them here. Although the political process that leads to a legislative decision may be of very high quality, it very often is not, as the recent debates in the United States about health care reform and gun control show. Even when the debate is illuminating, moreover, the majoritarian process encourages compromises that may subordinate important issues of principle. Constitutional legal cases, by contrast, can and do provoke a widespread public discussion that focuses on political morality. The great American debate about civil rights and affirmative action, which began in the 1950s and continues today, may well have been more deliberative because the issues were shaped by adjudication, and the argument over *Roe v. Wade,* discussed in Part I, for all its bitterness and violence, may have produced a better understanding of the complexity of the moral issues than politics alone would have provided.

I put the suggestion that judicial review may provide a superior kind of republican deliberation about some issues tentatively, as a possibility, because I do not believe that we have enough information for much confidence either way. I emphasize the possibility, nevertheless, because the communitarian argument simply ignores it, and assumes, with no pertinent evidence, that the only or most beneficial kind of "participation" in politics is the kind that looks toward elections of representatives who will then enact legislation. The character of recent American elections, and of contemporary national and local legislative debate and deliberation, hardly makes that assumption self-evident. Of course we should aim to improve ordinary politics, because broad-based political activity is essential to justice as well as dignity. (Rethinking what democracy means is, as I said, an essential part of that process.) But we must not pretend, when we evaluate the impact of judicial review on deliberative democracy, that what should happen has happened. In any case, however, as I emphasize in Chapter 17, whether great constitutional issues provoke and guide public deliberation depends, among much else, on how these issues are conceived and addressed by lawyers and judges. There is little chance of a useful national debate over constitutional principle when constitutional decisions are considered technical exercises in an arcane and conceptual craft. The chances would improve if the moral reading of the Constitution were more openly recognized by and in judicial opinions.

I do not mean, of course, that only judges should discuss matters of high political principle. Legislatures are guardians of principle too, and that includes constitutional principle.[21] The argument of this section aims only to show why the ideal of community does not support the majoritarian premise, or undermine the moral reading, any more effectively than do liberty and equality, the two senior members of the revolutionary brigade. We must set the majoritarian premise aside, and with it the majoritarian conception of democracy. It is not a defensible conception of what true democracy is, and it is not America's conception.

What Follows?

In a decent working democracy, like the United States, the democratic conditions set out in the Constitution are sufficiently met in practice so that there is no unfairness in allowing national and local legislatures the powers they have under standing arrangements. On the contrary, democracy would be extinguished by any general constitutional change that gave an oligarchy of unelected experts power to overrule and replace any legislative decision they thought unwise or unjust. Even if the experts always improved the legislation they rejected—always stipulated fairer income taxes than the legislature had enacted, for example—there would be a loss in self-government which the merits of their decisions could not extinguish. It is different, however, when the question is plausibly raised whether some rule or regulation or policy itself undercuts or weakens the democratic character of the community, and the constitutional arrangement assigns *that* question to a court. Suppose the legislature enacts a law making it a crime for someone to burn his own American flag as an act of protest.[22] Suppose this law is challenged on the ground that it impairs democratic self-government, by wrongly constricting the liberty of speech, and a court accepts this charge and strikes down the law. If the court's decision is correct—if laws against flag-burning do in fact violate the democratic conditions set out in the Constitution as these have been interpreted and formed by American history—the decision is not anti-democratic, but, on the contrary, improves democracy. No moral cost has been paid, because no one, individually or collectively, is worse off in any of the dimensions we have now canvassed. No one's power to participate in a self-governing community has been worsened, because everyone's power in that respect has been improved. No one's equality has been compromised, because equality, in the only pertinent sense, has been strengthened. No one has been cheated of the ethical advantages of a role in principled deliberation if he or she had a chance to participate in the public discussion about whether the decision was right. If the court had not intervened—if the legislature's decision had been left standing—everyone would have been worse off, in all the dimensions of democracy, and it would be perverse to regard that as in any way or sense a democratic victory. Of course, if we assume that the court's decision was wrong, then none of this is true. Certainly it impairs democracy when an authoritative court makes the wrong decision about what the democratic conditions require—but no more than it does when a majoritarian legislature makes a wrong constitutional decision that is allowed to stand. The possibility of error is symmetrical. So the majoritarian premise is confused, and it must be abandoned.

These are important conclusions. They show the fallacy in the popular argument that since judicial review of legislation is undemocratic the moral reading, which exacerbates the damage to democracy, should be rejected. But it is crucial to realize the limits of our conclusions. We do not yet have a positive argument in *favor* of judicial review, either in the form that institution has taken in the United States or in any other form. We have simply established a level playing field on which the contest between different institutional structures for interpreting the democratic conditions must take place, free from any default or presupposition whatsoever. The real, deep difficulty the constitutional argument exposes in democracy is that it is a procedurally *incomplete* scheme of government. It cannot prescribe the procedures for testing whether the conditions for the procedures it does prescribe are met.

How should a political community that aims at democracy decide whether the conditions democracy requires are met? Should it have a written constitution as its most fundamental law? Should that constitution describe a conception of the democratic conditions in as great detail as possible, trying to anticipate, in a constitutional code, all issues that might arise? Or should it set out very abstract statements of the democratic conditions, as the American Constitution and many other contemporary constitutions do, and leave it to contemporary institutions to interpret these generation by generation? If the latter, which institutions should these be? Should they be the ordinary, majoritarian parliamentary institutions, as the British constitution has for so long insisted? Or should they be special constitutional chambers, whose members are elected but perhaps for much longer terms or in different ways than the ordinary parliamentarians are? Or should they consist in a hierarchy of courts, as John Marshall declared natural in *Marbury v. Madison?*

A community might combine these different answers in different ways. The United States Constitution, as we noticed, combines very specific clauses, about quartering soldiers in peacetime, for example, with the majestically abstract clauses this book mainly discusses. It is settled in the United States that the Supreme Court does have authority to hold legislation invalid if it deems it unconstitutional. But of course that does not deny that legislators have a parallel responsibility to make constitutional judgments themselves, and to refuse to vote for laws they think unconstitutional. Nor does it follow, when courts have power to enforce some constitutional rights, that they have power to enforce them all. Some imaginative American constitutional lawyers argue, for example, that the power of the federal courts to declare the acts of other institutions invalid because unconstitutional is limited: they have power to enforce many of the rights, principles, and standards the Constitution creates, on this view, but not all of them.[23]

The moral reading is consistent with all these institutional solutions to the problem of democratic conditions. It is a theory about how certain clauses of some constitutions should be read—about what questions must be asked and answered in deciding what those clauses mean and require. It is not a theory about who must ask these questions, or about whose answer must be taken to be authoritative. So the moral reading is only part, though it is an important part, of a general theory of constitutional practice. What shall we say about the remaining questions, the institutional questions the moral reading does not reach?

I see no alternative but to use a result-driven rather than a procedure-driven standard for deciding them. The best institutional structure is the one best calculated to produce the best answers to the essentially moral question of what the democratic conditions actually are, and to secure stable compliance with those conditions. A host of practical considerations are relevant, and many of these may argue forcefully for allowing an elected legislature itself to decide on the moral limits of its power. But other considerations argue in the opposite direction, including the fact that legislators are vulnerable to political pressures of manifold kinds, both financial and political, so that a legislature is not the safest vehicle for protecting the rights of politically unpopular groups. People can be expected to disagree about which structure is overall best, and so in certain circumstances they need a decision procedure for deciding that question, which is exactly what a theory of democracy cannot provide. That is why the initial making of a political constitution is such a mysterious matter, and why it seems natural to insist on supermajorities or even near unanimity then, not out of any conception of procedural fairness, but rather out of a sense that stability cannot otherwise be had.

The situation is different, however, when we are interpreting an established constitutional practice, not starting a new one. Then authority is already distributed by history, and details of institutional responsibility are matters of interpretation, not of invention from nothing. In these circumstances, rejecting the majoritarian premise means that we may look for the best interpretation with a more open mind: we have no reason of principle to try to force our practices into some majoritarian mold. If the most straightforward interpretation of American constitutional practice shows that our judges have final interpretive authority, and that they largely understand the Bill of Rights as a constitution of principle—if that best explains the decisions judges actually make and the public largely accepts—we have no reason to resist that reading and to strain for one that seems more congenial to a majoritarian philosophy.

Comments and Cautions

I have not revised the essays that make up the rest of this book, except to correct a few mistakes of reference. Hindsight is tempting, and in many cases I would put arguments, and especially predictions, differently now. Substantial revision would also have avoided much of the repetition that collecting essays inevitably generates. Arguments and examples sometimes appear in more than one essay (though they take different forms, and have been, I hope, improved over time). But most of the original essays have been commented on by others, and changing them now might cause confusion.

This is not in any sense a textbook on constitutional law. I discuss relatively few cases, and I do not attempt to prove my general claims by citations to secondary sources. Scholars and lawyers disagree about constitutional theory not because some of them have read more cases than others, or read them more carefully, but because they disagree about the philosophical and jurisprudential issues that I emphasize. So I discuss a few cases as illustrations of principles rather than attempting to derive principles from many cases.

Nor do I much discuss technical legal doctrine, except when this is absolutely necessary. Every part of law, including constitutional law, makes use of special invented devices and categories in an attempt to discipline abstract legal principles with a technical vocabulary. Principles resist such discipline, however, and the technical devices have a finite—often very short—shelf life. Each begins as a useful and modest strategy showing the implications of general principles for a limited set of problems. But some then develop a life and force of their own, and become aging tyrants whose patching and grooming is more trouble than it is worth, until they are finally dispatched—sans teeth, sans everything—by a creative judge with new devices. The apparatus of "strict," "relaxed," and "intermediate" levels of "scrutiny," which the Supreme Court has used for decades in its equal protection decisions, for example, once served a useful purpose by offering working presumptions about discriminations that did or did not signal likely failures of equal concern. It no longer does. This book neglects such doctrinal devices to concentrate on the underlying principles they are supposed to serve.

I should like, finally, to reply to an objection that has been made to my arguments before, and that I anticipate will be made again. It is said that the results I claim for the moral reading, in particular constitutional cases, magically coincide with those I favor politically myself. As one commentator has put it, my arguments always seem to have happy endings. Or, at any rate, liberal endings—my arguments tend to endorse the Supreme Court decisions that are generally regarded as liberal ones, and to reject, as mistakes, those generally seen as conservative. This is suspicious, it is said, because I insist that law is different from morality, and that legal integrity often prevents a lawyer from finding in the law what he wishes were there. Why, then, is the American Constitution, as I understand it, so uniform a triumph of contemporary liberal thought?

I should make plain, first, that my arguments do not by any means always support people or acts or institutions I admire or approve. Much of Part II defends pornographers, flag-burners, and Nazi marchers, and Part I defends a general right of abortion, though I believe, for reasons I have described in another book, that even early abortion is often an ethical mistake.[24] Nor do I read the Constitution to contain all the important principles of political liberalism. In other writings, for example, I defend a theory of economic justice that would require substantial redistribution of wealth in rich political societies.[25] Some national constitutions do attempt to stipulate a degree of economic equality as a constitutional right, and some American lawyers have argued that our Constitution can be understood to do so.[26] But I have not; on the contrary, I have insisted that integrity would bar any attempt to argue from the abstract moral clauses of the Bill of Rights, or from any other part of the Constitution, to any such result.

But though the objection is wrong in assuming that I find the Constitution to be exactly what I would wish, I mainly want to resist the objection's other premise—that it is embarrassing for the moral reading when those who accept it find happy endings to their constitutional journeys. Of course my constitutional opinions are influenced by my own convictions of political morality. So are the opinions of lawyers who are more conservative and more radical than I am. As Chapter 6 shows, conservative judges are much readier than political liberals to use the abstract moral language of the Fourteenth Amendment to strike down affirmative action programs, and the radical view of the First Amendment that Part II discusses is at least as much driven by political instincts as my liberal understanding is.

I not only concede but emphasize that constitutional opinion is sensitive to political conviction. Otherwise, as I said, we would not be able to classify jurists as conservative or moderate or liberal or radical with even the success we have. The question is rather whether the influence is disreputable. Constitutional politics has been confused and corrupted by a pretense that judges (if only they were not so hungry for power) could use politically neutral strategies of constitutional interpretation. Judges who join in that pretense try to hide the inevitable influence of their own convictions even from themselves, and the result is a costly mendacity. The actual grounds of decision are hidden from both legitimate public inspection and valuable public debate. The moral reading offers different counsel. It explains why fidelity to the Constitution and to law *demands* that judges make contemporary judgments of political morality, and it therefore encourages an open display of the true grounds of judgment, in the hope that judges will construct franker arguments of principle that allow the public to join in the argument.

So of course the moral reading encourages lawyers and judges to read an abstract constitution in the light of what they take to be justice. How else could they answer the moral questions that abstract constitution asks them? It is no surprise, or occasion for ridicule or suspicion, that a constitutional theory reflects a moral stance. It would be an occasion for surprise—and ridicule—if it did not. Only an unbelievably crude form of legal positivism—a form disowned by the foremost positivist of the century, Herbert Hart—could produce that kind of insulation.[27] Text and integrity do act as important constraints, as I have been emphasizing throughout this discussion. But though these constraints shape and limit the impact of convictions of justice, they cannot eliminate that impact. The moral reading insists, however, that this influence is not disreputable, so long as it is openly recognized, and so long as the convictions are identified and defended honestly, by which I mean through proper arguments of principle not just thin slogans or tired metaphors.

This book does indeed offer a liberal view of the American Constitution. It provides arguments of liberal principle and claims that these provide the best interpretations of the constitutional tradition we have inherited and whose trustees we now are. I believe, and try to show, that liberal opinion best fits our constitutional structure, which was, after all, first constructed in the bright morning of liberal thought. My arguments can certainly be resisted. But I hope they will be resisted in the right way: by pointing out their fallacies or by deploying different principles—more conservative or more radical ones—and showing why these different principles are better because they are grounded in a superior morality, or are more practicable, or are in some other way wiser or fairer. It is too late for the old, cowardly, story about judges not being responsible for making arguments like these, or competent to do so, or that it is undemocratic for them to try, or that their job is to enforce the law, not speculate about morality. That old story is philosophy too, but it is bad philosophy. It appeals to concepts—of law and democracy—that it does not begin to understand.

It is in the nature of legal interpretation—not just but particularly constitutional interpretation—to aim at happy endings.[28] There is no alternative, except aiming at unhappy ones, because once the pure form of originalism is rejected there is no such thing as neutral accuracy. Telling it how it is means, up to a point, telling it how it should be. What is that point? The American constitutional novel includes, after all, the Supreme Court's *Dred Scott* decision, which treated slaves as a kind of property, and the Court's twentieth-century "rights of property" decisions, which nearly swamped Roosevelt's New Deal. How happy an overall view of that story is actually on offer? Many chapters raise that question, and it cannot be answered except through detailed interpretive arguments like those they provide. But political and intellectual responsibility, as well as cheerfulness, argue for optimism. The Constitution is America's moral sail, and we must hold to the courage of the conviction that fills it, the conviction that we can all be equal citizens of a moral republic. That is a noble faith, and only optimism can redeem it.

I

LIFE
DEATH
AND
RACE

▾

THREE OF THE ESSAYS in this part are about abortion, the issue that has dominated constitutional argument in the United States for decades. Do women have a right to abort fetuses they are carrying, if they judge this right or necessary? When and how far may government regulate such abortions? These are issues of searing importance to a wide variety of groups and interests—to women's rights groups, who see them as issues of equality, to religious institutions and movements, who think abortion a terrible desecration, and, above all, to individual women, many of them poor and powerless, who find themselves in tragic circumstances and for whom they are fundamentally issues of individual freedom. No constitutional issue has seemed so important to so many people before, not even, perhaps, the great civil rights cases of the 1950s and 1960s.

The Supreme Court's 1973 decision in *Roe v. Wade*, which announced that women do have a right to an abortion within the first two trimesters of their pregnancy, seemed to many lawyers—not just those who objected to abortion on moral grounds themselves—a step too far down the road of government by judiciary. The Constitution says nothing explicit about abortion, and though certain of the Court's past decisions—in particular its earlier decision that people have a right to use contraceptives—seemed relevant, it struck those lawyers that it was unjustified for a Court to attempt to decide so bitterly contested a social and political issue as abortion had become. These doubts about the Supreme Court's proper role in government quickly became part of the larger public argument about abortion, and people took sides in the legal controversy about the Court and the Constitution that reflected, not only in direction but in passion, their convictions about that larger argument. So constitutional jurisprudence has become densely intertwined with the abortion issue in these decades, and that issue not only dominates this part of the book, but breaks out in other parts as well, particularly in the discussion of Part III, about judges.

The essay in Chapter 1 was first published in 1989, sixteen years after *Roe* had been decided. The composition of the Supreme Court had changed, principally through the conservative appointments that President Reagan had made in his two terms. The state of Missouri had challenged *Roe* in a new case, *Webster v. Reproductive Health Services,* and the Bush Administration had joined with that state in asking the Court formally to overrule *Roe*. I wrote the essay after oral argument in the case, but before the decision was handed down. Chapter 2 was written later in the year, after the Court had made and published its decision, upholding a variety of restrictions that Missouri had imposed on abortions, but declining, in this case, expressly to overrule *Roe.* I argued, in that essay, that *Roe* had survived intact, and remained good law, though other constitutional lawyers insisted that it had been all but repealed.

The great battle lay ahead. By 1992, only one of the justices who had voted for abortion rights in *Roe*—Justice Harry Blackmun, who had written the majority opinion in that case—remained on the Court. Two other firm defenders of the decision—Justices William H. Brennan and Thurgood Marshall—had resigned, and President Bush, an outspoken opponent of *Roe,* had replaced them with Justices Souter and Thomas. A new abortion case, *Casey v. Planned Parenthood of Pennsylvania,* was being argued before the new Court, and most commentators thought that *Roe* would finally be repealed outright, or at least further eviscerated. I wrote the essay in Chapter 3, which was first presented as part of an exchange with Judge Richard Posner, to argue against overruling *Roe,* and to recommend a different and more powerful rationale for that decision, explicitly based on the moral reading of the Constitution. That chapter anticipated some of the arguments of the Introduction, though the Introduction makes them, in somewhat different form, as part of a more general argument for the moral reading and for the constitutional conception of democracy.

To the surprise of most commentators, the Court did reaffirm *Roe,* and did give it a new and better foundation, along the lines that Chapter 3 (which was cited in one opinion) described, though without explicit reference to one of the doctrinal bases—the First Amendment—mentioned there. In Chapter 4, published directly after that decision, I described the various opinions in the *Casey* decision, and explained why the decision represents a clear endorsement of the moral reading.

Abortion was not the only issue of conscience and personal freedom that has figured in constitutional adjudication in recent decades. Chapter 5 describes another such issue—euthanasia. It discusses the Supreme Court's 1990 decision in the heart-breaking *Cruzan* case, in which the Court upheld Missouri's right to set strict conditions on the manner in which people, when competent, may specify what methods may be used to sustain their lives if they fall into a persistent vegetative state. The various opinions that made up the Court's decision have implications that extend beyond the immediate issue that the justices faced. I have added an addendum to the chapter which is a short article I published in 1994, discussing a dramatic and potentially revolutionary decision by a Seattle district court judge, who relied on the *Casey* abortion decision to rule that it is unconstitutional for a state to deny terminally ill patients, in all circumstances, the right to the help of a doctor in committing suicide. The Ninth Circuit Court of Appeals, in a decision by Judge John Noonan, who is a noted Catholic theorist, reversed that decision, and the Supreme Court will have soon to confront the stark questions the district court raised.[1]

Though Chapter 6 touches on abortion, because it discusses the part Reagan's solicitor general played in the cases discussed in earlier chapters, it mainly discusses a different issue that has also continued to play a major role in constitutional argument—affirmative action. This is once again a political issue, as newly powerful Republicans have vowed sharply to curtail the various programs through which different institutions have tried to reduce the balkanization of American society by improving the number and visibility of women and members of minority groups in employment, particularly in skilled jobs and professions. The issue is important in the constitutional argument, as I emphasized in the Introduction, not only because of its social and political importance, but because it is an issue which tempts politically conservative judges to rely on the moral reading of the Constitution to strike down decisions of more majoritarian institutions, not out of hypocrisy, but rather out of a sense of the power and point of that reading when what *they* take to be political injustice appears. The Court's radical decision in *Adarand Constructors, Inc. v. Pena* (announced on June 12, 1995) is a superb illustration of that point.[2]

1

▼

Roe in Danger

No judicial decision in our time has aroused as much sustained public outrage, emotion, and physical violence, or as much intemperate professional criticism, as the Supreme Court's 1973 decision in *Roe v. Wade,* which declared, by a seven to two majority, that women have a constitutionally protected right to abortion in the early stages of pregnancy.[1] In the years since, anti-abortion groups and political conservatives have campaigned with single-minded conviction to reverse that decision. They proposed without success a series of constitutional amendments, sponsored unsuccessful bills asking Congress to declare that a fetus's life begins at conception, persuaded President Reagan to appoint anti-abortion judges to the federal courts, waged single-issue political campaigns against candidates who support a right to abortion, and disrupted and bombed abortion clinics.[2] The public at large is divided in different ways about different aspects of the abortion issue. A *Los Angeles Times* national survey reported that 61 percent of Americans think abortion morally wrong—57 percent think it murder—and yet 74 percent nevertheless believe that "abortion is a decision that has to be made by every woman for herself."

The composition of the Supreme Court has changed dramatically since 1973,[3] and now, in *Webster v. Reproductive Health Services,* the state of Missouri and the Bush administration ask the Court to reverse *Roe v. Wade.* The Missouri legislature had enacted a statute designed to discourage abortions in spite of that decision. The statute, among other things, declared that human life begins at conception; it required doctors, as part of determining whether a fetus is viable before undertaking an abortion, to

44

perform expensive, often irrelevant, and sometimes dangerous tests; and it prohibited any abortion in hospitals or medical facilities that employ assets owned, leased, or controlled by the state. Lower federal courts declared all these provisions unconstitutional under *Roe v. Wade.* Missouri appealed to the Supreme Court, asking the Court to overrule that decision or, failing that, to curtail or restrict it in such a way that the Missouri statute would then be constitutional.

Oral argument was heard on April 26, 1989, while protesters on both sides of the issue organized long and noisy demonstrations outside the Court. Charles Fried, who was solicitor general in the Reagan administration and has now returned to the Harvard Law School faculty, defended in a brief and in oral argument the Bush administration's claim that *Roe v. Wade* should now be discarded. Seventy-eight other briefs—more than in any previous case—were filed by a wide variety of concerned groups. These include, for example, briefs on various aspects of the litigation on behalf of 25 United States senators and 115 congressmen, the American Medical Association and other medical groups, 281 academic historians, 885 law professors, and a large number of anti-abortion groups. The Court is expected to hand down its decision before it adjourns in July, though it might wait until next year. Whatever decision it reaches will frustrate and anger millions of Americans.

Is the human fetus a person from the moment of conception? That question has been argued by theologians and moral philosophers and ordinary people for many centuries. It cannot be resolved by legal research or scientific evidence or conceptual analysis; it will continue to divide people, as it divides Americans now, so long as deep disagreements remain about God and morals and metaphysics. It therefore seems an exceptionally poor issue to ask any court, including the Supreme Court, to decide, and that fact best explains, I think, the immediate appeal many people find in the idea that the abortion issue is best decided politically, through the ordinary processes of legislation. It seems offensive that a majority of judges on a single court should declare one answer for everyone. It seems more democratic, and also better suited to the inherent complexity of the issue, that different groups of Americans should be permitted to decide, through political action state by state, which solution fits their own convictions and needs best.

That first impression is misguided in several ways, however. Leaving the abortion issue to state-by-state politics will not, of course, mean that each woman will be able to decide which solution best fits *her* convictions and needs. It means that if the anti-abortion lobby is sufficiently powerful in a particular state, the women of that state will be denied that opportunity, as they were before *Roe v. Wade*.[4] It is doubtful that there were fewer abortions then, relative to the number of pregnancies, even though most of them were illegal. But there were many more deaths: abortion-related fatalities were 40 percent higher before *Roe v. Wade*.[5] Blacks suffered most. In New York, for example, a black woman was nine times as likely to die in an illegal abortion as a white one. Of course if *Roe v. Wade* were reversed, women who were rich and knowledgeable enough could still decide to have an abortion by traveling to the nearest or most convenient place where it was legal, as thousands did before 1973 by traveling to Britain, for example. But a poor woman who found herself pregnant might have to choose between the danger of illegal abortion and the misery imposed by and on a child she could not support or raise.

The first impression is misguided not just practically, but legally and logically as well. The key question in the debate over *Roe v. Wade* is not a metaphysical question about the concept of personhood or a theological question about whether a fetus has a soul, but a legal question about the correct interpretation of the Constitution which in our political system *must* be settled one way or the other judicially, by the Supreme Court, rather than politically. It is the question whether the fetus is a *constitutional* person, that is, a person whose rights and interests must be ranked equally important with those of other people in the scheme of individual rights the Constitution establishes. That is a complex and difficult question, and it does involve moral issues. But it is nevertheless different from the metaphysical question philosophers and theologians debate; it is entirely consistent to think, for example, that a fetus is just as much a human being as an adult, or that it has a soul from the moment of conception, and yet that the Constitution, on the best interpretation, does not grant a fetus rights competitive with the rights it grants other people.

Courts cannot avoid deciding the legal question whether a fetus is a constitutional person because it makes no sense to consider what constitutional rights some people do or do not have, in any area of constitutional law, without first deciding who *else* has rights a state must or may also recognize. The Supreme Court has held, for example, that the citizens of each state have a constitutional right that state elections be conducted under districting arrangements that ensure one person one vote, and a state could not undermine that principle by counting as people whole classes of entities that the Constitution, properly interpreted, does not. A state could not declare corporations persons, for instance, by providing separate votes for them, and cut down the voting power of real people. The question of whether and in what sense corporations are constitutional persons, with rights of their own, has been much debated throughout constitutional history. But it has never been doubted that because that question affects the rights of everyone else, it must be decided judicially, at the national constitutional level. Of course a state may promote the interests of its corporations in a wide variety of ways. But it cannot endow them with rights whose force is to curtail the constitutional rights enjoyed by others. Only the Constitution can do that.[6]

So the question of who is a constitutional person must be settled at the constitutional level, by the Supreme Court, as part of deciding what constitutional rights anyone has, and the question whether a fetus is a constitutional person is pivotal to the abortion debate. In *Roe v. Wade* the Court decided that a fetus is not a constitutional person before birth, and though its opinion has been criticized by several academic lawyers, it is largely persuasive once that premise is accepted. Earlier Supreme Court decisions had established that a person has a fundamental constitutional right to control his or her own role in procreation—the Court had decided, for example, that for this reason a state may not prohibit the sale of contraceptives. If a fetus is not a constitutional person, then a fetus's right to live cannot be cited as a justification for denying that right after pregnancy begins, though of course a state can nevertheless protect the fetus's interests in a great variety of other ways.

But if the fetus is a constitutional person, then *Roe v. Wade* is plainly wrong, as the Court's opinion in that case conceded. The Fourteenth Amendment declares that no state may deny any person "equal protection of the laws." If the fetus is protected by that clause, then of course a state is entitled to protect its life in the same way it protects the lives of other people under its care, and for that reason is entitled to say that a woman's right to control the use of her body for procreation ends, at least when her health is not at stake, when pregnancy begins. Indeed, it would be difficult to resist a very much stronger conclusion: that a state is not only entitled but *required* to take that view, so that states like New York, which decided to permit abortion in early pregnancy even before *Roe v. Wade* was decided, would be constitutionally *prohibited* from doing so.

The equal protection clause requires states to extend the protection of their laws against murder and assault equally to all persons, and if fetuses were constitutional persons any state legislation that discriminated against them in that respect, by permitting abortion, would be "suspect," under equal protection principles, and the Supreme Court would have an obligation to review such legislation to determine whether the state's justification for that discrimination was "compelling." In some cases it would be: when a state permitted abortion to protect the health of a mother, for example, or perhaps in cases of rape or incest. But if a woman is well aware of the physical and emotional consequences of pregnancy and voluntarily has sexual intercourse knowing that she risks becoming pregnant, a state that permits her or her doctor to abort her fetus has no compelling justification for doing so if the fetus is entitled to equal protection of the laws. For a state fails to show equal concern for both mother and fetus when it allows the mother to regain the freedom of her body at the expense of the fetus's life.

It is true, as a number of legal scholars have pointed out, that the law does not generally require people to make any sacrifice at all to save the life of another person who needs their aid. A person ordinarily has no legal duty to save a stranger from drowning even if he can do so at no risk to himself and with minimal effort.[7] But abortion normally requires a physical attack on a fetus, not just the failure to come to its aid. And in any case parents are invariably made an exception to the general doctrine under which people are not required to save others. Parents have a legal duty to care for their children, and if a fetus is a person from conception a state would not be justified in discriminating between fetuses and infants. If it did not permit killing infants or abandoning them in circumstances in which they would inevitably die, it could not permit abortion either.[8] The physical and emotional and economic burdens of pregnancy are intense, of course, but so are the parallel burdens of parenthood.

I stress this point because it is important to notice that those who urge the Supreme Court to leave the question of abortion to the states, to decide as their politics dictate, have in effect conceded that a fetus is *not* a constitutional person. In oral argument, Justice Byron White asked Charles Fried whether in his view there is "some problem about the state permitting abortion." Fried replied, "Oh, no," and said very firmly that it would be a serious mistake for the Court to "constitutionalize" the issue at any "point in the spectrum" by requiring constitutional scrutiny of permissive abortion legislation by a state. That position is preposterous except on the assumption that the Constitution itself offers a fetus's life no protection at all.[9]

But Fried could hardly have given White's question any other answer. It would be political madness for the Court to try to force unwilling states to outlaw abortion; and neither the government nor any other responsible group has asked it to do so. The damage to the community, to the Court's authority, and to the Constitution would be far greater if it did try to force the states to outlaw abortion than if it simply left the law where it stands. But the Court can avoid that inconceivable decision, legitimately, only by confirming *Roe v. Wade's* explicit decision that a fetus is not a constitutional person. So the most complex and difficult of the legal issues in the abortion dispute has been removed from the controversy by a kind of practical necessity. I do not mean to suggest, by emphasizing these practical arguments for that view, that it is not the correct view in law. On the contrary, I think that it is.

The question is one of legal interpretation. The principle that the fetus is not a constitutional person fits better with other parts of our law and also with our sense of how related issues would and should be decided if they arose than the rival principle that it is. Even if the fetus is a human being, it is in a unique situation politically as well as biologically for a reason that could properly be thought sufficient to deny it constitutional status. The state can take action that affects it, in order to protect or advance its interests, only through its mother, and only through means that would necessarily restrict her freedom in ways no man's or other woman's freedom could constitutionally be limited; by dictating her diet and other personal and intimate behavior, for example. Apart from anti-abortion statutes, there are few signs in our law of the kind of regulation of pregnancy that would be appropriate if the fetus were a constitutional person, and the Supreme Court has never suggested any constitutional requirement of such protection.

The best historical evidence shows, moreover, that even anti-abortion laws, which were not prevalent in the United States before the middle of the nineteenth century, were adopted to protect the health of the mother and the privileges of the medical profession, not out of any recognition of a fetus's rights.[10] Even states that had the most stringent anti-abortion laws before *Roe v. Wade,* moreover, did not punish abortion as severely as murder, as they should have done if they thought a fetus a constitutional person. Nor did they try to outlaw or penalize a woman's procuring an abortion in another state or abroad.

So the better interpretation of our constitutional law and practice holds that a fetus is not a constitutional person. That conclusion could be accepted, as I suggested, even by someone who thinks abortion a heinous sin: not every sin is or could be punished by law. But it will of course be easier to accept for someone who believes that a human being has no moral right to life until it has developed self-consciousness as a being whose life extends over time.[11] On the assumption that this condition is not reached until some time after birth, the interpretive conclusion, that a human being becomes a constitutional person no earlier than at that point, seems even sounder.

It is therefore not an acceptable argument, against the claim that women have a constitutional right to choose an abortion in early pregnancy, that the fetus is a constitutional person whose competing right to live would overcome any such right. I have already mentioned the argument *for* the claim that women do have a constitutional right of that character. In a series of previous cases relating to sterilization, marriage, and contraception, the Supreme Court recognized that all citizens have a general right, based in the Fourteenth Amendment's guarantee of due process of law, to decide for themselves ethical and personal issues arising from marriage and procreation.[12] Justice Blackmun relied heavily on these previous decisions, which have come to be called "privacy" decisions, in his opinion for the Court in *Roe v. Wade*. He argued that though abortion raises questions different from those raised by these other issues, the general principle that people have a right to control their own role in procreation plainly applied to abortion as well.[13] Neither Missouri nor the Bush administration has argued that these precedents should be overruled.[14] Fried, in oral argument, said that the case of *Griswold v. Connecticut,* which upheld a right of contraception, was correct and should not be disturbed. He said that *Roe v. Wade* could be overruled without affecting that case or the other privacy precedents, that *Roe v. Wade* could be pulled from the fabric woven by these past decisions like a single thread.

Abortion cannot be disentangled from contraception even medically, however, because the IUD and the most popular and safest birth control pills act as abortifacients; that is, they destroy fertilized ova. So the Court could not hold that a woman's right to control her role in procreation ends with fertilization without permitting states to outlaw the contraceptives now in use. That would be in effect to overrule *Griswold,* which Fried said was a correct decision. Even if contraception and abortion did not overlap medically in that way, they could not be distinguished in principle, once it is assumed that a fetus is not a constitutional person.

The Court's previous privacy decisions can be justified only on the assumption that decisions affecting marriage and childbirth are so important, so intimate and personal, so crucial to the development of personality and sense of moral responsibility, and so closely tied to religious and ethical convictions protected by the First Amendment, that people must be allowed to make these decisions for themselves, consulting their own conscience, rather than allowing society to thrust its collective decision on them. The abortion decision is at least as much a private decision in that sense as any other the Court has protected. In many ways it is more private, because the decision involves a woman's control not just of her connections to others, but of the use of her own body, and the Constitution recognizes in a variety of ways the special intimacy of a person's connection to her own physical integrity.[15]

If a fetus were a constitutional person, then abortion could of course be distinguished from at least contraception that did not involve abortifacients, because a state could properly cite a compelling interest in protecting the fetus's right to life and to be treated with equal concern. But given the assumption that a fetus is not a constitutional person, that reason for distinguishing abortion from contraception, and from other activities permitted by decisions protecting privacy, fails. Fried tried to distinguish the contraception cases on the ground that *Griswold v. Connecticut* was based not on any general right to control one's own procreation, but on the different basis that the police could enforce a prohibition on the use of contraceptives only by searching the marital bedroom, which would be offensive. It is true that one opinion in *Griswold v. Connecticut* mentioned that reason for invalidating a prohibition on married couples using contraceptives. But it is a silly reason, not only because prohibitions on the use of contraceptives could be enforced without breaking down bedroom doors, but because the Court has upheld other criminal statutes that might be thought just as difficult to enforce without offensive and impermissible searches.[16]

In any case, the later contraception cases rejected that interpretation of *Griswold v. Connecticut,* and they are inconsistent with it. In *Eisenstadt v. Baird,* Justice Brennan, for the Court, stated the point of the past privacy cases this way: "If the right of privacy means anything, it is the right of the *individual,* married or not, to be free from government intrusion into matters so fundamentally affecting a person as the decision whether to bear or beget a child."

And one of the justices who dissented in the *Griswold* case, Potter Stewart, joined the majority in *Roe v. Wade,* on the ground that if one accepts the *Griswold* decision, as he then did on grounds of precedent, one has to accept *Roe v. Wade* as well. Fried's claim that the privacy decisions were really only about searching bedrooms proved too bizarre for him to defend with any confidence. When Justice Sandra Day O'Connor asked a direct question, "Do you say there is no fundamental right to decide whether to have a child or not?" he could only answer, "I would hesitate to formulate the right in such abstract terms."

So the argument from precedent in favor of *Roe v. Wade* seems a strong one: Supreme Court precedents established a constitutional right of control over one's own role in childbirth, and, if a fetus is not a constitutional person, that right naturally extends to abortion. But we must now consider the opposing arguments made by those lawyers, including the justices dissenting in that case, who insist it was wrong and should now be discarded. They say that the right to abortion is "judge-made" and has "little or no cognizable roots in the language or design of the Constitution."[17] Or that the right has "no moorings in the text of our Constitution or in familiar constitutional doctrine, and cannot be sustained by 'the interpretive tradition of the legal community.'"[18] Or that the right does not exist because the subject of abortion is "one upon which the Constitution is silent."[19]

But these various complaints beg the question. Of course if the judges who decided *Roe v. Wade* made up the constitutional rights they announced, or if those rights have no roots in the language or design of the Constitution, or if they cannot be established as drawn from the Constitution by interpretive methods traditional to legal reasoning, then the decision was certainly wrong. But we cannot decide whether these complaints are justified without some theory of how judges *should* interpret the abstract provisions of the Constitution, such as the provision that requires due process of law. How should judges decide which rights do and which do not have "roots" in the abstract language?

The various government briefs in *Webster* sometimes suggest an answer to that question which our legal tradition has decisively rejected: that abstract language should never be interpreted to yield a right that the historical framers who enacted the abstract provision did not accept themselves. The briefs argue that the Fourteenth Amendment cannot be thought to include a right to abortion because abortion laws were being enacted by states throughout the country when that amendment was added to the Constitution.[20] But the Congress that enacted the Fourteenth Amendment itself segregated the public schools of the District of Columbia, and no one now argues that *Brown v. Board of Education,* which held that segregation violated the rights provided by that amendment, was wrong.

The briefs of the Bush administration and the state of Missouri also rely on a variety of other interpretive suggestions. They propose that the Constitution should be understood to contain only "enumerated" rights, that is, rights explicitly mentioned in the text. But that ignores the fact that the same legal situation can be described in different ways. The Supreme Court decided, in 1952, that the police may not pump out a suspect's stomach for evidence. Shall we say that the Court decided that the right to due process of law, which is mentioned in the text of the Constitution, applied to the particular facts of that case? Or that it decided that people have a right not to have their stomachs pumped, which is derived from the due process clause but which is not itself mentioned in the text? There is only a verbal difference between these two formulations and neither is more accurate than the other.

In any case, if we must reject the right to an abortion because abortion is not mentioned in the Constitution, then we must also reject a great number of other, unquestioned constitutional rights that lawyers frequently describe in language not to be found there either. These include the right to use contraceptives, which the government now argues is part of the Constitution in spite of the fact that contraception is not mentioned. They also include the right to vote, to marry, to travel between states, to live with one's extended family, to educate one's children privately in schools meeting educational standards, and to attend racially desegregated schools. If these are all "unenumerated" rights, and so "judge-made" constitutional law, it hardly counts against *Roe v. Wade* that it falls into the same category.

One of the government briefs replies to that objection with a metaphor. It says that the supposed right of abortion "travels further from its point of departure in the text" than these other rights. But how do we measure the distance between a right and the constitutional language from which it is drawn? How can we tell whether the distance between abortion and the constitutional language of due process is greater than the distance between contraception or stomach pumping and that language? Or the distance between the other "unenumerated" rights I listed and the constitutional language in which these were rooted?

Our legal tradition gives a very different, less metaphorical and superficial, answer to the question how abstract constitutional provisions should be interpreted. Judges should seek to identify the principles latent in the Constitution as a whole, and in past judicial decisions applying the Constitution's abstract language, in order to enforce the same principles in new areas and so make the law steadily more coherent. In that way, the principles that have been relied on to justify rights for one group or in one situation are extended, so far as that is possible, to everyone else to whom they equally apply. That common law process was used in *Roe v. Wade* to argue that the principles latent in the earlier privacy decisions about sterilization and family and contraception must be applied to the abortion case as well. These earlier privacy decisions can themselves be defended in a similar way, as part of a broader project of the Court, begun earlier in the century, to identify and enforce the principles implicit in what the Court called "the concept of ordered liberty," which means the principle a society truly committed to individual liberty and dignity must recognize. A right to control one's part in procreation finds support in that general project, as well as in the more closely related decisions protecting privacy, because that right is crucially important to the moral, social, and economic freedom of women.

These are the arguments that the opponents of *Roe v. Wade* must meet, and they should try to meet them in the traditional way, by explaining why principles different from those mentioned, which do not yield a right to abortion, provide a more satisfactory interpretation of the Constitution as a whole and of the Court's past decisions under it. Of course different judges will come to very different conclusions about which principles provide the best interpretation of the Constitution, and since there is no neutral standpoint from which it can be proved which side is right, each justice must in the end rely on his or her convictions about which argument is best. But that is an inevitable feature of a political system, like ours, which conceives of its Constitution as a charter of principle rather than a particular collection of political settlements.

Certainly the present critics of *Roe v. Wade* offer no alternative. Since their question-begging rhetoric about "judge-made law" and "new rights" rests on no reasoned intellectual basis, it provides even less discipline than the traditional interpretive method, because the latter does demand coherent and extended argument, not just name-calling. The question-begging rhetoric, on the contrary, leaves lawyers free to accept constitutional rights now popular in the community, such as the right to legally integrated education and to the use of contraceptives, and to oppose rights politically more troublesome, such as the right to abortion, without having to explain what the difference between the constitutional standing of these rights actually is.

Though *Roe v. Wade* held that women have a right in principle to control their part in procreation, it added that states have a legitimate interest in protecting "potential life," and that any statement of a woman's constitutional right to an abortion must take that interest into account. It decided that the state's interest becomes compelling enough in late pregnancy, when the fetus has become viable, to permit the state to regulate or prohibit abortions after that point, except as necessary to protect the mother's health. Unfortunately, the Court did not satisfactorily explain what kind of interest a state is permitted to take in "potential life," or why its concern grows stronger or more legitimate after a fetus becomes viable.

The Court did not mean, of course, that a state has a legitimate interest in increasing the birth rate, because that interest would apply with equal strength at all times in pregnancy and, indeed, would justify a state's opposing contraception as vigorously as abortion. Nor did the Court mean that a state may legitimately decide that a being with potential life has rights of its own which the state may take an interest in protecting. As we saw, the Court rightly held that the question whether a fetus is a constitutional person, and thus a person whose rights can be competitive with the constitutional rights of others, must be settled at the constitutional level, not by state legislation, and it then held that the fetus is not such a person. What else could a state's interest in "potential life" mean?

The most persuasive answer which takes the Court's subsequent decisions into account, is, I believe, the following. Even though a fetus is not a constitutional person, it is nevertheless an entity of considerable moral and emotional significance in our culture, and a state may recognize and try to protect that significance in ways that fall short of any substantial abridgment of a woman's constitutional right over the use of her own body. A state might properly fear the impact of widespread abortion on its citizens' instinctive respect for the value of human life and their instinctive horror at human destruction or suffering, which are values essential for the maintenance of a just and decently civil society. A political community in which abortion became commonplace and a matter of ethical indifference, like appendectomy, would certainly be a more callous and insensitive community, and it might be a more dangerous one as well.

A state's concern for the moral significance of a fetus increases as pregnancy advances, and it is particularly intense after viability, when the fetus has assumed a post-natal baby's form. This is a matter of resemblance.[21] People's instinctive respect for life is unlikely to be lessened significantly if they come to regard the abortion of a just-fertilized ovum as permissible, any more than it is lessened when they accept contraception.

But the assault on instinctive values is likely to be almost as devastating when a nearly full-term baby is aborted as when a week-old child is killed.

So the state's concern is greatest after the point at which a fetus, under present technology, is viable, and a prohibition on elective abortion after that time will not significantly burden or compromise a woman's constitutional right.[22] Her right is a right to make fundamental decisions for herself, and that right is satisfied when she has had ample time after discovering her pregnancy to consider whether she wishes to continue it, and to arrange a safe and convenient abortion if she does not.[23] *Roe v. Wade,* understood in that way, did not balance a woman's rights against the competing rights of a fetus or of anyone else. Rather it identified a scheme of regulation that could meet a state's most powerful needs without substantially compromising a woman's rights at all.

The Court had to pick a particular event or period of pregnancy in constructing that scheme in order to make it clear enough to be administered by officials and judges.[24] If the Court had said simply that a state must allow a woman "ample" or "reasonable" time after the discovery of pregnancy to decide about abortion, it would have faced a succession of test cases provoked by state legislatures defining the cut-off line earlier and earlier, so that it would eventually have been forced to draw a line in any case. The Court's decision to make the crucial event viability, which occurs at approximately twenty-three or twenty-four weeks, has much to recommend it. Viability marks a distinct stage of pregnancy after which the difference between a fetus and a premature infant is a matter not of development but only of environment. Since viability follows "quickening," or the point at which a pregnant woman feels movement in her womb, it is late enough to provide her a reasonable opportunity for an abortion after pregnancy is discovered. (Teenage women, particularly, may easily be unaware of pregnancy before quickening; their periods may have been erratic or missing before pregnancy and they may not "show," or look pregnant, before then.)

Some critics feared that advances in medical technology would make fetuses viable much earlier, requiring the Court to change its standard; in an earlier case Justice O'Connor said that *Roe v. Wade* was for that reason on "a collision course" with itself. But a consensus of medical opinion now declares that fear unfounded: there is, according to the brief filed in the *Webster* case by the American Medical Association and other medical groups, an "anatomical threshold for fetal survival of about twenty-three to twenty-four weeks of gestation . . . because the fetal lung does not mature sufficiently to permit normal or even mechanically-assisted respiration before [that time]."

An established Supreme Court decision, particularly one that recognizes individual constitutional rights, should not be overruled unless it is clearly wrong or has proved thoroughly unworkable.[25] *Roe v. Wade* is not wrong, and it certainly is not clearly wrong. Justice Blackmun's opinion might have been clearer in some respects, and the Court might have chosen an event in pregnancy other than viability but which occurs at roughly the same time, such as neocortical functioning, to mark the point at which abortion might be prohibited.[26] But these are hardly reasons to tear apart constitutional law by overturning the decision now. The Court should refuse to nourish the cynical view, already popular among its critics, that constitutional law is only a matter of which President appointed the last few justices.

If the Court declines to overrule or substantially restrict *Roe v. Wade,* as it should, it must decide the more limited constitutional issues raised by the *Webster* case. As I said, the lower courts declared unconstitutional a variety of clauses in Missouri's statute. The state does not now contest some of these rulings, and urges implausible but benign interpretations of others in order to save them from unconstitutionality. The important remaining controversy concerns the state's ban on the use of public facilities in connection with abortion even when the abortion is performed by a private doctor and paid for by private funds.

The statute defines public facilities very broadly as "any public institution, public facility, public equipment, or any physical asset owned, leased, or controlled by this state or any agency or political subdivision thereof." So it would forbid abortion in the Truman Medical Center in Kansas City—where 97 percent of all hospital abortions at sixteen weeks or later in Missouri were performed in 1985—in spite of the fact that the center is a private hospital staffed mainly by private doctors, and administered by private corporations, just because that hospital is located on ground leased from a political subdivision of the state.[27]

Missouri defends the provision by appealing to earlier decisions of the Supreme Court. In *Maher v. Roe,*[28] the Court sustained a state's right to provide medical assistance funds for childbirth but not for abortion, and in *Poelker v. Doe*[29] it allowed a state to provide childbirth but not abortion facilities in a public city hospital. The Court said that although a state may not forbid abortions, it need not go into the abortion business itself. It might constitutionally adopt a preference for childbirth to abortion, and provide funds only for the former.

The decisions in the *Maher* and *Poelker* cases have been criticized because they permit states to take action to discourage people from exercising their constitutional rights. But even if we accept these decisions as sound they do not support Missouri's broad prohibition. Of course a state need not subsidize or support the exercise of every constitutional right, and it may pursue policies of its own choice in the benefits it awards. It may without violating anyone's rights to free speech publish literature encouraging conservation while refusing to distribute other political material.

But Missouri's argument overlooks a crucial distinction. It is one thing for a state to decline to participate in some act it disapproves in circumstances in which it would itself be the author of the act, or would plausibly be taken to be, if it did. A state, for example, may refuse to distribute political criticism of its own government without violating anyone's rights to free speech. It is quite another thing for a state to use its economic power or control of crucial resources to discourage citizens from exercising their constitutional rights when there is no question of the state being seen as the author of, or as in any way supporting, what they do. A city cannot force newsstands in shopping centers built on public land to sell only papers it approves. It cannot force theaters it supplies with water and power and police protection to perform only plays it likes.

Perhaps a state that itself pays for abortions, or provides them in free public hospitals, will in effect have declared itself neutral between abortion and childbirth, or will be understood to have done so. For the state is necessarily the author of its own public funding and public medical provision. But it is preposterous that a state should be understood as itself performing abortions carried out by private doctors on their own initiative and paid for with private funds, just because the hospital in which this is done is in other ways state-supported, or because it is on land the state, as it happens, owns.

The true explanation of why Missouri adopted its stringent prohibition is not, of course, that it wants to avoid declaring itself neutral about abortion, but that it wants to make abortion as difficult and as expensive as possible in order to discourage its residents from exercising their constitutional rights. It enacts whatever measures to that end its officials can devise and the federal courts have not yet condemned, including measures so obviously unconstitutional that its lawyers do not seriously defend them when they are challenged. That is impermissible: a state must not declare war on its own people because it is angry that the law is on their side.

Unhappily, if the Court in any way now signals itself more ready to accept constraints on abortion than it has been in the past, that dismal spectacle will continue. Other states will adopt more and more restrictive statutes to provoke more and more test cases to see how far the Court will actually go. Charles Fried anticipated exactly that at the close of his oral argument. He asked the justices, even if they did not overrule *Roe v. Wade*, at least not to say anything "that would further entrench this decision as a secure premise for reasoning in future cases." The justices would do best for constitutional order and decorum, as well as principle, if they refused to take that bad advice.

June 29, 1989

2

▼

Verdict Postponed

On July 3, 1989, the Supreme Court decided *Webster v. Missouri Reproduction Services,* the abortion case that had been the subject of unprecedented political campaigns, demonstrations, and public debate for months. By a five to four vote, the Court left standing every provision of the Missouri statute restricting abortion that had been brought before it, reversing lower federal courts which had declared these provisions unconstitutional.

The most important of the Missouri provisions prohibits abortion altogether in any "public facility," defined very broadly to include "any public institution, public facility, public equipment, or any physical asset owned, leased, or controlled by this state or any agency or political subdivision thereof." Since the statute forbids abortion in any such facility even when paid for privately and performed by a private doctor, the effect will be to deny abortions to many women too poor or otherwise unable to find a doctor and hospital with no state connections.[1] That is a serious and discriminatory constraint, which other states can now be expected to follow.

Nevertheless, the Court's decision did not go as far in restricting women's rights to have an abortion as anti-abortion groups had hoped it would. The state of Missouri and the Bush administration had both invited the Court to take the opportunity to overrule *Roe v. Wade,* the famous and much criticized 1973 Supreme Court decision which struck down a Texas statute that prohibited abortion at any time except to save the mother's life. The Court said then that states cannot prohibit abortion, except to

60

protect the mother, before the third trimester of pregnancy. The main opinion in *Webster*, written by Chief Justice William Rehnquist, said that the Court was not overruling *Roe v. Wade* because it was not deciding that states could make abortion criminal even in early pregnancy. But the opinion also said that the Court was abandoning the "rigid trimester structure" of *Roe*, which prohibited any regulation of abortion before the third trimester except in the mother's interests. The opinion left open the possibility that the Court would overrule *Roe* completely in a future case, and in effect it invited states to enact even more restrictive legislation than Missouri had. State politics has been dominated by the abortion issue since the decision was announced.

Rehnquist's opinion was supported in full by only two other justices—White and Kennedy. Since Justices Scalia and O'Connor agreed with the Rehnquist group that the Missouri provisions restricting abortion were constitutional, the decision to reverse the lower courts was a majority decision and therefore the decision of the Court as a whole. But Scalia and O'Connor each rejected important parts of Rehnquist's opinion, and four justices, joining or supporting a fierce and persuasive opinion by Justice Blackmun, dissented from almost all of it. So the opinion represents the full views of only three justices, and it is wrong to assert, as many commentators have, that its remarks about *Roe v. Wade* have already changed constitutional law. Nevertheless, the opinion must be studied carefully because it suggests how a crucial group of justices will vote in later cases, not just about abortion but also about other individual liberties the Supreme Court has protected from majority interference in recent decades.

Justice Scalia, in an indignant concurring opinion, said that it was irresponsible of the Court not to overrule *Roe v. Wade* outright. He said that Rehnquist's approach left states in doubt as to their rights, and left the Court subject to continuing and unseemly political pressure. Justice O'Connor, on the contrary, criticized the Rehnquist opinion for saying too much rather than too little about *Roe*. She said that Rehnquist had simply invented a false conflict between the Missouri statute and the *Roe v. Wade* trimester structure, and she cited ample authority, including statements from earlier opinions by Rehnquist himself, that the Supreme Court should not pronounce on issues of constitutional law not raised by the case before it. "When the constitutional invalidity of a State's abortion statute actually turns on the constitutional validity of *Roe v. Wade*," she said, "there will be time enough to reexamine *Roe*. And to do so carefully."[2]

O'Connor was plainly right.[3] Rehnquist claimed only that one section of the Missouri statute was inconsistent with the theory of *Roe v. Wade*: section 188.029, which requires doctors, before performing an abortion on any woman they have reason to think is twenty or more weeks pregnant, to determine whether the fetus is viable by performing "such medical examinations and tests as are necessary to make a finding of [its] gestational age, weight, and lung maturity."

Lower federal courts had held this clause unconstitutional on the ground that it required expensive and sometimes dangerous tests even when there would be no medical point in performing them. If that were the correct interpretation, the clause would be unconstitutional because irrational quite apart from *Roe v. Wade*. But Rehnquist saved the clause by interpreting it in a different way: he said that in spite of its apparently imperative language it should be read as requiring only those tests that a "careful and prudent" doctor would use in the circumstances.[4] Then he said that since the statute required doctors to perform such tests even when they had reason to think a fetus had reached only twenty weeks, it violated the strict structure of *Roe v. Wade*, because if the fetus did turn out to be only twenty weeks of age the state, by requiring tests, would have intervened in a second-trimester abortion, which *Roe* does not permit.

This is a stunningly bad argument. Rehnquist himself quoted the lower court's findings that "the medical evidence is uncontradicted that a 20-week fetus is *not* viable," and that "$23\frac{1}{2}$ to 24 weeks gestation is the earliest point in pregnancy where a reasonable possibility of viability exists." But he added that the lower court "also found that there may be a 4-week error in estimating gestational age . . . [and the possibility of such an error] supports testing [when doctors have reason to think that the fetus is twenty weeks old]." If so, then, contrary to Rehnquist's argument, Missouri's medical requirement can be assigned a purpose wholly consistent with the trimester structure; indeed it *must* be assigned that purpose in order not to be thought irrational. It attempts to ensure that doctors do not carelessly abort viable fetuses. Briefs filed by both an anti-abortion medical group and the American Medical Association pointed out that noninvasive and relatively inexpensive tests, like ultrasound examinations, can confirm a doctor's judgment that a fetus has not reached twenty-four weeks, and so allow him to make all the other findings the statute requires by inference. If his judgment is confirmed, he is free to abort with no further tests. If it is not, then the fetus is viable, and Missouri may prohibit the abortion under the *Roe v. Wade* structure.

Roe v. Wade recognizes that the states have a "compelling" interest in preventing the abortion of viable fetuses, and it therefore permits a state to adopt reasonable regulations to ensure that viable fetuses are not aborted negligently. A requirement that doctors perform whatever tests a careful and prudent doctor would perform to ensure that a fetus is not viable is plainly a reasonable regulation to that end. Justice Blackmun, who wrote the opinion in *Roe v. Wade,* said on behalf of himself and Justices Brennan and Marshall that if section 188.029 were interpreted as Rehnquist interpreted it, it would plainly be constitutional under the trimester structure, and Justice Stevens, in his separate dissent, agreed. Even the brief for Missouri Reproduction Services, the plaintiff who had challenged the statute, itself conceded that point. It argued that the interpretation Rehnquist ultimately adopted was implausible, but it said that if *that* interpretation were adopted it would no longer have any constitutional objection to the clause.

So Rehnquist offered his bad argument in an effort not to reconcile his decision with judicial precedent, as judges often do, but to show that his decision was *inconsistent* with precedent, which is extraordinary. The conclusion is irresistible that he had determined in advance somehow to damage *Roe v. Wade* without explicitly overruling it, and the crucial question, for those concerned with the future of constitutional law in individual rights, is why he did so. Scalia hinted at a depressing explanation in his bitter prediction that Rehnquist's opinion would be hailed as a "triumph of judicial statesmanship." It is possible that Rehnquist hoped to satisfy as many of the parties in the abortion debate as possible by saying both that the Court was leaving *Roe v. Wade* "undisturbed," and that it was abandoning the fundamental logic of that case, ignoring the contradiction.

Blackmun's angry but powerful dissent suggested a different explanation, Machiavellian rather than Solomonic: that Rehnquist, White, and Kennedy do intend eventually to overrule *Roe* altogether, and leave women with no constitutional rights to an abortion at all, but that they intend to do so not directly and in plain terms, having to confront strong arguments and strong contrary public opinion, but indirectly and in stages. Blackmun may be right.[5]

Some commentators find evidence for a more favorable interpretation of the Rehnquist opinion, however.[6] They suggest that Rehnquist and his colleagues may have attacked *Roe v. Wade*'s structure to prepare the way for substituting, in future cases, a new set of principles that would adjust the rights of the state and individual women somewhat differently: to give states greater power to regulate abortion than they have under *Roe*'s trimester doctrine, and yet confirm that a woman has some constitutional right to make her own decision whether to continue an unwanted pregnancy, even though it is a more limited right than *Roe* recognized.

Is there evidence in Rehnquist's opinion that he and the justices who joined him intend to allow women some limited right to an abortion? He said that he and they regard abortion as a "liberty interest protected by the due process clause," and that any difference between that description and saying that women have a fundamental right to an abortion would be "abstract." That does seem to suggest at least some constitutional protection for a woman's right to choose. But other lawyers fear exactly the opposite: that the terminological shift from the language of protected rights to the language of liberty interests, far from being academic, means that the Rehnquist group will in the end accept no significant limits on the state's power to regulate or even forbid abortion.

We must notice a point of constitutional practice in order to understand that fear. The Supreme Court has distinguished between two tests it uses to decide whether a state has the constitutional power to limit the liberty of individuals in order to pursue some collective policy or objective. The first is the "compelling interest" test which it used in *Roe v. Wade* and in other cases when important personal liberties were at stake, and which permits liberty to be abridged only when necessary to protect some important state interest, in this case preventing the abortion of viable fetuses.

The second is the much weaker "rational relationship" test it has used in judging economic legislation, which requires only that the state's policy be "valid" or "legitimate" and that there be some rational connection between abridging liberty and advancing that policy. In practice, state legislation almost always passes the weak rational relationship test, because almost any statute can be shown to be related to some goal a state is allowed to pursue. But legislation curtailing liberty almost never passes the "compelling interest" test, because some less restrictive means can invariably be found that would have adequately served any essential state policy. Prohibiting unpopular political protests might well make it easier for the state to maintain law and order in the streets, for example, but that would not justify a prohibition because political protests are protected by the compelling interest test and less drastic means of preventing riots are available. So in practice constitutional cases are decided not *after* choosing between the two standards, but by choosing between them. (The Court has sometimes adopted an intermediate test more demanding than the rational relationship test but less demanding than the compelling interest test. It has done so in gender discrimination cases, for example.)

Rehnquist's description of abortion as a "liberty interest" suggests that he means to switch to the weaker test in deciding future abortion cases because it echoes his original dissent in *Roe v. Wade*.[7] He also said, in that dissent, that abortion is a liberty interest protected by the due process clause, and then added:

> But that liberty is not guaranteed absolutely against deprivation, only against deprivation without due process of law. The test traditionally applied in the area of social and economic legislation is whether or not a law such as that challenged has a rational relation to a valid state objective . . . If the Texas statute were to prohibit an abortion even where the mother's life is in jeopardy, I have little doubt that such a statute would lack a rational relation to a valid state objective under the [rational relation] test stated [above]. But the Court's sweeping invalidation of any restrictions on abortion during the first trimester is impossible to justify under that standard.

Even if the Court does switch to the weaker, rational relationship, test in some future abortion cases, however, that will not necessarily mean that women will receive no constitutional protection. For if a justice accepts that test, his opinions about which state objectives are valid in regulating abortion may very well already embody some recognition of rights that will therefore survive that test. Rehnquist's declaration that a statute forbidding abortion even when the mother's life was in danger would lack a rational relation to a valid objective illustrates the point. If we define a state's valid objective simply as protecting the lives of all fetuses, then it cannot be denied that prohibiting abortion even when necessary to save the mother bears a rational relationship to that goal. Rehnquist's conclusion follows only if he defines the state's legitimate interest in a narrower way, as an interest in protecting not all fetuses but at most only those that can be protected without endangering the mother's life.

Of course once the state's interest is stated that way, then the conclusion that a woman has a right to an abortion needed to save her life follows immediately. That is not because the rational relationship test supports or justifies that right, however, but only because the right is then artificially built into the test in advance, as an assumption that in effect makes the rational relationship test somewhat more like the compelling interest one.[8] So even if a majority of the Court says it is shifting to the weak rational relationship test in abortion cases, they can still recognize significant abortion rights, beyond the right of a woman to save her own life, if they define a state's legitimate interests in a way that already presupposes those further rights.

It is therefore important to consider whether Rehnquist's opinion suggests that he, White, and Kennedy might be prepared to define a state's proper interests in that way, and we should begin by noticing remarks that might indicate otherwise. The entire Court is agreed that at some stage in pregnancy the state has what in *Roe v. Wade* it called a legitimate interest in protecting "potential human life." That often-repeated claim is ambiguous, however, because it does not indicate the character of that interest. In *Roe,* the Court said that the interest became compelling only after viability. Rehnquist's *Webster* opinion challenged that thesis. "We do not see why," he said, "the State's interest in protecting potential human life should come into existence only at the point of viability, and that there should therefore be a rigid line allowing state regulation after viability but prohibiting it before viability." He quoted White's remark in an earlier case that "the State's interest, if compelling after viability, is equally compelling before viability."

These remarks might indicate that Rehnquist and the others have a view of the state's interest in political life that would mean the end of any significant right of women to control their own pregnancies: that the state has a legitimate interest in preventing the destruction of any fertilized ovum except when necessary to save the mother's life. If a state may properly seek that goal, then, according to the rational relationship test, it may prohibit abortion at any stage of pregnancy, because total prohibition is a reasonable, indeed necessary, means of preventing a fetus's destruction.[9] If a majority of the Court accepted that analysis in a future case, states would be free to return to the pre-*Roe* era: a woman too poor to travel to another state where abortion is legal would have only the miserable choice between an illegal and unsafe abortion and an unwanted child that might ruin her life.

Nevertheless, in spite of the evident danger that Rehnquist and his colleagues do have this chilling view of a state's legitimate interests in mind, his opinion leaves some room for them to construct a narrower account of those interests that would recognize important abortion rights. They might accept that a state has a legitimate interest only in protecting the fetus by means that do not deny women a genuine opportunity to terminate a pregnancy, and that therefore a state may not forbid abortion altogether before viability or, perhaps, before some other stage of pregnancy late enough to allow a woman a reasonable chance to make that decision. That would, after all, be only an extension—though a very significant one—of Rehnquist's artificial restriction of a state's interest to cases in which a mother's life is not at stake.[10] Moreover, since only 0.5 percent of the approximately 1.6 million annual abortions now take place after twenty weeks, and only 3.7 percent after sixteen weeks, and since many of these very late abortions are medical emergencies, Rehnquist and the others could allow total prohibition of almost all abortions substantially earlier than *Roe v. Wade* does without much changing the practical impact of that decision.

But they would then insist that a state has *other* legitimate concerns that are equally valid throughout a whole pregnancy. They might argue, for example, that a state has a proper interest in protecting the mother's health even during an early abortion, and therefore that a state can adopt medical regulations made in good faith at any point in pregnancy, contrary to *Roe*, which forbids such regulations before the second trimester. (Rehnquist's remark in his *Roe* dissent that the due process clause would not justify "sweeping invalidation of any restrictions on abortion during the first trimester" would be consistent with that view.)

Or they might argue that a state has a legitimate interest in ensuring that every woman considering an abortion at any stage of pregnancy understands the moral gravity of that decision, its impact on others beyond herself, and the range of the reasons her parents, the father, and the community as a whole might have for opposing it. It might follow from that view, based on the rational relationship test, that though a state may not prohibit abortion altogether before some advanced stage of pregnancy, it may insist on mandatory waiting periods, or require doctors to provide women seeking an abortion with material setting out arguments against it, or impose an absolute requirement of parental consent in the case of even mature teenaged women, for example, all of which were declared unconstitutional in Supreme Court decisions following *Roe v. Wade* and citing its authority.[11]

I do not mean that overruling these decisions would be sound or desirable. Though some of the post-*Roe* cases might have gone too far, any regulation that significantly increases the risk that a woman will be denied a fair opportunity to control her own reproductive life, as mandatory waiting periods or a requirement of parental consent might do, is in my view inconsistent with the best interpretation of what the Constitution requires. Nor am I predicting that Rehnquist, White, and Kennedy will adopt the comparatively moderate view of a state's legitimate interests I just described rather than the extreme view that would allow states to forbid abortion altogether, except in cases of medical emergency. Rehnquist's opinion is for the most part not a sustained argument but a string of unexplored and ambiguous assertions that offer little basis for confident prediction.[12] (Perhaps divisions among the three justices for whom it spoke made a less opaque opinion impossible.) I mean only that the relatively moderate approach is perfectly consistent, so far as I can tell, with what that opinion actually says.

In any case, the Court's next term will provide more than enough opportunity for these justices to clarify their intentions. The Court has agreed to hear three new abortion cases. One raises the question, among other very serious issues, whether a state may require a teenage woman to notify both parents before an abortion, even when the parents are divorced and one of them lives in a distant city and has no responsibility for her, without allowing a judge or some other official to exempt her from that requirement when exemption would be in her best interests.[13] An absolute requirement that a parent who has neither interest nor responsibility nor connection be notified in advance does not seem rationally related to any proper interest a state has in protecting minors or promoting family integrity or ensuring that a teenager is properly informed of the moral gravity of and alternatives to abortion. If Rehnquist, White, and Kennedy accept Minnesota's claim that it has the power to insist on that requirement, they will have embraced a particularly feeble version of a feeble standard.

Another of the new cases may be even more revealing. It tests Illinois's statute requiring clinics that provide abortion only in the first trimester to meet expensive operating room, equipment, space, personnel, and other medical standards that the lower court found to have absolutely no medical justification.[14] Satisfying these requirements would increase the cost of early abortions and make it impossible for many private abortion clinics to continue to function. Since the *Webster* decision holds that states may forbid abortion in any public hospital or facility, upholding the Illinois statute would have the same effect, for many women, as denying them any right even to an early abortion. The statute cannot be sustained as rationally related to any goal except the goal of in effect overruling *Roe v. Wade* in Illinois. If the three justices vote to sustain it, they will have confirmed Blackmun's view of their motives in *Webster*.

"The goal of constitutional adjudication," Rehnquist said, summing up, "is to hold true the balance between that which the Constitution puts beyond the reach of the democratic process and that which it does not. We think we have done that today." His remark was unhelpful as an explanation of his opinion, because he had not said where that balance should be struck, except that *Roe v. Wade* had struck it in the wrong way. But the remark nevertheless reminds us of the claim justices who want to overturn established constitutional rights often make: that their decisions will make America more democratic because they will return power to the people. They believe that constraints on majority will are inherently undemocratic, and that a view of the Constitution that shrinks those constraints is therefore a more democratic one.

They offer no arguments of either jurisprudence or history, but only question-begging assertions, for their claim that the Constitution supports their view about the right balance between democratic power and constitutional constraint. And their assumption that the Constitution is only a list of a few discrete checks on ordinary politics was rejected by the original authors of the Constitution, whose opinions they claim to make decisive.[15] But the immediate aftermath of the *Webster* decision raises the question whether the new Court's recent decisions decreasing constitutional protection for individuals have even the benefit its authors claim, whether they really are making America more democratic.

Different aspects or conceptions of the democratic ideal have different consequences for the division of power between legislatures and courts; a decision that makes a community more democratic on one conception, because it increases the power of officials who are elected by a majority or plurality of voters, may make it less democratic on another, because, for example, it decreases the efficiency of the political process as a means for revealing and executing the popular will. The sudden dominance of the abortion issue in state politics and elections in all regions of the country has driven crucial economic and social issues from the political agenda. Fundamentalists and other anti-abortion groups, accepting the Court's invitation, are already preparing a variety of new and restrictive laws to place before state legislatures across the country, laws they hope will pass whatever standards the Court finally announces.[16] These groups are dedicated and effective single-issue minorities who in many parts of the country destroy politicians they target for attack, not because their views are so popular but because most voters are concerned with a variety of issues and are unwilling to allow their politics to be governed by only one.

The Court's decision has therefore forced groups concerned with the rights of women to counterattack with single-issue politics of their own, hoping to persuade women generally that they too must concentrate their political interests exclusively on the abortion issue. The counterattack will fail in some states, succeed in others, and force anti-abortion groups to settle for marginal new constraints on abortion in the rest. It is not clear that Republicans will gain politically from President Bush's clumsy attempt to make the issue one of party politics; many commentators think it will hurt his party not only in selected states but nationally, because most women who have grown up since *Roe v. Wade* are outraged at his assault on a right they have taken for granted, and believe crucial to women's social and financial independence.

But in any case American democracy will be made poorer by the corruption of single-issue politics. Political decisions will be less sensitive to the complexities of the popular will, because ordinary voters are in a worse, not better, position to express their convictions and preferences across the range of political issues when politicians are forced to treat one issue as the only one that counts.[17] Of course I do not mean that the Supreme Court should remove any issue from ordinary politics that it believes is receiving disproportionate attention or is in some other way preventing democracy from working well. I mean only that if the Court has good constitutional reasons for denying majorities the power to limit some personal liberty, that decision may also advance rather than defeat democratic values.

The question whether cutting down constitutional protection promotes democracy raises an even more fundamental and important issue, moreover. Since the Enlightenment, political philosophers have debated the merits of two rival views about what democracy—government by the people rather than some electoral aristocracy—really is. The first is a majoritarian conception: that a majority of voters should always have the power to do anything it thinks right or in its own interests. The second is communal: it insists that democracy is government of, by, and for not the majority but the people as a whole. The communal conception of democracy requires that each citizen have not only an equal part in government but an equal place in its concern and respect. Democracy, on that conception, is not undermined by but requires a system of individual rights guaranteeing the integrity of each person's basic interests and needs. On this view, majority tyranny is not just a possible vice of democracy, but a denial of it.

A radical attack on established constitutional rights would indeed promote the first, majoritarian conception of democracy. But it would do so at the expense of the second, communal conception, and it is the second that America chose at its birth and that a majority of citizens want to retain. The first polls indicate that most Americans think the *Webster* decision was wrong, and Judge Bork's surprising unpopularity, in his unsuccessful Supreme Court nomination battle in 1986, suggests that few Americans accept his view that day-to-day majoritarian politics is the best instrument for deciding when the majority should let individual people alone.

François Furet said recently, in a bicentennial lecture on the French Revolution, that the most important development in democratic theory since World War II was the continuing change, not only in Europe but in democracies across the world, from a majoritarian to a communal democratic system, in which the basic rights of men and women are adjudicated by judges under an abstract written constitution.[18] He rightly credited that most important development to the ideas of the American rather than the French Revolution. Of course if the justices who reject *Roe v. Wade* are right, that the Constitution, properly interpreted, gives women less substantial rights to control their own lives than the Supreme Court had previously recognized, then these reflections about the nature of democracy offer no argument to the contrary. But it is no argument *for* their view, or for other recent and troubling Supreme Court decisions, that deference to temporary majorities on matters of individual right makes America more democratic. The version of democracy these decisions serve is brutal and alien, and many other nations with firm democratic traditions now reject it as fake. They cite our leadership and inspiration, and it would be a historic shame if we begin now to abandon our most distinctive and valuable contribution to democratic theory.

September 28, 1989

3

▼

What the Constitution Says

*J*udge Richard Posner and I have been asked to debate the subject of unenumerated rights. I am at a disadvantage, because I think that the distinction between enumerated and unenumerated constitutional rights, a distinction presupposed by our assignment, is bogus. I shall explain why, but it would be unfair to end my contribution to the expected debate with that explanation. The topic "unenumerated rights" on a conference menu leads the audience to expect some discussion of abortion, the most violently debated constitutional issue of our era. So I shall try to explain how that constitutional issue should be resolved once the distinction between enumerated and unenumerated rights is safely shut up with other legal concepts dishonorably discharged for bad philosophy.

The Real Bill of Rights

We are celebrating the Bill of Rights, which we take to include the Civil War amendments. I begin by asking you, in your imagination, to read that part of the Constitution. Some parts of the Bill of Rights are very concrete, like the Third Amendment's prohibition against quartering troops in peacetime. Others are of medium abstraction, like the First Amendment's guarantees of freedom of speech, press, and religion. But key clauses are drafted in the most abstract possible terms of political morality. The Fourteenth Amendment, for example, commands "equal" protection of the laws, and also commands that neither life nor liberty nor property be taken without "due" process of law. That language might, in some contexts, seem wholly concerned with procedure—in no way restricting the laws government might enact and enforce, but only stipulating how it must enact and enforce whatever laws it does adopt. Legal history has rejected that narrow interpretation, however, and once we understand the constitutional provisions to be substantive as well as procedural, their scope is breathtaking. For then the Bill of Rights orders nothing less than that government treat everyone subject to its dominion with equal concern and respect, and that it not infringe citizens' most basic freedoms, those liberties essential, as one prominent jurist put it, to the very idea of "ordered liberty."[1]

The Natural Reading of the Bill of Rights

On its most natural reading, then, the Bill of Rights sets out a network of principles, some extremely concrete, others more abstract, and some of near limitless abstraction. Taken together, these principles define a political ideal: they construct the constitutional skeleton of a society of citizens both equal and free. Notice three features of that striking architecture. First, this system of principle is comprehensive, because it commands both equal concern and basic liberty. In our political culture these are the two major sources of claims of individual right. It therefore seems unlikely that anyone who believes that free and equal citizens would be guaranteed a particular individual right will not also think that our Constitution already contains that right, unless constitutional history has decisively rejected it. That is an important fact about constitutional adjudication and argument, to which I shall return.

Second, since liberty and equality overlap in large part, each of the two major abstract articles of the Bill of Rights is itself comprehensive in that same way. Particular constitutional rights that follow from the best interpretation of the equal protection clause, for example, will very likely also follow from the best interpretation of the due process clause. So (as Justice John Paul Stevens has reminded us)[2] the Supreme Court had no difficulty in finding that, although the equal protection clause does not apply to the District of Columbia, racial school segregation in the District was nevertheless unconstitutional under the due process clause of the Fifth Amendment, which does apply to it. Indeed, it is very likely that, even if there had been no First Amendment, American courts would long ago have found the freedoms of speech, press, and religion in the Fifth and Fourteenth Amendments' guarantees of basic liberty.

Third, the Bill of Rights therefore seems to give judges almost incredible power. Our legal culture insists that judges—and finally the justices of the Supreme Court—have the last word about the proper interpretation of the Constitution. Since the great clauses command simply that government show equal concern and respect for the basic liberties—without specifying in further detail what that means and requires—it falls to judges to declare what equal concern really does require and what the basic liberties really are. But that means that judges must answer intractable, controversial, and profound questions of political morality that philosophers, statesmen, and citizens have debated for many centuries, with no prospect of agreement. It means that the rest of us must accept the deliverances of a majority of the justices, whose insight into these great issues is not spectacularly special. That seems unfair, even frightening. Many people think that judges with that kind of power will impose liberal convictions on less liberal majorities. But they are equally likely to impose conservative convictions on less conservative majorities, as the Supreme Court did in *Lochner v. New York,* and is now doing again in, for example, its affirmative action decisions. The resentment most people feel about unelected judges having that kind of power is bipartisan.

Constitutional Revisionism

In any case, many academic constitutional theorists have for a long time thought that their main job is to demonstrate to themselves, the legal profession, and the public at large that the Constitution does not mean what it says—that it does not, properly understood, actually assign that extraordinary and apparently unfair power to judges. The revisionist strategy is a simple one. It denies that the Bill of Rights has the structure I said was its natural interpretation. It aims to picture it differently, not as defining the skeleton of an overall conception of justice, but as being only an antique list of the particular demands that a relatively few people long ago happened to think important. It hopes to turn the Bill of Rights from a constitutional charter into a document with the texture and tone of an insurance policy or a standard form of commercial lease.

In one way this collective revisionist effort has been remarkably success-ful. It has achieved the Orwellian triumph, the political huckster's dream, of painting its opponents with its own shames and vices. It has persuaded almost everyone that turning the Constitution into an out-of-date list is really protecting that document, and that those who stubbornly read the

Constitution to mean what it says are the actual inventors and usurpers. Even judges who accept the broad responsibility the Constitution imposes on them still adopt the misleading names their revisionist opponents assign them. They call themselves "activists," or "noninterpretivists," or champions of "unenumerated rights," who wish to go "outside" the "four corners" of the Constitution to decide cases on a "natural law" basis.

In that important political way, the massive effort to revise and narrow the Bill of Rights has been successful. But in every substantive way, it has failed—not because it has constructed coherent alternative interpretations with unattractive consequences, but because it has failed to construct any coherent alternative interpretations at all.

Part of the revisionist effort has not even attempted an alternative interpretation. I refer to what I call the "external" revisionist strategy, which does not propose an account of what the Constitution itself actually means, but rewrites it to make it more congenial to what the revisionists consider the best theory of democracy. In its rewritten version, the Constitution leaves as much power to government as is possible, consistent with genuine majority rule and with what the text of the Constitution uncontroversially forbids. Learned Hand held a version of this theory,[3] and John Hart Ely has provided its most elaborate form.[4] The external revisionist strategy plainly begs the question. "Democracy" is itself the name of an abstraction: there are many different conceptions of democracy, and political philosophers debate which is the most attractive. The American conception of democracy is whatever form of government the Constitution, according to the best interpretation of that document, establishes. So it begs the question to hold that the Constitution should be amended to bring it closer to some supposedly purer form of democracy.[5]

For the most part, however, the revisionists have indeed tried to disguise their revisionism as only "better" interpretations of the actual Constitution. They argue that the natural interpretation I described—that the Constitution guarantees the rights required by the best conceptions of the political ideals of equal concern and basic liberty—is not in fact the most accurate interpretation. They say that that natural interpretation neglects some crucial semantic fact, some property of language or communication or linguistic interpretation which, once we grasp it, shows us that the abstract language of the great clauses does not mean what it seems to mean. Constitutional scholars have ransacked the cupboard of linguistic philosophy to find semantic constraints of that character and power. They found in that cupboard, for example, the important idea that what philosophers call the "speaker's meaning" of an utterance may differ from the meaning an audience would likely assign the utterance if it were ignorant of any special information about the speaker.

Some constitutional lawyers try to transform that point into a so-called framers' intention theory of constitutional interpretation. They argue that the great constitutional clauses should be understood not to declare abstract moral requirements, as they do if read acontextually, but in the supposedly different and much less expansive sense which some presumed set of "framers" supposedly "intended."

That suggestion is self-destructive, however, as Robert Bork's unsuccessful attempt to defend it (largely by abandoning it) in his recent book shows.[6] We must take care to make a distinction on which the philosophical idea of speaker's meaning crucially depends: the distinction between what someone means to say and what he hopes or expects or believes will be the consequence for the law of his saying it. Many of the framers undoubtedly had beliefs different from mine about what equality or due process requires, just as my beliefs about that differ from yours. They thought that their abstract commands about equality and due process had legal implications for concrete cases different from the implications you or I think those abstract commands have. But it does not follow that they meant to say anything different from what you or I would mean to say if we used the same words they did. We would normally use those words to say not that government is forbidden to act contrary to the speakers' own conceptions of equality and justice, but that it is forbidden to act contrary to the soundest conception of those virtues. All the evidence (and common sense) suggests that that is what they meant to say as well: they meant to use abstract words in their normal abstract sense. If so, then strict attention to speakers' meaning only reinforces the broad judicial responsibility that the revisionists hope to curtail.

Enumerated and Unenumerated Rights

The distinction I am supposed to be discussing, between enumerated and unenumerated rights, is only another misunderstood semantic device. Constitutional lawyers use "unenumerated rights" as a collective name for a particular set of recognized or controversial constitutional rights, including the right of travel; the right of association; and the right to privacy, from which the right to an abortion, if there is such a right, derives. They regard this classification as marking an important structural distinction, as the terms "enumerated" and "unenumerated" obviously suggest. If the Bill of Rights only enumerates some of the rights necessary to a society of equal concern and basic liberty, and leaves other such rights unmentioned, then judges arguably have only the power to enforce the rights actually enumerated.

Some lawyers accept the distinction, but deny the inference about judicial power. They say that judges do have the power to enforce unenumerated rights, and claim that the Supreme Court has often done so in the past. But lawyers who argue in this way have conceded a very great deal to their opponents who deny that judges should have this kind of power. Their opponents are then able to say that judges have no authority to add to the enumerated rights. If we allow judges to roam at will beyond the "four corners" of the Constitution, they add, we abandon all hope of limiting judicial power. That is the argument made by Justice White in *Bowers v. Hardwick,* for example, to explain why the Court should not recognize a right of homosexual sodomy.[7] He said that judge-made constitutional law was particularly suspect when it had "little or no cognizable roots in the language or design of the Constitution";[8] and he presumably had in mind the putative right of abortion, as well as that of homosexual sodomy.

So the distinction between enumerated and unenumerated rights is widely understood to pose an important constitutional issue: the question whether and when courts have authority to enforce rights not actually enumerated in the Constitution as genuine constitutional rights. I find the question unintelligible, however, as I said at the outset, because the presumed distinction makes no sense. The distinction between what is on some list and what is not is of course genuine and often very important. An ordinance might declare, for example, that it is forbidden to take guns, knives, or explosives in hand luggage on an airplane. Suppose airport officials interpreted that ordinance to exclude canisters of tear gas as well, on the ground that the general structure of the ordinance, and the obvious intention behind it, prohibits all weapons that might be taken aboard and used in hijacks or terrorism. We would be right to say that gas was not on the list of what was banned, and that it is a legitimate question whether officials are entitled to add "unenumerated" weapons to the list. But the distinction between officials excluding pistols, switchblades, and hand grenades, on the one hand, and tear gas, on the other, depends upon a semantic assumption: that tear gas falls within what philosophers call the reference of neither "guns" nor "knives" nor "explosives."

No comparable assumption can explain the supposed distinction between enumerated and unenumerated constitutional rights. The Bill of Rights, as I said, consists of broad and abstract principles of political morality, which together encompass, in exceptionally abstract form, all the dimensions of political morality that in our political culture can ground an individual constitutional right. The key issue in applying these abstract principles to particular political controversies is not one of reference but one of interpretation, which is very different.

Consider the following three constitutional arguments, each of which is very controversial. The first argues that the equal protection clause creates a right of equal concern and respect, from which it follows that women have a right against gender-based discriminations unless such discriminations are required by important state interests. The second argues that the First Amendment grants a right of symbolic protest, from which it follows that individuals have a right to burn the American flag. The third argues that the due process clause protects the basic freedoms central to the very concept of "ordered liberty," including the right of privacy, from which it follows that women have a constitutional right to abortion. By convention, the first two are arguments (good or bad) for enumerated rights: each claims that some right—the right against gender discrimination or the right to burn the flag—is an instance of some more general right set out, in suitably abstract form, in the text of the Constitution. The third argument, by contrast, is thought to be different and more suspect, because it is thought to be an argument for an unenumerated right. The right it claims—the right to an abortion—is thought to bear a more tenuous or distant relationship to the language of the Constitution. It is said to be at best implied by, rather than stated in, that language.

But the distinction cannot be sustained. Each of the three arguments is interpretive in a way that excludes the kind of semantic constraints the distinction assumes. No one thinks that it follows just from the meaning of the words "freedom of speech" either that people are free to burn flags, or that they are not. No one thinks it follows just from the meaning of the words "equal protection" that laws excluding women from certain jobs are unconstitutional, or that they are not. In neither case does the result follow from the meanings of words in the way it follows from the meaning of "gun" that it refers to pistols but not to canisters of gas. Nor are the three arguments different in how they are interpretive. Each conclusion (if sound) follows not from some historical hope or belief or intention of a "framer," but because the political principle that supports that conclusion best accounts for the general structure and history of constitutional law. Someone who thinks that this manner of constitutional argument is inappropriate—who thinks, for example, that the framers' expectations should play a more decisive role than this view of constitutional argument allows—will have that reservation about all three arguments, not distinctly about the third. If he thinks that the third argument is wrong, because he abhors, for example, the idea of substantive due process, then he will reject it, but because it is wrong, not because the right it claims would be an unenumerated one.

In his reply to my remarks, Judge Posner constructs a Socratic dialogue in which the straight man is brought to see that "speech" in the First Amendment includes flag-burning, though Posner concedes that the argument might have gone the other way.[9] He does not construct a parallel dialogue in which another dupe is made to agree that gender is a suspect category under the equal protection clause, though it is easy to see how that second dialogue might go. And it would be equally easy to construct a third dialogue ending with a straight man's startled recognition that abortion is, after all, a basic liberty protected by the due process clause. Posner does suggest that this argument might take us "further" from the text. But the metaphor of distance is wholly opaque in this context: it means or suggests nothing. Posner cannot mean, for example, that a right to abortion is further away from the Constitution's language than a right against gender discrimination is, in the sense that "tear gas" is further from the meaning of "gun" than "pistol" is. "Pistol" is closer because "gun" refers to a pistol and does not refer to tear gas. But since neither a right to abortion nor a right against gender discrimination follows from the meanings of textual words, neither can be closer to or further from the text than the other in that sense.

It is sometimes said that the Constitution does not "mention" a right of travel, or of association, or of privacy, as if that fact explained why these rights are usefully classified as unenumerated. But the Constitution does not "mention" flag-burning or gender discrimination either. The right to burn a flag and the right against gender discrimination are supported by the best interpretation of a more general or abstract right that is "mentioned." It is true that the phrase "right to privacy" is itself more abstract than the phrase "right to burn a flag as protest," and that the former phrase therefore figures more in the conversation and writing of constitutional scholars than the latter. But these facts reflect accidents (or highly contingent features) of usage. Scholars have found it useful to develop a name of middling abstraction—the right of privacy—to describe a stage in the derivation of particular concrete rights from the even more abstract rights named in the constitutional text. But it hardly follows that those concrete rights—including the right to abortion—are more remote from their textual beginnings than are concrete rights—such as the right to burn a flag—that are derived by arguments that do not employ names for rights of middling abstraction. Constitutional lawyers might well have adopted the middling terms "right of symbolic protest" or "right of gender equality" in the way they have adopted "right of privacy." It is hardly a deep fact of constitutional structure that they have not.

I must be clear. I am not arguing that the Supreme Court should enforce unenumerated as well as enumerated constitutional rights, any more than I meant to argue, in my remarks about a speaker's meaning, that the Court is right to ignore or modify what the framers said. I mean that the distinction between enumerated and unenumerated rights, as it is commonly used in constitutional theory, makes no sense, because it confuses reference with interpretation.

I should say—to complete this exercise in provocation—that I take much the same view of a variety of other distinctions popular among constitutional lawyers, including those Posner discusses in his reply. He distinguishes between what he calls a "top-down" and a "bottom-up" method of legal reasoning, and also between a "clause-by-clause" and a "holistic" approach. He apparently regards the second of these distinctions as more important than the first. Though he says he agrees with me that "there isn't much to bottom-up reasoning,"[10] he thinks that I am wrong to criticize Bork's "clause-by-clause" approach,[11] and also that I would do better to make my own arguments about abortion more explicitly "holistic."[12]

Neither of the two distinctions makes any sense, however. We cannot understand a particular precedent, for example, except by construing that decision as part of a more general enterprise, and any such constructive interpretation must, as I argued at length in *Law's Empire*, engage the kind of theoretical hypothesis characteristic of what Posner calls top-down reasoning.[13] So bottom-up reasoning is automatically top-down reasoning as well. The same point also erodes the distinction between clause-by-clause and holistic constitutional interpretation. Legal interpretation is inherently holistic, even when the apparent target of interpretation is a single sentence or even a single clause rather than a document. Any interpreter must accept interpretive constraints—assumptions about what makes one interpretation better than another—and any plausible set of constraints includes a requirement of coherence. An interpretation of the Bill of Rights which claims that a moral principle embedded in one clause is actually rejected by another is an example not of pragmatist flexibility, but of hypocrisy.

Law's Integrity

Where do we stand? The most natural interpretation of the Bill of Rights seems, as I said, to give judges great and frightening power. It is understandable that constitutional lawyers and teachers should strive to tame the Bill of Rights, to read it in a less frightening way, to change it from a systematic abstract conception of justice to a list of discrete clauses related to one another through pedigree rather than principle. These efforts fail, however, and are bound to fail, because the text and history of the Bill of Rights will not accept that transformation. They are bound to fail, moreover, in a paradoxical and disastrous way. Because the semantic distinctions on which the efforts are based have no sense as they are used, they are powerless themselves to define any particular set of constitutional rights. As the recent history of the Court amply demonstrates, a judge who claims to rely on a speaker's meaning, "enumeration," or a preference for clause-by-clause interpretation must actually choose which constitutional rights to enforce on grounds that have nothing to do with these semantic devices, but that are hidden from view by his appeal to them. The search for limits on judicial power ends by allowing judges the undisciplined power of the arbitrary.

Posner's reply acknowledges that fact, with typical candor. He says that the semantic devices beloved of conservative lawyers "could end up with a document that gave answers only to questions that no one was asking any longer,"[14] and that judges who say they are constrained by those useless devices will necessarily decide according to their own "personal values"[15]—according, he says, to what makes them "puke."[16] His own personal values endorse "stretching" the due process clause to yield *Griswold*, and, if I read correctly between the lines, *Roe v. Wade* as well. But he knows that other judges have stronger stomachs about society dictating sexual morality: their puke tests will flunk affirmative action programs instead.[17] The idea that the Constitution cannot mean what it says ends in the unwelcome conclusion that it means nothing at all.

What is to be done? We can finally, after two hundred years, grow up and begin to take our actual Constitution seriously, as those many nations now hoping to imitate us have already done. We can accept that our

Constitution commands, as a matter of fundamental law, that our judges do their best collectively to construct, reinspect, and revise, generation by generation, the skeleton of liberal equal concern that the great clauses, in their majestic abstraction, demand. We will then abandon the pointless search for mechanical or semantic constraints, and seek genuine constraints in the only place where they can actually be found: in good argument. We will accept that honest lawyers and judges and scholars will inevitably disagree, sometimes profoundly, about what equal concern requires, and about which rights are central and which only peripheral to liberty.

We will then acknowledge, in the political process of nomination and confirmation of federal judges, what is already evident to anyone who looks: that constitutional adjudicators cannot be neutral about these great questions, and that the Senate must decline to confirm nominees whose convictions are too idiosyncratic, or who refuse honestly to disclose what their convictions are. The second stage of the Thomas confirmation hearings was, as most people now agree, physically revolting. But the first stage was intellectually revolting, because candidate and senators conspired to pretend that philosophy had nothing to do with judging, that a nominee who said he had abandoned convictions the way a runner sheds clothing was fit for the office he sought.[18]

The constitutional process of nomination and confirmation is an important part of the system of checks through which the actual Constitution disciplines the striking judicial power it declares. The main engines of discipline are intellectual rather than political, however, and the academic branch of the profession has a responsibility to protect that intellectual discipline, which is now threatened from several directions. Of course, we cannot find a formula which will guarantee that judges will all reach the same answer in complex or novel or crucial constitutional cases. No formula can protect us from a *Lochner*, which Posner tells us stinks, or from a *Bowers v. Hardwick*, which upheld a law making consensual homosexual sodomy a crime. The stench of those cases does not lie in any jurisdictional vice or judicial overreaching. After a near century of treating *Lochner* as a whipping boy, no one has produced a sound mechanical test that it fails. The vice of bad decisions is bad argument and bad conviction; all we can do about those bad decisions is to point out how and where the arguments are bad. Nor should we waste any more time on the silly indulgence of American legal academic life: the philosophically juvenile claim that, since no such formula exists, no one conception of constitutional equality and liberty is any better than another, and adjudication is only power or visceral response.[19] We must insist, instead, on a principle of genuine power: the idea, instinct in the concept of law itself, that whatever their views of justice and fairness, judges must also accept an independent and superior constraint of integrity.[20]

Integrity in law has several dimensions. First, it insists that judicial decision be a matter of principle, not compromise or strategy or political accommodation. That apparent banality is often ignored: the Supreme Court's present position on the politically sensitive issue of affirmative action, for example, cannot be justified on any coherent set of principles, however conservative or unappealing.[21] Second, integrity holds vertically: a judge who claims a particular right of liberty as fundamental must show that his claim is consistent with the bulk of precedent, and with the main structures of our constitutional arrangement. Third, integrity holds horizontally: a judge who adopts a principle must give full weight to that principle in other cases he decides or endorses.

Of course not even the most scrupulous attention to integrity, by all our judges in all our courts, will produce uniform judicial decisions, or guarantee decisions you approve of, or protect you from those you hate. Nothing can do that. The point of integrity is principle, not uniformity: We are governed not by a list but by an ideal, and controversy is therefore at the heart of our story. We are envied for our constitutional adventure, and increasingly imitated, throughout the democratic world: in Delhi and Strasbourg and Ottawa, even, perhaps, in the Palace of Westminster and, perhaps tomorrow or the day after, in Moscow and Johannesburg. In all those places people seem ready to accept the risk and high promise of government by ideal, a form of government we created in the Constitution. We have never fully trusted that form of government. But unless we abandon it altogether, which we will not do, we should stop pretending that it is not the form of government we have. The energy of our best academic lawyers would be better spent in making, testing, and evaluating different conceptions of liberal equality, to see which conception best fits our own history and practice. They should try to guide and constrain our judges by criticism, argument, and example. That is the only way to honor our great constitutional creation, to help it prosper.[22]

Abortion: What Is the Argument About?

In the discussion of abortion that I promised, I shall try to illustrate the role that integrity should play in legal argument. I begin by briefly summarizing claims about the constitutional status of that issue that I have argued elsewhere,[23] and will argue in much more detail in a book I am writing about abortion and euthanasia.[24] A woman, I assume, has a constitutionally protected right to control the use of her own body. (I shall later consider the constitutional source of that right.) Therefore, a pregnant woman has a right to an abortion unless her state's government has some legitimate and important reason for prohibiting it. Many people think governments do have such a reason, and would have no difficulty in saying what it is.

A state must make abortion a crime, they say, in order to protect human life. That is indeed what many state officials have said, in preambles to regulatory statutes, in legal briefs, and in political rhetoric. That is, moreover, what the Supreme Court justices who dissented in *Roe v. Wade,* or who later announced their view that it is wrong, say a state's reason for forbidding abortion is. And even justices and lawyers who support that decision say something similar. In his opinion for the Court in *Roe v. Wade,* Justice Blackmun recognized that a state had an interest in protecting what he called "fetal life."[25] He said that a state's interest in protecting life did not give it a compelling reason for prohibiting abortion until the third trimester, but he conceded that it did have that interest throughout pregnancy.[26] The premise on which so many people rely is, however, dangerously ambiguous, because there are two very different aims or purposes a state might have, each of which might be described as protecting human life. A good part of the confusion that surrounds both the legal and the moral argument about abortion is the result of ignoring that ambiguity. Consider the difference between two kinds of reasons a government might have for prohibiting murder within its territory. First, government has a responsibility to protect the rights and interests of its citizens, and chief among these, for most people, is an interest in staying alive and a right not to be killed. I shall call this a derivative reason for prohibiting murder, because it presupposes and derives from individual rights and interests. Government sometimes claims, second, a very different kind of reason for prohibiting murder. It sometimes claims a responsibility not just to protect the interests and rights of its citizens, but to protect human life as an objective or intrinsic good, a value in itself, quite apart from its value to the person whose life it is or to anyone else. I shall call this responsibility a detached one, because it is independent of, rather than a derivative of, particular people's rights and interests.

If government does have a detached responsibility to protect the objective, intrinsic value of life, then its laws against murder serve both its derivative and detached responsibility at once. They protect the rights and interests of particular victims, and they also recognize and respect the intrinsic value of human life. In some cases, however, the two supposed responsibilities might conflict: when someone wishes to kill himself because he is in terrible pain that doctors cannot relieve, for example, or when relatives wish to terminate the mechanical life support of someone who is permanently unconscious. In such cases, suicide or terminating life support might be in the best interests of the person whose life ends, as he or his relatives think it is. These acts nevertheless seem wrong to many people, because they think that any deliberate killing, or ever allowing someone to die who might be kept alive longer, is an insult to the intrinsic value of human life. It makes a great difference, in such cases, whether a government's legitimate reasons for protecting human life are limited to its derivative concern or whether they include a detached concern as well. If the latter, then government is entitled to forbid people to end their lives, even when they rightly think they would be better off dead.

We have identified two different claims a state that proposes to forbid abortion in order to protect human life might be making: a derivative claim and a detached claim. The derivative claim presupposes that a fetus already has rights and interests. The detached claim does not, though it does presuppose that the intrinsic value of human life is already at stake in a fetus's life. You will notice that I did not describe either of these claims as claims about when human life begins or about whether a fetus is a "person," because those runic phrases perpetuate rather than dissolve the ambiguity I described.

Though scientists disagree about exactly when the life of any animal begins, it seems undeniable that in the ordinary case a fetus is a single living creature by the time it has become implanted in a womb, and that it is human in the sense that it is a member of the animal species Homo sapiens. It is, in that sense, a human organism whose life has begun. It does not follow that it also has rights and interests of the kind that government might have a derivative responsibility to protect. Nor that it already embodies the intrinsic value of a human life that a government might claim a detached responsibility to guard. But when people say that a fetus is already a living human being, they often mean to make either or both of these further claims.

"Person" is an even more ambiguous term. We sometimes use it just as a description (in which use it is more or less synonymous with human being) and sometimes as a term of moral classification, to suggest that the creatures so described have a special moral standing or importance that marks them out from other species. So someone who said that a just-conceived fetus is already a person might simply mean that it is a member of the human—rather than some other animal—species. Or he might mean, not just that a fetus is alive and human, but that it already has that special kind of moral importance. But even the latter claim is ambiguous in the way I described. It might mean that a fetus is already a creature with the interests and moral rights we take persons, as distinct from other creatures, to have. Or it might mean that a fetus is already a creature whose life has the intrinsic moral significance the life of any person has. So the clarity of the public debate is not improved by the prominence of the questions "Is a fetus a person?" and "When does human life begin?" We do better to avoid that language so far as we can. I suggest that we consider, instead, whether states can justify anti-abortion legislation on one of the two grounds—derivative or detached—that I described.

Most people think that the great constitutional debate about abortion in America is obviously and entirely about a state's derivative grounds. They think the argument is about whether a fetus is a person in the sense in which that means having a right to life. That is why one side claims, and the other denies, that abortion is murder. (Some might add that the detached ground I described is too mysterious or metaphysical even to make sense, let alone to provide a plausible ground for anti-abortion legislation.) Not just the political argument, but the legal and academic discussion as well, seems to assume that view of the controversy. Lawyers and philosophers discuss whether a fetus is a person with rights. They speculate about whether abortion is morally permissible even if a fetus does have a right to life. But they almost all assume that if it does not, then there is no moral objection even to consider.

In the following two sections I shall assess the constitutional argument understood in that familiar and popular way. I shall interpret the claim that states have a responsibility to protect life to mean that they have a derivative responsibility to protect the right to life of a fetus. I shall argue, however, that if we do understand the dispute that way, then the constitutional argument is a relatively simple one. On that basis, *Roe* was not only correct but obviously correct, and its many critics are obviously wrong. I conclude that the constitutional debate about abortion is actually not about whether a fetus has rights and interests. It must be understood, if at all, as about the different claim I just conceded some people may find mysterious: that a state can legitimately claim a detached responsibility to protect the intrinsic value of human life.

Is a Fetus a Constitutional Person?

The national Constitution defines what we might call the constitutional population. It stipulates who has constitutional rights that government must respect and enforce, and therefore whose rights government must take into account in curtailing or limiting the scope of other people's constitutional rights in cases of conflict. States would of course have a derivative reason for forbidding abortion if the Constitution designated a fetus as a constitutional person, that is, as a creature with constitutional rights competitive with those of a pregnant woman. Our analysis must therefore begin with a crucial threshold question. Is a fetus a constitutional person? In *Roe v. Wade*, the Supreme Court answered that question in the only way it could: in the negative. If a fetus is a constitutional person, then states not only may forbid abortion but, at least in some circumstances, must do so. No justice or prominent politician has even advanced that claim.

It is true, as a number of legal scholars have pointed out, that the law does not generally require people to make any sacrifice at all to save the life of another person who needs their aid. A person ordinarily has no legal duty to save a stranger from drowning even if he can do so at no risk to himself and with minimal effort.[27] But abortion normally requires a physical attack on a fetus, not just a failure to come to its aid. And in any case parents are invariably made an exception to the general doctrine. Parents have a legal duty to care for their children; if a fetus is a person from conception, a state would discriminate between infants and fetuses without any justification if it allowed abortion but did not permit killing infants or abandoning them in circumstances when they would inevitably die.[28] The physical and emotional and economic burdens of pregnancy are intense, but so are the parallel burdens of parenthood.

We may safely assume, then, that the national Constitution does not declare a fetus to be a constitutional person whose rights may be competitive with the constitutional rights of a pregnant woman. Does this leave a state free to decide that a fetus shall have that status within its borders? If so, then *Roe v. Wade* could safely be reversed without the politically impossible implication that states were required to prohibit abortion. The

Supreme Court could then say that while some states have chosen to declare fetuses persons within their jurisdiction, other states need not make the same decision.

There is no doubt that a state can protect the life of a fetus in a variety of ways. A state can make it murder for a third party intentionally to kill a fetus, as Illinois has done, for example, or "feticide" for anyone willfully to kill a quickened fetus by an injury that would be murder if it resulted in the death of the mother, as Georgia has. These laws violate no constitutional rights, because no one has a constitutional right to injure with impunity.[29] Laws designed to protect fetuses may be drafted in language declaring or suggesting that a fetus is a person or that human life begins at conception. The Illinois abortion statute begins, for example, by declaring that a fetus is a person from the moment of conception.[30] There can be no constitutional objection to such language, so long as the law does not purport to curtail constitutional rights. The Illinois statute makes plain, for example, that it does not intend to challenge or modify *Roe v. Wade* so long as that decision remains in force.[31]

So qualified, a declaration that a fetus is a person raises no more constitutional difficulties than states raise when they declare, as every state has, that corporations are legal persons and enjoy many of the rights real people do, including the right to own property and the right to sue. States declare that corporations are persons as a shorthand way of describing a complex network of rights and duties that it would be impossible to describe in any other way, not as a means of curtailing or diminishing constitutional rights that real people would otherwise have.

The suggestion that states are free to declare a fetus a person, and thereby justify outlawing abortion, is a very different matter, however. That suggestion assumes that a state can curtail some persons' constitutional rights by adding new persons to the constitutional population. The constitutional rights of one citizen are of course very much affected by who or what else also has constitutional rights, because the rights of others may compete or conflict with his. So any power to increase the constitutional population by unilateral decision would be, in effect, a power to decrease rights the national Constitution grants to others.

If a state could not only create corporations as legal persons but endow each of those corporations with a vote, it could impair the constitutional right of ordinary people to vote, because the corporations' votes would dilute theirs. If a state could declare trees to be persons with a constitutional right to life, it could prohibit publishing newspapers or books in spite of the First Amendment's guarantee of free speech, which could not be understood as a license to kill. If a state could declare the higher apes to be persons whose rights were competitive with the constitutional rights of others, it could prohibit its citizens from taking life-saving medicines first tested on those animals. Once we understand that the suggestion we are considering has that implication, we must reject it. If a fetus is not part of the constitutional population, under the national constitutional arrangement, then states have no power to overrule that national arrangement by themselves declaring that fetuses have rights competitive with the constitutional rights of pregnant women.

I am uncertain how far Posner disagrees with that conclusion. He says that states can indeed create new persons. But he adds that it remains an open question how far they can treat these new persons' interests as if they were the interests of real people. This leaves mysterious what he thinks creating a new person amounts to. Perhaps he means only to agree with me that though a state can create persons for a variety of purposes, it cannot thereby acquire a power to abridge constitutional rights that it would not otherwise have had.

That position would be consistent with the examples he offers. He says, for example, that states can create property and liberty in ways that affect people's procedural rights under the due process clause.[32] These are not, however, powers to decrease constitutional rights by adding competing rights-holders to the constitutional scheme. They are powers to create new rights under state law that, once created, satisfy standing conditions for constitutional protection without decreasing the constitutional rights of others. He also says that states can decide whether "death means brain death" or "a stopped heart"[33] and that it follows that they can "decide when life begins."[34] A state can certainly decide when life begins and ends for any number of reasons, as I said a moment ago. It can fix the moment of death for purposes of the law of inheritance, for example, just as it can declare that life begins before birth in order to allow people to inherit through a fetus. But it cannot change constitutional rights by its decisions about when life begins or death happens. It cannot escape its constitutional responsibilities to death-row prisoners by declaring them already dead, or improve its congressional representation by declaring deceased citizens still alive for that purpose. I cannot think of any significant constitutional rights that would be curtailed by treating someone as dead when his brain was dead, however. So none of Posner's examples suggests that he really accepts the position I reject.

Nor, I dare say, do many of even the strongest opponents of *Roe v. Wade* really accept it, because it is inconsistent with other views they hold. Chief Justice Rehnquist, who dissented in that case, had "little doubt" that a state could not constitutionally forbid an abortion that was necessary to save a pregnant woman's life.[35] Of course if a state could declare a fetus a constitutional person, it could prohibit abortion even when the pregnancy threatens the mother's life, just as it normally forbids killing one innocent person to save the life of another.

Do Fetuses Have Interests?

Consider this argument, however. "Even if a fetus is not a constitutional person, and states have no power to make it one, a state can nevertheless legislate to protect a fetus's interests, just as it can legislate to protect the interests of dogs, who are not constitutional persons either." States can protect the interests of nonpersons. But it is extremely doubtful whether a state can appeal to such interests to justify a significant abridgment of an important constitutional right, such as a pregnant woman's right to control her own body. It can do that only in deference to the rights of other constitutional persons, or for some other "compelling" reason.

But it is important to see that this argument fails for another reason as well: a fetus has no interests before the third trimester. Not everything that can be destroyed has an interest in not being destroyed. Smashing a beautiful sculpture would be a terrible insult to the intrinsic value that great works of art embody, and also very much against the interests of people who take pleasure in seeing or studying it. But a sculpture has no interests of its own; a savage act of vandalism is not unfair to it. Nor is it enough, for something to have interests, that it be alive and in the process of developing into something more mature. It is not against the interests of a baby carrot that it be picked early and brought to table as a delicacy. Nor even that it is something that will naturally develop into something different or more marvelous. A butterfly is much more beautiful than a caterpillar; but it is not better for the caterpillar to become one. Nor is it enough, for something to have interests, even that it is something en route to becoming a human being. Imagine that, just as Dr. Frankenstein reached for the lever that would bring life to the assemblage of body parts on the table before him, someone appalled at the experiment smashed the apparatus. That act, whatever we think of it, would not have been harmful to the assemblage, or against its interests, or unfair to it.

These examples suggest that nothing has interests unless it has or has had some form of consciousness—some mental as well as physical life.[36] Creatures that can feel pain of course have an interest in avoiding it. It is very much against the interests of animals to subject them to pain, by trapping them or experimenting on them, for example. Causing a fetus pain would be against its interests too. But a fetus cannot feel pain until late in pregnancy, because its brain is not sufficiently developed before then. Even conservative scientists deny that a fetal brain is sufficiently developed to feel pain until approximately the twenty-sixth week.[37]

Of course many things that are against people's interests cause them no physical pain. Someone acts against my interests when he chooses someone else for a job I want, or sues me, or smashes into my car, or writes a bad review of my work, or brings out a better mousetrap and prices it lower than mine, even when these things cause me no physical pain and, indeed, even when I am unaware that they have happened. In these cases my interests are in play not because of my capacity to feel pain but because of a different and more complex set of capacities: to enjoy or fail to enjoy, to form affections and emotions, to hope and expect, to suffer disappointment and frustration. I do not know when these capacities begin to develop, in primitive or trace or shadowy form, in animals, including humans. Infants may have them in at least primitive form, and therefore so may late-stage fetuses, whose brains have been fully formed. But of course such capacities are not possible before sentience, and therefore, on conservative estimates, not before the twenty-sixth week.

We must beware the familiar but fallacious argument that abortion must be against the interests of a fetus because it would have been against the interests of almost anyone now alive to have been aborted. Once a creature develops interests, then it becomes true, in retrospect, that certain events would have been against those interests if they had happened in the past. It obviously does not follow that these events were therefore against interests someone had when they happened. Suppose we assume that it was good for me that my father was not sent on a long business trip the night before my parents conceived me, rather than, as in fact happened, two days later. It does not follow that it would have been bad for anyone, in the same way, had he left on the earlier date. There never would have been anyone for whom it could have been bad.

Of course in the case of abortion, there is something—the fetus—for whom someone might think this bad, a candidate, as it were. But the fetus's existence makes no difference to the logical point. If the fact that I would not now exist had my father left early does not entail that there was some creature for whom it would have been bad if he had, as it plainly does not, then the fact that I would not exist if I had been aborted doesn't entail that either. Whether abortion is against the interests of a fetus must depend on whether the fetus itself has interests, not on whether interests will develop if no abortion takes place.

This distinction may help explain what some observers have found puzzling. Many people who believe that abortion is morally permissible nevertheless think it wrong for pregnant women to smoke or drink or otherwise to behave in ways injurious to a child they intend to bear. Critics say that this combination of views is contradictory: since killing something is worse than injuring it, it cannot be wrong to smoke and yet not wrong to abort. But if a woman smokes during pregnancy, someone will later exist whose interests will have been seriously damaged by her behavior. If she aborts, no one will exist against whose interests that will ever have been.

The Real Issue in *Roe v. Wade*

An important conclusion follows from my argument so far: If the only issue at stake in the constitutional debate were whether states could treat a fetus as a person whose rights are competitive with those of a pregnant woman, then *Roe v. Wade* would plainly be right. But that is not the only issue at stake, and (though this is widely misunderstood) that is not even the central issue in the underlying national debate about the morality of abortion. Most people, it is true, say that both the moral and the legal debate turns on some question about the moral personality, or rights, or interests of a fetus. They say that it turns, for example, on whether a fetus is a metaphysical or moral person, or whether a fetus has interests of its own, or how its interests should rank in importance with those of a pregnant woman, or some other question of that sort. In fact, however, most people's actual views about the morality of abortion in different circumstances make no sense if we try to understand these views as flowing from a set of consistent answers they give to questions about fetal personhood or rights or interests.

Most people think, for example, that abortion is always morally problematic, and must never be undertaken except for very good reason, but that it is nevertheless sometimes justified. Some think it justified only to save the life of the mother. Other overlapping but nonidentical groups think it justified in other circumstances as well: to protect the mother from non-life-threatening physical impairment, for example, or in cases of rape and incest, or in cases of serious fetal deformity. Some people who think abortion always morally problematic also think it justified when childbirth would severely cripple a mother's chances for a successful life herself. Many people also think that a pregnant woman should be free to decide about abortion for herself, even when she chooses abortion in circumstances in which they believe it morally impermissible. None of these complex positions flows from a consistent answer to the question whether a fetus is a moral person, or how its interests compare in importance to other people's interests.

Most people's views about abortion can only be understood as responses to a very different set of issues. They assume that human life is intrinsically valuable, and worthy of a kind of awe, just because it is human life. They think that once a human life begins, it is a very bad thing—a kind of sacrilege—that it end prematurely, particularly through someone's deliberate act. That assumption does not presuppose that the creature whose life is in question is a person with rights or interests, because it does not suppose that death is bad for the creature whose life ends. On the contrary, the assumption explains why some people think suicide morally wrong even in circumstances in which they believe suicide would be best for the person who dies. Most people take a parallel view about the destruction of other things they treat as sacrosanct, which plainly involve no moral personhood: works of art, for example, and particular animal species. Our attitude toward the destruction of human life has the same structure, though it is, understandably, much more intense.

Though most people accept that human life is sacrosanct, and must be respected as such, the American community is divided about what that respect actually requires in the kinds of circumstances I just described: rape, incest, fetal deformity, and cases in which motherhood would have a serious and detrimental impact on the potential mother's own life. Some Americans think that respect for life forbids abortion in some or all of these circumstances; others think that respect for life recommends and even requires abortion in some or all of them.[38] As I argue in the book about abortion and euthanasia I mentioned, these differences reflect profound differences in people's views about the relative importance of divine, natural, and human contributions to the overall intrinsic value of a human life. They also reflect, as Kristin Luker has argued, different convictions about the appropriate lives for women to lead in our society.[39] The public is deeply divided about these matters. It is divided, however, not into two bitterly opposed groups—one of which affirms and the other of which denies that a fetus is a person—but in a much more complex way, because judgments about whether abortion dishonors or respects the intrinsic value of life in different circumstances involve a large variety of separate issues.

So what I take to be the uncontroversial propositions that a fetus is not a constitutional person, and that a state may not enlarge the category of constitutional persons, do not, after all, entail that *Roe v. Wade* was right. Neither paintings nor animal species nor future human beings are constitutional persons. But no one doubts that government can treat art and culture as having intrinsic value, or that government can and should act to protect the environment, endangered animal species, and the quality of life of future generations of people. The majority in a community can levy taxes that will be used to support museums. It can forbid people to destroy their own buildings if it deems these to be of historical or architectural value. It can prohibit building or manufacturing that threatens endangered species or that will injure future generations. Why should a majority not have the power to enforce a much more passionate conviction—that abortion is a desecration of the inherent value that attaches to every human life?

So the most difficult constitutional issue in the abortion controversy is whether states can legitimately claim a detached interest in protecting the intrinsic value, or sanctity, of human life. Does our Constitution allow states to decide not only what rights and interests people have and how these should be enforced and protected, but also whether human life is inherently valuable, why it is so, and how that inherent value should be respected? We cannot dispose of that question in the quick way some liberals might prefer: we cannot say that an individual woman's decision whether or not to have an abortion affects only herself (or only herself and the fetus's father) and that it is therefore none of the community's business which decision she makes. Individual decisions inevitably affect shared collective values. Part of the sense of the sacred is a sense of taboo, a shared sense of horror at desecration, and it is surely harder to maintain a sense of taboo about abortion in a community in which others not only reject the taboo but violate it openly, especially if they receive official financial or moral support. It is plainly more difficult for a parent to raise his or her children to share the conviction that abortion is always a desecration in such a community than in one in which abortion is branded a crime.

The constitutional question I describe therefore lies at the intersection of two sometimes competing traditions, both of which are part of America's political heritage. The first is the tradition of religious and personal freedom. The second is a tradition that assigns government responsibility for guarding the public moral space in which all must live. A good part of constitutional law consists in reconciling these two ideas. What is the appropriate balance in the case of abortion?

Government's Legitimate Concerns

One idea deployed in both the majority and dissenting opinions in *Roe* might have seemed mysterious: that a state has an interest in "protecting human life." I have now assigned a particular sense to that idea. A community has an interest in protecting the sanctity of life—in protecting the community's sense that human life in any form has enormous intrinsic value—by requiring its members to acknowledge that intrinsic value in their individual decisions. But that statement is ambiguous. It might describe either of two goals, and the distinction between them is extremely important. The first is the goal of responsibility. A state might aim that its citizens treat decisions about abortion as matters of moral importance, that they recognize that fundamental intrinsic values are at stake in their decision, and that they decide reflectively, not out of immediate convenience but out of examined conviction. The second is the goal of conformity. A state might aim that all its citizens obey rules and practices that the majority believes best capture and respect the sanctity of life, that they abort only in circumstances, if any, in which the majority thinks abortion is appropriate or at least permissible.

These goals of responsibility and conformity are not only different; they are antagonistic. If we aim at responsibility, we must leave citizens free, in the end, to decide as they think right, because that is what moral responsibility entails. If, on the other hand, we aim at conformity, we deny citizens that decision. We demand that they act in a way that might be contrary to their own moral convictions, and we discourage rather than encourage them to develop their own sense of when and why life is sacred.

The traditional assumption that states have a derivative interest in preventing abortion, which I have rejected, submerges the distinction between the two goals. If a fetus is a person, then of course the state's dominant goal must be to protect that person, just as it protects all other people. The state must therefore subordinate any interest it has in developing its citizens' sense of moral responsibility to its interest that they reach, or at least act on, a particular moral conclusion: that killing people is wrong.

But when we shift the state's interest, as we have, to its interest in protecting a particular intrinsic value, then the contrast and opposition between the two goals move into the foreground. The sanctity of life is, as I said, a highly contestable value. What it requires in particular cases is controversial: when a fetus is deformed, for example, or when having a child would seriously depress a woman's chance to make something valuable of her own life. Does a state protect a contestable value best by encouraging people to accept the value as contestable, with the understanding that they are responsible for deciding for themselves what it means? Or does the state protect that value best by itself deciding, through the political process, which interpretation is the right one, and then forcing everyone to conform? The goal of responsibility justifies the first choice; the goal of conformity the second. A state cannot pursue both goals at the same time.

I can think of no reason, grounded in a plausible conception of either equal concern or basic liberty, why government should not aim that its citizens treat decisions about human life and death as matters of serious moral importance. The benefits of such a policy are evident and pervasive. So in my view the Constitution allows states to pursue the goal of responsibility, but only in ways that respect the distinction between that goal and the antagonistic goal of wholly or partly coercing a final decision. May a state require a woman contemplating abortion to wait twenty-four hours before the operation? May it require that she receive information explaining the gravity of a decision to abort? May it require a pregnant teenage woman to consult with her parents, or with some other adult? Or a married woman to inform her husband if she can locate him? Must the government provide funds for abortion if, and on the same terms as, it provides funds for the costs of childbirth for those too poor to bear those costs themselves? Constitutional lawyers have tended to discuss these issues as if they were all governed by *Roe*, as they would be if the only pertinent issue were whether a fetus is a person. If that were the only issue, and if *Roe* is right that a fetus is not a constitutional person, then on what ground could a state require women contemplating abortion to wait, or to discuss the question with an adult? On what ground could Congress aid women who wanted to bear their fetuses but not those who wanted to abort?

Much of the media discussion about how far the Supreme Court has amended *Roe* in its recent decisions presupposes that questions about responsibility and questions about conformity are tied together in that way. That explains why the Court's decision in *Webster*[40] was widely viewed as in itself altering *Roe*,[41] why the *New York Times* said that the Third Circuit's recent *Casey* decision upholding a comprehensive Pennsylvania regulatory statute assumed that *Roe* would soon be overturned,[42] and why so many commentators expect the Supreme Court, which has agreed to review the Third Circuit decision, to use that opportunity further to narrow *Roe* or perhaps to overrule it altogether, even though the Court requested parties only to brief issues the Third Circuit had actually addressed.[43]

Many of these commentators say that *Roe* gave women a fundamental right to abortion, which states need a compelling reason to curtail, and that *Webster* undermined *Roe*, and *Casey* will undermine it further, by allowing states to curtail the right without such a reason. But when we understand *Roe* as I suggest, this analysis becomes too crude. The fundamental right *Roe* upheld is a right against conformity. It is a right that states not prohibit abortion before the third trimester, either directly or through undue burdens on a woman's choice to abort. *Roe* itself did not grant a right, fundamental or otherwise, that states not encourage responsibility in the decision a woman makes or that states not display a collective view of which decision is most appropriate.

It is a further question, certainly, whether a particular regulation—say, a mandatory waiting period or mandatory notification or consultation— makes abortion much more expensive or dangerous or difficult to secure, and so does unduly burden the right against conformity.[44] And of course I agree that it would be naive to read the Court's recent decisions as carrying no threat to *Roe* at all. The past statements of at least four justices, and the likely views of the two newest appointees, are threatening indeed. But we do no favor to the crucial right *Roe* recognized by insisting that every decision pro-life groups applaud is automatically another nail in *Roe*'s coffin.

The real question decided in *Roe*, and the heart of the national debate, is the question of conformity. I said that government sometimes acts properly when it coerces people in order to protect values the majority endorses: when it collects taxes to support art, or when it requires businessmen to spend money to avoid endangering a species, for example. Why (I asked) can the state not forbid abortion on the same ground: that the majority of its citizens thinks that aborting a fetus, except when the mother's own life is at stake, is an intolerable insult to the inherent value of human life?

Conformity and Coercion

I begin my reply to that question by noticing three central and connected reasons why prohibiting abortion is a very different matter from conservation or aesthetic zoning or protecting endangered species. First, the impact on particular people—pregnant women—is far greater. A woman who is forced by her community to bear a child she does not want is no longer in charge of her own body. It has been taken over for purposes she does not share. That is a partial enslavement, a deprivation of liberty vastly more serious than any disadvantage citizens must bear to protect cultural treasures or to save troubled species. The partial enslavement of a forced pregnancy is, moreover, only the beginning of the price a woman denied an abortion pays. Bearing a child destroys many women's lives, because they will no longer be able to work or study or live as they believe they should, or because they will be unable to support that child. Adoption, even when available, may not reduce the injury. Many women would find it nearly intolerable to turn their child over to others to raise and love. Of course, these different kinds of injury are intensified if the pregnancy began in rape or incest, or if a child is born with grave physical or mental handicaps. Many women regard these as not simply undesirable but terrible consequences, and would do almost anything to avoid them. We must never forget that a great many abortions took place, before *Roe v. Wade,* in states that prohibited abortion. These were illegal abortions, and many of them were very dangerous. If a woman desperate for an abortion defies the criminal law, she may risk her life. If she bows to it, her life might be destroyed, and her self-respect compromised.

Second, it is a matter of deep disagreement within our culture, as I said, what someone who is anxious to respect the intrinsic value of human life should therefore do about abortion. There is no parallel disagreement in the case of the other values I mentioned. No one could plausibly claim that respect for future generations sometimes means leaving the planet uninhabitable for them or that respect for animal species sometimes means allowing their extinction. When the law requires people to make sacrifices for those values, it requires them, at most, to sacrifice for something that they do not believe to be important, but that the rest of the community does. They are not forced to act in ways that they think are not only disadvantageous to them but ethically wrong.[45] A woman who must bear a child whose life will be stunted by deformity, or a child who is doomed to an impoverished childhood and an inadequate education, or a child whose existence will cripple the woman's own life, is not merely forced to make sacrifices for values she does not share. She is forced to act not just in the absence of, but in defiance of, her own beliefs about what respect for human life means and requires.

Third, our convictions about how and why human life has intrinsic importance, from which we draw our views about abortion, are much more fundamental to our overall moral personality than the other convictions about inherent value I mentioned. They are decisive in forming our opinions about all life-and-death matters, including not only abortion but also suicide, euthanasia, the death penalty, and conscientious objection to war. Their power is even greater than this suggests, moreover, because our opinions about how and why our own lives have intrinsic value crucially influence every major choice we make about how we should live.[46] Very few people's opinions about architectural conservation or endangered species are even nearly so foundational to the rest of their moral personality, even nearly so interwoven with the other major structural convictions of their lives.

These interconnections are most evident in the lives of people who are religious in a traditional way. The connection between their faith and their opinions about abortion is not contingent but constitutive: their convictions about abortion are shadows of more general foundational convictions about why human life itself is important, convictions at work in all aspects of their lives. A particular religion, like Catholicism, could not comprehensively change its views about abortion without becoming a significantly different faith, organized around a significantly different sense of the ground and consequences of the sacrosanct character of human life. People who are not religious in the conventional way also have general, instinctive convictions about whether, why, and how any human life—their own, for example—has intrinsic value. No one can lead even a mildly reflective life without expressing such convictions. These convictions surface, for almost everyone, at exactly the same critical moments in life—in decisions about reproduction and death and war. Someone who is an atheist, because he does not believe in a personal god, nevertheless has convictions or at least instincts about the value of human life in an infinite and cold universe, and these convictions are just as pervasive, just as foundational to moral personality, as the convictions of a Catholic or a Moslem. They are convictions that have, in the words of a famous Supreme Court opinion, "a place in the life of its possessor parallel to that filled by the orthodox belief in God."[47]

For that reason we may describe people's beliefs about the inherent value of human life, beliefs deployed in their opinions about abortion, as essentially religious beliefs. I shall later try to defend that claim as a matter of constitutional interpretation: I shall argue that such beliefs should be deemed religious within the meaning of the First Amendment. My present point is not legal but philosophical, however. Many people, it is true, think that no belief is religious in character unless it presupposes a personal god. But many established religions—some forms of Buddhism and Hinduism, for example—include no commitment to such a supreme being. Once we set aside the idea that every religious belief presupposes a god, it is doubtful that we can discover any defining feature that all but only religious beliefs have. We must decide whether to classify a belief as religious in a less rigid way: by asking whether it is similar in content to plainly religious beliefs.[48] On that test, the belief that the value of human life transcends its value for the creature whose life it is—that human life is objectively valuable from the point of view, as it were, of the universe—is plainly a religious belief, even when it is held by people who do not believe in a personal deity. It is, in fact, the most fundamental purpose of traditional religions to make exactly that claim to their faithful, and to embody it in some vision or narrative that makes the belief seem intelligible and persuasive.

Religion in that way responds to the most terrifying feature of human life: that we have lives to lead, and death to face, with no evident reason to think that our living, still less how we live, makes any genuine difference at all. The existential question whether human life has any intrinsic or objective importance has been raised in many ways. People ask about the "meaning" or "point" of life, for example. However it is put, the question is foundational. It cannot be answered by pointing out that if people live in a particular recommended way—observing a particular moral code, for example, or following a particular theory of justice—this will make them, individually or collectively, safer or more prosperous, or that it will help them fulfill or realize their human nature, as understood in some particular way. The existential question is deeper, because it asks why any of that matters.

In that way beliefs about the intrinsic importance of human life are distinguished from more secular convictions about morality, fairness, and justice. The latter declare how competing interests of particular people should be served or adjusted or compromised. They rarely reflect any distinctive view about why human interests have objective intrinsic importance, or even whether they do.[49] That explains why people with very different views about the meaning or point of human life can agree about justice, and why people with much the same views about that religious issue can disagree about justice dramatically. Of course many people believe that fairness and justice are important only because they think that it is objectively important how a human life goes.[50] But their particular views about what justice requires are not, for that reason, themselves views about why or in what way that is true.

Religions attempt to answer the deeper existential question by connecting individual human lives to a transcendent objective value. They declare that all human lives (or, for more parochial religions, the lives of believers) have objective importance through some source of value outside human subjective experience: the love of a creator or a redeemer, for example, or nature believed to give objective normative importance to what it creates, or a natural order understood in some other but equally transcendental way. People who think that abortion is morally problematic, even though a fetus has no interests of its own, all accept that human life is intrinsically, objectively valuable. Some think that human life is intrinsically important because it is created by a god, others because human life is the triumph of nature's genius, and others because human life's complexity and promise is in itself awe-inspiring. Some people in each of these groups believe that because human life has intrinsic importance abortion is always, or almost always, wrong. Others in each group have reached a contrary conclusion: that abortion is sometimes necessary in order truly to respect life's inherent value.[51] In each case the belief affirms the essentially religious idea that the importance of human life transcends subjective experience.

The Right of Procreative Autonomy

These three ways in which abortion is special, even among issues that involve claims about inherent value, suggest an interpretation of the much-discussed constitutional right of privacy. That constitutional right limits a state's power to invade personal liberty when the state acts not to protect the rights or interests of other people, but to safeguard an intrinsic value. A state may not curtail liberty, in order to protect an intrinsic value, (1) when the decisions it forbids are matters of personal commitment on essentially religious issues, (2) when the community is divided about what the best understanding of the value in question requires, and (3) when the decision has a very great and disparate impact on the person whose decision is displaced.[52]

I should say again (though by now you will be tired of the point) that the principle of privacy I just defined would not guarantee a right to abortion if a fetus were a constitutional person from the moment of conception. The principle is limited to circumstances in which the state claims authority to protect some inherent value, not the rights and interests of another person. But once we accept that a fetus is not a constitutional person, and shift the ground of constitutional inquiry to the different question of whether a state may forbid abortion in order to respect the inherent value of human life, then the principle of privacy plainly does apply.

It applies because ethical decisions about procreation meet the tests the principle provides. That is why procreative decisions have been collected, through the common law method of adjudication, into a distinct principle we might call the principle of procreative autonomy. That principle, understood as an application of the more general principle of privacy, provides the best available justification for the Court's decisions about contraception, for example. In the first of these cases—*Griswold v. Connecticut*[53]—the justices who made up the majority provided a variety of justifications for their decision. Justice John Harlan said that laws forbidding married couples to use contraceptives violated the Constitution because they could only be enforced by police searches of marital bedrooms, a practice that struck him as repulsive to the concept of ordered liberty.[54]

This justification was inadequate even for the decision in *Griswold*—a prohibition on the purchase or sale of contraceptives could be enforced without searching marital bedrooms, just as a prohibition on the sale of drugs to or the use of drugs by married couples can be enforced without such a search. And it was plainly inadequate for the later decisions in the series. In one of these, Justice Brennan, speaking for the Court, offered a different and more general explanation. "If the right of privacy means anything," he said, "it is the right of the individual, married or not, to be free from government intrusion into matters so fundamentally affecting a person as the decision whether to bear or beget a child."[55]

I take the principle of procreative autonomy to be an elaboration of Brennan's suggestion. It explains the sense in which individual procreative decisions are, as he said, fundamental. Many decisions, including economic decisions, for example, have serious and disparate impacts. Procreative decisions are fundamental in a different way, because the moral issues on which a procreative decision hinges are religious in the broad sense I defined. They are issues touching the ultimate point and value of human life itself. The state's power to prohibit contraception could plausibly be defended only by assuming a general power to dictate to all citizens what respect for the inherent value of human life requires: that it requires, for example, that people not make love except with the intention to procreate.

The Supreme Court, in denying the specific power to make contraception criminal, presupposed the more general principle of procreative autonomy I am defending. That is important, because almost no one believes that the contraception decisions should now be overruled. It is true that Bork had challenged *Griswold* and the later decisions in speeches and articles before his nomination.[56] But during his hearings, he hinted that *Griswold* might be defended on other grounds.[57]

The law's integrity demands, as I said, that principles necessary to support an authoritative set of decisions must be accepted in other contexts as well. It might seem an appealing political compromise to apply the principle of procreative autonomy to contraception, which almost no one now thinks the states can forbid, but not to apply it to abortion, which powerful conservative constituencies violently oppose. But the point of integrity—the point of law itself—is exactly to rule out political compromises of that kind. We must be one nation of principle: our Constitution must represent conviction, not the tactical strategies of justices anxious to satisfy as many political constituencies as possible.

Integrity does not, of course, require that justices respect principles embedded in past decisions that they and others regard as mistakes. It permits the Court to declare, as it has several times in the past, that a particular decision or string of decisions was in error, because the principles underlying those decisions are inconsistent with more fundamental principles embedded in the Constitution's structure and history. The Court cannot declare everything in the past a mistake: that would destroy integrity under the pretext of serving it. It must exercise its power to disregard past decisions modestly. But it must also exercise that power in good faith. It cannot ignore principles underlying past decisions it purports to approve, decisions it would ratify if asked to do so, decisions almost no one, not even rabid critics of the Court's past performance, now disapproves or regards as mistakes. The contraception cases fall into that category, and it would be both dangerous and offensive for the Court cynically to ignore the principles presupposed in those cases in any decision it now reaches about abortion.

So integrity demands general recognition of the principle of procreative autonomy, and therefore of the right of women to decide for themselves not only whether to conceive but whether to bear a child. If you remain in doubt, then consider the possibility that in some state a majority of voters will come to think that it shows disrespect for the sanctity of life to continue a pregnancy in some circumstances—in cases of fetal deformity, for example. If a majority has the power to impose its own views about the sanctity of life on everyone, then the state could require someone to abort, even if that were against her own religious or ethical convictions, at least if abortion had become physically as convenient and safe as, for example, the vaccinations and inoculations states are now recognized as having the power to require.

Of course, if a fetus were a person with a right to live, it would not follow from the fact that one state had the right to forbid abortion that another would have the right to require it. But that does follow once we recognize that the constitutional question at stake in the abortion controversy is whether a state can impose a canonical interpretation of the inherent value of life on everyone. Of course it would be intolerable for a state to require an abortion to prevent the birth of a deformed child. No one doubts, I think, that that requirement would be unconstitutional. But the reason why—because it denies a pregnant woman's right to decide for herself what the sanctity of life requires her to do about her own pregnancy—applies with exactly equal force in the other direction. A state just as seriously insults the dignity of a pregnant woman when it forces her to the opposite choice, and the fact that the choice is approved by a majority is no better justification in the one case than in the other.

Textual Homes

My argument so far has not appealed to any particular constitutional provision. But, as I said, the general structure of the Bill of Rights is such that any moral right as fundamental as the right of procreative autonomy is very likely to have a safe home in the Constitution's text. Indeed, we should expect to see a principle of that foundational character protected not just by one but by several constitutional provisions, because these must necessarily overlap in the way I also described.

The right of procreative autonomy follows from any competent interpretation of the due process clause and of the Supreme Court's past decisions applying that clause. I have already indicated, in my discussion of the contraception cases, my grounds for that claim. I shall now argue, however, for a different and further textual basis for that right. The First Amendment prohibits government from establishing any religion, and it guarantees all citizens the free exercise of their own religion. The Fourteenth Amendment, which incorporates the First Amendment, imposes the same prohibition and the same responsibility on the states. These provisions guarantee the right of procreative autonomy. I do not mean that the First Amendment defense of that right is stronger than the due process clause defense. On the contrary, the First Amendment defense is more complex and less demonstrable as a matter of precedent. I take it up because it is, as I shall try to show, a natural defense, because it illuminates an important dimension of the national debate about abortion, and because the argument for it illustrates both the power and the constraining force of the ideal of legal integrity.

Locating the abortion controversy in the First Amendment would seem natural to most people, who instinctively perceive that the abortion controversy is at bottom essentially a religious one. Some of you may fear, however, that I am trying to revive an old argument now rejected even by some of those who once subscribed to it. This argument holds that since the morality of abortion is a matter of controversy among religious groups, since it is declared immoral and sinful by some orthodox religions—conspicuously the Catholic Church—but permissible by others, the old idea of separation of church and state means that government must leave the subject of abortion alone. That would indeed be a very bad argument if states were permitted to treat a fetus as a person with rights and interests competitive with the rights of a pregnant woman. For the most important responsibility of government is to identify the differing and sometimes competing rights and interests of the people for whom it is responsible, and to decide how these rights may best be accommodated and these interests best served. Government has no reason to abdicate that responsibility just because (or when) organized religion also takes an interest in those matters. Religious bodies and groups were among the strongest campaigners against slavery, and they have for centuries sought social justice, the eradication of suffering and disease, and a vast variety of other humanitarian goals. If the distinction between church and state barred government from also taking up those goals, the doctrine would paralyze government altogether.

But we are now assuming that the issue whether a fetus is a person with rights and interests of its own has already been decided, by secular government, in the only way that issue can be decided under our constitutional system. Now we are considering a different constitutional issue: whether states may nevertheless prohibit abortion in order to endorse a controversial view about what respect for the intrinsic value of human life requires. That is not an issue about who has rights, or how people's competing interests should be balanced and protected. If states are forbidden to prohibit conduct on the ground that it insults the intrinsic value of human life, they are not therefore disabled from pursuing their normal responsibilities. On the contrary, it is one of government's most fundamental duties, recognized throughout Western democracies since the eighteenth century, to ensure that people have a right to live their lives in accordance with their own convictions about essentially religious issues. So the reasons for rejecting the bad argument I described are not arguments against my suggestion that the First Amendment forbids states to force people to conform to an official view about what the sanctity of human life requires.

We must now consider arguments for that suggestion. It is controversial how the establishment and free exercise clauses should be interpreted, and the Supreme Court's rulings on these clauses are somewhat unclear.[58] I cannot offer an extended consideration of those rulings here, and my immediate purpose is not to compose a full and detailed legal argument for the First Amendment defense, but rather to indicate the main structural lines of that defense. Any satisfactory interpretation of the religion clauses of the amendment must cover two issues. First, it must fill out the phrase "free exercise of religion" by explaining which features make a particular belief a religious conviction rather than a nonreligious moral principle or a personal preference. Second, it must interpret "establishment" by explaining the difference between secular and religious aims of government.

Difficult cases arise when government restricts or penalizes conduct required by genuinely religious convictions, but for the secular purpose of serving and protecting other people's interests.[59] Such cases require courts to decide how far the right of free exercise prevents government from adopting policies it believes would increase the general secular welfare of the community. It is a very different matter, however, when government's only purpose is to support one side of an argument about an essentially religious issue. Legislation for that purpose which substantially impaired anyone's religious freedom would violate both of the First Amendment's religion clauses at once.

Of course if a fetus were a constitutional person, with interests government is obliged and entitled to protect, then legislation outlawing abortion would fall into the first of these categories even if convictions permitting or requiring abortion are genuinely religious in character. Such legislation would plainly be constitutional: rights of free exercise would not extend to the killing of a fetus any more than they extend to human sacrifice in religious ritual. But a fetus is not a constitutional person. If people's convictions about what the inherent value of human life requires are religious convictions, therefore, any government demand for conformity would be an attempt to impose a collective religion, and the case would fall into the second category.

What makes a belief a religious one for purposes of the First Amendment? The great majority of eighteenth-century statesmen who wrote and ratified the Constitution may have assumed that every religious conviction presupposes a personal god. But, as the Supreme Court apparently decided in *United States v. Seeger,* that restriction is not now acceptable as part of a constitutional definition of religion, in part because not all the major religions represented in this country presuppose such a being.[60] Once the idea of religion is divorced from that requirement, however, courts face a difficulty in distinguishing between religious and other kinds of conviction. There are two possibilities: a conviction can be deemed religious because of its content—because it speaks to concerns identified as distinctly religious—or because it has very great subjective importance to the person who holds it, as orthodox religious convictions do for devout believers. In *Seeger,* the Court suggested that a scruple is religious if it has "a place in the life of its possessor parallel to that filled by the orthodox belief in God of one who clearly qualifies for the exemption."[61] That statement, taken by itself, is ambiguous. It might mean that a conviction is religious if it answers the same questions that orthodox religion answers for a believer, which is a test of content, or that it is religious if it is embraced as fervently as orthodox religion is embraced by a devout believer, which is a test of subjective importance.

The opinion as a whole is indecisive about which of these two meanings, or which combination of them, the Court intended, and the ambiguity has damaged the development of constitutional law in this area. In any case, however, a subjective importance test is plainly inadequate, by itself, to distinguish religious from other forms of conviction, or indeed from intensely felt preferences. Even people who are religious in the orthodox way often count plainly nonreligious affiliations, like patriotism, as equally or even more important. Some test of content is at least necessary, and may be sufficient.

I argued, earlier, that a belief in the objective and intrinsic importance of human life has a distinctly religious content. Convictions that endorse that objective importance play the same role, in providing an objective under-pinning for concerns about human rights and interests, as orthodox relig-ious beliefs provide for those who accept them. Several of the theologians the Court cited in *Seeger* made the same claim. The Court called the following statement from the Schema of a recent Ecumenical Council, for example, "a most significant declaration on religion": "Men expect from the various religions answers to the riddles of the human condition: What is man? What is the meaning and purpose of our lives?"[62]

I can think of no plausible account of the content a belief must have, in order to be religious in character, that would rule out convictions about why and how human life has intrinsic objective importance, except the abandoned test that requires a religious belief to presuppose a god. It is, of course, essential that any test of religious content allow a distinction between religious beliefs, on the one hand, and nonreligious political or moral convictions, on the other. I have already suggested, however, how the belief that human life has intrinsic objective importance, and other beliefs that interpret and follow directly from that belief, differ from most people's opinions about political fairness or the just distribution of eco-nomic or other resources.[63]

We can see the distinction at work in the Supreme Court's disposition of the conscientious objector cases. In *Seeger*, the Court presumed that the Constitution would not allow exempting men whose opposition to all war was based on theistic religion but not men whose similar opposition was grounded in a nontheistic belief. In *Gillette*, on the other hand, the Court upheld Congress's refusal to grant exemption to men whose opposition to war was selective, even to those whose convictions condemning a particu-lar war were supported by their religion.[64] Though the Court offered various practical grounds for the distinction, these were unpersuasive. The distinction can in fact be justified—if it can be justified at all—only by supposing that though a flat opposition to all war is based on a conviction that human life as such is sacred—which is a distinctly religious convic-tion—selective opposition is at least normally based on considerations of justice or policy, which justify killing in some cases but not others, and which are not themselves religious in content even when they are endorsed by a religious group. As the Court said, "A virtually limitless variety of beliefs are subsumable under the rubric, 'objection to a particular war.' All the factors that might go into nonconscientious dissent from policy, also might appear as the concrete basis of an objection that has roots in conscience and religion as well. Indeed, over the realm of possible situations, opposition to a particular war may more likely be political and nonconscientious, than otherwise."[65]

So the popular sense that the abortion issue is fundamentally a religious one, and some lawyers' sense that it therefore lies outside the proper limits of state action, is at bottom sound, though for reasons somewhat more complex than is often supposed. It rests on a natural—indeed irresistible—understanding of the First Amendment: that a state has no business prescribing what people should think about the ultimate point and value of human life, about why life has intrinsic importance, and about how that value is respected or dishonored in different circumstances. In his reply, Posner objects that if my view of the scope of the free exercise clause were correct, government could not forbid "an aesthete to alter the exterior of his landmark house."[66] But he has misunderstood my view: he apparently thinks that I use a test of subjective importance to identify religious convictions. He points out, as a reductio ad absurdum of my argument, that "economic freedom is a religion" to a variety of libertarians,[67] suggesting that taxation, which libertarians find particularly offensive, would on my argument violate their religious freedom.

I argued, however, that convictions about the intrinsic value of human life are religious on a test of content, not subjective importance. A law forbidding people to tear down Georgian houses does not raise essentially religious issues, no matter how much some people would prefer to build post-modern pastiches instead, because that law does not presuppose any particular conception of why and how human life is sacred, or take a position on any other matter historically religious in character.[68] It is even plainer that my argument would not justify exempting Milton Friedman from tax on grounds of his free-market faith. Government collects taxes in order to serve a variety of secular interests of its citizens, not to declare or support a particular view about any essentially religious matter. It is, of course, true that some people resist paying taxes for reasons that do implicate their convictions about the intrinsic value of human life. Some people refuse to pay taxes to finance war on that basis, for example. In such cases compulsory taxation does plausibly impair the free exercise of religion. But the problem falls into the first of the two categories I distinguished, and the appropriate balancing sustains the tax, given the limited character of the infringement of free exercise and the importance of uniform taxation.

I conclude that the right to procreative autonomy, from which a right of choice about abortion flows, is well grounded in the First Amendment.[69] But it would be remarkable, as I said, if so basic a right did not figure in the best interpretation of constitutional liberty and equality as well. It would be remarkable, that is, if lawyers who accepted the right did not think it fundamental to the concept of ordered liberty, and so protected by the due process clause, or part of what government's equal concern for all citizens requires, and so protected by the equal protection clause. Posner is amused that different scholars who endorse a right of procreative autonomy have offered a variety of textual homes for it: he says that in my account, *Roe v. Wade* "is the Wandering Jew of constitutional law."[70] But of course, as he would agree, it is hardly an embarrassment for that right that lawyers have disagreed about which clause to emphasize in their arguments for it. Some constitutional lawyers have an odd taste for constitutional neatness: they want rights mapped uniquely onto clauses with no overlap, as if redundancy were a constitutional vice. Once we understand, however, that the Bill of Rights is not a list of discrete remedies drawn up by a parsimonious draftsman, but a commitment to an ideal of just government, that taste makes no more sense than the claim that freedom of religion is not also liberty, or that the protection of freedom for everyone has nothing to do with equality.

Dignity and Concern

I pause for a brief summary. We must abandon the traditional way of understanding the constitutional argument about abortion. It is not an argument about whether a fetus is a person. It is rather a dispute about whether and how far government may enforce an official view about the right understanding of the sanctity of human life. I described a constitutional right—the right of procreative autonomy—which denies government that power. I suggested that this right is firmly embedded in our constitutional history. It is the best available justification of the "privacy" cases, including the contraception cases. Those cases are conventionally understood as residing, by way of textual home, in the due process clause of the Fourteenth Amendment. I argued that they might also rest on the religion clauses of the First Amendment.

Posner suggests that my argument is more powerful construed holistically, that is, as an argument about what the Constitution as a whole requires. I do not, as I said, see a difference between clause-by-clause and holistic interpretations of the Bill of Rights. But I nevertheless accept the spirit of his suggestion—that it is important to notice the place the right I have been describing holds not only in the structure of the Constitution, but in our political culture more generally. Cardinal in that culture is a belief in individual human dignity: that people have the moral right—and the moral responsibility—to confront for themselves, answering to their own consciences and convictions, the most fundamental questions touching the meaning and value of their own lives. That assumption was the engine of emancipation and of racial equality, for example. The most powerful arguments against slavery before the Civil War, and for equal protection after it, were framed in the language of dignity: the cruelest aspect of slavery, for the abolitionists, both religious and secular, was its failure to recognize a slave's right to decide issues of value for himself or herself. Indeed, the most basic premise of our entire constitutional system—that our government shall be republican rather than despotic—embodies a commitment to that conception of dignity.

So the principle of procreative autonomy, in the broad sense, is a principle that any remotely plausible explanation of our entire political culture would have to recognize. It is also a principle we would want our Constitution to contain even if we were starting on a clean slate, free to make any constitution we wanted. I want to guard against an interpretation of my argument that I would disown, however. It does not suppose that people either are or should be indifferent, either as individuals or as members of a political community, to the decisions their friends or neighbors or fellow citizens or fellow human beings make about abortion. On the contrary, it recognizes several reasons why they should not be indifferent. As I have already noted, individual choices together create a moral environment that inevitably influences what others can do. So a person's concern for his own life, and for that of his children and friends, gives him a reason for worrying about how even strangers treat the inherent value of human life. Our concern that people lead good lives is not naturally limited, moreover, nor should it be, to concern for our own lives and those of our family. We want others, even strangers, not to lead what we regard as blighted lives, ruined by a terrible act of desecration.

But the most powerful reason we have for wanting others to respect the intrinsic value of human life, in the way we think that value demands, is not our concern for our own or other people's interests at all, but just our concern for the value itself. If people did not think it transcendentally important that human lives not be wasted by abortion, then they would not have the kind of commitment my argument assumes people do have. So of course Americans who think that almost all abortion is immoral must take a passionate interest in the issue: liberals who count such people as deranged busybodies are insensitive as well as wrong. Nevertheless, we must insist on religious tolerance in this area, as in other issues about which people once cared just as passionately and in the same way, and once thought sufficiently important to wage not just sit-ins but wars. Tolerance is a cost we must pay for our adventure in liberty. We are committed, by our Constitution, to live in a community in which no group is deemed clever or spiritual or numerous enough to decide essentially religious matters for everyone else. If we have genuine concern for the lives others lead, moreover, we will also accept that no life is a good one lived against the grain of conviction, that it does not aid someone else's life but spoils it to force values upon him he cannot accept but can only bow before out of fear or prudence.

Roe Reconsidered

We must now take a fresh look at *Roe v. Wade*. *Roe* did three things. First, it reaffirmed a pregnant woman's constitutional right of procreative autonomy, and declared that states do not have the power simply to forbid abortion on any terms they wish. Second, it recognized that states nevertheless do have a legitimate interest in regulating abortion. Third, it constructed a detailed regime for balancing that right and that interest: it declared, roughly, that states could not forbid abortion for any reason in the first trimester of pregnancy, that they could regulate abortion in the second trimester only out of concern for the health of the mother, and, finally, that they could outlaw abortion altogether after fetal viability, that is, after approximately the beginning of the third trimester. We must inspect those three decisions against the background of our argument so far.

Our argument confirms the first decision. The crucial issue in the constitutional abortion controversy is not whether a fetus is a person—*Roe* was plainly right in holding that a fetus is not a person within the meaning of the Constitution—but whether states have a legitimate power to dictate how their members must respect the inherent value of life. Since any competent interpretation of the Constitution must recognize a principle of procreative autonomy, states do not have the power simply to forbid abortion altogether.

Roe was also right on the second score. States do have a legitimate interest in regulating the abortion decision. It was mysterious, in *Roe* and other decisions, what that interest was. Our account identifies it as a legitimate interest in maintaining a moral environment in which decisions about life and death, including the abortion decision, are taken seriously, treated as matters of moral gravity.

It remains to consider whether *Roe* was right on the third score. Does the trimester scheme it announced allow states to pursue their legitimate interests while adequately protecting a pregnant woman's right of autonomy? That trimester scheme has been criticized as arbitrary and overly rigid, even by some lawyers who are sympathetic to the narrowest decision in *Roe*: that the Texas statute was unconstitutional. Why is the point of viability the crucial point? We might put that question in two ways. We might ask why viability should mark the earliest time at which a state is entitled to prohibit abortion. If it can prohibit abortion then, why not earlier, as a majority of citizens in some states apparently wish? Or we might ask why viability should mark the end of a woman's right to protection. If a state cannot prohibit abortion before viability, then why may it prohibit it after that point? Both questions challenge the point of viability as arbitrary, though from different directions. I shall first pursue the second form of the question. What happens at viability to make the right I have been describing—the right of procreative autonomy—less powerful or effective?

Two answers to that question might figure in any defense of the *Roe v. Wade* scheme. First, at about the point of viability, but not much before, fetal brain development may be sufficient to allow pain.[71] So at the point of viability, but not much before, a fetus can sensibly be said to have interests of its own. That does not mean, I must emphasize, that a state is permitted to declare a fetus a person at that point. The question who is a constitutional person, with independent constitutional rights in competition with the rights of others, must be decided nationally, as I argued. But a state may nevertheless act to protect the interests even of creatures—animals, for example—who are not constitutional persons, so long as it respects constitutional rights in doing so. At the point of viability, therefore, the state may claim a legitimate derivative interest that is independent of its detached interest in enforcing its collective conception of the sanctity of life.

Second, choosing the point of viability gives a pregnant woman, in most cases, ample opportunity to reflect upon and decide whether she believes it best and right to continue her pregnancy or to terminate it. Very few abortions are performed during the third trimester—only about 0.01 percent[72]—and even fewer if we exclude emergency abortions necessary to save a mother's life, which almost no one wants to prohibit even near the end of pregnancy. It is true that a very few women—most of whom are very young women—are unaware of their pregnancy until it is nearly complete. But in almost all cases, a woman knows she is pregnant in good time to make a reflective decision before viability. That suggests that a state does not violate most women's right to choose by insisting on a decision before that point, and it also suggests an important reason why a state might properly so insist.

It is an almost universal conviction that abortion becomes progressively morally more problematic as a fetus develops toward the shape of infanthood, as the difference between pregnancy and infancy becomes more a matter of location than development. That widespread conviction seems odd so long as we suppose that whether abortion is wrong depends only on whether a fetus is a person from the moment of conception. But the belief is compelling once we realize that abortion is wrong, when it is, because it insults the sanctity of human life. The insult to that value is greater when the life destroyed is further advanced, when, as it were, the creative investment in that life is greater. Women who have a genuine opportunity to decide on abortion early in pregnancy, when the impact is much less, but who actually decide only near the end, may well be indifferent to the moral and social meaning of their act. Society has a right, if its members so decide, to protect its culture from that kind of indifference, so long as the means it chooses do not infringe the right of pregnant women to a reflective choice.

Taken together, these two answers provide, I believe, a persuasive explanation of why government is entitled to prohibit abortion, subject to certain exceptions, after the sixth month of pregnancy. But do they provide an answer to the question asked from the other direction? Why may government not prohibit abortion earlier? The first answer would not justify any much earlier date, because, as I said, the central nervous system is not sufficiently developed much before the end of twenty-six weeks of pregnancy to admit of pain.[73] But must that be decisive? The second answer does not depend on attributing interests to a fetus, and, by itself, seems an adequate justification of state power to prohibit abortion after a sufficiently long period. Would women not have a sufficient opportunity to exercise their right of autonomy if they were forbidden abortion after just five months? Four? Three?

Blackmun chose a point in pregnancy that he thought plainly late enough to give women a fair chance to exercise their right, in normal circumstances, and that was salient for two other reasons, each captured in the overall explanation I gave. As I said, viability seems, on the best developmental evidence, the earliest point at which a fetus might be thought to have interests of its own, and the point at which the natural development of a fetus is so far continued that deliberately waiting until after that point seems contemptuous of the inherent value of life. These three factors together indicate viability as the most appropriate point after which a state could properly assert its interests in protecting a fetus's interests, and its responsibility. Blackmun's decision should not be overruled. So important a decision should not be overruled, after nearly twenty years, unless it is clearly wrong, and his was not clearly wrong. On the contrary, the arguments for choosing viability as the key date remain impressive.

But it is important to acknowledge that a different test, bringing the cut-off date forward by some period, would have been acceptable if it had afforded women enough time to exercise their right to terminate an unwanted pregnancy. Of course, the earlier the cut-off time, the more important it would be to provide realistic exceptions for reasons the mother could not reasonably have discovered earlier. Suppose that the Court had substituted for the fixed scheme of *Roe* not another fixed scheme, but rather a constitutional standard drafted in terms of overall reasonableness, which the federal courts would enforce case by case. Such a standard might have provided, in effect, that any prohibition would be unconstitutional if it did not provide women a reasonable time to decide upon an abortion after discovering that they were pregnant, or after discovering medical information indicating defects in the fetus or an increased risk to the mother of pregnancy, or other facts pertinent to the impact of childbirth on their lives.

In the end, as Blackmun no doubt anticipated, the Court would have had to adopt more rigid standards that selected at least a prima facie point in pregnancy before which prohibition would be presumptively unconstitutional. But the Court might have developed those standards gradually, perhaps deciding, in the first instance, that any statute that forbade second-term abortions would be subject to strict scrutiny to see whether it contained the exceptions necessary to protect a woman's right to a reflective choice. That approach still would have struck down the Texas law in *Roe*. It would also strike down the equally strict laws that some states and

Guam have recently adopted, each hoping to provide the lawsuit that will end *Roe.*

Would it make much practical difference if the Supreme Court now substituted such a case-by-case test for *Roe*'s rigid structure? A case-by-case test might not, in fact, much reduce legal abortion. In 1987, only 10 percent of abortions took place in the second trimester,[74] and many of these were on medical or other grounds that would still be permitted in any legislation acceptable under the more flexible test I have described. If a more flexible test were adopted, publicity might bring home to more women the importance of deciding and acting early. Medical developments in the technology of abortion might soon increase the percentage of very early abortions anyway. For instance, the abortion pill being developed in France, RU 486, which permits a safe abortion at home early in pregnancy, will allow pregnant women a more private method of abortion, if they decide and act in a timely way.[75] Of course no statute that banned that pill would be constitutional, even under the more flexible standard.

I believe, as I said, that *Roe v. Wade* should not be substantially changed. The line it draws is salient and effectively serves the legitimate state purpose of promoting a responsible attitude toward the intrinsic value of human life. But the most important line, as I said, is the line between that legitimate goal and the illegitimate goal of coercion. It will be disappointing, but not intolerable, if *Roe* is amended in some such way as I have been discussing. But it would be intolerable if *Roe* is wholly reversed, if the constitutional right of procreative autonomy is denied altogether. Some of you already think that recent appointments to the Court, and recent decisions by it, signal a dark age for the American constitutional adventure. I hope that your bleak judgment is premature. But it will be confirmed, spectacularly, if the Supreme Court declares that American citizens have no right to follow their own reflective convictions in the most personal, conscience-driven, and religious decisions many of them will ever make.

Winter 1992

4

▼

Roe Was Saved

The Supreme Court's ruling in *Planned Parenthood of Southeastern Pennsylvania et. al. v. Casey,* the abortion decision handed down on June 29, 1992, was a great surprise, and astounded many observers. It may prove to be one of the most important Court decisions of this generation, not only because it reaffirmed and strengthened the reasoning behind the Court's 1973 decision in *Roe v. Wade,* that a woman has a constitutional right to an abortion until the fetus is viable, but because three key justices also reaffirmed a more general view of the nature of the Constitution which they had been appointed to help destroy. Justices Sandra Day O'Connor, Anthony Kennedy, and David Souter, all of whom were appointed by Ronald Reagan or George Bush, and two of whom had expressed substantial reservations about *Roe v. Wade* in the past, joined the two remaining liberal justices, Harry Blackmun and John Paul Stevens, in a strong reaffirmation of *Roe.* But the three Reagan-Bush appointees also voted to uphold certain regulations of abortion that pro-choice groups deplore, and that Blackmun and Stevens, in separate opinions, voted to strike down.

Though there are good reasons, which Blackmun and Stevens described, to disagree with parts of the decision of the three justices, it would be wrong to underestimate the importance for women of their clear endorsement of a basic right to free choice about abortion until the fetus is viable.[1]

They set out their views in a joint opinion that drew partial dissents from the Chief Justice, William Rehnquist, and Justice Antonin Scalia. Each of these dissents was joined by Justices Byron White and Clarence Thomas.[2] Scalia's dissent, which was particularly bitter and heavy with sarcasm,

117

emphasized what many observers have come to realize: that the three justices who signed the joint opinion, and who this term have rejected orthodox conservative positions not only about abortion but about freedom of religion and other issues as well,[3] seem to have formed a surprising new force reasserting a traditional legal attitude toward constitutional interpretation, a force that has so far partially frustrated the right wing's desire to make the Constitution less effective in protecting individual rights against the majority will.

The *Casey* decision concerned the Abortion Control Act that Pennsylvania had adopted in 1982 to regulate abortion. Among other things, the act required doctors to give prescribed information to women contemplating abortion, forbade doctors to perform an abortion until at least twenty-four hours after the patient had received that information, required parental consent for a teenager's abortion (though with a bypass procedure allowing a judge to find a teenager mature enough to make her own decision), and required married women to inform their husbands before any abortion. Five abortion clinics and one doctor sued for a declaration that the statute was unconstitutional because it violated *Roe v. Wade.* The federal district court for the Eastern District of Philadelphia agreed that the statute was unconstitutional and struck down all the provisions of which the plaintiffs complained. But the Third Circuit Court of Appeals substantially reversed the district court: it agreed that the requirement to notify spouses was unconstitutional, but denied that any of the other provisions were unconstitutional, even on the assumption that *Roe v. Wade* remained good law. Both sides appealed to the Supreme Court: the clinics arguing once again that all the restrictions were unconstitutional, and Pennsylvania arguing that even the provision requiring that spouses be notified was not.

The Bush administration filed a separate brief urging the Court to take the opportunity to overrule *Roe v. Wade* outright, as Reagan and Bush administrations had asked the Court to do in five previous cases. Many lawyers and commentators expected the Court to overrule *Roe* soon, because they thought that at least two of four recent appointees—O'Connor, Kennedy, Souter, and Thomas—would join Rehnquist, White, and Scalia, all of whom had expressed opposition to the decision, to provide the five votes for overruling. Most commentators expected the Court not to take that step in *Casey,* which it could decide without reviewing *Roe,* and to wait until one of the statutes more directly challenging *Roe* came before it next year, after the election.[4]

O'Connor, Kennedy, and Souter confounded both these predictions. They sustained the Third Circuit's decision upholding most of the Pennsylvania restrictions but striking down the requirement that married women notify their spouses.[5] But they insisted both on reviewing *Roe* in the present case rather than waiting—they said that a "jurisprudence of doubt" is bad for liberty—and on reaffirming rather than condemning *Roe*'s central holding.[6] It may exaggerate the future coherence of these three justices to describe them, as the media have, as now forming a new, moderate center for the Court. I suspect that they will divide again, as they have in the past, over specific constitutional issues, and that one or another will make decisions, as each has in the past, that will strike liberals as conservative rather than as moderate.

But the three justices do indeed seem united, as their joint opinion makes plain, in a crucial and fundamental conviction that separates all of them from the four conservative justices who voted to overrule *Roe*. O'Connor, Kennedy, and Souter emphatically believe that the principal individual rights protected by the Constitution should be understood not as a list of discrete and limited rules hammered out in past political compromises, with only the force that the politicians who created them expected them to have, but rather as defining an overall national commitment to liberty and justice.

They ended their joint opinion with a commanding restatement of that ideal. "Our Constitution is a covenant," they said, "running from the first generation of Americans to us and then to future generations . . . We accept our responsibility not to retreat from interpreting the full meaning of the covenant in the light of all our precedents." They said that the due process clause of the Fourteenth Amendment, which forbids states to curtail liberty except through due process of law, must therefore be understood as protecting all of the most fundamental personal liberties, whether or not these are specifically mentioned in some other clause of the Constitution.[7] They conceded that applying that test requires judgment, and that reasonable judges could disagree about which liberties were among the most important. But it is a great merit of their joint opinion that they were able considerably to strengthen the case for *Roe* by adding a crucial argument as to why freedom of choice about abortion is fundamental, an argument that Blackmun's opinion in *Roe* had not emphasized, but that two decades of national reflection and debate about abortion has since brought to the foreground.

The three justices recognized that the fate of a fetus is rightly of very great personal concern to many Americans. But they said that decisions about abortion nevertheless deserve special constitutional protection because such decisions involve "the most intimate and personal choices a person may make in a lifetime." "At the heart of liberty," they said, "is the right to define one's own concept of existence, of meaning, of the universe, and of the mystery of human life."

The argument summarized in that language is complex.[8] As Stevens made plain in his independent, supporting opinion, the argument presupposes that a fetus is not a person within the meaning of the Constitution, and also presupposes that states have no power to declare it a person, within their territory, so as to limit women's rights under the national Constitution. Obviously, if a state can designate a fetus as a person, and protect it the way it protects other people, then the fact that a woman's decision about abortion draws on her metaphysical or religious views would provide no reason for denying a state power to stop her killing what it is entitled and obliged to protect.

But once we assume that a fetus is not a person from the perspective of the Constitution, and that states have no power to declare it one, then the fact that a decision about abortion implicates profound personal convictions does provide a strong reason why the state must leave that decision to individual conscience. Some people who are strongly pro-life do think that even an early fetus is already a person from the moral point of view. Other opponents of abortion, though they do not think that an early fetus is even morally a person, or that it has rights or interests of its own, insist that it nevertheless embodies an important intrinsic value because it is already a form of human life, a stage in the development of a full person, and that abortion is therefore inconsistent with what the joint opinion called "reverence for the wonder of creation."

People who take a different view of abortion, and believe that it is sometimes morally justified, do not necessarily deny that a fetus embodies an intrinsic value. They may rather think that on some occasions—the joint opinion mentions cases in which a child, if born, would lead a deprived life—the appropriate "reverence" for human creation argues for abortion rather than childbirth.

It would be wrong, the three justices declare, for a state to form official, collective convictions about essentially ethical and religious issues like these, and to impose those official convictions on individual women, forcing them to suffer great personal hardship for particular metaphysical beliefs, about the meaning or inherent value of life, that they do not share. Any decent society committed to liberty will leave such decisions, their opinion said, to an individual woman's "own conception of her spiritual imperatives." "Beliefs about such matters," it said, "could not define the attributes of personhood were they formed under the compulsion of the State."

That argument is important not just because it provides an even more secure basis for *Roe*'s judgment that women have a right, in principle, to freedom of choice about abortion, but because it also provides a natural basis for the joint opinion's other main ambition: to redefine and assess a state's competing interest in regulating a woman's decisions about abortion. Blackmun's opinion in *Roe* had conceded the existence of such a state interest, but had not satisfactorily defined it, and though several justices in later decisions had also referred to a presumed state interest in regulating abortion, the content of that interest had remained mysterious.

It would not be consistent with recognizing a woman's right to freedom of choice about abortion, after all, also to recognize that the state had a legitimate interest in protecting a fetus's right to live, the way it protects the interests of ordinary persons. If a state were entitled to protect the life of a fetus in that way, then women would of course not have a right to freedom of choice about abortion at all. But it is certainly consistent with the joint opinion's explanation of why women do have such a right—that a decision about abortion implicates a woman's most profound convictions about human existence and the cosmic meaning of life—to insist that a state has a legitimate interest in attempting to persuade its citizens to take decisions about abortion seriously, to understand that such decisions do involve fundamental moral issues. So long, that is, as the state stops short of dictating to its citizens which decision they must ultimately make.

It is the second great merit of the joint opinion that it clearly defines the state's interest in regulating abortion in just those terms. "What is at stake is the woman's right to make the ultimate decision, not a right to be insulated from all others in doing so," it said, and therefore "States are free to enact laws to provide a reasonable framework for a woman to make a decision that has such profound and lasting meaning." The state may reasonably think, moreover, that a woman tempted to abortion should be at least aware of arguments against it that others in the community believe important and persuasive, so that "even in the earliest stages of pregnancy, the State may enact rules and regulations designed to encourage her to know that there are philosophic and social arguments of great weight that can be brought to bear in favor of continuing the pregnancy."

But of course a state cannot be permitted to appeal to its interest in its citizens making informed and reflective decisions about abortion as a justification for forcing them ultimately to make the decision that the majority, as represented by the legislature, prefers. The joint opinion therefore adopted the test that O'Connor had endorsed in an earlier case: it said that a state regulation about abortion is unconstitutional, even if it does not purport to dictate an ultimate decision, if either its purpose or its effect is to create an "undue burden" on a woman who chooses abortion by posing "substantial obstacles" to that choice.

The line between a regulation that imposes such an obstacle and one that only makes an abortion somewhat more expensive or inconvenient, which the joint opinion declared permissible, is plainly a difficult one to draw in practice. The joint opinion had no trouble agreeing with the Third Circuit that requiring a married woman to notify her husband before an abortion does unduly burden her decision. Even though the Pennsylvania statute provided an exception for women who reasonably feared a husband's physical attack, the three justices agreed with the district court that many women have reason to fear psychological or economic intimidation as well.[9]

The group also held, however, that Pennsylvania's mandatory twenty-four-hour delay, after a doctor had given the patient prescribed information, had not been shown, at least on the record before the Supreme Court, to impose an undue burden. Women's groups were particularly angered by that decision. The clinics had pointed out, in their briefs and arguments, that the mandatory waiting period means that women who live at a considerable distance from an abortion clinic, as many do in rural areas, will have to make two possibly expensive trips rather than one. They may have to explain two trips to those they may not wish to know about the abortion; and they may have to endure the gauntlet of pro-life protesters outside the clinic twice. The clinics said that this requirement might indeed deter some women from an abortion who would otherwise want one.

The joint opinion found this argument "troubling," and its decision on the point was tentative in a way that many newspaper reports have not made sufficiently clear. It emphasized that the district court had not actually made a finding that the mandatory waiting period imposed "substantial obstacles," and said that it might well respect such a finding in a later case. (Justice Blackmun, in his separate opinion, said he was encouraged by that remark and expected that district courts could be persuaded to make the appropriate finding in a future case.) The joint opinion's remark about the district court finding was perhaps disingenuous, however—the district court had not used the phrase "substantial obstacle," but its findings clearly implied that the waiting period might impose such obstacles.

In any case the joint opinion might well have explored the question whether Pennsylvania could have achieved substantially the same success in its aim of inducing women to think seriously about arguments against abortion in a way that imposed far less difficulty for women living far from abortion facilities. Could Pennsylvania not have provided, for example, that in the case of women living a stipulated distance from such facilities, the required information might be given by doctors over the telephone, at least twenty-four hours before an abortion? Doctors could make a tentative judgment about probable fetal age based on information provided over the telephone, and could confirm that judgment, and display any graphic material the state wished women contemplating abortion to see, on the day of the abortion itself, when a woman reflecting on the previous telephone conversation could still change her mind. Whether a state has the constitutional power to impose a particular kind of regulation, such as a particular form of mandatory waiting period, must surely depend on whether it might achieve substantially the same legitimate result with fewer regrettable side effects.

The joint opinion suggests (though perhaps only for the sake of the argument) that one or more of its members "may" have "reservations" about the soundness of *Roe*'s central holding—that a woman has a constitutionally protected right to choose abortion at any point before the fetus becomes viable. Since each justice who signed the opinion presumably supports the strong substantive arguments for that holding the opinion offers, it is not clear what those reservations could be. But various parts of the joint opinion suggest the following, at least theoretical, possibility. Though all three justices are convinced that women have a constitutional right to an abortion, and that the state's interest in regulating the exercise of that right is limited to attempting to persuade women to exercise it responsibly, at least one member of the group believes that the best accommodation of that right and that partially conflicting state interest would permit states to prohibit abortion altogether at some point well along in pregnancy but earlier than viability, as many European statutes regulating abortion do.[10]

But whatever reservation one or more members of the three-justice group might have had about *Roe*'s central holding, if he or she were free to think about the matter on a clean slate, the group was united in thinking that a sound respect for *stare decisis*—the legal tradition that a court ought not lightly to alter its own past decisions—barred any reconsideration of that holding now. "The reservations any of us may have in reaffirming the central holding of *Roe* are outweighed," the joint opinion said, "by the explication of individual liberty we have given combined with the force of *stare decisis*."

The opinion devotes an entire section to elaborating the force of the latter consideration. It argues, first, that a generation of women has come to rely on a right to an abortion until viability; it says that *Roe* "facilitated" the "ability of women to participate equally in the economic and social life of the Nation." That seems an odd claim understood as an argument about reliance on past decisions. The fact that the *Roe* rule has improved the equality of women is a strong substantive reason for thinking it sound, not a reason why it should be protected even if it was, as an original matter, unsound. In any case, the strongest argument the joint opinion provides for respecting *stare decisis* is not an argument about the unfairness of reversal for those who have relied on past decisions, but rather that reversing *Roe* now, whatever the consequences for particular people, would be damaging to the integrity of the law and therefore to the legitimacy of the Supreme Court.

That is a crucial claim, because it underscores the group's commitment to the view I described earlier: that the Constitution must be understood not as a list of discrete rules but as a charter of principle that must be interpreted and enforced as a coherent system. That view of the Constitution entails two central judicial responsibilities. First, judges must decide particular cases in the light of general principles they can responsibly assign to the text of the abstract clauses of the Constitution, and they must respect those principles even when the decisions the principles dictate are controversial or unpopular. As O'Connor, Kennedy, and Souter made plain, they were guided by that responsibility in applying the principle established in the *Griswold* case, and other cases everyone now accepts, to abortion as well.

Second, the vast power judges have in assigning principles of such sweep to the abstract constitutional provisions must be disciplined, if the

Court is to be understood as an institution of law and not just another venue for politics, by a respect for the integrity of its decisions over time. When the Court changes its mind, the joint opinion suggests, and argues that it was mistaken in the past, it chips away at an important part of that restraint, and it cannot do so too often without undermining its legitimacy as an unelected forum committed to basing its decisions on principle.

So the Court should hesitate to change its mind, and should do so only when the overall goal of principled integrity itself demands the change. Integrity did demand a change, as the joint opinion argues, in the two most celebrated reversals in the Court's history: when it overruled the infamous *Lochner* decision, which denied states the power to improve working conditions and otherwise regulate the economic market, and when, in the *Brown* case of 1954, it overruled *Plessy v. Fergusson*'s holding that racially segregated public facilities did not violate the equal protection clause. In both cases, decades of experience had shown that the past decision was inconsistent with more general principles the law and the community had come to adopt, both about the moral responsibilities of government and about the psychological and social meaning of discrimination. Overruling was absolutely necessary in order to protect the coherence of constitutional law as a whole. There is no such justification for overruling *Roe*, the joint opinion said: nothing has happened to indicate that enforcing a woman's right to choose abortion until a fetus is viable offends more general principles of liberty or equality that other past decisions presuppose. So overruling *Roe* would undermine the valuable general constraint of precedent with no offsetting justification drawn from the same command to respect principles presupposed by previous decisions.

The importance of the joint opinion's commitment to the vision of the Constitution as a system of principle is underscored by the dissenting opinions of Rehnquist and Scalia, who fervently embrace the opposite view. They insist that the rights set out in the Constitution, including the right that liberty not be limited except by due process of law, are only a set of discrete rules which neither appeal to nor presuppose any more general principles. They say that the force of these rights is limited to the highly specific expectations of the politicians who created them, and that the rights therefore must be interpreted so as not to condemn any political practices in general force when they were adopted.

Rehnquist begins his partial dissent in *Casey* by declaring a firm belief that *Roe* should be overruled. He makes no genuine attempt to dispute the majority's claim that *Roe* is supported by general principles implicit in the Court's past decisions about contraception, marriage, and private education. He only points out that no particular language in these opinions declared an "all-encompassing" right of privacy. He means, apparently, that since none of the previous cases concerned abortion, no past decision explicitly included it.[11] But it hardly follows that the principle those decisions presuppose does not extend to abortion, as the majority insists they plainly do.

Rehnquist does say, as he has before, that abortion is different from contraception because abortion involves the destruction of a fetus; he compares abortion to "firing a gun where the case at hand happens to involve its discharge into another person's body." These claims presuppose, however, that the Constitution entitles states to treat a fetus as a person, and Rehnquist makes no attempt whatever to reply to or even acknowledge the majority's reasons, carefully set out by Stevens in his own opinion, for supposing that states may not do so. Nor does Rehnquist explain how his own previously announced view, that states have no right to prohibit abortion when the mother's life is at stake, is consistent with a state's power to declare a fetus a person. States plainly have the power to forbid a doctor's "firing a gun" into one innocent person even to save the life of another.

Scalia, in his own partial dissent, makes even plainer his contempt for the view that the Constitution creates a system of principle. He reaches the conclusion that abortion is not a liberty protected by the Constitution, he says, "not because of anything so exalted as my views concerning the 'concept of existence, of meaning of the universe, and of the mystery of human life,'" but "because of two simple facts: (1) The Constitution says absolutely nothing about it, and (2) the long-standing traditions of American society have permitted it to be legally proscribed." Scalia's flat assertion that the Constitution says nothing about abortion begs the question, of course. The Fourteenth Amendment does explicitly forbid states to abridge liberty without due process of law, and the question, in this case as in any other case involving that clause, is whether the state legislation in question does in fact do exactly that. If it does, then the Constitution does say something about it: the Constitution forbids it. The majority argues that if we accept the principles that underlie past Supreme Court decisions everyone accepts, we must also accept that forbidding abortion before viability denies liberty without due process. Scalia says nothing at all that undermines or even challenges that claim.

So Scalia's entire argument depends on his assertion that since a majority of states had outlawed abortion before the Fourteenth Amendment was adopted, it would be wrong to interpret the due process clause as denying them the power to do so now. He refuses to consider whether laws outlawing abortion, no matter how popular they were or are, offend other, more general principles of liberty that are embedded in the Constitution's abstract language and in the Court's past decisions. He disdains inquiries of that character because, he says, they involve "value judgments." Of course they do. How can any court enforce the abstract moral command of the Constitution that states may not violate fundamental liberties without making judgments about "values"? Judges have had to make such judgments since law began.

It is exactly because the Constitution requires courts to exercise moral judgment that the joint opinion of O'Connor, Kennedy, and Souter lays such great emphasis on the traditional constraints lawyers in our tradition have always observed: integrity of principle and respect for precedent. Scalia and Rehnquist reject those constraints. But of course their decisions reflect moral judgments just as much as the majority's do, because they pick and choose which traditions to accept as defining the content of constitutional rights and which to reject as inconsistent with it. They both, presumably, now accept the Court's past decisions striking down, under the Fourteenth Amendment, various forms of racial and gender discrimination that were widely practiced when that amendment was enacted. Scalia insists that racial classifications are different from prohibitions on abortion because the former are "contradicted by a text"—the equal protection clause. But that clause does not explicitly condemn separate public facilities for different races, or racial school segregation, both of which were widely practiced when the clause was adopted, and those who adopted it probably did not have gender discrimination in mind at all.

Nothing in Scalia's opinion suggests why he does not treat the racially or sexually discriminatory practices that flourished when the Fourteenth Amendment was adopted as fixing the content of that amendment, rather than being condemned by it, or why he takes a different view of the force of the practices that outlawed abortion. In this case, as well as in others I have described elsewhere,[12] treating the Constitution as only a set of independent and historically limited rules masks a freewheeling judicial discretion that is guided only by a justice's own political or moral convictions, unchecked by the constraints that treating the Constitution as a charter of principle would necessarily impose.

That vision of the Constitution as principle, whose importance I have been emphasizing, is a jurisprudential conviction rather than a distinctly liberal or even moderate position. Justice Harlan, who was widely regarded as a conservative justice, embraced it, as I said, and the fact that O'Connor, Kennedy, and Souter have endorsed it in *Casey* and other recent decisions does not signal that the future decisions of any of those justices will please liberals or displease conservatives. The vision of a principled constitution does strongly support a constitutional right to abortion, for all the reasons I described, and it is not surprising that the only justices who have rejected that right also reject that vision.[13] But there is no equally strong connection between the view that the Constitution is a system of principle and liberal positions about many other controversial constitutional issues.

The principled view of the Constitution is, however, a great national heritage and treasure, and people of all political convictions should join in endorsing and protecting it. Many of us feared that recent appointments to the Supreme Court, by Presidents who expressly rejected that view of the Constitution, had buried it for a generation. *Casey* and the other dramatic decisions at the close of the last Court term show that the fear was premature, that the principled view of the Constitution remains robust and effective.

That fact is itself a tribute to the great emotional strength of that view. If a President appoints justices who love and respect their craft and its history, then those justices will be drawn to the principled view of the Constitution, whatever expectations the President may have had. O'Connor, Kennedy, and Souter are only the latest examples of that cheering fact: Justices Warren and Brennan were appointed by Eisenhower, and Blackmun by Nixon. These examples refute the cynics who insist that since Court appointments are politically motivated the Court is inevitably just another political institution.

But of course Presidents who know what they are about, and care about nothing else, can still appoint justices who take the same demeaning view of the Constitution as they do. Justice Thomas, on the record so far, shows what Presidents of that cast of mind can do. We must not forget that in the *Casey* decision four justices announced themselves still determined to overrule *Roe v. Wade* and to undermine the principled view of the Constitution on which that decision was based. Justice Blackmun took care to remind us, in his separate opinion, that he is now eighty-three years old and cannot serve forever. When he leaves the Court, a President determined to change the character of our Constitution could do so with a single appointment. The *Casey* decision did not, as some commentators have suggested it might have, take abortion and the Supreme Court out of the election debate. On the contrary, the decision showed the breathtaking importance of the very next nomination to that Court, and of which President will make it.

August 13, 1992

5

▼

Do We Have a Right to Die?

*T*he tragedy of Nancy Cruzan's life is now part of American constitutional law. Before her automobile accident in 1983, she was an energetic twenty-four-year-old recently married woman. Her injuries deprived her brain of oxygen for fourteen minutes, and left her in what doctors describe as a permanent vegetative state. Only the lower part of her brain stem continued to function. She was unconscious and oblivious to the environment, though she had reflexive responses to sound and perhaps to painful stimuli. She was fed and hydrated through tubes implanted in her stomach, and other machines performed her other bodily functions. She was washed and turned regularly, but all of her limbs were contracted and her fingernails cut into her wrists.

For months after the accident her parents and her then husband pressed doctors to do everything possible to restore her to some kind of life. But when it became plain that she would remain in a vegetative state until she died, which might mean for thirty more years, her parents, who had become her legal guardians, asked the state hospital to remove the tubes and allow her to die at once. Since the hospital refused to do so without a court order, the parents petitioned a Missouri court, which appointed a guardian *ad litem* (a special guardian appointed to represent her in these proceedings) to offer arguments why it should not grant that order. After a hearing the court granted the order on the ground that it was in Cruzan's best interests to be permitted to die with some dignity now rather than to live on in an unconscious state.

The guardian *ad litem* felt it his duty to appeal the order to the Missouri supreme court, though he told that court that he did not disagree with the decision. But the supreme court reversed the lower court's decision: it held that Cruzan's legal guardians had no power to order feeding stopped without "clear and convincing" evidence that she herself had decided, when competent, not to be fed in her present circumstances. Though a friend had testified that Cruzan had said, in a conversation soon after the death of her grandmother, that she would not want to be kept alive if she could not really live, the supreme court held that this testimony was not adequate evidence of the necessary decision.

Cruzan's parents appealed to the United States Supreme Court: their lawyers argued that the Missouri decision violated her right not to be subjected to unwanted medical treatment. The Court had not previously ruled on the question how far states must respect that right. On June 25, 1990, by a five to four vote, the Court refused to reverse the Missouri decision: it denied that Cruzan had a constitutional right that could be exercised by her parents in these circumstances.

The main opinion was written by Chief Justice Rehnquist, and he was joined by Justices Kennedy and White. Many newspaper reports and comments on the case declared that, although the Court had refused the Cruzan family's request it had nevertheless endorsed a general constitutional right of competent people to decide that they should not be kept alive through medical technology. The *New York Times,* for example, said that the Court had decided that "the Constitution protects a person's liberty to reject life-sustaining technology," and congratulated the Court for a "monumental example of law adjusting to life." The *Washington Post* headline read "Court Rules Patient's Wishes Must Control 'Right to Die.'"

It is important to notice, however, that Rehnquist took care to say that he and the two justices who joined his opinion were not actually deciding that people have a right to die. He said they were assuming such a right only *hypothetically,* "for purposes of this case," and he emphasized that he thought it still an open question whether even a competent person's freedom to die with dignity could be overridden by a state's own constitutional right to keep people alive.[1] Although the logic of past cases would embrace a "liberty interest" of a competent person to refuse artificially delivered food and water, he said, "the dramatic consequences involved in refusal of such treatment would inform the inquiry as to whether the deprivation of that interest is constitutional."

Even if we do assume that people have a constitutional right to refuse to be kept alive if they become permanently vegetative, Rehnquist said,

Missouri did not infringe that right. It only insisted that people must exercise the right for themselves, while still competent, and do so in a formal and unmistakable way, by executing a "living will," for example. The United States Constitution does not prohibit states from adopting strict evidentiary requirements of that sort, he said. The Constitution does not require Missouri to recognize what most people would think was very strong evidence of Cruzan's convictions, that is, her serious and apparently well-considered statements to a close friend soon after a relative's death.

Justices O'Connor and Scalia, though they agreed to uphold the Missouri supreme court's decision, filed separate concurring opinions. O'Connor made an important practical point: that instead of drafting a living will describing precisely what should not be done to keep them alive, many people would prefer to designate someone else—a relative or close friend—to make those decisions for them when the need arises.[2] She stated her own view that the Constitution gave people that right, and emphasized that the Court's decision against Cruzan's parents was not to the contrary, since Cruzan had made no formal designation.

Scalia's concurring opinion was of a very different character. He repeated his extraordinarily narrow view of constitutional rights: that the Constitution, properly interpreted, allows the states to do anything that it does not expressly forbid. Since, he said, the Constitution "says nothing" about people's rights to control their own deaths, there is no question of any constitutional right of that sort, and state legislatures are free to make any decision they wish about what can be done to people to keep them technically alive. Scalia left little doubt about his own views of what a sensible state legislature would decide; he said that no reasonable person would wish to inhabit a body that was only technically alive. But, he said, the Constitution does not require state legislatures to be either reasonable or humane.

Justice Brennan dissented in an opinion joined by Justices Marshall and Blackmun. Brennan's opinion, one of the last he delivered before his retirement, was a valedictory address that made even plainer how much his humanity and intelligence will be missed. He pointed out the main fallacy in Rehnquist's opinion: it is inconsistent to assume that people have a constitutional right not to be given medical care contrary to their wishes, and yet to allow the state to impose evidentiary rules that make it unlikely that an incompetent person's past wishes will actually be discovered. "Even someone with a resolute determination to avoid life-support under circumstances such as Nancy's," he said, "would still need to know that such things as living wills exist and how to execute one . . . For many, the thought of an ignoble end, steeped in decay, is abhorrent. A quiet, proud death, bodily integrity intact, is a matter of extreme consequence."

Justice Stevens dissented separately. He criticized the majority for not having enough regard for Cruzan's best interests, and stressed the religious basis of Missouri's case. "Not much may be said with confidence about death," he wrote, "unless it is said from faith, and that alone is reason enough to protect the freedom to conform choices about death to individual conscience."

In August 1990 Cruzan's parents petitioned the lower court that had initially decided in their favor with what they called new evidence: three more friends of Cruzan had come forward prepared to testify that she had told them, too, that she would not want to live as a vegetable. Though this evidence was of the same character as that which the Missouri supreme court had earlier said was not sufficiently "clear and convincing," the state attorney general decided this time not to oppose the parents' petition. On December 14, the lower court granted the parents' petition. Within a few days feeding and hydration were stopped, and Cruzan was given medication to prevent pain. She died on December 26.

When competent people refuse medical treatment that is necessary to save their lives, doctors and legal officials may face a dilemma. They have an ethical and legal obligation both to act in the patient's best interests and to respect his autonomy, his right to decide for himself what will be done with or to his body. These obligations may be in conflict, because a patient may refuse treatment the doctors think essential. Rehnquist introduced a third consideration into the constitutional issue. He contrasted the patient's autonomy not just with his or her own best interests but also with the *state's* interest in "protecting and preserving life." In most cases when a competent person refuses life-saving aid—for example, when he refuses an essential blood transfusion on religious grounds—there is no difference between what most people would regard as his best interests and the state's interest in keeping him alive, because it is assumed that it is in his best interests to live. But in some cases—when the patient is in great pain, for example, and cannot live very long even with treatment—the state's supposed interest in keeping him alive may conflict with his own best interests, not only as he but as most people would judge these.

If we accept that some state policy might be served by prolonging life even in such cases, then two constitutional issues are presented. Does a state have the constitutional power to impose life-saving medical treatment on a person against his will, that is, in defiance of his autonomy, when it believes that treatment is in his own best interests? Does it have the constitutional power to impose such treatment for its own purposes, even when it concedes that this is *against* his best interests, that is, in defiance of the normal rule that patients should not be given medical treatment that is bad for them?

The law of most American states seems settled that the autonomy of a competent patient will be decisive in all such cases, and that doctors may not treat him against his will either for his sake or for the sake of some social interest in keeping him alive. The Supreme Court had never explicitly decided that the Constitution compels states to take that position, though in the present case, as I said, Rehnquist assumed hypothetically that it does.

In the case of people who are unconscious or otherwise incompetent, however, and who did not exercise their right of self-determination when they were able to do so, the distinction between their own best interest and the alleged interest of the state in keeping them alive is of great importance, as Rehnquist's opinion, carefully examined, makes clear. He offered two different, though not clearly distinct, arguments why Missouri has a right to tip the scales in favor of keeping comatose people alive by demanding "clear and convincing" evidence that they had decided they would rather die. His first argument appealed to the best interests of incompetent people. He said that a rule requiring evidence of a formal declaration of a past decision to die, before life support can be terminated, benefits people who have become comatose because it protects them against guardians who abuse their trust, and because a decision not to terminate is always reversible if documented evidence of a formal past decision emerges later. His second argument is very different: it appeals not to the interests of comatose patients but to Missouri's supposed independent interests in keeping such patients alive. He said that a state has its own legitimate reasons for protecting and preserving life, which "no one can gainsay," and that Missouri is therefore entitled for its own sake to tip the evidentiary scales against termination.

He treats these as cumulative arguments: he thinks that taken together they justify Missouri's evidentiary rule. I shall consider them separately, however, because they raise very different issues, and because, though

Rehnquist mentions the second only obliquely and in passing, it has important implications for other constitutional issues, including the abortion controversy, and so deserves separate study.

Rehnquist devotes most of his opinion to the first argument: that the Missouri rule is in the best interests of most of the thousands of people who live in a permanent vegetative state and did not sign living wills when they could. That seems implausible. Many people who are now in that position talked and acted in ways that make it very likely that they would have signed a living will had they anticipated their own accidents, as Nancy Cruzan did in conversations with her friends. The Missouri rule flouts rather than honors their autonomy. Many others, at least in the opinions of their family and others who know them best, almost certainly would have decided that way if they had ever considered the matter. The Missouri rule denies them what they probably would have chosen. Why is so indiscriminate a rule necessary? Why would it not be better to allow lower courts to decide each case on the balance of probabilities, so that a court might decide that on the best evidence Nancy Cruzan would have chosen to die, as the initial Missouri court in fact did decide?

While Rehnquist concedes that Missouri's rigid rule may sometimes lead to a "mistake," he says that the Constitution does not require states to adopt procedures that work perfectly. But his arguments that the Missouri rule would even in general work to the benefit of incompetent people are question-begging: they reflect a presumption that it is normally in the best interests of permanently comatose people to live, so that they should be kept alive unless there is decisive evidence that they have actually decided to the contrary. It is true that in some situations a presumption of that kind is sensible. A state need not accept the judgment of devout Jehovah's Witnesses, for example, that it would be in the best interests of an unconscious relative not to have a blood transfusion that would bring him back to conscious life, even if the state would accept his own decision not to be treated were he conscious. But we think that because we believe that life and health are fundamentally so important that no one should be allowed to reject them on behalf of someone else.

No such assumption is plausible when the life in question is only the insensate life of the permanently vegetative. That kind of life is not valuable to anyone. Some people, no doubt, would want to be kept alive indefinitely in such a state out of religious convictions: they might think that failing to prolong life as long as possible is insulting to God, for example. But even they do not think that it is in *their* interests to live on; most such people would hope, I think, for an early death in that situation, though one in which everything had been done to prolong life. They would regard an early death as an instance of God's mercy.

But Rehnquist is so far in the grip of the presumption that life is of great importance even to people in a vegetative state that he argues, at times, as if the Cruzan family's petition were a proceeding *against* their daughter. He says that the state is entitled to act as a "shield" for the incompetent, and he cites cases in which the Supreme Court required that government have "clear and convincing" evidence of fault before deporting someone, or depriving him of citizenship, or terminating his parental rights. In such cases constitutional law properly tips the scales against punitive action, because, as in an ordinary criminal trial, a mistake on one side, against the defendant, is much more serious than a mistake on the other. Cruzan's case is not an adversary proceeding, however. Her own parents are seeking relief on her *behalf*, and fairness argues for only one thing: the most accurate possible identification of what Nancy Cruzan's wishes were and where her interests now lie.

Some of Rehnquist's arguments depend not on the assumption that it is normally in the interests of a permanently comatose person to continue living, but on the equally implausible assumption that continued life in those circumstances is never against such a person's interests. This is the premise of his argument, for example, that it is better to keep a comatose patient alive than to allow her to die, even if the chances of recovery are infinitesimal, because the latter decision is irreversible. He assumes that someone in Nancy Cruzan's position suffers no disadvantage in continuing to live, so that if there is only the barest conceivable possibility of some extraordinary medical discovery in the future, however remote that may seem now, it must be on balance in the patient's interests to continue living as long as possible.

If the only things people worried about, or wanted to avoid, were pain and other unpleasant physical experiences, then of course they would be indifferent about whether, if they became permanently comatose, their bodies continued to live or not. But people care about many other things as well. They worry about their dignity and integrity, and about the view other people have of them, how they are conceived and remembered. Many of them are anxious that their relatives and friends not have to bear the burdens, whether emotional or financial, of keeping them alive. Many are appalled by the thought of resources being wasted on them that might be used for the benefit of other people who have genuine, conscious lives to lead.

These various concerns explain the horror so many people feel at the idea of existing pointlessly for years as a vegetable. They think that a bare biological existence, with no intelligence or sensibility or sensation, is not a matter of indifference, but something bad for them, something that damages their lives considered as a whole. This was the view Nancy Cruzan expressed to her friend after her grandmother's death. Rehnquist seems depressingly insensitive to all these concerns. In any case his assumption—that people lose nothing when permission to terminate their lives is refused—ignores them. A great many people, at least, believe the contrary: that a decision to keep them alive would cheat them forever of a chance to die with both dignity and consideration for others, and that to be deprived of that chance would be a great and irreversible loss.

Of course, given the devastating importance of the decision to terminate life support, a state may impose strenuous procedural constraints on any doctor's or guardian's decision to do so. The state may require guardians to show, for example, in an appropriate hearing before a judge or hospital committee or some other suitable body, and with appropriate medical support, that there is no genuine hope that the victim will ever become competent again. It may require guardians to show, moreover, that there is no persuasive reason to think the patient would have preferred to have life support continued. It may also adopt suitable precautions to ensure that the decision is made by people solely concerned with the patient's wishes and interests; it may specify, for example, that the decision not be made by guardians who would gain financially by the patient's early death. Though these and other procedural constraints may somewhat increase the chance that a patient who would have wished to die is kept alive, they can plausibly be described as in the best interests of patients overall, or in the interests of protecting their autonomy.

The Cruzan family satisfied all such requirements, however. There is no evidence that Nancy Cruzan had any religious beliefs that would have led her to prefer mere biological life to death. On the contrary, the evidence of her serious conversations strongly suggested—to put it at its weakest—that she would vigorously oppose being kept alive. Since Missouri itself paid the full cost of her treatment, the family had no financial incentive to allow her to die. So the state's evidentiary procedures cannot reasonably be said to have been in Cruzan's best interests, or in the best interests of vegetative patients generally. If Missouri's rule is constitutional, it must be for some other reason.

We must therefore turn to Rehnquist's second, much less developed, argument: that Missouri can impose evidentiary requirements, even if that is against Cruzan's interests and those of other permanently incompetent people, in order to protect its own interests in preserving life. Rehnquist said that "societal" and "institutional" issues are at stake, as well as individual ones, that no one can "gainsay" Missouri's "interest in the protection and preservation of human life."

No doubt Missouri pressed this argument, and perhaps Rehnquist adopted it, with an eye to the abortion controversy. In 1989's abortion case, *Webster v. Missouri Reproductive Services,* Missouri cited its own sovereign interest in preserving all human life as justification for refusing to allow abortions to be performed in state-financed medical facilities. Even *Roe v. Wade,* the 1973 decision that established a woman's limited right to an abortion, acknowledged that a state has a legitimate concern with protecting the life of a fetus. Though Justice Blackmun said, in that case, that a state's right to protect a fetus is outweighed by a woman's right of privacy during the first two trimesters of pregnancy, he held that the state's right was sufficiently strong thereafter to allow a state to make most third-trimester abortions illegal. In the *Webster* decision, several justices said that the state's legitimate interest in protecting human life is more powerful than Blackmun recognized, and justifies more sweeping regulation of abortion than he allowed.

Nevertheless, in spite of the crucial part that the idea of a legitimate state interest in preserving all human life now plays in constitutional law, there has been remarkably little attention, either in Supreme Court opinions or in the legal literature, to the question of what that supposed interest is or why it is legitimate for a state to pursue it. It is particularly unclear how the supposed state interest bears on the questions that were at stake in the *Cruzan* case. Of course government is properly concerned with the welfare and well-being of its citizens, and it has the right, for that reason, to try to prevent them from being killed or put at risk of death from disease or accident. But the state's obvious and general concern with its citizens' well-being does not give it a reason to preserve someone's life when his or her welfare would be better served by being permitted to die in dignity. So the state interest that Rehnquist has in mind, as justifying Missouri's otherwise unreasonable evidentiary rule, must be a different, less familiar, one: it must supply a reason for forcing people to accept medical treatment when they or their guardians plausibly think they would be better off dead.

Scalia, in his concurring opinion, said that we must assume that states are constitutionally entitled to preserve people's lives, even against their own interests, because otherwise familiar laws making either suicide or aiding suicide a crime, which no one doubts are valid, would be unconstitutional. As I said, he disagreed with Rehnquist's hypothetical assumption that, at least, competent people have a constitutional right to refuse life-saving medical treatment. But Scalia's argument is doubly suspect.

First, his assumption that states have the constitutional power to prevent suicide in all circumstances is too broad and it is premature. It is true that both suicide and assisting suicide were crimes according to common law, and Scalia relies heavily on the views of William Blackstone, the famous and influential eighteenth-century legal commentator, who declared that it was a crime even for someone suffering a terminal illness and in terrible pain to take his own life. But there are many examples in constitutional history of constraints on liberty that were unquestioned for long periods of history but were then reexamined and found unconstitutional because lawyers and the public as a whole had developed a more sophisticated understanding of the underlying ethical and moral issues.[3] That is particularly likely when the historical support for the constraint has been mainly religious. It was long unquestioned that states have the power to outlaw contraception, for example, before the Supreme Court held otherwise in 1965 in *Griswold v. Connecticut.*

Longstanding practice is an even worse guide to constitutional law when technological change has created entirely new problems or exacerbated old ones. Doctors can now keep people alive in terminal illness for long periods that would have seemed incredible in the recent past, and their new abilities have made the position of people who would rather die than continue living in pain both more tragic and more common. So when the Supreme Court is next asked to rule on whether states can constitutionally forbid someone in that position from taking his own life, or can make it criminal for a doctor to assist him, even if the doctor takes every precaution to be sure that the person has freely decided to commit suicide, the Court will face a very different situation from that in which the common law principles about suicide developed. It seems premature for Scalia simply to declare that the power of states to forbid suicide has no exceptions at all. Government is entitled to try to prevent people from killing themselves in many circumstances—in periods of severe but transient depression, for example. But it does not follow that it has the power to prolong the suffering of someone in terrible and pointless pain.

In any case, it is bizarre to classify as suicide someone's decision to reject treatment that would keep him alive but at a cost he and many other people think too great. Many people whose lives could be lengthened through severe amputations or incapacitating operations decide to die instead, and they are not thought to have taken their own lives for that reason. It seems plain that states have no constitutional power to direct doctors to perform such operations without the consent and against the wishes of the patient. People imagining themselves as permanently comatose are in the same position: their biological lives could then be prolonged only through medical treatment they would think degrading, and only in a form they would think worse than death. So it is a mistake, for that reason, to describe someone who signs a living will as committing hypothetical suicide. It seems a mistake for another reason as well.

Even if Scalia were right, that a conscious and competent patient who refuses an amputation that would prolong his life should be treated as a suicide, it would still not follow that someone who decides to die if he becomes a permanent vegetable is in fact taking his own life, because it is at least a reasonable view that a permanently comatose person is, for all that matters, dead already.

Scalia's argument is therefore a red herring, and in spite of Rehnquist's confident remark that no one can "gainsay" Missouri's interest in protecting and preserving life, we still lack an explanation of what that interest is and why it is proper for Missouri to pursue it. It might be said that keeping people alive, even when they would be better off dead, helps to protect the community's sense of the importance of life. I agree that society is better and more secure when its members share a sense that human life is sacred, and that no effort should be spared to save lives. People who lack that sense may themselves be more ready to kill, and will be less anxious to make sacrifices to protect the lives of others. That seems to me the most powerful available argument why states should be permitted to outlaw elective abortion of very late-stage fetuses, for example.[4] But it is extremely implausible that allowing a permanently comatose patient to die, after a solemn proceeding devoted only to her wishes and interests, will in any way erode a community's sense of the importance of life.

So a state cannot justify keeping comatose people alive on the instrumental ground that this is necessary to prevent murder or to encourage people to vote for famine relief. If Rehnquist is right that a state has a legitimate interest in preserving all human life, then this must be in virtue not of any instrumental argument but of the *intrinsic* value of such life, its importance for its own sake. Most people do believe that human life has intrinsic importance, and perhaps Rehnquist thinks it unnecessary either to clarify or to justify that idea.[5] It is unclear, however, that they accept the idea on any ground, or in any sense, that supports his case. For some people, for example, life has intrinsic value because it is a gift of God; they believe, as I said, that it is wrong not to struggle to prolong life, because this is an insult to Him, who alone should decide when life ends. But the Constitution does not allow states to justify policy on grounds of religious doctrine; some more secular account of the intrinsic value of life would be needed to support Rehnquist's second argument.

It will be helpful to distinguish two forms that a more secular version of the claim might take. The first supposes that a human life, in any form or circumstance, is a unique and valuable addition to the universe, so that the stock of value is needlessly diminished when any life is shorter than it might be. That does not seem a convincing view. Even if we think that a conscious, reflective, engaged human life is inherently valuable, we might well doubt that an insensate, vegetative life has any value at all.

The view that all forms of life are inherently valuable is also disqualified for a different reason. On that view we would have as much reason to bring new lives into being, increasing the population, as for prolonging lives already in progress. After all, people who think that great art is inherently valuable have the same reason for encouraging the production of more masterpieces as for preserving art that now exists. But most people who think life has intrinsic significance do not think that they therefore have any general duty to procreate or to encourage procreation. In any case, the Supreme Court's decision in *Griswold*, which is now accepted by almost everyone, holds that the states have no power to prohibit contraception.

People who think that life has intrinsic value or importance, but do not think that this fact offers any reason for increasing the population, understand life's value in a second and more conditional way. They mean, I think, that once a human life has begun it is terribly important that it go well, that it be a good rather than a bad life, a successful rather than a wasted one. Most people accept that human life has inherent importance in that sense. That explains why they try not just to make their lives pleasant but to give them worth and also why it seems a tragedy when people decide, late in life, that they can take neither pride nor satisfaction in the way they have lived.[6] Of course nothing in the idea that life has intrinsic importance in this second sense can justify a policy of keeping permanently comatose people alive. The worth of their lives—the character of the lives they have led—cannot be improved just by keeping the bodies they used to inhabit technically alive. On the contrary, that makes their lives worse, because it is a bad thing, for all the reasons I described earlier, to have one's body medicated, fed, and groomed, as an object of pointless and degrading solicitude, after one's mind is dead. Rehnquist's second argument is therefore a dramatic failure: Missouri's policy is not supported but condemned by the idea that human life is important for its own sake, on the only understanding of that idea that is available in our constitutional system.

It is a relatively new question how the medical technology that now allows doctors to keep wholly incompetent people alive for decades should be used. Of course the Constitution leaves considerable latitude to the state legislatures in fixing detailed schemes for regulating how and what doctors and guardians decide. But the Constitution does limit a state's power in certain ways, as it must in order to protect the autonomy and the most fundamental interests of the patient.

In the *Cruzan* case the Supreme Court recognized, even if only hypothetically, an important part of that constitutional protection: that in principle a state has no right to keep a comatose patient alive against his previously expressed wish that he be allowed to die in the circumstances he has now reached. But the Court undercut the full value of that principle by allowing Missouri to impose an evidentiary rule that substantially decreases the chance a patient will receive only the treatment he or she would have wanted. Even worse, the justification the Chief Justice offered for the Court's decision put forward two principles that, unless they are soon rejected, will damage the rest of the law as it develops. It is therefore worth summarizing the argument I have made against these principles.

Rehnquist assumed that it is in the best interests of at least most people who become permanent vegetables to remain alive in that condition. But there is no way in which continued life can be good for such people, and several ways in which it might well be thought bad. He also assumed that a state can have its own legitimate reasons for keeping such people alive even when it concedes that this is against their best interests. But that judgment rests on a dangerous misunderstanding of the irresistible idea that human life has intrinsic moral significance. We do not honor that idea—on the contrary we insult it—when we waste resources in prolonging a bare, technical, insensate form of life.

More than just the right to die, or even the right to abortion, is at stake in these issues. In the next decades the question of why and how human life has intrinsic value is likely to be debated, by philosophers, lawyers, and the public, not just with respect to those issues but others as well, including genetic engineering, for example. Constitutional law will both encourage and reflect the debate, and though it is far too early to anticipate what form that law will take, Rehnquist's unreasoned opinion was a poor beginning.

ADDENDUM

A lawsuit decided on May 3, 1994, in Seattle might well become the *Roe v. Wade* of euthanasia. In *Compassion in Dying v. State of Washington,* Federal District Court Judge Barbara Rothstein struck down Washington state's 140-year-old anti–assisted-suicide law, and declared that competent terminal patients have a constitutional right to a willing doctor's help in killing themselves.

She decided, that is, that the laws of almost all the states, which make assisting suicide a crime, are unconstitutional. Once again the courts are at the center of a bitter moral and religious controversy.

Americans have been arguing about euthanasia for decades. Two states, Washington and California, recently rejected voluntary euthanasia schemes in fairly close votes; another such measure will be on the ballot in Oregon later this year. In Michigan, a special statute was passed to stop Dr. Jack Kevorkian from helping patients to die, but a jury, expressing the depth of the public's sympathy for patients dying in pain, refused to convict him of violating that statute even though he admitted he had. The Michigan supreme court then invalidated the special statute on technical grounds. But it also reinstated murder charges against him.

If Judge Rothstein's decision (or a similar one) is upheld in the Supreme Court, the Constitution will have preempted part of this sprawling debate: every state will have to recognize that, though it can regulate doctor-assisted suicide, it may not prohibit it altogether. That result will outrage millions of conscientious citizens who think euthanasia an abomination in any form. Great constitutional cases, in the United States, are also great public arguments, and it is crucial that we all begin to think about the issues Judge Rothstein has raised.

She said that the Supreme Court's 1992 decision in *Planned Parenthood v. Casey,* which reaffirmed *Roe v. Wade,* "almost" compelled her own decision. *Casey*'s central opinion declared that "matters involving the most intimate and personal choices a person may make in a lifetime ... are central to the liberty protected by the Fourteenth Amendment. At the heart of liberty is the right to define one's own concept of existence, of meaning, of the universe, and of the mystery of human life." Judge Rothstein observed, correctly, that the freedom of a competent dying person to hasten his own death falls under that description at least as clearly as does the right of a pregnant woman to choose abortion.

Many opponents of euthanasia try to distinguish the two issues, however, by appealing to a "slippery-slope" argument. They say, for example, that voluntary euthanasia will so habituate doctors to killing that they will begin executing sick, old, unwanted people whose care is expensive but who plainly want to live. That contradicts common sense: doctors know the moral difference between helping people who beg to die and killing those who want to live. If anything, ignoring the pain of terminal patients pleading for death seems more likely to dull a doctor's humane instincts than trying to help.

Some critics worry about the practice in Holland, where doctors have given lethal injections to unconscious or incompetent terminal patients who had not explicitly asked to die. But Judge Rothstein's opinion applies only to assisted suicide, which demands a contemporary request, and even if a legislature were to allow for such injection, for patients incapable of taking pills or killing themselves in any other humane way, it could stipulate that a contemporary request was still essential.

A more plausible version of the slippery-slope argument supposes that if euthanasia is legalized, dying people whose treatment is expensive or burdensome may ask help in suicide only because they feel guilty, and that family members may perhaps try to coax or shame them into that decision. But states plainly have the power to guard against requests influenced by guilt, depression, poor care, or economic worries. (The main plaintiff in the case, the organization Compassion in Dying, helps only terminal patients who have repeated their request three times and have expressed no ambivalence or uncertainty.) States also have the power to discourage distasteful, near-assembly-line suicides like those orchestrated by Dr. Kevorkian. Patients only go to him—and juries only acquit him—because there is no better alternative.

No set of regulations can be perfect. But it would be perverse to force competent people to die in great pain or drugged stupor for that reason, accepting a great and known evil to avoid the risk of a speculative one. In the *Cruzan* decision discussed above, the Supreme Court held that states must respect some form of "living will" that allows people to specify in advance that certain procedures not be used to keep them alive, in spite of the fact that patients can also be coaxed or shamed into signing such documents. No one thinks, moreover, that the fact that doctors sometimes deliberately give dying patients large enough doses of pain-killing drugs to kill them—a covert decision much more open to abuse than a scheme of voluntary euthanasia would be—is a good reason for withholding all dangerous pain-killers from terminal patients in torment.

These slippery-slope arguments, then, are very weak ones; they seem only disguises for the deeper convictions that actually move most opponents of all euthanasia. Fr. Matthew Habiger, president of Human Life International, described as the largest "pro-life" organization in the world, denounced the Compassion in Dying decision in terms that made those deeper convictions explicit. "The march toward a complete antilife philosophy," he said, "can now be easily mapped: from contraception to abortion to euthanasia. Once life is no longer treated as a sacred gift from God, a society inevitably embraces death in all its forms."

In this view, all euthanasia—even when fully voluntary and rational—is wrong because human life has an objective, intrinsic, value as well as a subjective value for the person whose life it is, and euthanasia dishonors that intrinsic value. That conviction underlies most opposition to abortion as well. Many people, particularly those who agree with Fr. Habiger that human life is a divine gift, believe that ending it deliberately (except, perhaps, as punishment) is always, at any stage, the most profound insult to life's objective value.

It would be wrong to think, however, that those who are more permissive about abortion and euthanasia are indifferent to the value of life. Rather, they disagree about what respecting that value means. They think that in some circumstances—when a fetus is terribly deformed, for example—abortion shows more respect for life than childbirth would. And they think dying with dignity shows more respect for their own lives—better fits their sense of what is really important in and about human existence— than ending their lives in long agony or senseless sedation.

Our constitution takes no sides in these ancient disputes about life's "meaning." But it does protect people's right to die as well as to live, so far as possible, in the light of their own, intensely personal, convictions about "the mystery of human life." It insists that these values are too central to personality, too much at the core of liberty, to allow a majority to decide what everyone must believe. Of course the law must protect people who think it would be appalling to be killed, even if they had only painful months or minutes to live anyway. But the law must also protect those with the opposite conviction: that it would be appalling not to be offered an easier, calmer death with the help of doctors they trust. Making someone die in a way others approve, but he believes contradicts his own dignity, is a serious, unjustified, unnecessary form of tyranny.

January 31, 1991
Addendum, May 17, 1994

6

Gag Rule and
Affirmative Action

*T*he right-wing lawyers Reagan appointed to the Department of Justice early in his presidency promised a "Reagan revolution" in constitutional law. They tried to pack federal courts at all levels with judges who survived the most stringent political tests for judicial appointment ever used in this country; and they asked these judges to make decisions that would overturn decades of constitutional precedent and leave the Constitution no longer an important source of minority or individual rights against unjustified public authority.

The revolution is beginning to bear fruit. In its recent decisions the Supreme Court (which now seems safely in the hands of justices whom conservatives regard as politically correct) has repealed or undercut traditional constitutional rights in major respects. It has adopted new rules that sharply limit the number of times people sentenced to death can ask federal courts to look at fresh evidence or new arguments.[1] It has decided that it may be merely "harmless error" for police to beat a confession out of a criminal defendant.[2] It has rejected the use of plainly pertinent statistics in deciding whether race has played any role in a decision to execute a black defendant.[3] It has granted states the power to restrict abortions in ways particularly harmful to poor women, and, most recently, in *Rust v. Sullivan,* it has approved as constitutional an executive order forbidding doctors in any clinic financed with federal funds to discuss or offer information about abortion, or to indicate where such information might

147

be available, even for women who specifically ask to discuss abortion and have no other access to medical advice.[4]

The last of these decisions seems particularly appalling to constitutional scholars. For the first time the Court has upheld the power of government to impose restrictions not only on what people who accept government money might do with that money, which are often reasonable, but on what they may say in the performance of their professional duties, which strikes close to the nerve of free speech, particularly in a society like ours in which medicine, research, and education are so densely intertwined with government funding.

The Court did this, moreover, in a particularly crude way: it upheld a Reagan bureaucrat's reinterpretation of a congressional statute that had always been understood not to carry that implication, in spite of the fact that, as Justice O'Connor pointed out in a stinging dissent, the Court traditionally avoids interpreting congressional acts in a way that would raise difficult constitutional issues unless Congress insists that it means to raise them. Congress can—and may very well—enact another statute declaring that the administration's interpretation is wrong. But Bush can veto that statute, and a minority of legislators, who are "pro-life," can sustain his veto.

Not just this decision, but each of those I have mentioned, is revolutionary: in each the Court has ignored decades of precedent, and each would have been inconceivable until recent years. (In 1981, for example, the other eight justices all voted against Justice Rehnquist's attempt to limit the number of appeals from a death sentence.) Conservative lawyers say, however, that in spite of the fact that ordinarily past Court decisions should be respected, the new decisions are justified, indeed required, as a matter of law. They argue that the past decisions being overruled were illegitimate, the result of past efforts to amend the Constitution to serve a "left-liberal" point of view.

Charles Fried, Reagan's last solicitor general, who recently announced his approval of the *Rust* decision, puts it this way in his interesting and instructive memoir of his years in office, *Order and Law: Arguing the Reagan Revolution:* "The tenets of the Reagan Revolution were clear: courts should be more disciplined, less adventurous and political in interpreting the law, especially the law of the Constitution."

But why should we accept that the Court's new decisions are "more disciplined" or "less political" than its former ones? The key clauses of the Constitution's Bill of Rights, after all, are very abstract: they say, for example, that "due process" is not to be denied, and that all people are to receive "equal protection of the laws," but they do not specify what process is due or what counts as equal protection. The past decisions that the revolutionaries want to repeal were based not on ignoring these abstract clauses, but on interpreting them in a certain way. The earlier decisions supposed, for example, that convicting a person partly on the basis of a confession beaten out of him denies due process of law even if there is ample other evidence of his guilt. The Reagan revolutionaries interpret the abstract clauses of the Constitution very differently, but it begs the question simply to declare that their new interpretations are more accurate or less political than the old ones were. We need to ask what theory of constitutional interpretation would justify that assertion.

The most popular answer to that question, among the revolutionaries, was given by Reagan's attorney general, Edwin Meese, and defended by Robert Bork, Reagan's unsuccessful nominee to the Supreme Court. They said that the Constitution means only what its framers intended their abstract language to entail. It is true, Bork conceded, that present-day judges must exercise judgment in applying the general principles that the framers intended to new circumstances, like electronic wiretapping, for example. But the general principles themselves must be taken from those intentions, and it is plain, according to conservatives like Bork, that the framers intended no principle that would protect abortion or allow murderers to delay their execution through repeated appeals.

Fried, who has returned to his former job as professor of law at Harvard, ridicules this view of "original intention" and he is right. The framers' opinions, he says, are both unknowable and, as they themselves thought, irrelevant. "It is a public text they put in force," he adds, "and it is as a public text we must try to understand it." Bork's recent book, *The Tempting of America,* which tried to defend that view, was so spectacular a failure that, as I have suggested elsewhere, it may mark the end of the original intention thesis as a serious position among constitutional lawyers.[5]

Fried also rejects a second argument that other conservative lawyers often make to justify overruling past decisions. They say that the earlier tradition was undemocratic, because when judges force states to permit abortion or to abandon programs or decisions that disadvantage minorities, for example, the judges are substituting their own judgment for that of democratically elected officials, and so restricting the power of the majority to govern itself. Fried replies, correctly, that crude majority rule has been the source of great tyranny in the past. In any case, this conservative argument begs the question of what our form of democracy, properly understood, really is. America's principal contribution to political theory is a conception of democracy according to which the protection of individual rights is a precondition, not a compromise, of that form of government.

It is to Fried's great credit, therefore, that he rejects the two most familiar defenses of the revolutionary decisions that he approves of. His book is important because he adopts a much more sophisticated and attractive thesis about constitutional interpretation. He says that judges enforcing the Constitution must interpret that document constructively, by trying to identify general principles of political morality that provide the best justification for the document not clause by clause but as a whole, conceived as a fundamental structure for just government. "In interpreting the broad language of the Fourteenth Amendment," he says, "the Constitution as a whole should serve as a guide. The particular guarantees specified in the Bill of Rights are like the points on a graph, which the judge joins by a line to describe a coherent and rationally compelling function."

Fried concedes that this interpretive method will lead to different results in the hands of different judges, because judges whose convictions of political morality are different will connect the points with very different principles. It is the same method, he concedes, that produced *Roe v. Wade,* the famous abortion decision disliked by conservatives, which he says "gave legal reasoning a bad name" because it was based on a "morally inadequate vision," and because its legal argument connecting that vision to the Constitution was deeply flawed. Still, he says, the interpretive method is the only defensible one, and good, conservative, legal reasoning consists not in using any different method but in using that method well, in grounding an overall constitutional interpretation in attractive and convincing conservative principles, and in elaborating and applying these principles with logic and care.

So Fried's project in this book—the project defined in its subtitle—is to argue for the Reagan revolution in a different way: to show how it can be justified not as the blind application of some rule about the framers' intentions, or of some fetish about majority rule, but as the natural consequence of political principles that can plausibly be said to be embedded in the nation's constitutional history. That is a project of the first importance. If we can identify a plausible conservative moral reading of the Constitution, a reading that purports to justify the Court's new direction, then the national constitutional debate would be much improved. We could then decide which of the two competing visions—the new or the old—is more persuasive as an interpretive understanding of our constitutional history, or which side has been more successful in elaborating its vision into concrete legal decisions.

Order and Law is more, I should add, than a jurisprudential defense along those lines. Fried wrote it also as a political memoir, and it is a very good and useful one. With great candor he describes how, as a Harvard Law School professor with a conservative reputation, he campaigned for years for a job in the Reagan administration before he finally secured one; how he became acting solicitor general when the incumbent, Rex E. Lee, who had been criticized by conservatives as too independent of the administration's policies, left; how he then deferred to the administration's wish that he submit a brief in an abortion case asking the Supreme Court to overrule *Roe v. Wade,* in spite of the fact that no party in the case had asked for that step; and how he was appointed as solicitor general shortly thereafter, the abortion brief having put him "in a leadership position in the Department." He recalls the political battles he fought and the enemies he made within the administration, and defends his view, which has been sharply criticized by other former holders of the office, that a solicitor general owes loyalty to the President's own constitutional theories, as any lawyer owes loyalty to a client. The book is clear, lively, and exceptionally well written. But its main ambition, and its importance, lie in its legal and philosophical argument.

That argument occupies the three chapters in which Fried discusses abortion, race, and the separation of powers. In the last of these, he argues that the independent counsel law, under which Congress appointed special prosecutors to investigate the Iran-Contra and Wedtech scandals, was unconstitutional because the prosecutors were not appointed and could not be dismissed by the President; and he defends the Sentencing Guidelines Commission, which is appointed by the President but is declared to be part of the judiciary. His argument is of great theoretical interest, but he concedes that the Supreme Court has not accepted the position he believes to be the right one. The heart of his defense of the Reagan revolution is therefore in his chapters about abortion and race.

Fried was at the center of the administration's campaign to persuade the Supreme Court to overrule *Roe v. Wade:* he argued that view in one case, as I said, as acting solicitor general and in another by special appointment after he had returned to Harvard. (Though the Court did not accept his argument in those cases, it might well do so in some other case soon.) Many of *Roe v. Wade*'s strongest critics accuse the justices who decided that case of simply inventing the right to privacy, which the justices said guaranteed choice about abortion in early pregnancy. According to these critics, since the Constitution nowhere mentions privacy, and since there is no evidence that the framers intended any such right, no such right exists.

Fried, on the other hand, accepts the right to privacy as a genuine and important one. He approves the main precedent on which the Court relied in *Roe v. Wade:* the 1965 decision, in *Griswold v. Connecticut,* that the states cannot forbid married couples the use of contraceptives.[6] He also disapproves—and this is even more significant—the Court's 1986 decision in *Bowers v. Hardwick,* which permitted states to make homosexuality between consenting adults a crime. (The decision in *Bowers* was five to four, and a key member of the majority, Justice Powell, who has since retired, said recently in a lecture at New York University that he has changed his mind and now thinks the decision wrong.) Fried says that Justice White's opinion for the majority in that case was "stunningly harsh," and that even though homosexuality is widely thought immoral, and does not involve marital intimacy as contraception does, it is private conduct that the Constitution, properly interpreted, protects.

So Fried agrees that the Constitution recognizes a general right of freedom of choice in matters not directly affecting other people, freedom even to make choices others think immoral. But why, then, does he regard *Roe v. Wade,* which applied that principle to the case of abortion, so serious a mistake that it must be overruled though it has been in force for almost two decades? He recognizes the moral impulse behind that decision: he says that the Court was "evidently moved by the truly horrible spectacle of women—especially poor and ignorant women—suffering mutilation and death in desperate attempts to end unwanted pregnancies." But he says that this "conviction of moral rectitude" does not rest on any "broad and simple and clear" moral principle. Why not? Why does it not rest on the broad, simple, and clear principle of privacy which makes legislation against homosexuals, in his view, unconstitutional? Why should not the same principle protect women from being made to suffer in a terrible way for abstract philosophical or ethical or religious views they do not share?

He offers only one argument in reply to these questions: he says that "the constitutional problem with abortion" is different because it "turns on whether the life of an innocent person is at stake."[7] Of course, if the

Constitution, properly understood, does recognize a fetus as a person whose life is at stake, then abortion is indeed a very different matter in principle from homosexuality, and perhaps also from contraception. But the Supreme Court decided that the Constitution does not recognize a fetus as a person, and Fried accepts that conclusion as obviously right: he insists that the Constitution is neutral about abortion, which of course it would not be if it declared fetuses entitled to the benefit of the Fourteenth Amendment's guarantee of equal protection of the law for all "persons."

He argues, however, that even though the Constitution does not recognize fetuses as persons, it does not insist that they are not persons, so any state has the constitutional power to declare them persons within its own borders, and to prohibit abortion on that ground.[8] He assumes, that is, that a state has the power to add creatures to the category of persons whose rights may compete with, and justify restricting or compromising, the rights that the federal Constitution grants to others.

That is surely wrong: if a state had that power it could undercut the most fundamental rights granted by the national Constitution, simply by recognizing new persons. States might dilute the voting power of ordinary citizens by declaring corporations to be genuine persons, for example, who are also entitled to votes under the one-person-one-vote principle. It is essential to the whole idea of a national constitutional structure of rights that the full population of the constitutional community—those whose rights and interests could justify limiting the constitutionally protected rights of others—be fixed nationally. If women in principle have the same rights of privacy that Fried says married couples contemplating contraception or homosexuals do, then states cannot subvert those rights by inventing new persons, not so recognized under the national scheme of principle, whose own supposed rights then justify compromising that right of privacy.

So Fried's single argument why abortion is a different matter seems very weak. It is also an argument that no one, not even the strongest critics of *Roe v. Wade*, actually believes. Rehnquist, who dissented in that case, conceded that it would be obviously unconstitutional for states to refuse a woman an abortion necessary to save her life. But a state would surely have that power if it had the power to designate a fetus a person: it would then, presumably, be free to follow the familiar rule that it is not permissible to take the life of one innocent person to save the life of another.[9] And Fried himself, barely nine pages after he announces his view that states have the power to declare fetuses persons, makes plain that he does not really believe that either. In a quite extraordinary passage he imagines that after the Court has finally reversed *Roe v. Wade*, it might find an acceptable compromise that would defuse the abortion issue that now occupies so much judicial attention:

> Having one day abandoned *Roe*, the Court may reasonably distinguish between statutes forbidding abortions outright and statutes requiring a delay of a few days in which a woman may consider alternatives to abortion, which the clinic is obliged to tell her about; or between statutes regulating abortion services and statutes punishing women who undergo abortions. This last is a distinction that might have considerable practical importance with the greater availability of safe, simple, self-administered pharmaceuticals to induce early-term abortions. In fact, medical discoveries might then make this whole constitutional episode moot.

If the Supreme Court accepted Fried's announced view that a state has the power to declare a fetus a person, then it could not possibly make the distinctions he imagines and condones. How could it then decide that states can do no more, by way of protecting creatures that the states regard as persons, than just requiring women to wait a few days before killing them? How could the Supreme Court then justify a rule that allows states to make abortions in clinics and hospitals a crime, but not abortions that take place at home? What moral difference could the *location* of the abortion possibly make? And how, if a state had the power to declare a fetus a person, could the constitutional issue become moot just because science had discovered a way for a woman to abort herself with no one else's help? Why should a state not be free to prohibit the prescription or sale, within its borders, of drugs whose only purpose is to kill someone the state regards as a person?

The bizarre and morally arbitrary compromises that Fried imagines suggest not only that he does not really believe his own explanation of why the right to privacy does not apply in the case of abortion but that his opposition to *Roe v. Wade* may not be based on principle at all. He acknowledges the Reagan administration's concern with abortion as one of the "contradictions and cross-currents" in the revolution. "How does the impulse to reduce the intrusion of government into people's lives work with the abortion issue?" he asks. And he says, at the end of the chapter, that he regrets the attention the Reagan administration gave to the abortion issue. He says the administration's "apparent obsession with the subject distracted attention from what I conceive to have been its real project: restoring reasonableness and responsibility to the practice of judging"—an odd comment, because he had earlier described *Roe v. Wade* as a prime example of unreasonable and irresponsible judging.

It is hard to resist the conclusion that Fried actually saw the project of reversing *Roe v. Wade* as a narrowly political one: something that the administration had promised an important part of its constituency, and a goal that Fried, as lawyer for the administration, was therefore responsible for pursuing. In any case his attempt to base that project on constitutional principle, on an interpretation of the whole Constitution as a coherent system of moral rights, is a conspicuous failure.

Fried plainly has more personal enthusiasm for the second main element of the revolution he discusses: changing the law of racial discrimination. The Constitution and the Civil Rights Act that Congress enacted in 1964 clearly condemn what lawyers call *subjective* racial discrimination: the deliberate, racially motivated exclusion of members of minorities from public schools or universities or industries. Many prominent constitutional scholars argued that those fundamental laws also condemned *structural* discrimination: the intractable social and economic patterns of American society, created by generations of injustice, through which poorer education, lower expectations, and instinctive and unacknowledged prejudice ensure that race continues to be a dominant, pervasive factor affecting the lifetime prospects of individual citizens. The prospects of a nonwhite child now are still, on average, dramatically bleaker than those of a white child, and though that is the result of centuries of injustice and bias, it would remain true, a stagnant feature of economic and social practice, even if all the illegal acts of deliberate, subjective discrimination were miraculously to disappear.

In the 1970s and early 1980s, the Supreme Court seemed to accept that the Civil Rights Act was intended to attack structural as well as subjective discrimination, and that the Constitution recognized the eradication of structural discrimination as a compelling public goal. Its decisions were best interpreted as reflecting two fundamental principles. The first declared illegal any hiring tests or procedures that perpetuate structural discrimination by offering nonwhites disproportionately few jobs, relative to the population from which job applicants are drawn, unless the employers can show that these tests or procedures are required for sound business reasons. The Court announced that principle in *Griggs v. Duke Power Co.*, in 1971, in which the Nixon-appointed Chief Justice, Warren Burger, said for the majority that "the objective of Congress in the enactment of Title VII [of the Civil Rights Act] is plain . . . Practices, procedures, or tests neutral on their face, and even neutral in . . . intent cannot be maintained if they operate to 'freeze' the status quo of prior discriminatory practices."

The *Griggs* case principle is now widely admired in other countries struggling with different forms of discrimination: it was adopted in the British Sex Discrimination Act of 1975 and Race Relations Act of 1976, for example, and by the Court of Justice of the European Communities as the proper test of whether employment, social security, or pay provisions are illegal because they promote or perpetuate gender discrimination.

The second principle implicit in the Court's decisions was permissive rather than mandatory: it permitted both private and public institutions to give some preference, in hiring or admission decisions, to individual members of minority groups in order to help overcome the structural consequences of generations of injustice. The Court was, of course, concerned about the fairness of such programs to white applicants or workers who would be disadvantaged, and it tried to find appropriate restrictions. In the famous *Bakke* case, for example, it ruled that though a state university might take race into account as one factor among others, in order to promote student diversity it might not use rigid quotas for admitting minorities.[10]

The particular decisions that the Court made to carry out these two implicit principles, and the regulations that different departments of government issued to enforce them, were complex and often criticized—by some as too rigid or too open to bureaucratic or political abuse, and by others as not sufficiently protective of minorities. But the Reagan revolution in race law is aimed not at improving the application of the two principles, but at, in Fried's phrase, "clarifying" the law so as to read these principles out of it altogether, and, so it seems, at denying that structural discrimination is inconsistent with the Constitution's vision of an acceptable society. That aim is evident in two recent decisions in which Fried participated, both of which he now defends.

In 1989, in *Wards Cove Packing Co. v. Alioto*, the *Griggs* principle was seriously compromised.[11] An Alaska cannery's hiring practices resulted in a racial split between two kinds of work: difficult, unpleasant, and poorly paid cannery jobs were held predominantly by nonwhites, while the more attractive and better-paid jobs at some distance from the cannery were held predominantly by whites, who had different living accommodations and a different mess. (Justice Stevens, dissenting from the Court's opinion, described the result as a "plantation" economy.) The Court of Appeals had held that the cannery therefore had the burden of showing that the employment practices that produced this brutal disparity were required by business necessity. The Supreme Court disagreed, by the now familiar five to four margin. Justice White's majority opinion, in the course of arguing that the Court of Appeals had misapplied the *Griggs* principle, took the opportunity to change that principle dramatically by reversing its allocation of the burden of proof. Henceforth, he said, nonwhites complaining of racial disparity would first have to "demonstrate that the disparity they complain of is the result of one or more of the employment practices that they are attacking . . . specifically showing that each challenged practice has a significantly disparate impact on employment practices for whites and nonwhites."

The difference in the burden of proof between the two approaches is of crucial importance. The principle in the *Griggs* case was understood to be based on the assumption that great racial disparities in employment, which perpetuate structural discrimination, are bad in themselves, and that Congress intended to require employers to reduce those disparities unless they could show that business necessity prevented them from doing so. On that principle, once it is established that the cannery's practices and hiring decisions, taken together, have created a plantation economy, the cannery must show that it could have done nothing commercially rational to avoid that result. Under what are apparently the Court's new rules, however, the plaintiffs, who may be able to obtain only very sketchy information about how a particular company's often subjective employment decisions are actually made, must sustain what would often be an impossible burden. They must identify particular employment practices as those that have produced particular degrees or aspects of racial imbalance. That would be a sensible allocation of proof, perhaps, if the law aimed only at preventing subjective discrimination: it might then be fair that plaintiffs should bear the burden of showing which particular practices they believe to be evidence of intentional bias. But it is not a sensible allocation of proof on the assumption, which the Court appears now to have rejected, that structural discrimination is an evil in itself.[12]

The Court appears to have dealt an equally serious blow to the second of its two former principles: the principle that authorizes affirmative action as a mechanism of combating structural discrimination. Many American cities have adopted minority "set-aside" programs, which stipulate that a certain percentage of government contracts be reserved for construction firms owned in substantial part by nonwhites. In *City of Richmond v. Croson*, in 1989, the Court struck down a set-aside plan, of Richmond, Virginia, which reserved 30 percent of such contracts, an unusually high figure. It decided in favor of a white contractor who had been denied a contract; it held that the set-aside program denied the contractor's rights under the equal protection clause, because Richmond had not proved that the low percentage of local black entrepreneurs who had in the past been bidding for or receiving construction contracts was the direct result of any past racial discrimination in the local construction industry by the city or others, rather than just economic conditions and "societal" discrimination generally.[13] Once again that is a perverse decision if the point of affirmative action programs is the practical goal of relieving structural discrimination. An economic hierarchy in which few blacks are entrepreneurs is guaranteed to perpetuate that form of injustice.

Civil rights groups and others concerned with urban racial problems were therefore appalled by the Court's decision, and a group of distinguished law school deans and specialists in constitutional law wrote a joint article in the *Yale Law Journal* urging that cities interpret the *Croson* decision narrowly and not disband their programs immediately.[14] Fried replied with an article of his own, suggesting that the decision was much more sweeping than the deans and professors recognized, that it did revolutionize the constitutionality of affirmative action, and might well invalidate a great many set-aside programs.[15]

It is therefore crucial to Fried's project in *Order and Law* to provide a principled defense of the "clarification" that the Civil Rights Act requires plaintiffs to prove which specific hiring practice caused a racial disparity in employment, and that a public body can undertake affirmative action constitutionally only when there has been some specific historical discrimination against the particular group being benefited. What principle of justice or of individual right can he find embedded in our constitutional structure that would justify those constraints on government's ability to reduce structural discrimination? He offers only one argument that can be understood as a response to that question. He says that the principles the law seemed to many to be following in the past threatened a collectivist rather than an individualistic society, and were "a threat to liberty and to the basic right of every person to be considered as a distinct individual and not in terms of the groups to which government says he belongs." But that statement of a constitutional or moral right is plainly much too broad. Almost all legislation treats people not as "distinct" individuals but as members of some group or other: voter-qualification rules do not test individual qualifications of maturity, for example, but treat all those below a certain age in the same way. If the equal protection clause forbade *any* classification by groups, all such legislation would be unconstitutional, which is absurd.

Fried means, presumably, only that people have a right not to be treated as members of *racial* groups. He never explains, however, why it is an automatic offense to liberty to classify people racially though not by other categories equally not of their own choosing, such as age or income level or formal educational qualifications or other categories government and private institutions use instead of more individual assessments. Of course racial classifications are inherently dangerous, and must be carefully scrutinized, because they may reflect prejudice or naked favoritism by people in control. But it seems perverse to insist that racial classifications are wrong not just in those circumstances, but inherently, when the effect of that special severity toward racial classification is to perpetuate structural discrimination, that is, the situation in which individuals' fates are so largely governed by their race that our society remains divided on collectivist racial lines.

So once again Fried's crucial claim of principle seems undefended. Once again, moreover, his crucial claim seems inconsistent with his own more fully developed position. For Fried does not oppose all affirmative action programs using racial criteria. He endorses Justice O'Connor's assumption, in her majority opinion in the *Croson* case, that a public body may use appropriate racial classifications if it can prove the existence of specific past discrimination against the particular group it now seeks to help. He thinks that Richmond, for example, would have been entitled to adopt a set-aside program if it could have shown that the low number of black firms bidding for construction contracts was the result of specific past municipal or private discriminatory practices in the construction industry, even though the particular black firms benefiting from the program would not be those who had suffered from the past discrimination, and the particular white contractors put at a disadvantage would not be those who had gained anything by it.

So Fried distinguishes between cases in which specific past local discriminatory acts can be identified, and affirmative action is permitted, and the more frequent cases in which the disadvantages minority individuals suffer are the result of general and pervasive structural discrimination throughout the nation, and affirmative action is therefore to be forbidden.

That distinction might strike Fried and others as a useful political compromise in which those who hate affirmative action are appeased but minorities are given something. The compromise is unprincipled, however, because the distinction is arbitrary from the point of view of both legitimate political goals and individual moral or constitutional rights. Why should a community suffering from structural discrimination care whether it was caused by specific and identifiable private or public discriminatory acts or by historical prejudice and injustice more generally? Why should its eradication be a more compelling goal in the former than the latter case? Why are the supposed rights of white citizens, who might suffer from affirmative action, any less powerful in the former than the latter case?

Certainly the distinction cannot be justified if we accept the principle Fried cites: that individuals have a fundamental right not to be treated as members of a racial group. If individuals have that right, then *all* programs that give some people advantages denied to others because their race is different would violate that right; the violation is no more justified, with respect to any particular white job applicant or white construction contract bidder, when someone is denied that right on the ground that other whites behaved badly to other members of the same minority in the past. So the idea accepted by Fried and many other conservatives—that affirmative action programs are justified when they are "remedial" of past discrimination in the proper way—is itself deeply offensive to the principle he cites as the supposed basis of the revolution in race law. He seems left with no principled justification for his position at all.

He does have a good deal to say against most affirmative action programs, and against the *Griggs* principle, which is based not on any fundamental principles of racial justice, but on more pragmatic and political grounds. Like other conservatives, he disapproves of the economic and other side effects of policies that attack structural discrimination. He talks, for example, about the resentments such programs cause to whites who feel themselves disadvantaged, about the damage they may do to the self-esteem of some blacks, and about the economic cost to businessmen of defending actions under the principle of the *Griggs* case, which he says prompts them to avoid the problem by aiming at racial balance for its own sake. He says that it was a cardinal aim of the Reagan revolution to prevent affirmative action programs from "distorting the system of opportunity and reward for merit on which the morale of a free-enterprise system depends." These might be proper arguments to press before Congress and state and city legislatures, but no matter how passionately Fried and others may embrace them, they are not arguments of constitutional principle. They do not rest on principles that Fried can claim are embedded in the Constitution, principles that leap out at us when we draw lines from one individual right to another on the constitutional graph.

Fried confesses that the administration had to turn to the courts to suppress affirmative action because it was clear that it would not win what it wanted from Congress. "With the loss of the Senate in the 1986 midterm election," he says, "legislative relief became unthinkable, so that the Supreme Court was the only available forum for our views." That is a revealing statement: in matters concerning race, as well as in the *Rust* case mentioned earlier, which concerned free speech and abortion, the Reagan revolutionaries have treated the Court in the improper way they accuse liberals of having treated it in the past—as offering another opportunity to secure legislative policy goals, not involving constitutional principle, that they could not achieve more democratically.

Fried's book is, as I have said, candid about the political pressures that the White House and Department of Justice officials exerted to influence his decisions about which cases to argue in the Supreme Court, and what arguments to make. He reports, for example, about his decision as acting solicitor general to file a brief asking the Court to overrule *Roe v. Wade*, that "it was clear to me, that . . . I could not succeed in heading off an anti-*Roe* brief, even if I had been convinced that that was the right thing to do." He compromised over another issue—whether plaintiffs who ultimately win cases accusing state governments of taking their property without proper compensation should receive damages for the losses they incurred while the controversy was pending—and filed a brief he did not think right. (He considered resigning, but decided that the issue was too "Mickey Mouse" for that.) He held firm on another matter, however: he refused to argue to the Supreme Court that it was illegal for unions to use their members' dues for political purposes, even though he was told that the White House and various right-wing groups were angry with his decision, and that he would do himself good by changing it.

Some readers have been surprised by Fried's reports of such political interference with his judgment. Many lawyers believe that a solicitor general's responsibility is to interpret and protect the Constitution, not his administration's view of it. Another former solicitor general, Erwin Griswold, who was dean of the Harvard Law School for many years, wrote, in a review of Fried's book,[16] that he is worried by the degree to which that distinction seems to have been eroded in Fried's view of the office.

I find it even more worrying, however, that Fried was unable to deliver the principled defense of the Reagan revolution he promised. As I have said, he agrees that such a defense is necessary. He acknowledges that the Supreme Court's new direction cannot be justified by a conception of the Constitution that relies on "original intention" or by any appeal to the supposed primacy of majority rule in a democracy. But his attempt to justify the abortion and race decisions in the more principled way he proposes is just as complete a failure, in spite of his considerable skill and philosophical background.

It remains to be seen, therefore, whether the depressing Supreme Court decisions that are now beginning to change the character of our constitutional law can be defended in that way, whether they can be seen to reflect some general, coherent, even if very conservative, account of the Constitution as a moral system. The new decisions are strikingly consistent with the various political goals of major elements of the political constituency of Reagan and Bush. No one would count that as an adequate justification or defense, of course. But it is far from clear that anything jurisprudentially more impressive can be said on their behalf.

July 18, 1991

II

SPEECH
CONSCIENCE
AND SEX

THE FIRST AMENDMENT'S guarantee of the "freedom of speech, or of the press" is a constitutional provision that patently cannot be understood other than as an abstract moral principle. Lawyers and judges who apply it to concrete cases must ask and answer a variety of questions of political morality. What is the point of a special guarantee for speech and press? Is the point exclusively or dominantly one of improving the democratic process? Is this freedom particularly important because free speech and a free press provide the public with information it needs properly to govern itself? Or because fairness requires that everyone over whom a democratic government exercises dominion, even those with unpopular or distasteful or prejudiced opinions, have an unconstrained opportunity to influence both the formal and informal processes through which collective decisions are made and the political and moral environment is formed? Or does neither of these suggestions exhaust the main structural justifications for a special right? These are deep questions because they implicate the controversies about the nature of democracy that I described in the Introduction.

Particularly in the second half of this century, the Supreme Court has defended an expansive, essentially liberal, view of the First Amendment. Its decisions have been criticized from both the right and the left, and the chapters of this part defend the centrist liberal view from attacks on both these flanks. Chapter 7 describes a pair of lawsuits in which famous generals—William C. Westmoreland, who commanded American forces in Vietnam, and Ariel Sharon, who commanded Israeli troops in Lebanon—demanded libel damages for what they charged was unfair and inaccurate reporting. Many conservative groups, angered at what they took to be the press's liberal bias, supported the plaintiffs in those cases, and were particularly critical of the main doctrinal hurdle the plaintiffs faced—the Supreme Court's earlier decision in *New York Times v. Sullivan,* which declared that public figures could collect damages in libel only if they showed not simply that what was said about them was false, but that it was published either with the knowledge it was false or in "reckless disregard" of whether it was. I wrote the essay to evaluate the charge of recklessness made in those two lawsuits, but also to defend the *Sullivan* rule.

Chapter 8, which is a review essay of a book about the *Sullivan* decision, discusses its background and structure, and argues that it would have been a better decision had the main opinion relied less on the instrumental idea that free speech makes democracy work better, and more on the different idea I just distinguished, that free speech is itself a constitutive element of democratic fairness.[1] I recognize, in that chapter, that the *Sullivan* rule has made it difficult for many plaintiffs adequately to correct the record after they have been unfairly accused, and I suggest revisions in the law.

Chapter 9 concentrates on a very different kind of objection to First Amendment law, from a different political quarter. It continues the discussion, begun in Chapter 8, of the charge that freedom of speech as traditionally construed conflicts with the different and more urgent value of equality, and that for that reason the Constitution should be reinterpreted so as not to permit the publication of at least certain forms of pornography or of literature directed against minority races or groups. I have added a new addendum to that chapter, which discusses what is surely one of the most tempting of all occasions for censorship: the absurd and insulting charge, now soberly defended by individuals and groups in many countries, including Germany, that the Holocaust never took place, but is an invention of Jews and their allies.

Catharine MacKinnon has become the most publicized proponent of the view that free speech must be restricted in the interests of equality, and particularly that its protection must be withdrawn from pornography. Chapter 10 evaluates the arguments presented in her book, *Only Words*. MacKinnon wrote a letter to the editor in response to the chapter's initial publication, and I add, as an addendum to Chapter 10, my reply to her letter, which might help to clarify the argument in the chapter. (I believe the contents of her letter are sufficiently explained by my letter, but readers can consult her text in the March 3, 1994, issue of *The New York Review of Books*.) A very recent article, Chapter 11, broadens the discussion to include not only free speech but the different ideal of academic freedom, and it therefore considers one aspect of what has come to be called "political correctness."

7

▼

The Press on Trial

*R*enata Adler's fierce book about two recent libel suits—*Westmoreland v. CBS* and *Sharon v. Time*—has revived the debates they provoked and become a cause célèbre of its own. The lawsuits themselves attracted great public attention and were widely covered in both the American and foreign press. Both cases involved commanding generals, unpopular wars, and powerful press institutions. On January 23, 1982, CBS broadcast a documentary, called "The Uncounted Enemy," about the war in Vietnam. It claimed to report "a conscious effort—indeed a conspiracy at the highest levels of American military intelligence—to suppress and alter critical intelligence on the enemy in the year leading up to the Tet offensive," and showed General William C. Westmoreland, who commanded American forces in Vietnam, at the center of that "conspiracy." In February 1983, *Time* ran a cover story about the massacre of Palestinian refugees by Christian Phalangist troops in Sabra and Shatila in Lebanon following the assassination of the Phalangist leader Bashir Gemayel. It said that the Israeli defense minister, General Ariel Sharon, had "reportedly discussed with the Gemayels the need for the Phalangists to take revenge for the assassination of Bashir."

Westmoreland and Sharon both sued for enormous sums. Westmoreland's suit was financed by the conservative Capital Legal Foundation, which approached him after several firms had declined to take his case. Sharon's principal lawyer, Milton Gould, volunteered his firm's services. (Westmoreland said he would donate whatever compensation he won to charity.) CBS and *Time* were both represented by Cravath, Swaine and

167

Moore, one of New York's most prestigious law firms. David Boies of that firm headed the CBS team, and Thomas Barr the *Time* team. The trials were held at the same time (Sharon's began later and finished earlier) on different floors of the United States Courthouse in Foley Square in Manhattan before two exceptionally able judges—Pierre Leval for Westmoreland's trial, and Abraham Sofaer, who is now legal adviser to the State Department, for Sharon's. These judges earned the virtually unqualified admiration of both sides and of all commentators on the cases I have read. The plaintiffs were under a severe legal burden. The Supreme Court had held, in the famous 1964 case of *New York Times v. Sullivan,* that a public official cannot win compensation for libel unless he proves not only that the charge published against him was false but also that it was published with "actual malice," by which the Court meant that the publisher knew it to be false, or published it with "reckless disregard" for its truth. Sharon's jury decided, at the end of his trial, that *Time*'s statement about him was false, but that since *Time* had not known it to be false, he was not entitled to compensation. Westmoreland settled his suit just before his trial was to end, in exchange for no compensation—not even a contribution toward his expenses—and for a CBS statement that said only that it had not meant to call him unpatriotic or disloyal.

Renata Adler is a well-known journalist, essayist, and novelist. She is also a graduate of the Yale Law School, and therefore has formidable credentials to examine these lawsuits and their implications. She first published most of her book, *Reckless Disregard,* in 1986 in two long *New Yorker* articles that were very critical of CBS, *Time,* and Cravath. She said that they should not have defended the lawsuits so "aggressively," and that they cared too much about protecting themselves and too little about the truth or falsity of what they had said. And she seemed to suggest, though never quite explicitly, that the cases therefore call into question the Supreme Court's interpretation of the First Amendment guarantee of freedom of the press, including the rule in *New York Times v. Sullivan* about "actual malice," which she believes grants the press almost a sovereign immunity from the consequences of its mistakes.

CBS and *Time* each prepared rebuttals (CBS's, which Cravath helped prepare, ran to fifty pages) and sent these to William Shawn, the editor of *The New Yorker,* asking for corrections or an opportunity to reply. (Shawn rejected the rebuttals, refused to print any reply, and pronounced his magazine content with the articles as published.) CBS also sent its rebuttal to Knopf, which was to publish the book version, and Adler charges, in the coda she added to the book as finally published, that it did so to intimidate her and Knopf by covertly threatening *them* with a libel suit. The *Time* and CBS replies delayed the publication of *Reckless Disregard*, while Adler checked each of the charges they made.

There is indeed much to admire in *Reckless Disregard*. It provides fascinating sketches of the familiar courtroom theater of testimony and cross-examination, and of the less familiar offstage depositions and "side-bar" conferences, which took place out of the jury's hearing, between judge and counsel. (Adler attended, I believe, only some sessions of the actual trials, and her report is gathered from the considerable labor, for which she deserves much credit, of studying trial and other transcripts that, together with documents some of which she must also have studied, ran to a fearsome length of hundreds of thousands of pages.) She sets out testimony that should destroy any faith her more credulous readers might have had in the shrewdness of military intelligence or the infallibility of major news organizations, and some of her observations about the contemporary American press are refreshing and valuable. Adler's nonlegal readers will learn a good deal about libel law and, through the lines, even more about the law governing what evidence is admissible in court and how it must be presented. Her images are often arresting: she describes the giant *Time* organization, for example, which relied on one journalist's report of "confidential sources," as "perched, like an improbable ballerina, on a single toe."

But Adler often writes in dense and clotted prose, in sentences of amazing length and bewildering syntax. She writes about both trials together, moreover, jumping back and forth between the two in modern cinematographic style, letting light dawn only gradually over both lawsuits together. Though this device is presumably meant to suggest that her target is larger than the two cases, and is nothing less than the state of journalism and press law as a whole, its main effect is to obscure crucial differences between the two cases, and between the position, performance, and achievements of the two news organizations. And she too often surrenders to the very journalistic vices she excoriates. *Reckless Disregard* is marred by the same one-sided reporting, particularly in its account of *Westmoreland,* and its coda displays the same intransigence in the face of contrary evidence that we would rightly condemn in the institutional press.

Adler's main charge is summarized in this passage:

> Neither suit should ever have been brought. Once brought, neither suit
> should have been so aggressively defended. Because neither the ninety
> minutes nor the paragraph should have been broadcast or published,
> either. Whether it was Cravath, or the press defendants, or some unexam-
> ined, combative folly the clients and their law firm embarked upon
> together, the refusal to acknowledge, or even to consider, the possibility
> of human error caused both CBS and *Time* and their attorneys to spare
> no expense, and experience, apparently, no doubt or scruple, in trans-
> forming both suits into a contest not of mistakes but of legal and journal-
> istic shams.

It is not clear what Adler means by the key word "aggressively." Sometimes she seems to be objecting mainly to the manner in which the suits
were defended, that is, to the demeanor and evasiveness of the press's
witnesses, and to what she considers the boorishness or craftiness of its
lawyers. But sometimes she argues a graver and more important objection,
more relevant to her later serious charge that the defense "trivialized" the
First Amendment: that the defendants should not have tried to defend the
truth of what they had broadcast or published but should have defended
only their lack of "reckless disregard" in broadcasting or publishing it.

The first of these objections—about the press's demeanor—in turn
harbors two rather different accusations that should be distinguished. The
more serious is that the journalists who became witnesses for the defense
actually obstructed the search for truth by evasions and devious if not
downright false testimony, as if all that mattered, once the lawsuits had
begun, was winning them at any cost. (Though she several times implies
that the witnesses for both *Time* and CBS were guilty of this impropriety,
her more plausible examples are all drawn from the *Time* case.) She
analyzes, in much detail, the testimony of David Halevy, the "single toe"
Israeli reporter in *Time*'s Jerusalem office, who kept changing his story
about his sources. She spends several pages on the testimony of Richard
Duncan, *Time*'s chief of correspondents, who said he could not recall what
was in Halevy's personnel file (which in fact contained the record of a past
inaccurate story by Halevy for which he had been put on probation), a
failure of memory Adler, with justice, finds implausible. Duncan also said
that he had stopped making inquiries about Halevy's sources when the
litigation began because "at that point the role to make that kind of
investigation had passed from me to the lawyers."

Adler makes much of these evasions, and of this apparent abdication of responsibility, and she is right to find them lamentable. But they are also, I fear, perfectly understandable. *Time*'s executives and reporters did not become tricky or guarded or cautious or unenterprising because its story had been challenged—the magazine had conducted a thorough and successful investigation of Halevy's previous mistake, and published a retraction—but because *Time* had been sued for $50 million by a powerful man with considerable financial resources at his disposal and powerful emotional support at his back.

Lawsuits are frightening: they can be lost even with a sound case, and they are, in folklore and in fact, dangerous places where one incautious word or ventured fact will be seized upon by relentless lawyers on the other side and made to seem much more damaging or incriminating than it really is. Lawsuits are also, at an even cruder and more dramatic level, inescapably and deeply adversarial: the defendant finds himself confronted not by a partner in the search for truth but by an announced enemy bent on crushing him. Plaintiff and defendant are both, from the moment a complaint is filed, symbolically and actually locked into a process in which any end, even settlement, will be assessed as vindication for one and humiliation for the other. It is hardly surprising that almost everyone turns defensive (or, what is much the same thing, mock-arrogant) when he or his team is sued, and docile in the hands of his lawyers, who, in turn, are expected by client and colleagues to play their own scripted role, fighting fire with fire, in the sad drama.

Litigation, in short, is a culture of its own, and the behavior of *Time*'s officers and witnesses must be judged, in all fairness, against the standards of that culture rather than the higher and more attractive standards of their normal profession. I do not mean, of course, to condone the evasiveness and lack of candor Adler reports; nor do I disagree with her that it would have been admirable had all *Time*'s employees carried journalistic integrity across the litigation barrier. The more important point, however, is that the plaintiffs have their own kind of responsibility for turning reporting into caginess; both generals had other opportunities for redress, as we shall see, and their decision for litigation itself risked sacrificing accuracy in the public record for a chance at vengeance in court. The *Westmoreland* and *Sharon* cases did show a defect in the jurisprudence of libel; this was not, however, that libel law is too favorable to journalists, but that a trial's publicity and prospect of enormous damages make it too tempting for plaintiffs to try to take history to court.

I said that Adler's complaints about the demeanor of the defendants contained two accusations: the second is a much more diffuse and heated complaint not just about how journalists behave in court, but about what their courtroom behavior reveals about them as people:

> As early as the first depositions in *Sharon,* it was evident that witnesses with a claim to any sort of journalistic affiliation considered themselves a class apart, by turns lofty, combative, sullen, lame, condescending, speciously pedantic, but, above all, socially and, as it were, Constitutionally arrogant, in a surprisingly unintelligent and uneducated way. Who *are* these people? . . . Above all, the journalists, as witnesses, looked like people whose minds it had never crossed to be ashamed.

I do not know how much of this savage opinion Adler formed in her, I believe, selective visits to the trials, how much she constructed from reading transcripts (which are a notoriously unreliable guide to the figures witnesses actually cut), and how much it reflects the general impressions she has formed of her colleagues in her own career as a journalist. But it goes far beyond any evidence she supplies. She supports it mainly by quoting from the testimony of two witnesses: Halevy and George Crile, the producer of CBS's documentary.

Halevy is (to use one of her favorite expressions) what he is: a buccaneer foreign reporter who no doubt felt himself to be (as Judge Sofaer said he was) himself at risk in the trial, and who was indeed evasive and misleading. But I found nothing socially arrogant in his testimony Adler quotes, or anything that justifies calling him unintelligent or uneducated or condescending, or supposing that he considered himself a member of a class apart. His "Constitutional arrogance" consisted only in his sometimes inapposite appeals to a New York State statute (not a constitutional provision) designed to protect reporters unwilling to reveal sources. And though Adler does find passages in Crile's long testimony that make him seem arrogant or evasive, and others in which he went far beyond questions put to him, nothing she cites demonstrates he is unintelligent or uneducated. It is worth noting that her picture of Crile is contradicted by one of the jurors in *Westmoreland,* Patricia Roth, a school teacher who has written her own valuable account of the trial,[1] and who found Crile persuasive, patient, clear, and helpful.

I am more concerned here, however, with Adler's more interesting claim about the scope rather than the manner of the press's defense of the two lawsuits. Were *Time* and CBS wrong to try to prove, in court, that what they had published and broadcast was substantially true? Were they right to think, as they did, that this was necessary in order to protect the role of the First Amendment in American journalism? Or did their decision, as Adler claims, trivialize the First Amendment?

Bashir Gemayel was assassinated on September 14, 1982. Sharon visited Gemayel's relatives in Bikfaya the next day, to offer his and his government's sympathy. A day later the occupying Israeli forces allowed Phalangist troops to enter two refugee camps in Lebanon, where these troops massacred hundreds of unarmed Palestinians, including women and children. International opinion blamed Israel, whose government then established a commission, under an Israeli Supreme Court justice, Yitzhak Kahan, to investigate the tragedy. The Kahan Commission issued its report on February 8, 1983, with one appendix that was never made public. The published report assigned Sharon "indirect responsibility" for the massacre, and recommended that he resign his office, which he was then forced to do.

Time made the Kahan report the cover story for its next issue. It reported the commission's finding of Sharon's indirect responsibility, and then added these sentences:

> *Time* has learned that [Secret Appendix B to the Report] contains further details about Sharon's visit to the Gemayel family on the day after Bashir Gemayel's assassination. Sharon reportedly told the Gemayels that the Israeli army would be moving into West Beirut and that he expected the Christian forces to go into the Palestinian refugee camps. Sharon also reportedly discussed with the Gemayels the need for the Phalangists to take revenge for the assassination of Bashir, but the details of the conversation are not known.

Sharon called this statement a "blood libel," and sued *Time* for $50 million.

David Halevy had worked for *Time* in Jerusalem for many years, had excellent connections within the Israeli government and military (he had fought as an officer beside many of those he might have used as sources, and remained a lieutenant colonel in the military reserve), and had supplied reports, using these connections, for many stories published in *Time*, though one of his reports—a 1979 account of Prime Minister Menachem Begin's supposed ill health—turned out to be false. Halevy had filed an internal memorandum of December 6, 1982, reporting that according to his confidential source, Sharon had "given the Gemayels the feeling," in the condolence meeting, that he "understood" their need for revenge, and that the Israelis would not hinder them. When the February cover story was being written, Halevy was asked whether the secret Appendix B supported that claim. He telephoned his "source," and then reported, apparently with a "thumbs-up" gesture, that it did. William Smith, a *Time* writer in New York, then changed Halevy's phrase, about giving the Gemayels the feeling that Israel understood their need for revenge, to the rather different claim, which *Time* published, that Sharon "discussed" revenge with them.

Time defended itself against Sharon's suit by claiming not just that it believed, in good faith, that its cover story was true when it published it, but that the story was in fact true. Halevy was the key witness, and he was unconvincing, constantly changing his claims about the number and character of the sources on whom he had relied in his initial memorandum. And under skillful questioning—partly conducted by Judge Sofaer—he admitted that he had never actually *asked* the "source" he called to confirm the contents of Appendix B whether that document in fact reported what *Time* said it did. He had only, he conceded, "inferred" that Appendix B confirmed his earlier memorandum by "reading between the lines" of what his source suggested it contained. Just before the trial's end, and after patient negotiation by Judge Sofaer and direct appeals by Sharon, the Israeli government allowed Israeli lawyers for both sides to read, in the presence of Justice Kahan, not only Appendix B but also the notes and minutes about the Bikfaya meeting that had been submitted to the Kahan Commission. The appendix did not contain what *Time* said it had "learned" was there, and the notes and minutes did not mention any discussion of revenge.

Judge Sofaer gave the jury a highly specific set of instructions: he asked them to decide and report separately on each of the issues in the case. Did *Time*'s statement defame Sharon? If so, had Sharon's lawyers demonstrated by clear and convincing evidence that *Time*'s statement that he had "discussed" revenge with the Gemayels was false? If so, did *Time* publish that false statement with actual malice, that is, knowing it to be false or in reckless disregard of its truth? The jury answered the first question "yes." (*Time* had maintained that its statement was not defamatory because, it said, the most natural reading of the statement did not imply that Sharon had encouraged, instigated, or condoned the massacres, or was aware that they would take place. The jury disagreed.) Two days later the jury answered the second question "yes" as well: the jury thought that *Time* was wrong, not only about Appendix B, which it conceded it was, but about the Bikfaya meeting. After several days of further suspense, the jury answered the third question "no," but it added (though this was not part of what it had been asked to decide) that it thought that "certain *Time* employees, particularly correspondent David Halevy, acted negligently and carelessly in reporting and verifying the information which ultimately found its way into the published paragraph."

So though *Time* lost the first two battles and was wounded in the third, it won the legal war. Adler declares that *Time* was *not* guilty of serious irresponsibility in preparing and publishing its story:

> With the arguably minor exception of Halevy (in misrepresenting the number, the reliability and the nature of his "sources"), all *Time* personnel conducted themselves professionally, and even honorably, up to and including the moment when the cover story reached the stands . . . Up to and through the moment of publication, in other words, *Time*'s position and its paragraph were well within the rules.

That seems to me a somewhat generous assessment: Halevy's "misrepresentations" were not, even arguably, "minor." And surely Harry Kelly, *Time*'s bureau chief in Jerusalem, should have pressed Halevy about what Halevy's various sources had actually said.

Adler absolves *Time* of any serious fault before publication to emphasize that her complaint is with its conduct after publication, that is, after Sharon had condemned the story and launched his suit. She thinks it was wrong of *Time* to defend the truth of its story, which she calls trying to "enforce" a scoop. But *Time* was apparently ready to accept a compromise before the start of the trial that would have qualified its story in an important way. Since *Time* insisted that it had not meant to suggest that Sharon had encouraged, instigated, condoned, or anticipated the massacres, Judge Sofaer proposed that *Time* sign a statement to that effect as part of a settlement. According to Sharon's press adviser, who was with him during the trial and has now written his own book,[2] Sharon's lawyers had great difficulty persuading the general to accept their amended draft of that statement. Sharon said that he wanted not a settlement, but to punish *Time*: "*Time* published a blood libel about me. How the hell do you *settle* a matter like this? A blood libel. A blood libel you *fight!*" And when *Time*'s lawyers drafted a different version, Sharon, according to his press adviser, declined further negotiations.[3] He gave the *Time* version only a brief glance and told his lawyers to say that they had not even shown it to him. "*Time* wants war," he declared, "and that's what they'll get—as of tomorrow morning, in court."[4]

Though *Time*'s story did seem to make the damaging charges *Time* denied it meant, its proposed settlement would in effect have retracted those charges; in any case *Time* continued to retract them, by denying it intended that meaning, throughout the trial. Why was it arrogant for *Time,* in those circumstances, to defend what it still believed to be true in substance: that the question of revenge had arisen at the meeting in Bikfaya? Why should it concede to be false what it still believed to be true?

In a mysterious passage Adler says, "To the question Why publish the story? the answer was easy: *Time* believed it to be true. To the question Why defend it . . . the answer *Time* still believes it to be true is not sufficient." But why is that answer not sufficient? Adler's answer is hard to extract from the long and dense passage, about not bearing false witness, that follows. But it comes to this: *Time*'s belief did not justify its defense of the suit because it had made no effort, after the story had been challenged, to verify its truth.

It is not clear that Adler has a fair basis for that claim.[5] *Time* had made itself a prisoner of the widespread practice, on which much investigative journalism is now based, of relying on confidential sources. Reporters assure sources that their names will be revealed to no one, including the reporters' own superiors; they think this necessary, even if it means going to jail for contempt, to get information from people who have a great deal to say and a great deal to lose if it is known that they said it. Since Watergate, at least, few commentators have seriously challenged the practice. Adler does not challenge it, for all her wry remarks about Halevy; she accepts that *Time* acted, in publishing its story, honorably and within the rules. But just as the practice severely limits the checking a responsible publication can do before it publishes, so, just as effectively, it limits the checking it can do afterward.

If *Time* and its lawyers had pressed Halevy as firmly as he was pressed at trial about the basis for his Appendix B claim, they might have learned that he had only inferred, and not been told in so many words, what he said the appendix contained. If they did learn this, they should have instructed him to be candid in deposition and at trial—as, of course, he should have been anyway. But, as *Time*'s editor in chief Henry Grunwald pointed out in a letter he wrote to selected journalists on other papers just before the trial ended, reporting is often based on inferences from what cagey sources say (Grunwald's letter recalled the inferential devices Bob Woodward and Carl Bernstein used in their Watergate reporting). It turned out, of course, that Halevy's inference was mistaken, but *Time* could not have known this before its lawyer in Israel was finally permitted to read the appendix.

The important charge against Sharon, in any case, was that revenge had been "discussed" at the condolence meeting, not that Appendix B said that it had. Justice Kahan's end-of-trial report does not absolutely dispose of that issue: some of the notes and minutes his commission's staff consulted may not have been supplied to the commission itself, and the "discussion" Halevy reported might never have been recorded in any minutes at all. *Time* claimed without contradiction that his confidential sources had proved reliable throughout his previous reporting of the Lebanon campaign, and his editors might very well have trusted what he said they said about a man whose reputation is very far from impeccable, and who, after all, had been found guilty, in the public portions of the Kahan report, of very grave and tragic errors of judgment.

As late as just before the trial's end, when the truth about Appendix B had been revealed, *Time* asked Halevy to consult his source about the Bikfaya meeting yet again, and he reported that the source stood by his previous report. That might seem an odd way for *Time* to investigate—Wittgenstein imagined a man who did not believe what he read in the paper and so bought another copy to check it—but how else could it confirm the truth of Halevy's report while respecting the practice of protecting confidential sources, while acting, that is, within the rules Adler says it behaved honorably in observing?

It is that practice, more than any special institutional arrogance on *Time*'s part, that *Sharon* calls into question, and Adler's analysis inverts the character and importance of *Time*'s mistakes before and after publication. Though the use of confidential sources has proved, in spite of its failures in this and other cases, to be a valuable, perhaps even indispensable, means of uncovering official deceit, *Sharon* does show that editors must be particularly vigilant in supervising it.[6] So long as the practice continues to be accepted by American journalists, however, it cannot be wrong—it does not "trivialize" the First Amendment—for a journal not to retract what it still honestly believes its reporter learned from such a source, just because the story has been denied or because it has been sued.

Sam Adams was a CIA intelligence analyst in Vietnam in 1966. He formed the view, based on raw intelligence data, that the official reports on enemy troop strength circulated by Westmoreland's command seriously and deliberately underestimated that strength. He pursued that thesis vigorously within the CIA, and devoted himself, in near obsessive fashion, to proving it after he left the agency in 1973, and in 1975 he defended his views in an article in *Harper's* and before Congressman Otis Pike's House Select Committee on Intelligence, which agreed that the scope of the Tet Offensive had been unanticipated because the military had had a "degraded image of the enemy." Adams's editor at *Harper's* was George Crile, who later became a CBS producer. Crile thought the article was a good basis for a documentary. He prepared, with Adams's help, a "blue sheet" outline of the program he had in mind, together with an account of the witnesses and interviews that Adams believed would support him. CBS tentatively authorized Crile to begin preparing the documentary, allowing him to hire Adams as a paid consultant.

"The Uncounted Enemy," as broadcast, made a strong case. Mike Wallace narrated the introduction, charging a "conspiracy at the highest levels of military intelligence" to deceive the American public and the President of the United States, Lyndon Johnson, about the true strength of the enemy in Vietnam. Wallace was then shown interviewing Westmoreland, who seemed shifty and made damaging admissions. Adams repeated his accusations.

General Joseph A. McChristian, who had been Westmoreland's intelligence chief until mid-1967, supported Adams's view. He said that he had prepared a cable reporting sharply increased enemy estimates and showed it to Westmoreland, who had just returned from a public relations trip to America during which he had made optimistic public statements that the "cross-over" point in the Vietnam War had been reached. Westmoreland, McChristian said, did not ask him for an explanation of the increased figures and only told him that the cable would be misunderstood and cause political problems. Other, more junior, intelligence officers, including Colonel Gains Hawkins, who had direct charge of preparing the enemy "Order of Battle," were shown saying that they had in one way or another been prevented from reporting what they considered to be an accurate estimate of the enemy's capacity.

Three days after the broadcast, however, Westmoreland held an emotional press conference, where he was joined by Ellsworth Bunker, who had been Johnson's ambassador in Vietnam, George Carver, the CIA's chief official responsible for Vietnam military intelligence, General Philip Davidson, who succeeded McChristian as Westmoreland's intelligence chief, and Colonel Charles Morris, Davidson's former assistant. They all denounced "The Uncounted Enemy." A long critical article on the documentary in *TV Guide* revealed that Crile had used questionable production and editing techniques to obtain the hard-hitting broadcast.

Some of these techniques violated CBS's own guidelines for fairness in broadcasting. He had rehearsed witnesses before filming, interviewed one witness twice, allowing that witness to see film of interviews with other people before his second interview. He had not given Westmoreland proper notice about the scope of the interview; and he had edited Westmoreland's interview to cut out qualifying remarks that might have made what the general said seem less damaging, and spliced an answer a witness had given to one question to make it appear an answer to an entirely different one. He had excluded from the broadcast, moreover, several interviews he had filmed with high officials who argued against the broadcast's claims, including Walt W. Rostow, who had been Johnson's national security adviser.

Even the less obviously wrong of these practices raise serious and difficult questions about journalistic propriety and constitutional libel law. Is factual advocacy—in which a newspaper or network presents the case for a view of events it itself, in good faith, has come to believe, ignoring or subordinating claims or arguments of others to the contrary—an acceptable part of journalism? If not, should the "actual malice" rule of the *New York Times* case be revised so that the media can be held liable for damages for a claim presented in that one-sided way if the claim can be shown to be false? Should different standards apply to newspapers and television broadcasters? Adler has very little to say about these issues, however, because her main complaint against CBS is not that Crile tailored his program to his thesis. She says that "easy as it may be, in retrospect (and particularly with the evidence in a lawsuit of this magnitude), to find fault with a ninety-minute broadcast, these might all have been good-faith editorial decisions, based on a firm conviction of some kind."

Her main complaint, here as also against *Time,* is with CBS's behavior after it was sued. She says that CBS acted in an aggressive, intransigent way; it behaved as if it were an affront to its high social responsibility and constitutional privilege for anyone, including itself, even to imagine that it might be wrong. But in fact CBS responded to criticism of its documentary in a way that hardly fits the description of arrogance and intransigence. It offered Westmoreland, just before he actually filed his suit, what seems an appropriate opportunity to air his rebuttal: it invited him, together with senior officials who supported him, to appear on a panel broadcast discussing the fairness and accuracy of "The Uncounted Enemy," and to begin that broadcast with a fifteen-minute uninterrupted statement of his own position. (Adler never mentions this piece of evidence against her thesis.) Westmoreland declined that invitation, preferring to sue instead (a decision she might have pondered before reporting that he had sued in the interests of historical truth).

After the *TV Guide* article appeared, CBS conducted its own internal investigation, on the basis of which Van Gordon Sauter, then president of CBS News, issued a public statement which conceded editorial misjudgments and admitted that the program would have been better had it not used the word "conspiracy." After the trial had begun, CBS offered a settlement under which it would have paid Westmoreland's legal fees and issued a partial retraction no doubt more generous than the innocuous statement for which Westmoreland ultimately settled. Westmoreland rejected the offer: at that point in the trial he wanted a full retraction, which CBS, believing what it believed, could not make.

Adler clearly cannot make the charge against CBS she makes against *Time,* that it did nothing to investigate the truth of its charges after they were challenged. Instead she argues that it should not have continued to believe in the truth of its documentary, which had been, in her view, proved false beyond question. The documentary could be understood as making two distinct assertions: that in Vietnam Westmoreland had attempted to deceive the press and public about enemy strength; and that he attempted to deceive his own military and civilian superiors. Westmoreland seemed particularly to resent the second of these charges. His lawyers, in their original complaint, said that both accusations were untrue; but they decided, just before the trial began, to contest only the second. So Adler means that CBS could not rationally have continued to believe that Westmoreland had tried to deceive his superiors.

She makes four arguments (spread over many isolated discussions) for that proposition: that the CBS thesis was absurd on its face; that the witnesses for Westmoreland who denied the thesis were distinguished senior officers and Cabinet or White House officials who were in an excellent position to judge; that the main witnesses CBS produced were destroyed by cross-examination at trial; and that one of the program's claims was actually shown to be dishonest, because it turned out that Crile and his associates had simply invented it to make their broadcast more exciting.

She says, in support of the first of these charges, that CBS's thesis that Westmoreland tried to deceive President Johnson was preposterous because generals always exaggerate rather than minimize enemy strength to their superiors. That argument ignores the most profound and obvious fact about America's peculiar war in Vietnam: it was a war the American public was willing to tolerate, certainly by the months before Tet, only if it was convinced the war could be won, and won reasonably soon, with no commitment of American troops or loss of American lives much beyond present numbers. Westmoreland himself made no effort to hide his view that press reports that the Vietcong were stronger than he claimed were damaging to his campaign. It is not incredible (although it might very well be false) that he thought it in the national interest to prevent new and higher estimates of enemy strength from reaching the press and public, even if that meant keeping those estimates from his superiors as well. Adler's first argument relies on a generalization contradicted by the particular circumstances of the Vietnam War.

Her second argument borders on the naive. Westmoreland was indeed supported by people formerly in high office who were—collectively—in a position to know the truth about most of CBS's charges. They testified that there was never any attempt, on the part of Westmoreland or anyone else, to hide accurate estimates. There was, they said, only a legitimate disagreement within the military, and for a time between the military and the CIA, about whether certain types of enemy personnel—in particular guerrillas and undercover villagers who planted booby traps that accounted for a considerable number of American casualties—should be listed within the number of ordinary enemy forces, as they had been earlier, or in independent categories listed elsewhere. This, they argued, was a matter of relative unimportance so long as the disputed enemy personnel were listed somewhere.

But if any deceit did take place, at least several of these witnesses, including Westmoreland's own high-ranking subordinates, had to be parties to it, and others, including administration officials, would have been irresponsible or incompetent not to have discovered it. I do not mean to suggest that any of them lied. Indeed, it may be that everything they said was true. Or perhaps (as Rodney Smolla has pointed out)[7] their positions and the distance of time have given them a different sense now of the implications of past statements and events than wholly detached observers would have had then. CBS, in any case, had collected an impressive number of other witnesses, including military witnesses of lower rank than Westmoreland's advocates, who were directly involved in the intelligence-gathering process, and who agreed that there was a cover-up. They said that intelligence reports were falsified, and two of them said that Westmoreland had resisted reporting high estimates on the sole ground that the report would be politically embarrassing.

These witnesses may, of course, be wrong; they may misremember, or they too may now misunderstand past ambiguous statements or actions of others. But nothing Adler cites in the testimony of the military witnesses, for example, shows them to be failed and disgruntled officers or men with personal grudges against Westmoreland or political critics of the Vietnam War or even (to use one of Adler's terms) that they are of the "left." They appeared to be soldiers with a sense of honor no less vivid than Westmoreland's. Some of them were confessing to what they regarded as failures of responsibility or initiative on their own part. And they had, to put the point at its weakest, no greater or more evident reason to lie, or to misremember through bias or self-interest, than those further up the chain of military and civilian command whom they contradicted. Crile and his associates had decided, in preparing the documentary, that they believed the military officers who reported that the figures were consciously distorted rather than those who said they were not, and even Adler concedes, as I said, that that could have been a judgment made in good faith. And nothing happened at the trial to force CBS to disbelieve all its key witnesses.

Adler's third argument disputes this last judgment: she thinks CBS's witnesses collapsed under cross-examination. In fact they fared no worse than the military witnesses on the other side: some of the strongest testimony for CBS was extracted, by Boies's skillful questioning, from Westmoreland and senior military witnesses favorable to him. Adler's argument centers on the testimony of General McChristian, whose appearance was reported as particularly distressing to Westmoreland because they were both West Point graduates, and Colonel Hawkins, who apparently impressed the jury a great deal. She examines the supposedly embarrassing parts of these two witnesses' testimony in meticulous detail, with special concern for their faults of diction.

McChristian testified that when he prepared a cable reporting much larger enemy figures than Westmoreland had announced during his American trip, Westmoreland asked for no explanations but said only that the cable would be a "political bombshell," words that, McChristian testified, were "burned" into his memory. Adler reports that cross-examination revealed that McChristian had said, before the trial, that he could not remember the exact words Westmoreland had used when presented with the cable. Adler claims that this "effectively disposed of the matter."

But this apparent important victory for Westmoreland turned into what some observers thought a disaster for him, and led Bob Brewin and Sydney Shaw, in their book about the trial, to call McChristian's evidence "potentially devastating."[8] For Boies brought out on reexamination not only that McChristian had felt it a point of honor not to quote verbatim from a private conversation with his superior until he felt forced to do so at the trial itself, but the much more damaging fact that Westmoreland had telephoned McChristian, just before or just after the CBS broadcast, saying, according to McChristian's notes, that "he thought our conversation was private and official between West Pointers" and that "he has stood up for and took the brunt of Vietnam for all of us," which might seem to indicate that Westmoreland himself understood the incriminating character of the 1967 conversation about the cable. (McChristian had not revealed Westmoreland's telephone call to CBS or its lawyers, feeling honor-bound to keep it private as well, and it came to light only when his papers, which included a memorandum of Westmoreland's call, were subpoenaed by Westmoreland's lawyers.)

After the trial, Westmoreland disputed McChristian's interpretation of his call, and Adler might herself have formed the view from her transcripts that McChristian was dissembling about his reasons for not reporting details of the "bombshell" conversation earlier. David Dorsen, a lawyer on Westmoreland's team, did shake other aspects of McChristian's testimony in his cross-examination. But omitting any account of McChristian's testimony about the telephone call from Westmoreland, while making so much of McChristian's discomfort about which words were or were not burned into his memory, demonstrates her own weakness for factual advocacy.

Adler calls Hawkins "cornball" and "boozy," and strongly suggests that his testimony, however engaging, came to nothing. Hawkins testified that he had briefed Westmoreland twice, in May and June of 1967, and that Westmoreland had said, in response to Hawkins's figures, "What will I tell the President? What will I tell the Congress? What will be the reaction of the press?" Hawkins said that his superior officers constantly sent his figures back for further work, and that he finally told them that they should tell him what rules to follow and that he would then come up with figures they liked. He said, with what observers felt was shame, that he thereafter began to shave figures down arbitrarily, to keep them below what he gathered was a maximum acceptable figure, and that he had ordered his own assistants to do the same thing.

Dorsen was able to show that Hawkins could remember little of his Westmoreland briefings beyond the dramatic statements he said he did remember; and Adler emphasizes that, although repeatedly pressed to do so, he never said that he was explicitly ordered to respect what he described as a "command position" setting a top limit on enemy estimates. The case was settled before Hawkins's testimony was finished, but if he had added nothing to what he had already said, the jury would have had to decide how to interpret his own confessed tampering with the figures. It seems incredible that he would have done this on his own initiative. Was he right in thinking that his superiors, by their frequent refusal to accept higher figures, meant him to understand they wanted him to observe a top limit, even if they had never explicitly commanded him to do so? Or did he misunderstand what was only their disagreement, in good faith, with his methods of estimating? Patricia Roth, the juror who wrote a book, seemed to accept the first of these interpretations: she thought Hawkins was a particularly destructive witness. And Rodney Smolla says that "without doubt . . . the witness who did the most damage to Westmoreland was Colonel Gains Hawkins."

So Adler's third argument, that key CBS witnesses were destroyed, is unpersuasive. Her fourth argument seems an example of something even stronger than factual advocacy. "The Uncounted Enemy" reported that Westmoreland's command had suppressed reports of large-scale infiltration of North Vietnamese soldiers along the Ho Chi Minh Trail into South Vietnam in the months preceding the 1968 Tet Offensive. Adler says that, whatever one might think of the other claims the documentary made, this particular charge was "plain dishonest," that the program's producers had no evidence whatever for this claim and simply invented it to make the program more exciting. Here is Adler's argument for this very grave charge: "In all [Sam Adams's] 'lists,' 'chronologies' and other notes, until just before he began working on the broadcast, he had never once (and neither had anybody else) so much as mentioned the more than a hundred thousand North Vietnamese who, the program alleged, infiltrated South Vietnam in the five months before Tet."

In fact two intelligence officers in Vietnam—Lieutenant Bernard Gattozzi and Colonel (then Major) Russell Cooley—had told CBS, in pre-broadcast interviews, that they believed infiltration had increased to the figures it later reported. They and another intelligence officer, Lieutenant Michael Hankins, made that claim in their testimony. And even a West Point textbook, published in 1969 and in use until 1974, which was introduced into the trial record, reports infiltration figures as high or higher than CBS cited. The author, General Dave Richard Palmer, wrote, "By November [1967], the monthly infiltration figure had reached some 30,000 men."[9] Adler does not mention this book, although Crile testified that he had partly relied on it.

So whether or not its infiltration figures were accurate—and they were challenged at the trial—CBS had apparently not invented them in an act of "plain dishonesty." It cited its evidence for the figures in the rebuttal memorandum that Adler studied before her final revision of *Reckless Disregard.* Her central complaint, against CBS as well as *Time,* is that they refused to acknowledge even proved mistakes. But she does not discuss, in her coda, several of the CBS arguments attempting to rebut her claim that it was dishonest about infiltration. She does discuss Hankins, Gattozzi, and Cooley, but her remarks, among other difficulties, are almost all irrelevant to the crucial question whether CBS acted dishonestly in relying on their statements. Gattozzi, she says, had a "total memory block" until Crile and Adams made contact with him, which might suggest that they fed him the higher infiltration figures. But Gattozzi testified that it was he who had first raised the issue of infiltration with Adams, rather than vice versa.

She says that Hankins, who she concedes was an infiltration expert, admitted that his figures were based on new techniques that he "could never fully validate." But that, as she makes plain elsewhere in the book, is true of almost everyone's opinion of almost everything about enemy intelligence, and hardly shows that it was dishonest of CBS to accept his opinions. Hankins testified that he "screamed bloody murder" about the constraints imposed on his reports. Cooley testified that he believed Hankins's methods were sound and that they had never been questioned by superiors who nevertheless did not accept Hankins's results.

She says that Cooley had never met Westmoreland, which hardly damages his testimony that he believed the infiltration figures Westmoreland was supplying were much lower than the true figures. She says that "Gattozzi, in any event, told what he thought he had overheard from Hankins to Major Russell Cooley"—which might suggest that the high infiltration idea was somehow the product of a one-shot and perhaps garbled communication among these three witnesses.

In fact, Cooley testified that he had learned about the understated official infiltration reports directly from Hankins, the expert, and that he, Hankins, and Gattozzi went over the great disparity between these figures and what they believed to be the truth together, not once or twice but—"continually. I mean, absolutely continually. This wasn't a matter of once a week I received a briefing from Mike Hankins. This was a daily, this was an hourly, this was a minute, this was a from midnight to noon to 3 o'clock to 8 o'clock in the morning type of thing, not only with me, but with Gattozzi."

Adler says she has prepared a document, which she does not include in her coda, that refutes the CBS rebuttal. It might contain additional evidence for her claim that CBS was dishonest; but the coda itself does not succeed in rehabilitating that serious charge.

So Adler's four arguments why CBS must have known its documentary to be false all fail to support that thesis, and fail badly. In fact, so far from damaging CBS's case, the trial struck some observers as greatly improving it.[10] The combination of forces Adler finds unholy—the press and its lawyers joining in an intense investigation financed by a much larger budget than CBS would ever devote to a single program, and aided by the adversarial techniques of subpoena, discovery, deposition, and cross-examination—produced a much more powerful case that the military had systematically deceived the public during the Vietnam War than CBS had had for its original broadcast. Members of the jury were interviewed after the trial had ended in a virtual Westmoreland surrender; these interviews suggested that several members of the jury thought, on the basis of the evidence and arguments so far, that Westmoreland had not shown that the CBS charges were false. Though Patricia Roth never says how she would have voted, her diary suggests that when the trial ended she believed CBS and not the general.

I do not mean, however, that *Westmoreland* proved the desirability of moving history from the study to the courtroom. We do know more, as a result of *Westmoreland,* than we probably otherwise would ever have known about the course of military intelligence in Vietnam; it is hard to imagine a group of scholarly historians discovering all the details that Cravath's litigation team did. But the trial's cost was unbelievably high, and, as Judge Leval told the jurors when he dismissed them after the settlement, even a unanimous jury verdict will not put a complex historical controversy to rest.

Adler does not agree that the trial made the CBS case stronger. But she is arguing—remember—not just that Westmoreland's side had the better of the historical argument, which she is entitled to think, but that CBS could not rationally continue to believe its side, and she is not entitled, on the basis of the arguments and material she presents in her book, to that conclusion. She therefore has no case that CBS's decision to defend its claims trivializes the First Amendment, or illustrates a general, institutional arrogance in the American press that requires reexamining the constitutional jurisprudence of press freedom.

Adler's comments about the First Amendment, and about the *New York Times v. Sullivan* rule that a public official must prove "actual malice" to win a libel suit, are brief, obscure, and dangerous. She says that the press in the eighteenth century, when the First Amendment was adopted, consisted of a number of small journals representing a wide range of radically different political points of view whose audience expected biased reporting. She concludes that "the Constitution can hardly have envisioned, on the part of the press, a power, a scale and, above all, a unity, which is in part, but by no means entirely, a result of technological advance."

She plainly does not intend what might seem a natural implication of these remarks: that the First Amendment guarantee of a free press does not extend to the contemporary institutional press at all. She presumably does intend these observations to have some force and relevance to her essay, however; she apparently thinks they justify a less generous measure of First Amendment protection than the press now claims, at least in libel suits, though she does not, so far as I could discover, say even that in so many words. In any case, the skepticism her remarks suggest about the importance of press freedom in contemporary American society will strike many readers, already hostile to that freedom, as the most important aspect of her book.

Why does it matter that today's press is very different, in power and influence as well as character, from the small publications and pamphlets with which eighteenth-century statesmen were familiar? Adler might be making the fallacious argument that the fact that "the framers can never have contemplated" the modern press is decisive about how the First Amendment should be understood. That argument relies on the discredited thesis Attorney General Meese has done his best to revive: that the abstract provisions of the Constitution, like the First Amendment, should be interpreted so as to protect individuals and institutions only in the concrete circumstances the statesmen who first adopted the provisions had in mind. It relies on that discredited thesis, moreover, without supplying any evidence that the framers intended to limit freedom of speech and press to the broadsheets and pamphlets that were familiar to them.[11]

It is more likely that Adler means, however, not just that the framers could not have anticipated the power and role of the modern press, but that the best understanding of the point and purpose of the freedom they created does not justify extending that freedom, at least in the most generous way, to the giants of international journalism. Even if she thinks it follows only that the press deserves less protection in libel suits, her argument is unacceptable, because the wisdom of the special burden the "actual malice" rule creates for public figures depends not on the character of the press alone, but on a comparison of the press's power with that of government and the other powerful institutions we expect the press to watch.

If the press has developed far beyond its eighteenth-century situation in power and resources and influence, government has developed much further, not only in the scope of its operations and enterprises, but also in its capacity to keep its crimes and abuses dark. Indeed, these two institutions have grown in power together, in a kind of constitutional symbiosis: the press has the influence it does in large part because much of the public believes, with good reason, that a powerful and free press is a wise constraint on official secrecy and disinformation. The most basic intention of the framers was to create a system of balanced checks on power; the political role of the press, acting under a kind of limited immunity for mistakes, now seems an essential element of that system, exactly because the press alone has the flexibility, range, and initiative to discover and report secret executive misfeasance, while allowing other institutions in the checks-and-balance system to pursue these discoveries if and as appropriate. Though the Iran-Contra affair was revealed after *Reckless Disregard* was published, it provides an excellent example of the press's role in the complex constitutional structure that America, distinctively, has evolved.

CBS's documentary, though marred by culpable editorial misjudgment and one-sided presentation, was another example of that role, because it placed before an American audience serious and apparently honest military officers who reported that their superiors had deceived the people about a terrible war that cost the nation heavily. Whether or not history finally judges that report to be true, it was obviously in the public interest that these officers be heard, and it was a small triumph of journalism to persuade them to speak. It is, of course, a further question whether the press would be significantly inhibited if it were subject to the ordinary rules of libel, before *New York Times v. Sullivan*. But the Supreme Court's judgment that it would be seems right: even rich papers and networks would hesitate before printing or broadcasting damaging statements they were not certain would not be thought false by a jury. Or even statements they knew were true but did not wish to defend in expensive and protracted litigation brought by public figures financed by political groups seeking political goals. That, in any case, was the Supreme Court's rationale in *New York Times*, and it is in no way damaged by Adler's claims, even if we accepted them, about the monolithic and arrogant press.

Adler says the *New York Times* case was "historic" and "fair" and "rightly decided"; but she also says that it was "strange" and "not very carefully reasoned" (she never even hints what its flaws of reasoning were), and that later Supreme Court decisions refining the doctrine of the case produced such "unintelligible formulation" that "something is seriously amiss."[12] And in her coda she suggests, in a backhanded way, that the rule should be changed; she notes, as a qualification, that any change the Rehnquist court made would likely be a radical change for the worse. If Adler is a critic of the *New York Times* rule, she has a lot of company, and though this includes right-wing antipress fanatics, it includes some serious scholars and Supreme Court justices as well.

The facts of the *New York Times* case show why it appealed to the Supreme Court when the case was decided. The *Times* had published an advertisement placed by a civil rights organization which contained some inaccurate statements about the police of Montgomery, Alabama. A Montgomery official who was charged with supervising the police sued the paper in an Alabama court, alleging libel, and the local jury awarded him half a million dollars in damages. The jury had been instructed that unless the defendant in a libel suit of this kind proves his statements true in every damaging detail, the plaintiff is entitled to damages, even though the defendant published the statements in good faith, that is, even if he believed them.

In the Supreme Court, the *Times* argued that the Alabama libel rule, as applied against it in this case, violated the First Amendment's guarantee against laws abridging freedom of the press.[13] Some lawyers argue that the First Amendment effectively abolishes the law of libel altogether, because *any* law allowing damages for *any* publication abridges freedom of speech, and Justices Hugo Black, William O. Douglas, and Arthur Goldberg voted to overturn the jury's verdict against the *Times* on the straightforward

ground that no state has a right, under the Constitution, to award damages
in libel for any statement defaming a public official. But the majority of the
Court rejected that simple rule, and instead constructed the more complex
"actual malice" rule. The Court held that since the Montgomery plaintiff
was a public official, and since the evidence did not show that the *Times*
either knew that the contested statements were inaccurate or was indifferent about their truth, the decision of the Alabama jury must be overruled.

No one denies that the actual malice rule has unattractive consequences. It
deprives many public figures of compensation for financial and other loss
when false reports are published about them. The rule has other costs as
well. In *Herbert v. Lando,* the Supreme Court decided, properly, that if a
plaintiff cannot succeed in a libel suit unless he proves that the defendant
had a certain state of mind when he published—that he believed his
statements false or acted in reckless disregard of whether they were true or
not—the plaintiff must be allowed to examine the defendant's reporters,
editors, and executives, in pretrial depositions as well as on the witness
stand, and to see at least some parts of their notes and other preparatory
material, to determine what their state of mind actually was.[14] This aspect
of the rule has proved disruptive to the ordinary activities of newspapers
and broadcasters who defend libel suits.

But these patent disadvantages do not in themselves prove that the *New
York Times* actual malice rule is a mistake; its opponents must show that
there is a better way to reconcile an individual's interest in his reputation
with the public's interest in open government. Adler contributes nothing of
value to the debate about the actual malice rule—and wastes a valuable
opportunity to do so—by seeming to trash it, at least in some of her
remarks about it, without offering any alternative rule against which it
might be tested. Worse, much of what she says about the rule is so
misleading that it can only injure public understanding of the problem.

She wildly exaggerates the legal force of the rule, for example. She says,
about Westmoreland and Sharon, that "the main legal point, however,
was this: that in the unlikely event that either of them should prevail before
a jury the decision would almost certainly be reversed upon appeal." And
she repeats this remarkable opinion later in the book: "Both would, as a
result [of the actual malice rule], if not immediately then at some appellate
level, have lost their cases." But people held to be public figures have won
libel cases: Carol Burnett's famous victory against *The National Enquirer*
was upheld on appeal, though her damages were reduced; and when

William Tavoulareas, the president of Mobil Oil, won a suit against the *Washington Post* largely, it seems, because the jury misunderstood or ignored the judge's instructions, the verdict was upheld in the D.C. Court of Appeals in a decision in which Antonin Scalia, who has since been promoted to the Supreme Court, concurred. (The case has been reheard by the entire D.C. Circuit, *en banc,* and the entire court's decision, when announced, may be appealed to the Supreme Court.)

If Adler were right, in this judgment about "the main legal point," each of the judges she praises would have made a very serious and expensive mistake of law. Both defendants, *Time* and CBS, moved for "summary judgment" before the trials; a summary judgment motion argues that even if every assertion of fact the plaintiff makes were accepted by a jury, the plaintiff would still not have established a valid legal claim, and that the judge should therefore save everyone time and expense by dismissing the lawsuit at the outset. If Adler were right, these motions should have been granted, in which case the long and expensive trials would never have taken place. She makes no effort to state, let alone answer, the arguments the judges made for refusing summary judgment. Moreover, she herself believes, as I said, that CBS simply invented one of its charges to make its broadcast more interesting. If Westmoreland had supplied clear and convincing evidence supporting that charge, and if the jury had accepted it and decided for him on that ground, there is no reason to think its verdict would have been overturned on appeal.[15]

Though Adler makes no suggestions for ameliorating the disadvantages of the actual malice rule, or amending or replacing that rule, others have made such suggestions. Judge Leval, for example, after the CBS trial had ended, proposed that if a public figure objected to a report about him in a newspaper or broadcast, he and the publisher might agree to a form of arbitration in which the only issue would be the truth of the report rather than the good faith of the publisher; the agreement would provide that if the report is found to be false in the arbitration, the publisher would report that fact publicly, in a fashion the agreement would stipulate. This suggestion would prove useful in some circumstances—the arbitration would be much less expensive than a trial that probed the motives of the defendant's various reporters and editors as well as the truth of its statements—but it would require the consent of both parties.

Justice White recently revealed that he has changed his mind about the *New York Times* rule he once warmly endorsed.[16] He said that the rule often works against the First Amendment goal of providing a free flow of information to the public, because it prevents a public official from challenging false information, and so allows falsehood to "pollute" the record on which the public makes its decisions. White made various suggestions. One of these is available under the *New York Times* rule as it stands: instructing the jury to announce decisions on the issues of truth and actual malice separately, so that a public figure might at least have the satisfaction and benefit of a declaration of his innocence even if his failure to prove reckless disregard prevents him from winning financial compensation. (Judge Sofaer, as I said, used that technique in the *Sharon* case, and it allowed Sharon the "moral" victory of a jury's finding that he had not discussed revenge with the Phalangists. Judge Leval wanted to use the same technique in *Westmoreland*, but—though Adler makes no mention of the fact—Westmoreland's lawyers joined with CBS in opposing it.)

White's other suggestions would require more doctrinal changes. He proposes, for example, that even a public official be permitted to win a libel suit without showing actual malice if he asks merely nominal damages, or compensatory damages to reimburse him for his legal costs and for any actual financial loss he proves he suffered. The *New York Times* decision was aimed at protecting the press from large, punitive damages, and White's suggestion has the merit of barring extravagant financial demands while at the same time allowing a defamed public official to recover something. But the costs of defending a libel suit, even one limited to the issue of truth, are very great, as *Sharon* and *Westmoreland* demonstrated, and White's suggestion might therefore reinstate a large part of the chilling effect prospective litigation would have on a newspaper's decision whether to publish information the public should have.

It might be more effective to amend the *New York Times* doctrine in a different and more comprehensive way. Many states (including California) have statutes providing that if a newspaper is challenged as having falsely defamed someone, and prints a timely retraction as prominent as the original story, that retraction will be an adequate defense to any suit for punitive damages. This strategy might be expanded, and brought into First Amendment law, through the following set of rules. A public figure who proposes to contest a defamatory statement published or broadcast about him must first challenge the publisher either to print or to broadcast a timely and prominent retraction, or to print, broadcast, or accurately report a rebuttal of reasonable length prepared by him. If the publisher refuses to do either, then the person defamed may sue and win substantial compensation if he persuades a jury that whatever evidence he cited or supplied, at the time he challenged the publisher to retract its statement or report his rebuttal, provides clear and convincing evidence that the publisher's statement about him was false.

This set of rules has clear advantages. Suppose they were adopted. If a retraction or rebuttal were published, then White's concern, that the public record might be forever corrupted by false information, would be met. If not, even a public figure would have an opportunity to defend himself in court, and the issue that under *New York Times* has proved to be both an imposing burden for plaintiffs and a source of great expense and wasted time for both parties—the issue of the state of mind of the defendant when it published—would play no role whatever in the litigation.

Instead argument would focus on the question that should, after all, be decisive: whether the statement the plaintiff challenges had been shown to be, on the state of the evidence the plaintiff was able to produce to support his challenge, a doubtful matter, in which case the plaintiff would and should lose, or plainly false, in which case he would and should win because the press should not deny its victim the opportunity to disprove what is patently not true. The press would be given somewhat less protection under these rules, at least in some respects, than it enjoys under *New York Times*. But it would be saved great expense and difficulty, if it is sued, by not having to defend its honesty and good faith or even the reasonableness of its judgment when it published. It would be free to provide the public with information that it believed to be true on the evidence then available, with no "chilling" fear that if better evidence later showed its report false it would be punished financially by a vengeful plaintiff.

There are, of course, objections to the suggested rules even in the rough form in which I have described them. It would be necessary to draft adequate guidelines for the adequacy of a retraction or report of a rebuttal; the experience of the states with retraction statutes suggests, however, that adequate guidelines could be constructed. The rules might encourage particularly unscrupulous papers to libel people at will, cheerfully printing retractions later. This could be avoided by further refinements, but the irritation such papers could provoke might be an acceptable price to pay for keeping libel law simpler. The suggested rules might help to make that law simpler in another way: I see no very strong reason why they should not be applied to private people as well as public officials and figures. The distinction between public and private figures, and the attempt to define a separate standard governing libel suits by the latter, have proved very difficult,[17] and it would be a considerable benefit to eliminate the distinction altogether.

It might be useful, finally, to consider how the Sharon and Westmoreland stories might have been different if something like these rules had been in force. CBS's offer of a panel broadcast, opened by an uninterrupted fifteen-minute presentation by Westmoreland, would presumably have counted as an adequate opportunity for rebuttal. So there would have been no *Westmoreland* case. *Time* might have been willing to publish the "interpretation" of its remarks it offered before and during the trial, which withdrew the most damaging implications of its report. Since Halevy insisted that his sources continued to confirm their report of the Bikfaya meeting, *Time* would not have conceded error in that report as reinterpreted. But it would have had strong reason to print or report Sharon's own denial, together with those of whatever witnesses he was permitted by Israeli security law to quote, as well as to report that it had had access neither to Appendix B nor to any official reports of the Bikfaya meeting. For its lawyers would very likely have told *Time* that there was a good chance, if Halevy's sources remained confidential, that a jury might decide that no reasonable person would believe their story in the face of these denials. (That is, after all, what the *Sharon* jury in effect decided, though, it is true, with the benefit of Justice Kahan's report about his commission's documents.)

So the *Sharon* case might never have occurred either; if so, the hypothetical rules would have spared our legal system much cost and effort. And Renata Adler's great talents and energy, and her flair for provocation, would have been put to what I am confident would have been better use.

February 26, 1987

8

▼

Why Must Speech Be Free?

T he United States stands alone, even among democracies, in the extraordinary degree to which its Constitution protects freedom of speech and of the press, and the Supreme Court's great 1964 decision in *New York Times v. Sullivan* is a central element in that constitutional scheme of protection.[1] The Constitution's First Amendment provides that government may "make no law . . . abridging the freedom of speech, or of the press." In its *Sullivan* decision, the Court said that it follows that a public official cannot win a libel verdict against the press unless he proves not only that some statement it made about him was false and damaging, but that it made that statement with "actual malice"—that its journalists were not just careless or negligent in researching their story, but published it either knowing that it was false or in "reckless disregard" of whether it was false or not. The decision imposed that strong burden of proof only on public officials; it left private individuals free to recover damages according to state law, which traditionally allows plaintiffs to win who prove only that statements about them are false and damaging.

The Court's decision freed the press to investigate and report news, without the "chilling" fear that a jury might seize on some factual mistake or some journalistic lapse to award a libel verdict that would bankrupt the publisher. The *Sullivan* rule has made the American press much less cautious in criticizing public officials than journalists tend to be in Britain, for example, where public figures commonly sue newspapers and often win large verdicts against them.[2] It is doubtful whether the Watergate investigation, or similar exposés, would have been possible if the Court

195

had not adopted something like the *Sullivan* rule. But as Anthony Lewis makes plain in *Make No Law,* his fascinating book about the case, the decision had even wider importance, because Justice Brennan, in his opinion for the Court, redefined the fundamental premises of the First Amendment in terms that affected not only libel but First Amendment law much more generally. Though I shall argue, later, that this redefinition was not as successful, in retrospect, as it might have been, Brennan's opinion is the modern foundation of the American law of free speech.

On March 29, 1960, the *New York Times* published a full-page advertisement titled "Heed Their Rising Voices," which described the treatment of protesting black schoolchildren by the Alabama police. The advertisement contained some mistakes of fact. It said that students in Montgomery had been expelled from school after singing "My Country 'Tis of Thee" on the state capitol steps, though they were actually expelled for a sit-in in the courthouse grill, and that the students had been locked out of their lunchroom to "starve them into submission," which was apparently not true. L. B. Sullivan, a Montgomery city commissioner in charge of the police, claimed that the advertisement would be understood to be critical of him, though he was not mentioned in it, and would harm his reputation. He sued the *Times* in an Alabama court. After a trial in which the judge ordered segregated seating in the courtroom, and praised the "white man's justice" brought to the country by the "Anglo-Saxon race," an all-white jury, whose names and photographs had been published in the local paper, agreed that Sullivan had indeed been libeled and awarded him $500,000 in compensatory and punitive damages. The *Times* appealed, finally, to the Supreme Court.

Had the verdict stood, the *Times* would have been seriously damaged, and few papers of national circulation would have dared to publish anything about race that a southern jury might be persuaded to think false and libelous. The Supreme Court was therefore presumably anxious somehow to overrule the Alabama decision. But the legal background was inauspicious.

Lewis traces the constitutional history of free speech in America from the adoption of the First Amendment in the eighteenth century to the eve of the decision in *Sullivan.* For most of that period, the amendment was thought to have established only a very limited principle, and therefore to offer citizens only very limited protection. William Blackstone, the eighteenth-century English jurist whom American lawyers treated as the oracle of the common law, had declared that the common law right of free speech was a right only against what he called "previous restraint." He said government must not prevent citizens from publishing what they wished, but was free to punish them *after* publication if what they had published was offensive or dangerous. That was the traditional English view of free speech: even John Milton, who had campaigned ferociously against prior restraint in his famous essay *Areopagitica,* insisted that speech disrespectful to the Church, once published, could be punished by "fire and the executioner."

The American federalists understood the First Amendment in the same way. In 1798, they adopted the Sedition Act, which made it a crime to publish intentionally "false, scandalous and malicious" reports about members of Congress or the President. Though Madison thought the Sedition Act violated the First Amendment, and Jefferson pardoned all those who had been convicted under it when he became President, the view that only "previous restraint" was impermissible remained the dominant interpretation of the First Amendment for over a century. Oliver Wendell Holmes, whose famous dissents later helped to bury that view forever, embraced it in 1907, when he upheld the contempt conviction of an editor who had criticized a judge. Holmes said that the main purpose of the First Amendment was to prohibit prior restraints, and he added that even true statements could be punished if they were harmful to the judicial process.

By World War I, however, some judges and scholars had adopted Madison's different view, at least partly in reaction to a wave of prosecutions under the 1917 Espionage Act, which made it a crime to "attempt to cause . . . refusal of duty in the military or naval forces." Lewis describes that development with reverent excitement. The early heroes of his book are Learned Hand, then a federal district court judge, who wrote a brilliant (though immediately overruled) opinion in the *Masses* case[3] arguing that the First Amendment barred prosecuting a magazine whose cartoons ridiculed the war and the draft, and Zechariah Chafee, a Harvard Law School professor who wrote an influential law review article arguing that the amendment was intended to abolish all political censorship except direct incitement to illegal acts.

Though Holmes, whose skepticism made him reluctant to overturn any legislative decision, was slower to be converted, he was a lion once he was. His great dissent in the *Abrams* case, which declared that the Constitution commits us to an "experiment" based on the assumption that "the best test of truth is the power of the thought to get itself accepted in the competition of the market," became one of the two classic endorsements of free speech before *Sullivan*.[4] The other was Louis Brandeis's careful, moving, and optimistic opinion in the *Whitney* case, concurring in the Court's refusal to overrule the conviction of Anita Whitney for supporting the Wobblies.[5]

By the 1960s, the great Holmes and Brandeis dissents had become orthodoxy. The old view that the First Amendment condemned only prior restraint had been replaced by the very different view summarized in Holmes's famous formula: that government could punish political speech only when that speech posed a "clear and present danger" to society. But the Supreme Court had been careful to say, throughout this revolutionary period, that not *all* speech benefited from that protection. In *Chaplinsky v. New Hampshire*, for example, in which the Court said that the First Amendment did not protect "fighting words" which provoked immediate violence, it added that the First Amendment also did not apply to obscenity or private suits for libel.[6]

The latter exception seemed especially secure. The historical purpose of libel law was not to censor or punish the expression of opinion, but to allow offended citizens to vindicate their reputations. Such suits were governed by state law, and state courts, not the Supreme Court, were the final judge of what their state's law was and how it should be applied. But the Alabama jury verdict showed that private libel suits could be used to restrict freedom of the press on crucial political matters, and Herbert Wechsler, a distinguished professor at the Columbia Law School whom the *Times* had hired to brief and argue its appeal to the Court, decided to make the revolutionary claim that the First Amendment did apply to state libel law, after all. The Court unanimously accepted that claim,[7] Brennan elaborated it in his landmark opinion, and the *Sullivan* rule was born.

Lewis has himself created the genre in which he writes. Early in his career as a journalist he spent a year at the Harvard Law School as a Nieman Fellow, and then covered Supreme Court decisions, including the *Sullivan* case, for the *New York Times*, earning his second Pulitzer Prize and raising the standard of Supreme Court reporting to a new level of legal sophistication. In 1964 he wrote *Gideon's Trumpet*, an account of *Gideon v. Wainwright*, the case in which the Supreme Court established the constitutional right of poor people accused of a felony to a court-appointed lawyer.

Make No Law is an even better book. Freedom of speech and press is Lewis's special constitutional concern. He taught the standard course in those subjects at the Harvard Law School for many years, and teaches it now at Columbia Law School as James Madison Visiting Professor. He has written several important law review articles on the subject. His account of the craftsmanship of a complex judicial opinion, and of the unique process through which one justice gathers others under a collective opinion all can sign, is itself a contribution to constitutional jurisprudence. Lewis has a journalist's and a historian's grasp of the subject, moreover, as well as a lawyer's, and his prose is lucid, confident, and dramatic. *Make No Law* is exciting history and it is brilliantly told.

Sullivan became a landmark case not just because it revised the constitutional law of libel, but because Brennan's language and images came to dominate the whole body of First Amendment law. Yet his opinion, for all its nobility, did not set out a complete intellectual basis for free speech law. In order to explain why it was incomplete, I must describe a controversial issue of constitutional theory.

The First Amendment, like the other great clauses of the Bill of Rights, is very abstract. It cannot be applied to concrete cases except by assigning some overall *point* or *purpose* to the amendment's abstract guarantee of "freedom of speech or of the press." That is not just a matter of asking what the statesmen who drafted, debated, and adopted the First Amendment thought their clauses would accomplish. Contemporary lawyers and judges must try to find a political justification of the First Amendment that fits most past constitutional practice, including past decisions of the Supreme Court, and also provides a compelling reason *why* we should grant freedom of speech such a special and privileged place among our liberties.

The old Blackstonian explanation that appealed to many of the First Amendment's framers—that the First Amendment was designed only to protect publication from prior restraint—is now obsolete. What new explanation, which accounts for the vastly greater protection the amendment is now understood to provide, should take its place? That is a central question, because judges' understanding of the point of protecting free speech will guide their decisions in difficult and controversial cases about, for example, how far the right of free speech applies to nonpolitical speech, like art or commercial advertising or pornography, or how far that right is consistent with legal limitations on political campaign expenditures, or whether the First Amendment protects racist or sexist speech.

Constitutional lawyers and scholars have proposed many different justifications for the free speech and press clauses. Most of them fall into one or the other of two main groups, however. The first treats free speech as important *instrumentally,* that is, not because people have any intrinsic moral right to say what they wish, but because allowing them to do so will produce good effects for the rest of us. Free speech is said to be important, for example, because, as Holmes declared in his *Abrams* dissent, politics is more likely to discover truth and eliminate error, or to produce good rather than bad policies, if political discussion is free and uninhibited. Or for the reason Madison emphasized: that free speech helps to protect the power of the people to govern themselves. Or for the more commonsense reason that government is less likely to become corrupt if it lacks the power to punish criticism. According to these various instrumental views, America's special commitment to free speech is based on a national endorsement of a strategy, a collective bet that free speech will do us more good than harm over the long run.

The second kind of justification of free speech supposes that freedom of speech is valuable, not just in virtue of the consequences it has, but because it is an essential and "constitutive" feature of a just political society that government treat all its adult members, except those who are incompetent, as responsible moral agents. That requirement has two dimensions. First, morally responsible people insist on making up their own minds about what is good or bad in life or in politics, or what is true and false in matters of justice or faith. Government insults its citizens, and denies their moral responsibility, when it decrees that they cannot be trusted to hear opinions that might persuade them to dangerous or offensive convictions. We retain our dignity, as individuals, only by insisting that no one—no official and no majority—has the right to withhold an opinion from us on the ground that we are not fit to hear and consider it.

For many people moral responsibility has another, more active, aspect as well: a responsibility not only to form convictions of one's own, but to express these to others, out of respect and concern for them, and out of a compelling desire that truth be known, justice served, and the good secured. Government frustrates and denies that aspect of moral personality when it disqualifies some people from exercising these responsibilities on the ground that their convictions make them unworthy participants. So long as government exercises political dominion over a person, and demands political obedience from him, it may not deny him either of these two attributes of moral responsibility, no matter how hateful the opinions he wishes to consider or propagate, any more than it may deny him an equal vote. If it does, it forfeits a substantial ground of its claim to legitimate power over him. The wrong is just as great when government forbids the expression of some social attitude or taste as when it censors explicitly political speech; citizens have as much right to contribute to the formation of the moral or aesthetic climate as they do to participate in politics.

Of course, the instrumental and constitutive justifications of free speech are not mutually exclusive.[8] John Stuart Mill endorsed both of them in *On Liberty*. So did Brandeis in his remarkably insightful and comprehensive concurring opinion in *Whitney*: he said that "those who won our independence believed that the final end of the state was to make men free to develop their faculties" and that "free speech is valuable both as an end and as a means," which is a classic endorsement of the constitutive view.[9] Brandeis was right that both kinds of justification are needed in order fully to explain First Amendment law; it is hardly surprising that so complex and fundamental a constitutional right as the right of free speech should reflect a variety of overlapping justifications.[10]

The two kinds of justification are moreover similar in many ways. Neither claims that freedom of speech is absolute; both allow that the values they cite may be overridden in special cases: in deciding, for example, how far military information may be censored. But the two justifications are nevertheless crucially different, because the instrumental justification is both more fragile and more limited. It is more fragile because, as we shall see, there are circumstances in which the strategic goals it appeals to might well be thought to argue for restricting rather than protecting speech. It is more limited because, while the constitutive justification extends, in principle, to all aspects of speech or reflection in which moral responsibility demands independence, the instrumental one, at least in its most popular versions, concentrates mainly on the protection of political speech.

If the point of freedom of speech is only to ensure that democracy works well—that people have the information they need in order to vote properly, or to protect democracy from usurping officials, or to ensure that government is not corrupt or incompetent—then free speech is much less important in matters of art or social or personal decisions. The First Amendment then protects sexually explicit literature, for example, only on the strained and easily resisted assumption that people need to read such literature in order to vote intelligently in national or local elections. Indeed, some scholars who accept the instrumental view as the exclusive justification of free speech have argued, as Robert Bork did, that the First Amendment protects nothing *but* plainly political speech, and does not extend to art or literature or science at all.[11] Even those who reject that view, on the ground that literature and science can sometimes bear on politics, nevertheless insist that the main burden of the First Amendment is the protection of political speech, and that any protection the amendment offers for other kinds of discourse is derivative from that principal function.

Brennan seemed to rely almost exclusively on the instrumental justification in his opinion for the Court in *Sullivan*. He limited First Amendment protection to cases involving libel of "public officials" rather than extending protection to all libel defendants. He quoted Madison's instrumental argument that free speech is necessary in order to make the people rulers of the government rather than the other way around. He quoted passages from earlier Supreme Court decisions emphasizing the different instrumental argument Holmes had made in his *Abrams* dissent, in which he said that truth emerges in a free market of ideas. He quoted, for example, Learned Hand's endorsement of the same instrumental claim: "[The First Amendment] presupposes that right conclusions are more likely to be gathered out of a multitude of tongues, than through any kind of authoritative selection. To many this is, and always will be folly; but we have staked our all on it."[12] Only at one point did Brennan suggest a constitutive justification for free speech. He spoke of "the citizen-critic" of government; he said, "It is as much his duty to criticize as it is the official's duty to administer," and cited Brandeis's opinion in *Whitney*, which, as I said, recognized that free speech is an end as well as a means. But Brennan limited even this isolated suggestion of a constitutive justification to the political context.[13]

He was not just following a rhetorical tradition in endorsing the instrumental view. As Lewis demonstrates, Brennan was anxious to make his decision seem as little radical as possible—perhaps he could not otherwise have collected five other justices to support his opinion—and he therefore wanted to overrule the traditional exemption of libel actions from the First Amendment only to the degree absolutely necessary to prevent states from using libel to muzzle political criticism. The instrumental justification was very well suited to that purpose, because it seems to explain why it is particularly important to protect speech that is critical of public officials. The goal of helping the marketplace of ideas generate the wisest public choice of officials and policies is particularly badly served when criticism of officials is driven from that market.

In retrospect, however, Brennan's near exclusive reliance on the instrumental justification, as well as his emphasis on the special role of political speech, seems regrettable even if it was necessary to collect a majority, because it may, unwittingly, have reinforced the popular but dangerous assumption that that is all there is to the First Amendment, and that the constitutive justification is either misplaced or unnecessary. In fact, relying exclusively on the instrumental justification is dangerous for free speech in ways that have already begun to be realized, and that may grow more serious now that Brennan and Thurgood Marshall, two of the most devoted defenders of free speech in the Court's history, have been replaced by David Souter and Clarence Thomas.

We should start, in considering that danger, by noticing that the Madisonian version of the instrumental justification, on which Brennan particularly relied, cannot provide an intellectually acceptable justification even for the First Amendment's political core. Madison's argument that free speech is necessary if the people are to be in charge of their own government does explain why government must not be allowed to practice clandestine censorship which the people would reject if they were aware of it. But that argument does not explain why the majority of people should not be allowed to impose censorship that it approves and wants. A referendum might well reveal, for example, that a majority of Americans would prefer government to have the power to censor what it deems to be politically and diplomatically sensitive material, such as the *Pentagon Papers*. If so, then the Court's obviously correct decision that government does not have that power[14] can hardly be justified by Madison's instrumental argument, except on the most implausibly paternalistic grounds. The great expansion of First Amendment protection in the decades after World War I plainly contracted, rather than expanded, the majority's power to have the form of government it itself wants.

Some of that expanded protection can of course be justified on the different instrumental argument made by Hand and Holmes: that the truth about political issues is more likely to emerge if no idea is excluded from the discussion. It is certainly plausible that the public will make more intelligent decisions about race and civil rights if newspapers are free to write about these matters without fear of libel suits, and better decisions about war and peace if newspapers cannot be stopped from publishing documents like the *Pentagon Papers*.

But even this form of the instrumental argument cannot justify some of the most important of the federal court decisions expanding First Amendment protection in recent decades, including the Supreme Court's decision, in *Brandenburg v. Ohio,* that states may not punish someone who says, wearing a hood at a Ku Klux Klan rally, that "the nigger should be returned to Africa, the Jew returned to Israel,"[15] and the Seventh Circuit's decision that a small band of neo-Nazis could not be prevented from marching with swastikas in Skokie, Illinois, where many Holocaust survivors lived.[16] Is our electorate really in a better position to choose its leaders or its policies because it permits speech of that kind? Would we be in a worse position to sift truth from falsity—would the marketplace of ideas be less efficient—if Klansmen or Nazis or sexist bigots were silent?

It might be said that we cannot trust legislators or judges to draw distinctions between valuable and worthless political comment, so that in order to protect serious newspapers discussing serious issues we must also protect Klansmen and Nazis spreading hate and causing pain. But that slippery-slope argument ignores the ability of lawyers to draw difficult distinctions here as they do in every other part of the law. If the Supreme Court can distinguish political speech from commercial speech, which it has decided enjoys much weaker constitutional protection, then it could also distinguish racist or sexist speech from other forms of political comment. It could uphold a statute carefully drafted to outlaw only speech that insults people on grounds of race, religion, or gender, in the manner of the British Race Relations Act, for example.

I emphasize this point not, of course, to recommend such a course, but to show that the instrumental justification does not offer much genuine protection against a statute of that character. In fact, the Supreme Court will soon rule on just such a statute. In December 1991, it heard oral argument in *R.A.V. v. St. Paul* and will presumably announce its decision sometime this spring. The City of St. Paul adopted an ordinance prohibiting display of a symbol that can be expected to cause "anger, alarm or resentment in others" on the basis of their race, religion, or sex, and providing a ninety-day jail sentence for that offense. Robert Viktora was prosecuted, under that ordinance, for burning a cross on a black family's lawn. Of course burning a cross on someone else's lawn is forbidden by ordinary criminal law, and Viktora will be tried for that ordinary crime even if the Supreme Court decides that he cannot be punished under the special ordinance. The *Viktora* case raises the question whether a state may constitutionally make an assault a special crime, carrying a larger sentence, because it is intended to express a conviction the community disapproves of. The Court's decision will undoubtedly have repercussions for the constitutionality of the regulations that many state universities, which are subject to the First Amendment, have recently adopted forbidding speech that expresses racial or sexual hatred or bias.[17]

It is very important that the Supreme Court confirm that the First Amendment protects even such speech; that it protects, as Holmes said, even speech we loathe. That is crucial for the reason that the constitutive justification of free speech emphasizes: because we are a liberal society committed to individual moral responsibility, and *any* censorship on grounds of content is inconsistent with that commitment. The instrumental arguments Brennan relied on in *Sullivan* are now being widely used, however, not to support but to undermine that view of liberal society. In a recent defense of campus constraints on "politically incorrect" speech, for example, Stanley Fish insisted, "Speech, in short, is never and could not be an independent value, but is always asserted against a background of some assumed conception of the good to which it must yield in the event of conflict." Fish rejects the very possibility of what I called a constitutive defense of free speech; he insists that any defense must be instrumental, and that censoring politically incorrect speech will serve the instrumental purpose better than freedom will.[18]

Catharine MacKinnon, Frank Michelman, and others have offered a similar argument for censoring pornography and other material offensive to women. They say that since women are more effective participants in the political process when they are not insulted by offensive material, the instrumental goal of effective democracy is actually better served by invading than protecting freedom of speech. They suggest, for example, that the ordinance Indianapolis adopted in response to a feminist campaign, which prohibited, among other kinds of literature, materials that "present women as enjoying pain or humiliation or rape," would have improved rather than compromised democracy, because such literature "silences" women and so decreases their voice and role in democratic politics. The Seventh Circuit Court of Appeals, in an opinion by Judge Frank Easterbrook which I have discussed elsewhere,[19] rejected that argument, and held the statute unconstitutional because it outlawed not obscene publications generally, but just those promoting a particular idea or attitude. Easterbrook tacitly relied on the constitutive rather than the instrumental justification for free speech, and the Supreme Court can honestly declare the St. Paul ordinance invalid, as it should, only if it too recognizes that justification as well as repeating the old instrumental rhetoric.

An instrumental argument is also used to support bills pending in several state legislatures, and a federal bill introduced by Republican Senator Mitch McConnell of Kentucky now being considered by the Senate Judiciary Committee, which would allow a victim of sexual assault to sue a pornographic film or video's producer or distributor for damages if she claimed the cause of the crime was that her attackers had watched that material.

The parallel with the Alabama libel law that *Sullivan* held unconstitutional is striking. If such antipornography laws are adopted, either federally or in particular states, juries in civil cases will be able to destroy a publisher or distributor by deciding that a rapist had watched a particular video, that that video is covered by the statute in question, and that it had incited his crime. Jurors who understandably despise violent pornography might well accept such a claim in spite of the fact that no respectable study or evidence has shown any causal link between pornography and actual violence.[20] Since the trial would be a civil action for damages, the ordinary protections of the criminal law process would not apply. A rapist might even cooperate by testifying that pornography did cause his crime: criminals have often claimed, as if it were a kind of excuse, that their acts were caused by something they read or saw.[21] Video shops would become extremely cautious about the films they stocked; they would be loath, for example, to stock *The Accused,* a much-praised film about gang rape, which would fall under the descriptions of pornography in some of the proposed laws.[22] As Leanne Katz, who has formed a feminist group to fight the legislation, has said, the idea "that there should be a legal cause of action for what is 'caused' by exposure to ideas, is a truly frightening prospect."[23]

In a recent decision, the Supreme Court of Canada accepted a different instrumental argument for upholding a statute censoring certain forms of pornography.[24] The Canadian Charter of Rights and Freedoms protects freedom of expression, though with qualifications the First Amendment does not recognize. The Canadian Court conceded that the effect of its ruling was to narrow that constitutional protection, but said that "the proliferation of materials which seriously offend the values fundamental to our society is a substantial concern which justifies restricting the otherwise full exercise of the freedom of expression." That is an amazing statement. It is the central, defining, premise of freedom of speech that the offensiveness of ideas, or the challenge they offer to traditional ideas, cannot be a valid reason for censorship; once that premise is abandoned it is difficult to see what free speech means. The Court added that some sexually explicit material harms women because "materials portraying women as a class as objects for sexual exploitation and abuse have a negative impact on the individual's sense of self-worth and acceptance." But that kind of harm is so close to mere offensiveness that it cannot count, by itself, as a valid reason for censorship either. Every powerful and controversial idea has a potential negative impact on someone's self-esteem. The Canadian Court, presumably, would not uphold a ban on nonpornographic literature whose purpose was explicitly to deny the equal worth of women, no matter how persuasive or effective that objectionable literature might be.[25]

These trends are ominous for liberty and for democracy. If Brennan had given a more prominent place to the constitutive justification in his restatement of the First Amendment premises in *Sullivan,* it would now be easier for American courts to reject the arguments that appealed to the Canadian Supreme Court, and to hold statutes like the St. Paul ordinance and laws providing tort actions against video distributors unconstitutional. The Supreme Court's more general treatment of sexually explicit literature might also have been different if he had done so. The Court has several times declared that obscenity falls outside the protection of the First Amendment altogether, on the instrumental ground that obscenity has no "redeeming social value." As the great First Amendment scholar Harry Kalven pointed out long ago, it strains common sense to think that a society in which hard-core pornography is freely available is better placed to discover the truth about anything for that reason.[26] But it has proved enormously difficult for the Court to distinguish obscenity from sexually explicit material that does have at least some redeeming value. The Court has changed its mind about the ground of distinction so often and produced so many unworkable tests that Justice Stewart's frank declaration that he couldn't define obscenity but knew it when he saw it became the most-quoted judicial pronouncement on the issue.[27]

Though Brennan had himself declared, in 1957, that the First Amendment did not protect obscene speech or publication,[28] he changed his mind in 1973, and declared in a dissenting opinion that, "in the absence of distribution to minors or obtrusive exposure to unconsenting adults," the Constitution prohibits government from suppressing any materials as obscene.[29] He tried to reconcile this view with the instrumental justification of free speech he had earlier endorsed by emphasizing the "institutional" difficulties courts face in distinguishing obscene from valuable work. But this, once again, was strained, and failed to persuade the Court. If, on the other hand, past decisions, and particularly his own *Sullivan* decision, had more clearly recognized the constitutive justification of free speech, he would have had a more natural and persuasive argument for his change of view. It is obviously inconsistent with respecting citizens as responsible moral agents to dictate what they can read on the basis of some official judgment about what will improve or destroy their characters, or what would cause them to have incorrect views about social matters.[30]

The worst and most threatening consequence of ignoring the constitutive justification is undoubtedly, however, the Supreme Court's appalling decision in *Rust v. Sullivan*.[31] The Court upheld the Reagan administration's reinterpretation of a 1970 congressional statute, which provides funds to a variety of hospitals for "family planning" services but forbids that any of the funds be used for abortions, to mean that personnel working in such services may not even discuss that procedure.[32] The administration's order forbade doctors, nurses, or counselors even to respond to patients' questions about abortion; it prohibited them from answering, for example, if a patient asked them where she could get abortion information, or whether abortions were legal.

In March 1992 the Bush administration amended the regulations to allow doctors in federally financed facilities, though not nurses or other personnel, to discuss abortion. (The director of National Right to Life, an anti-abortion group, said he did not object to the amendment because "very little of the abortion counseling has been done by physicians.")[33] But the Court's decision, which sustained the gag rule even when it did apply to doctors, is a dangerous precedent. The Court rejected the argument that the rule violated the First Amendment; it said that since doctors who wish to advise their patients about abortion are free to resign their positions in federally financed family planning services and seek jobs elsewhere, the government was not censoring anyone but simply dictating how money it supplied must be spent. The decision was very widely condemned as illogical and irresponsible, and we must hope that one day it will become as infamous an example of bad constitutional adjudication as the *Lochner* case, and other agreed Supreme Court mistakes. But the decision would not have been possible, I believe, except for the influence of the idea that the exclusive or cardinal purpose of the First Amendment is the instrumental purpose of ensuring a free flow of political expression.

No one thinks that the government could use its central role in helping finance health care in order to dictate the political opinions doctors working in hospitals supported by federal funds can express. Government could not allow such doctors to praise the government's health care policies but forbid them to criticize those policies, for example. From the standpoint of any competent constitutive justification of free speech, however, any distinction between such a plainly improper gag rule and the one the Court upheld is illegitimate. From that perspective, a doctor must be as free to give information he believes necessary for his patient's health or well-being as he is to express political opinions. Requiring doctors, as a condition of their employment, not to give their patients medical information the patients request denigrates the moral responsibility of doctor and patient alike.

Suppose Brennan had set out to base his decision in the *Sullivan* case not on the relatively narrow ground he chose, which emphasized the instrumental justification of free speech, but on the broader ground I have been recommending, which emphasizes the constitutive justification as well. He might nevertheless have restricted the scope of a broader ruling to libel suits by public officials, on the ground that no more general scope is necessary to protect the moral independence of journalists and their audience. But he would at least have considered a much wider rule, which would have applied the current requirement that plaintiffs who are public officials or public figures must show the defendant was guilty of "actual malice" to all libel suits for damages by all plaintiffs against all defendants. That wider rule would protect a newspaper that had honestly but mistakenly published damaging information about a professor or a dancer or a businessman as well as about a sheriff or a general. Anyone who claimed that he had been libeled would be required to prove that the defendant was malicious, and not just careless or unlucky, in publishing the information the plaintiff claimed was false.

In fact Brennan himself recommended a rule very nearly that broad in a later case, in which he said that even a private individual should be required to satisfy the *Sullivan* test if he sued over a statement discussing a matter "of public or general concern."[34] As Thurgood Marshall, who disagreed, pointed out, "all human events are arguably within the area of 'public or general concern,'" so very few plaintiffs would not be covered by Brennan's suggestion. In that same case, Justice Harlan recommended a rule extending the *Sullivan* limitations to private individuals who sought presumed or punitive damages for libel. Since plaintiffs seek such damages in almost all important cases, Harlan's suggestion would have had much the same effect as Brennan's. But neither suggestion was accepted by a majority of the Court, and there is no reason to think that a majority would ever have adopted the simpler and more straightforward rule I mentioned, which would apply the *Sullivan* test automatically to all plaintiffs. Nevertheless, it is worth considering the merits of such a rule.

It would hardly be unfair to require a libel plaintiff to show at least that the press was in some way at *fault* in publishing what it did. That is the normal standard in almost all other civil actions for damages. I cannot make you pay on every occasion when you do something that injures me in some way—by damaging my property, for example. I must show that the injury was your fault, that it was the result of your not having acted, as lawyers say, reasonably in the circumstances. The law of libel has historically been an exception to this general principle: according to common law the plaintiff needed to prove only that what the defendant said was damaging to him, not that the defendant behaved unreasonably in saying it; indeed, the burden fell on the defendant to prove that what he had said was true, not on the plaintiff to prove that it was false. That odd (and unjustifiable) exception for libel actions remains part of British law even now.

Plainly, a proper regard for freedom of speech requires at least that this exception be ended, for the benefit of all speakers or writers on any subject. The *Sullivan* rule, of course, goes further, because it demands that the plaintiffs it covers prove that the defendant was not just careless but published in bad faith or recklessly. But if the argument that justifies a more strenuous burden of proof in libel cases for public figures—the argument that such a rule is necessary if the press is to function fearlessly— is not unfair to them, it is difficult to see why extending that argument to ordinary plaintiffs would be unfair to them either. It is sometimes said that public figures have chosen to enter the kitchen and must not complain of the heat. But that argument has grown progressively weaker as the Court has expanded the range of the plaintiffs who fall under the *Sullivan* rule, from public officials to public figures who are defined as public in some other way. In any case, the argument begs the question: public officials have consented to a greater risk of being libeled only if there is some *other* reason why people in that position should have less protection than more private people.

There would have been no injustice, then, in a much more general revision of libel law. A more general revision would have saved the Court, moreover, from the hopeless task I just mentioned, the task it undertook, in the years after *Sullivan*, when it decided which plaintiffs were in fact subject to the higher burden of proof that the *Sullivan* rule created. As Lewis explains, Brennan's original distinction between public officials and all other plaintiffs gave way, first, in the Court's decision that Wally Butts—head coach of the University of Georgia, who, the *Saturday Eve-*

ning Post said, gave away his team's game plans to the Alabama coach, Bear Bryant, before the big game between the two schools—was a public "figure" though not an "official," and was therefore subject to the *Sullivan* rule.[35] Brennan's distinction gave way more comprehensively in the later *Gertz* case, when the Court created an intermediate category of protection: it held that though a liberal lawyer who had been libeled by a John Birch Society publication was not a public figure, and so did not have to meet the strict *Sullivan* test of proving actual malice, he nevertheless had to prove that the defendant was at least negligent in publishing falsehoods about him, because the statements he complained of concerned a matter of political interest.[36]

So the Court has found it difficult to make the various discriminations its rules now require, and its categories seem arbitrary from the perspective of the instrumental view of free speech they are supposed to reflect. Movie stars, for example, have been classified as public figures, and so must satisfy the actual malice standard when they sue tabloids for false reports about them, though, as Lewis points out, celebrity gossip hardly contributes to the efficiency of the political process in discovering truth or wisdom. Lewis would regret any general extension of the *Sullivan* rule to all libel plaintiffs, however, because he thinks that the Court would not be as zealous in protecting that rule if the rule had much more general application. But, as he recognizes, the significant extension of protection since the original decision has not so far caused any reduced enthusiasm for the rule. There is the important possibility, moreover, that a general extension would set in motion an even more radical reform of American libel law which, in the end, would benefit both libel plaintiffs and press freedom.

The *Sullivan* rule has not proved as effective a protection of the press's freedom to report on politics as commentators initially expected. As Lewis says, celebrations stopped when lawyers and the press realized that the rule gave well-financed public-figure plaintiffs an opportunity to inflict great damage on the press by claiming that what the press published was, indeed, malicious or reckless. The much-publicized suits by Ariel Sharon against *Time* and General William Westmoreland against CBS in 1984 illustrate the difficulty: though *Time* won a qualified jury victory and Westmoreland finally abandoned his suit, both *Time* and CBS were seriously damaged by the publicity, cost, and dislocations of long trials in which their honesty and competence were the chief topics of investigation.[37]

In another long and expensive trial, *Herbert v. Lando,* CBS argued that it should not be required to engage in the time-consuming task of producing volumes of confidential reports, internal memoranda, and other material that the plaintiff said he needed to review in order to prove actual malice.[38] The Supreme Court said that the press could not have it both ways: if the law required the plaintiff to prove that the defendant knew what it said was wrong, or that it published in disregard of its truth, then it would be unfair to allow the defendant to withhold any information the plaintiff might need to prove that. So the press is still in jeopardy of suffering great financial loss if it publishes what opponents with rich supporters are prepared to argue is false and malicious.

Lewis describes sensible proposals that several commentators have offered for revising libel law to help solve that problem, while also giving people reasonable protection against false and malicious statements.[39] Under the present law libel plaintiffs seek to redeem their reputation by winning huge jury awards whose purpose is not to compensate them for any actual financial loss they may have suffered, but to punish the press. Reformers hope to separate these two ingredients of a libel suit by allowing a plaintiff to sue, not for monetary reward, but simply for a judicial declaration that what the press said was false. Under one version of that proposal, someone who thinks he has been libeled must inform the publisher of facts which he believes show that what it published was false. Unless the publisher prints a sufficiently prominent correction, the plaintiff may sue for a judicial declaration of falsity, and an order requiring the defendant to report that declaration.[40] Since there would be no prospect of damages, the truth or falsity of what was published would be the only issue, and no question of the defendant's malice or negligence would be raised. The *Sullivan* rule would have no application. In most cases the trial would be expeditious and inexpensive, and an unfairly libeled plaintiff would be able to secure a judicial declaration that he had been unjustly attacked.

It is a further question how far such a declaration would help restore a plaintiff's reputation. Sensational statements in one newspaper, even one with a reputation for inaccuracy, are widely copied in other media, and a judicial declaration that the statement was an error might not be as widely reported, even if the offending paper was itself required to report that decision. So even if states were to adopt a new form of legal action, allowing a plaintiff to sue just for a judicial declaration of falsehood, they might continue to allow a plaintiff to sue for damages for loss of reputation as well, if he so wished. But there would then be no reason not to apply the *Sullivan* rule to all damage claims, so that both public figures and private individuals would have the option of suing for a judicial declaration, in which case they need prove nothing except the falsity of the publication, or for damages, in which case they must show that the press published the falsehood knowingly or recklessly.[41]

Reform of that general character would be more likely, in fact, if the Court did insist that the same rules apply to everyone. So far no state has changed its libel law in the way the reformers recommend. In 1985, Charles Schumer, a congressman from Brooklyn, introduced a federal bill along the lines of these suggestions, but his bill failed. The Supreme Court cannot itself order a change of that complex character in state libel law, though it might perhaps go some distance toward it, by ruling, for example, that a state must accept a prominently printed correction as a full defense. Congress or the states would be more likely to make the change themselves, however, if the Court had declared that ordinary people as well as public figures must meet the *Sullivan* test in order to collect damages for libel. Private individuals would then be anxious to find some quicker and less expensive means of vindicating their reputations, and a suit for a judicial declaration would be a valuable alternative. No legal scheme can provide an ideal solution to the inevitable conflict between free speech and the protection of private reputation. Nor is there any reason to think that the Supreme Court will expand the *Sullivan* rule in the way I suggest. But a unified system which treats all plaintiffs and all defendants alike seems more in the interests of everyone—press, public, and private citizens—than the present set of complex and unstable rules.

Sullivan was a monumental decision, for all the reasons Lewis skillfully reports. Brennan's decision freed the American press to play a more confident role in protecting democracy than the press plays anywhere else in the world. It does not detract from his achievement that the intellectual premises of his argument must now be expanded, in the face of very different threats to liberty from those he confronted in that case, and that the libel law he constructed, radical for its time, is now sufficiently well established to be simplified. *Sullivan* was a crucial battle in the defense of our first freedom. But now we have new battles to fight.

June 11, 1992

9

▼

Pornography and Hate

When Isaiah Berlin delivered his famous inaugural lecture as Chichele Professor of Social and Political Theory at Oxford, in 1958, he felt it necessary to acknowledge that politics did not attract the professional attention of most serious philosophers in Britain and America. They thought philosophy had no place in politics, and vice versa; that political philosophy could be nothing more than a parade of the theorist's own preferences and allegiances with no supporting arguments of any rigor or respectability. That gloomy picture is unrecognizable now. Political philosophy thrives as a mature industry; it dominates many distinguished philosophy departments and attracts a large share of the best graduate students almost everywhere.

Berlin's lecture, "Two Concepts of Liberty," played an important and distinctive role in this renaissance. It provoked immediate, continuing, heated, and mainly illuminating controversy. It became, almost at once, a staple of graduate and undergraduate reading lists, as it still is. Its scope and erudition, its historical sweep and evident contemporary force, its sheer interest, made political ideas suddenly seem exciting and fun. Its main polemical message—that it is fatally dangerous for philosophers to ignore either the complexity or the power of those ideas—was both compelling and overdue. But chiefly, or so I think, its importance lay in the force of its central argument. For though Berlin began by conceding to the disdaining philosophers that political philosophy could not match logic or the philosophy of language as a theater for "radical discoveries," in which "talent for minute analyses is likely to be rewarded," he continued by

214

analyzing subtle distinctions that, as it happens, are even more important now, in the Western democracies at least, than when he first called our attention to them.

I must try to describe two central features of his argument. The first is the celebrated distinction described in the lecture's title: between two (closely allied) senses of liberty. Negative liberty (as Berlin came later to restate it) means not being obstructed by others in doing whatever one might wish to do. We count some negative liberties—like the freedom to speak our minds without censorship—as very important and others—like driving at very fast speeds—as trivial. But they are both instances of negative freedom, and though a state may be justified in imposing speed limits, for example, on grounds of safety and convenience, that is nevertheless an instance of restricting negative liberty.

Positive liberty, on the other hand, is the power to control or participate in public decisions, including the decision how far to curtail negative liberty. In an ideal democracy—whatever that is—the people govern themselves. Each is master to the same degree, and positive liberty is secured for all.

In his inaugural lecture Berlin described the historical corruption of the idea of positive liberty, a corruption that began in the idea that someone's true liberty lies in control by his rational self rather than his empirical self, that is, in control that aims at securing goals other than those the person himself recognizes. Freedom, on that conception, is possible only when people are governed, ruthlessly if necessary, by rulers who know their true, metaphysical will. Only then are people truly free, albeit against their will. That deeply confused and dangerous, but nevertheless potent, chain of argument had in many parts of the world turned positive liberty into the most terrible tyranny. Of course, by calling attention to this corruption of positive liberty, Berlin did not mean that negative liberty was an unalloyed blessing, and should be protected in all its forms in all circumstances at all costs. He said, later, that on the contrary the vices of excessive and indiscriminate negative liberty were so evident, particularly in the form of savage economic inequality, that he had not thought it necessary to describe them in much detail.

The second feature of Berlin's argument that I have in mind is a theme repeated throughout his writing on political topics. He insists on the complexity of political value, and on the fallacy of supposing that all the political virtues that are attractive in themselves can be realized in a single political structure. The ancient Platonic ideal, of some master accommodation of all attractive virtues and goals, combined in institutions satisfying each in the right proportion and sacrificing none, is in Berlin's view, for all its imaginative power and historical influence, only a seductive myth. He later summed this up:

> One freedom may abort another; one freedom may obstruct or fail to create conditions which make other freedoms, or a larger degree of freedom, or freedom for more persons, possible; positive and negative freedom may collide; the freedom of the individual or the group may not be fully compatible with a full degree of participation in a common life, with its demands for cooperation, solidarity, fraternity. But beyond all these there is an acuter issue: the paramount need to satisfy the claims of other, no less ultimate, values: justice, happiness, love, the realization of capacities to create new things and experiences and ideas, the discovery of the truth. Nothing is gained by identifying freedom proper, in either of its senses, with these values, or with the conditions of freedom, or by confounding types of freedom with one another.[1]

Berlin's warnings about conflating positive and negative liberty, and liberty itself, with other values, seemed, to students of political philosophy in the great Western democracies in the 1950s, to provide important lessons about authoritarian regimes in other times and places. Though cherished liberties were very much under attack in both America and Britain in that decade, the attack was not grounded in or defended through either form of confusion. The enemies of negative liberty were powerful, but they were also crude and undisguised. Joseph McCarthy and his allies did not rely on any Kantian or Hegelian or Marxist concept of metaphysical selves to justify censorship or blacklists. They distinguished liberty not from itself, but from security; they claimed that too much free speech made us vulnerable to spies and intellectual saboteurs and ultimately to conquest.

In both Britain and America, in spite of limited reforms, the state still sought to enforce conventional sexual morality about pornography, contraception, prostitution, and homosexuality. Conservatives who defended these invasions of negative liberty appealed not to some higher or different sense of freedom, however, but to values that were plainly distinct from, and in conflict with, freedom: religion, true morality, and traditional and proper family values. The wars over liberty were fought, or so it seemed, by clearly divided armies. Liberals were for liberty, except, in some circumstances, for the negative liberty of economic entrepreneurs. Conservatives were for that liberty, but against other forms when these collided with security or their view of decency and morality.

But now the political maps have radically changed and some forms of negative liberty have acquired new opponents. Both in America and Britain, though in different ways, conflicts over race and gender have transformed old alliances and divisions. Speech that expresses racial hatred, or a degrading attitude toward women, has come to seem intolerable to many people whose convictions are otherwise traditionally liberal. It is hardly surprising that they should try to reduce the conflict between their old liberal ideals and their new acceptance of censorship by adopting some new definition of what liberty, properly understood, really is. It is hardly surprising, but the result is dangerous confusion, and Berlin's warnings, framed with different problems in mind, are directly in point.

I shall try to illustrate that point with a single example: a lawsuit arising out of the attempt by certain feminist groups in America to outlaw what they consider a particularly objectionable form of pornography. I select this example not because pornography is more important or dangerous or objectionable than racist invective or other highly distasteful kinds of speech, but because the debate over pornography has been the subject of the fullest and most comprehensive scholarly discussion.

Through the efforts of Catharine MacKinnon, a professor of law at the University of Michigan, and other prominent feminists, Indianapolis, Indiana, enacted an antipornography ordinance. The ordinance defined pornography as "the graphic sexually explicit subordination of women, whether in pictures or words," and it specified, as among pornographic materials falling within that definition, those that present women as enjoying pain or humiliation or rape, or as degraded or tortured or filthy, bruised or bleeding, or in postures of servility or submission or display. It included no exception for literary or artistic value, and opponents claimed that applied literally it would outlaw James Joyce's *Ulysses,* John Cleland's *Memoirs of a Woman of Pleasure,* various works of D. H. Lawrence, and even Yeats's "Leda and the Swan." But the groups who sponsored the ordinance were anxious to establish that their objection was not to obscenity or indecency as such, but to the consequences for women of a particular kind of pornography, and they presumably thought that an exception for artistic value would undermine that claim.[2]

The ordinance did not simply regulate the display of pornography so defined, or restrict its sale or distribution to particular areas, or guard against the exhibition of pornography to children. Regulation for those purposes does restrain negative liberty, but if reasonable it does so in a way compatible with free speech. Zoning and display regulations may make pornography more expensive or inconvenient to obtain, but they do not offend the principle that no one must be prevented from publishing or reading what he or she wishes on the ground that its content is immoral or offensive.[3] The Indianapolis ordinance, on the other hand, prohibited any "production, sale, exhibition, or distribution" whatever of the material it defined as pornographic.

Publishers and members of the public who claimed a desire to read the banned material arranged a prompt constitutional challenge. The federal district court held that the ordinance was unconstitutional because it violated the First Amendment to the United States Constitution, which guarantees the negative liberty of free speech.[4] The circuit court for the Seventh Circuit upheld the district court's decision,[5] and the Supreme Court of the United States declined to review that holding. The circuit court's decision, in an opinion by Judge Easterbrook, noticed that the ordinance did not outlaw obscene or indecent material generally but only material reflecting the opinion that women are submissive, or enjoy being dominated, or should be treated as if they did. Easterbrook said that the central point of the First Amendment was exactly to protect speech from content-based regulation of that sort. Censorship may on some occasions be permitted if it aims to prohibit directly dangerous speech—crying fire in a crowded theater or inciting a crowd to violence, for example—or speech particularly and unnecessarily inconvenient—broadcasting from sound trucks patrolling residential streets at night, for instance. But nothing must be censored, Easterbrook wrote, because the message it seeks to deliver is a bad one, or because it expresses ideas that should not be heard at all.

It is by no means universally agreed that censorship should never be based on content. The British Race Relations Act, for example, forbids speech of racial hatred, not only when it is likely to lead to violence, but generally, on the grounds that members of minority races should be protected from racial insults. In America, however, it is a fixed principle of constitutional law that such regulation is unconstitutional unless some compelling necessity, not just official or majority disapproval of the message, requires it. Pornography is often grotesquely offensive; it is insulting, not only to women but to men as well. But we cannot consider that a sufficient reason for banning it without destroying the principle that the speech we hate is as much entitled to protection as any other. The essence of negative liberty is freedom to offend, and that applies to the tawdry as well as the heroic.

Lawyers who defend the Indianapolis ordinance argue that society does have a further justification for outlawing pornography: that it causes great harm as well as offense to women. But their arguments mix together claims about different types or kinds of harm, and it is necessary to distinguish these. They argue, first, that some forms of pornography significantly increase the danger that women will be raped or physically assaulted. If that were true, and the danger were clear and present, then it would indeed justify censorship of those forms, unless less stringent methods of control, such as restricting pornography's audience, would be feasible, appropriate, and effective. In fact, however, though there is some evidence that exposure to pornography weakens people's critical attitudes toward sexual violence, there is no persuasive evidence that it causes more actual incidents of assault. The Seventh Circuit cited a variety of studies (including that of the Williams Commission in Britain in 1979), all of which concluded, the court said, "that it is not possible to demonstrate a direct link between obscenity and rape."[6] A recent report based on a year's research in Britain said: "The evidence does not point to pornography as a cause of deviant sexual orientation in offenders. Rather it seems to be used as part of that deviant sexual orientation."[7]

Some feminist groups argue, however, that pornography causes not just physical violence but a more general and endemic subordination of women. In that way, they say, pornography makes for inequality. But even if it could be shown, as a matter of causal connection, that pornography is in part responsible for the economic structure in which few women attain top jobs or equal pay for the same work, that would not justify censorship under the Constitution. It would plainly be unconstitutional to ban speech directly *advocating* that women occupy inferior roles, or none at all, in commerce and the professions, even if that speech fell on willing male ears and achieved its goals. So it cannot be a reason for banning pornography that it contributes to an unequal economic or social structure, even if we think that it does.

But the most imaginative feminist literature for censorship makes a further and different argument: that negative liberty for pornographers conflicts not just with equality but with positive liberty as well, because pornography leads to women's *political* as well as economic or social subordination. Of course pornography does not take the vote from women, or somehow make their votes count less. But it produces a climate, according to this argument, in which women cannot have genuine political power or authority because they are perceived and understood unauthentically—that is, they are made over by male fantasy into people very different from, and of much less consequence than, the people they really are. Consider, for example, these remarks from the work of the principal sponsor of the Indianapolis ordinance. "[Pornography] institutionalizes the sexuality of male supremacy, fusing the eroticization of dominance and submission with the social construction of male and female . . . Men treat women as who they see women as being. Pornography constructs who that is. Men's power over women means that the way men see women defines who women can be."[8]

Pornography, on this view, denies the positive liberty of women; it denies them the right to be their own masters by recreating them, for politics and society, in the shapes of male fantasy. That is a powerful argument, even in constitutional terms, because it asserts a conflict not just between liberty and equality but within liberty itself, that is, a conflict that cannot be resolved simply on the ground that liberty must be sovereign. What shall we make of the argument understood that way? We must notice, first, that it remains a causal argument. It claims not that pornography is a consequence or symptom or symbol of how the identity of women has been reconstructed by men, but an important cause or vehicle of that reconstruction.

That seems strikingly implausible. Sadistic pornography is revolting, but it is not in general circulation, except for its milder, soft-porn manifestations. It seems unlikely that it has remotely the influence over how women's sexuality or character or talents are conceived by men, and indeed by women, that commercial advertising and soap operas have. Television and other parts of popular culture use sexual display and sexual innuendo to sell virtually everything, and they often show women as experts in domestic detail and unreasoned intuition, and nothing else. The images they create are subtle and ubiquitous, and it would not be surprising to learn, through whatever research might establish this, that they indeed do great damage to the way women are understood and allowed to be influential in politics. Sadistic pornography, though much more offensive and disturbing, is greatly overshadowed by these dismal cultural influences as a causal force.

Judge Easterbrook's opinion for the Seventh Circuit assumed, for the sake of argument, however, that pornography did have the consequences the defenders of the ordinance claimed. He said that the argument nevertheless failed because the point of free speech is precisely to allow ideas to have whatever consequences follow from their dissemination, including undesirable consequences for positive liberty. "Under the First Amendment," he said, "the government must leave to the people the evaluation of ideas. Bald or subtle, an idea is as powerful as the audience allows it to be . . . [The assumed result] simply demonstrates the power of pornography as speech. All of these unhappy effects depend on mental intermediation."

That is right as a matter of American constitutional law. The Ku Klux Klan and the American Nazi party are allowed to propagate their ideas in America, and the British Race Relations Act, so far as it forbids abstract speech of racial hatred, would be unconstitutional in the United States. But does the American attitude represent the kind of Platonic absolutism Berlin warned against? No, because there is an important difference between the idea he thinks absurd, that all ideals attractive in themselves can be perfectly reconciled within a single utopian political order, and the different idea he thought essential, that we must, as individuals and nations, choose, among possible combinations of ideals, a coherent, even though inevitably and regrettably limited, set of these to define our own individual or national way of life. Freedom of speech, conceived and protected as a fundamental negative liberty, is the core of the choice modern democracies have made, a choice we must now honor in finding our own ways to combat the shaming inequalities women still suffer.

This reply depends, however, on seeing the alleged conflict within liberty as a conflict between the negative and positive senses of that virtue. We must consider yet another argument which, if successful, could not be met in the same way, because it claims that pornography presents a conflict within the negative liberty of speech itself. Berlin said that the character, at least, of negative liberty was reasonably clear, that although excessive claims of negative liberty were dangerous, they could at least always be seen for what they were. But the argument I have in mind, which has been offered by, among others, Frank Michelman of the Harvard Law School, expands the idea of negative liberty in an unanticipated way. He argues that some speech, including pornography, may be itself "silencing," so that its effect is to prevent other people from exercising their negative freedom to speak.

Of course it is fully recognized in First Amendment jurisprudence that some speech has the effect of silencing others. Government must indeed balance negative liberties when it prevents heckling or other demonstrative speech designed to stop others from speaking or being heard. But Michelman has something different in mind. He says that a woman's speech may be silenced not just by noise intended to drown her out but also by argument and image that change her audience's perceptions of her character, needs, desires, and standing, and also, perhaps, change her own sense of who she is and what she wants. Speech with that consequence silences her, Michelman supposes, by making it impossible for her effectively to contribute to the process Judge Easterbrook said the First Amendment protected, the process through which ideas battle for the public's favor. "It is a highly plausible claim," Michelman writes, "[that] pornography [is] a cause of women's subordination and silencing . . . It is a fair and obvious question why our society's openness to challenge does not need protection against repressive private as well as public action."[9]

He argues that if our commitment to negative freedom of speech is consequentialist—if we want free speech in order to have a society in which no idea is barred from entry, then we must censor some ideas in order to make entry possible for other ones. He protests that the distinction that American constitutional law makes between the suppression of ideas by the effect of public criminal law and by the consequences of private speech is arbitrary, and that a sound concern for openness would be equally worried about both forms of control. But the distinction the law makes is not between public and private power as such, but between negative liberty and other virtues, including positive liberty. It would indeed be contradictory for a constitution to prohibit official censorship while also protecting the right of private citizens physically to prevent other citizens from publishing or broadcasting specified ideas. That would allow private citizens to violate the negative liberty of other citizens by preventing them from saying what they wish.

But there is no contradiction in insisting that every idea must be allowed to be heard, even those whose consequence is that other ideas will be misunderstood, or given little consideration, or even not be spoken at all because those who might speak them are not in control of their own public identities and therefore cannot be understood as they wish to be. These are very bad consequences, and they must be resisted by whatever means our Constitution permits. But acts that have these consequences do not, for that reason, deprive others of their negative liberty to speak, and the distinction, as Berlin insisted, is very far from arbitrary or inconsequential.

It is of course understandable why Michelman and others should want to expand the idea of negative liberty in the way they try to do. Only by characterizing certain ideas as themselves "silencing" ideas—only by supposing that censoring pornography is the same thing as stopping people from drowning out other speakers—can they hope to justify censorship within the constitutional scheme that assigns a preeminent place to free speech. But the assimilation is nevertheless a confusion, exactly the kind of confusion Berlin warned against in his original lecture, because it obscures the true political choice that must be made. I return to Berlin's lecture, which put the point with that striking combination of clarity and sweep I have been celebrating:

> I should be guilt-stricken, and rightly so, if I were not, in some circum-stances, ready to make [some] sacrifice [of freedom]. But a sacrifice is not an increase in what is being sacrificed, namely freedom, however great the moral need or the compensation for it. Everything is what it is: liberty is liberty, not equality or fairness or justice or culture, or human happiness or a quiet conscience.

ADDENDUM:
A Compelling Case for Censorship?

Recently, an important free speech drama has been unfolding in Germany. In 1991, Guenter Deckert, leader of the ultra-right-wing National Demo-cratic party, organized a meeting at which Fred Leuchter (an American "expert" who has designed gas chambers for American prisons) presented his "research" purporting to show that the Auschwitz gassing of Jews never took place.

Though Leuchter's arguments were already well publicized around the world, Deckert was prosecuted and convicted for arranging the lecture, under a statute prohibiting incitement to racial hatred. In March of 1994, the Federal Court of Justice reversed on the ground that just denying the Holocaust does not automatically constitute incitement, and it ordered a new trial to determine whether the defendant "sympathized with Nazi beliefs" and was guilty of "insulting and denigrating the dead."

Deckert was tried and convicted again: three trial court judges said he did sympathize with Nazi beliefs and did insult the dead. But they gave him only a suspended one-year jail sentence and a light fine, declaring that his only crime consisted in expressing an opinion, and adding, incredibly, that he was a good family man, that his opinions were from "the heart," and that he was only trying to strengthen German resistance to Jewish demands. Two of the judges were soon relieved of their duties for "long-term illness," the only available ground for that action, and though they have quietly returned to their court they continue to be criticized by other judges, some of whom refuse to sit with them. In December 1994, the Federal Court of Justice overturned Deckert's light sentence, and ordered yet another trial.

The public was outraged by the series of events, and the law responded. In April 1994, the German constitutional court declared that denials of the Holocaust are not protected by free speech, and upheld an official ban on a right-wing conference where the controversial British historian of the Holocaust, David Irving, was to present his views. Early in 1995 the German parliament passed a new law declaring it a crime, punishable by five years in prison, to deny the Holocaust, whether or not the speaker believes the denial.

The new law has been vigorously enforced: in March, German police searched the headquarters of a far-right newspaper and seized copies of an issue reviewing a Danish Holocaust-denying book. The law has also produced problems of interpretation. In February, a Hamburg court decided that someone who left a message on an institutional answering machine stating that Steven Spielberg's *Schindler's List* won an Academy Award because it perpetuated the "Auschwitz myth" was not guilty of the crime. That decision, which generated a new furor, is now on appeal, but if it is reversed neo-Nazis will undoubtedly test the law with a variety of other locutions until they find one that is sustained and can become a new code phrase. They are, of course, delighted with trials turning on speech, because these provide brilliant forums for their views—the Munich trial of Ewald Althans, another Holocaust denier, featured hours of videos of Hitler's speeches and other neo-Nazi propaganda.

The German constitution guarantees freedom of speech. What justifies this exception? It is implausible that allowing fanatics to deny the Holocaust would substantially increase the risk of fascist violence in Germany. Savage anti-Semitic crimes are indeed committed there, along with equally savage crimes against immigrants, and right-wing groups are undoubtedly responsible for much of this. But these groups do not need to deny that Hitler slaughtered Jews in order to encourage Hitler worshipers to attack Jews themselves. Neo-Nazis have found hundreds of lies and distortions with which to inflame Germans who are angry, resentful, and prejudiced. Why should this one be picked out for special censorship, and punished so severely?

The real answer is clear enough: it was made explicit in the reactions of Jewish leaders to the legal events I described, and in the constitutional court's opinion. Denying that the Holocaust ever existed is a monstrous insult to the memory of all the Jews and others who perished in it. That is plainly right: It would be ghastly, not just for Jews but for Germany and for humanity, if the cynical "Auschwitz lie" were ever to gain credibility. It should be refuted publicly, thoroughly, and contemptuously whenever it appears.

But censorship is different. We must not endorse the principle that opinion may be banned when those in power are persuaded that it is false and that some group would be deeply and understandably wounded by its publication. The creationists who banned Darwin from the Tennessee public schools in the 1920s were just as convinced about biological history as we are about German history, and they, too, acted to protect people who felt humiliated at the center of their being by the disgraceful new teaching. The Moslem fundamentalists who banned Salman Rushdie were convinced that he was wrong too, and they, too, acted to protect people who had suffered deeply from what they took to be outrageous insult. Every blasphemy law, every book-burning, every witch hunt of the right or left, has been defended on the same ground: that it protects fundamental values from desecration. Beware principles you can trust only in the hands of people who think as you do.

It is tempting to say that Germany's situation is special, that the Holocaust was off history's graph and calls for exceptions to everything, including freedom of speech. But many other groups believe their situation special too, and some have good reason. There is nothing like the Holocaust in American history, but slavery is bad enough. Blacks find arguments like those of Richard Herrnstein and Charles Murray's book, *The Bell Curve,* which suggests that races differ genetically in intelligence, deeply offensive, and in some American universities, professors who teach a view of history that minorities believe insulting are ostracized and disciplined. We would not want people in power, who thought this biology or that history plainly wrong, to have the right to ban it. Censorship is often the child of grievance, and people who feel that history has been unjust to them—as many Moslem fundamentalists and other groups as well as blacks do—are unlikely to accept that their position is not special too.

I know how strong the case for censorship seems in Germany now; I know that decent people are impatient with abstract principles when they see hoodlums with pseudo-swastikas pretending that the most monumental, cold-blooded genocide ever was the invention of its victims. The hoodlums remind us of what we often forget: the high, sometimes nearly unbearable, cost of freedom. But freedom is important enough even for sacrifices that really hurt. People who love it should give no hostage to its enemies, like Deckert and his odious colleagues, even in the face of the violent provocations they design to tempt us.

August 15, 1991
Addendum, May/June 1995

10

▼

MacKinnon's Words

*P*eople once defended free speech to protect the rights of firebrands attacking government, or dissenters resisting an established church, or radicals campaigning for unpopular political causes. Free speech was plainly worth fighting for, and it still is in many parts of the world where these rights hardly exist. But in America now, free-speech partisans find themselves defending mainly racists shouting "nigger" or Nazis carrying swastikas or—most often—men looking at pictures of naked women with their legs spread open.

Conservatives have fought to outlaw pornography in the United States for a long time: for decades the Supreme Court has tried, though without much success, to define a limited category of "obscenity" that the Constitution allows to be banned. But the campaign for outlawing all forms of pornography has been given new and fiercer form, in recent years, by the feminist movement. It might seem odd that feminists have devoted such energy to that campaign: other issues, including abortion and the fight for women's equality in employment and politics, seem so much more important. No doubt mass culture is in various ways an obstacle to sexual equality, but the most popular forms of that culture—the view of women presented in soap operas and commercials, for example—are much greater obstacles to that equality than the dirty films watched by a small minority.

But feminists' concentration on pornography nevertheless seems easy to explain. Pornographic photographs, films, and videos are the starkest possible expression of the idea feminists most loathe: that women exist principally to provide sexual service to men. Advertisements, soap operas,

227

and popular fiction may actually do more to spread that idea in our culture, but pornography is the rawest, most explicit symbol of it. Like swastikas and burning crosses, pornography is deeply offensive in itself, whether or not it causes any other injustice or harm. It is also particularly vulnerable politically: the religious right supports feminists on this issue, though on few others, so feminists have a much greater chance to win political campaigns for censorship than any of the other campaigns they fight.

And pornography seems vulnerable on principle as well. The conventional explanation of why freedom of speech is important is Mill's theory that truth is most likely to emerge from a "marketplace" of ideas freely exchanged and debated. But most pornography makes no contribution at all to political or intellectual debate: it is preposterous to think that we are more likely to reach truth about anything at all because pornographic videos are available. So liberals defending a right to pornography find themselves triply on the defensive: their view is politically weak, deeply offensive to many women, and intellectually doubtful. Why, then, should we defend pornography? Why should we care if people can no longer watch films of people copulating for the camera, or of women being whipped and enjoying it? What would we lose, except a repellent industry?

Catharine MacKinnon's book of three short essays, *Only Words*, offers a sharp answer to the last of these questions: society would lose nothing if all pornography were banned, she says, except that women would lose their chains. MacKinnon is the most prominent of the feminists against pornography. She believes that men want to subordinate women, to turn them into sexual devices, and that pornography is the weapon they use to achieve that result. In a series of highly charged articles and speeches, she has tried to talk or shock other women into that view. In 1986, she wrote:

> Pornography constructs what a woman is as what men want from sex. This is what pornography means . . . It institutionalizes the sexuality of male supremacy, fusing the eroticization of dominance and submission with the social construction of male and female . . . Pornography is a harm of male supremacy made difficult to see because of its pervasiveness, potency, and principally, because of its success in making the world a pornographic place.[1]

Only Words is full of language apparently intended to shock. It refers repeatedly to "penises slamming into vaginas," offers page after page of horrifying descriptions of women being whipped, tortured, and raped, and begins with this startling passage:

> You grow up with your father holding you down and covering your mouth so that another man can make a horrible, searing pain between your legs. When you are older, your husband ties you to the bed and drips hot wax on your nipples and brings in other men to watch and makes you smile through it. Your doctor will not give you drugs he has addicted you to unless you suck his penis.

The book offers arguments as well as images, however, and these are presented as a kind of appeal, to the general public, from a judicial decision MacKinnon lost. In 1983, she and a feminist colleague, Andrea Dworkin, drafted an ordinance that outlawed or attached civil penalties to all pornography, defined as the "graphic sexually explicit subordination of women through pictures and/or words" that meet one or more of a series of tests (some of which are impossibly vague) including: "women are presented dehumanized as sexual objects, things, or commodities"; or "women are presented as sexual objects experiencing sexual pleasure in rape, incest, or other sexual assaults"; or women are depicted "in positions of sexual submission, servility, or display"; or "women's body parts—including but not limited to vaginas, breasts, or buttocks—are exhibited such that women are reduced to those parts."

In 1984, largely through their efforts, a similar ordinance was adopted by the Indianapolis legislature. The ordinance included no exception for literary or artistic value, and it could plausibly be interpreted to outlaw not only classic pornography like John Cleland's *Memoirs of a Woman of Pleasure*, but a great deal else, including, for example, D. H. Lawrence's novels and Titian's *Danae*. In 1985, the Seventh Circuit Court of Appeals held the ordinance unconstitutional on the grounds that it violated the First Amendment's guarantees of free speech and press; and in 1986, the Supreme Court declined to overrule the Seventh Circuit's decision.[2]

Only Words offers several arguments in favor of the Indianapolis ordinance and against the Seventh Circuit's ruling, though some of these are run together and must be disentangled to make sense. Some of MacKinnon's arguments are old ones that I have considered elsewhere.[3] But she devotes most of the book to a different and striking claim. She argues that even if the publication of literature degrading to women is protected by the First Amendment, as the Seventh Circuit declared, such material offends another, competing constitutional value: the ideal of equality embedded in the equal protection clause of the Fourteenth Amendment, which declares that no state may deprive any person of the equal protection of the laws. If so, she says, then the courts must balance the two constitutional values, and since pornography contributes nothing of any importance to political debate, they should resolve the conflict in favor of equality and censorship.

Unlike MacKinnon's other arguments, this claim has application far beyond the issue of pornography. If her analysis is right, national and state governments have much broader constitutional powers than most lawyers think to prohibit or censor any "politically incorrect" expression that might reasonably be thought to sustain or exacerbate the unequal positions of women or of racial, ethnic, or other minorities. I shall therefore concentrate on this new argument, but I shall first comment briefly on MacKinnon's more conventional points.

In *Only Words,* she repeats the now familiar claim that pornography significantly increases the number of rapes and other sexual crimes. If that claim could be shown to be even probable, through reliable research, it would provide a very strong though not necessarily decisive argument for censorship. But in spite of MacKinnon's fervent declarations, no reputable study has concluded that pornography is a significant cause of sexual crime: many of them conclude, on the contrary, that the causes of violent personality lie mainly in childhood, before exposure to pornography can have had any effect, and that desire for pornography is a symptom rather than a cause of deviance.[4] MacKinnon tries to refute these studies, and it is important to see how weak her arguments are. One of them, though repeated several times, is only a metaphysical sleight-of-hand. She several times insists that pornography is not "only words" because it is a "reality." She says that because it is used to stimulate a sexual act—masturbation—it is sex, which seems to suggest that a film or description of rape is itself a kind of rape. But obviously that does not help to show that pornography causes rape in the criminal sense, and it is only the latter claim that can count as a reason for outlawing it.

Sometimes MacKinnon relies on breathtaking hyperbole disguised as common sense. "Sooner or later," she declares, "in one way or another, the consumers want to live out the pornography further in three dimensions. Sooner or later, in one way or another, they do. *It* does make them want to; when they believe they can, when they feel they can get away, *they do*." (Confronted with the fact that many men who read pornography commit no rapes, she suggests that their rapes are unreported.)[5] Elsewhere she appeals to doubtful and unexamined correlations: In a recent article, for example, she declares that "pornography saturated Yugoslavia before the war," and suggests that pornography is therefore responsible for the horrifying and widely reported rapes of Croatian and Moslem women by Serbian soldiers.[6] But, as George Kennan has noted, rape was also "ubiquitous" in the Balkan wars of 1913, well before any "saturation" by pornography had begun.[7]

Her main arguments, however, are anecdotal: she cites examples of rapists and murderers who report themselves as having been consumers of pornography, like Thomas Shiro, who was sentenced to death in 1981 in Indiana for raping and then killing a young woman (and copulating with her corpse) and who pleaded that he was not responsible because he was a lifelong pornography reader. Such evidence is plainly unreliable, however, not just because it is so often self-serving, but because, as the feminists Deborah Cameron and Elizabeth Fraser have pointed out, criminals are likely to take their views about their own motives from the folklore of their community, whether it is sound or not, rather than from serious analysis of their motives. (Cameron and Fraser, who favor banning pornography on other grounds, concede that "arguments that pornography 'causes' violent acts are, indeed, inadequate.")[8]

MacKinnon's second argument for censorship is a radically different one: that pornography should be banned because it "silences" women by making it more difficult for them to speak and less likely that others will understand what they say. Because of pornography, she says,

> You learn that language does not belong to you . . . You learn that speech is not what you say but what your abusers do to you . . . You develop a self who is ingratiating and obsequious and imitative and aggressively passive and silent.[9]

In an earlier work she put the point even more graphically:

> Who listens to a woman with a penis in her mouth? . . . Anyone who cannot walk down the street or even lie down in her own bed without keeping her eyes cast down and her body clenched against assault is unlikely to have much to say about the issues of the day . . . Any system of freedom of expression that does not address a problem where the free

speech of men silences the free speech of women . . . is not serious about securing freedom of expression.[10]

On this view, which has been argued more elaborately by others,[11] it is women, not pornographers, who need First Amendment protection, because pornography humiliates or frightens them into silence and conditions men to misunderstand what they say. (It conditions them to think, for example—as some stupid judges have instructed juries in rape trials—that when a woman says no she sometimes means yes.) Because this argument cites the First Amendment as a reason for banning, not for protecting, pornography, it has the appeal of paradox. But it is premised on an unacceptable proposition: that the right to free speech includes a right to circumstances that encourage one to speak, and a right that others grasp and respect what one means to say.

These are obviously not rights that any society can recognize or enforce. Creationists, flat-earthers, and bigots, for example, are ridiculed in many parts of America now; that ridicule undoubtedly dampens the enthusiasm many of them have for speaking out and limits the attention others pay to what they say. Many political and constitutional theorists, it is true, insist that if freedom of speech is to have any value, it must include some right to the opportunity to speak: they say that a society in which only the rich enjoy access to newspapers, television, or other public media does not accord a genuine right to free speech. But it goes far beyond that to insist that freedom of speech includes not only opportunity to speak to the public but a guarantee of a sympathetic or even competent understanding of what one says.

MacKinnon's third argument centers on the production rather than the distribution or consumption of pornography: she argues that women who act in pornographic films suffer actual, direct sexual subordination, compounded by the fact that their degradation is recorded for posterity. She points out that some women are coerced or tricked into making pornographic films, and mentions the notorious "snuff" films, which are said to record the actual murder of women. But of course all these crimes can be prosecuted without banning pornography, and, as MacKinnon herself concedes, it would be wrong to "rely on the fact that some pornography is made through coercion as a legal basis for restricting all of it." Laws banning child pornography are indeed justified on the grounds that children may be damaged by appearing in pornographic films. But these laws, like many others that treat children differently, suppose that they are not competent to understand and consent to acts that may well be against their present and future interests.

It would plainly be a mistake to assume that women (or men) who appear in pornographic films do so unwillingly. Our economic system does, it is true, make it difficult for many women to find satisfactory, fulfilling employment, and may well encourage some of them to accept roles in pornographic films they would otherwise reject. The system, as MacKinnon grimly notes, works to the benefit of the pornographers. But it also works to the benefit of many other employers—fast-food chains, for example—who are able to employ women at low wages. There is great economic injustice in America, but that is no reason for depriving poor women of an economic opportunity some of them may prefer to the available alternatives.

I should mention a fourth consideration that MacKinnon puts forward, though it is difficult to find an argument in it. She says that much pornography is not just speech—it is not "only words"—because it produces erections in men and provides them with masturbatory fantasies. (She warns her readers never to "underestimate the power of an erection.") Her view of the psychology of sexual arousal is mechanical—she thinks men who read pornography "are sexually habituated to its kick, a process that is largely unconscious and works as primitive conditioning, with pictures and words as sexual stimuli." In any case, she thinks that pornography's physiological power deprives it of First Amendment protection: "An orgasm is not an argument," she says, "and cannot be argued with. Compared with a thought, it raises far less difficult speech issues, if it raises any at all." But that seems a plain non sequitur: a piece of music or a work of art or poetry does not lose whatever protection the First Amendment affords it when some people find it sexually arousing, even if that effect does not depend on its argumentative or aesthetic merits, or on whether it has any such merits at all.

The continued popularity of bad arguments such as those in *Only Words* testifies to the strength of the real but hidden reason why so many people despise pornography and want to ban it. The sado-masochistic genre of pornography, particularly, is so comprehensibly degrading that we are appalled and shamed by its existence. Contrary to MacKinnon's view, almost all men, I think, are as disgusted by it as almost all women. Because those who want to forbid pornography know that offensiveness alone does not justify censorship, however, they disguise their repulsion as concern that pornography will cause rape, or silence women, or harm the women who make it.

In the most interesting parts of *Only Words,* MacKinnon offers a new argument that is also designed to transcend mere repulsion. She says that the way in which pornography is offensive—that it portrays women as submissive victims who enjoy torture and mutilation—contributes to the unequal opportunities of women in American society, and therefore contradicts the values meant to be protected by the equal protection clause. She concedes, for the sake of this argument, that in spite of its minimal contribution to intellectual or political debate, pornography is protected under the First Amendment. But that First Amendment protection must be balanced, she says, against the Fourteenth Amendment's requirement that people be treated equally. "The law of equality and the law of freedom of speech are on a collision course in this country," she says, and she argues that the balance, which has swung too far toward liberty, must now be redressed.

The censorship of pornography, she says, should be regarded as like other kinds of government action designed to create genuine equality of opportunity. It is now accepted by almost everyone that government may properly prohibit discrimination against blacks and women in employment and education, for example. But such discrimination may take the form, not merely of refusing them jobs or university places, but of subjecting those who do manage to find jobs or places to an environment of insult and prejudice that makes work or education less attractive or even impossible. Government prohibits racial or sexual harassment at work—it punishes employers who subject blacks to racial insult or women to sexual pressures, in spite of the fact that these objectionable practices are carried out through speech—and many universities have adopted "speech codes" that prohibit racial insults in classrooms or on campus.

Banning or punishing pornography, MacKinnon suggests, should be regarded as a more general remedy of the same kind. If pornography contributes to the general subordination of women by picturing them as sexual or servile objects, as she believes it does, then eliminating pornography can also be defended as serving equality of opportunity even though it restricts liberty.[12] The "egalitarian" argument for censorship is in many ways like the "silencing" argument I described earlier: it supposes not that pornography significantly increases sexual crimes of violence, but that it works more insidiously to damage the standing and power of women within the community. But the "egalitarian" argument is in two ways different and apparently more cogent.

First, it claims not a new and paradoxical conflict within the idea of liberty, as the silencing argument does, but a conflict between liberty and equality, two ideals that many political philosophers think are often in conflict. Second, it is more limited in its scope. The "silencing" argument supposes that everyone—the bigot and the creationist as well as the social reformer—has a right to whatever respectful attention on the part of others is necessary to encourage him to speak his mind and to guarantee that he will be correctly understood; and that is absurd. The "egalitarian" argument, on the contrary, supposes only that certain groups—those that are victims of persisting disadvantage in our society—should not be subjected to the kind of insult, harassment, or abuse that has contributed to that disadvantage.

But the "egalitarian" argument is nevertheless much broader and more dangerous in its scope than might first appear. The analogies MacKinnon proposes—to sexual harassment laws and university speech codes—are revealing, because though each of these forms of regulation might be said to serve a general egalitarian purpose, they are usually defended on much more limited and special grounds. Laws against sexual harassment are designed to protect women not from the diffuse effects of whatever derogatory opinions about them are part of the general culture, but from direct sexual taunts and other degrading language in the workplace.[13] University speech codes are defended on a different ground: they are said to serve an educational purpose by preserving the calm and reflective atmosphere of mutual respect and of appreciation for a diversity of cultures and opinions that is essential for effective teaching and research.

I do not mean that such regulations raise no problems about free speech. They do. Even if university speech codes, for example, are enforced fairly and scrupulously (and in the charged atmosphere of university politics they often are not), they sometimes force teachers and students to compromise or suppress their opinions by erring on the side of safety, and some speech codes may actually be unconstitutional. I mean only that constraints on speech at work and on the campus can be defended without appealing to the frightening principle that considerations of equality require that some people not be free to express their tastes or convictions or preferences anywhere. MacKinnon's argument for banning pornography from the community as a whole does presuppose this principle, however,

and accepting her argument would therefore have devastating consequences.

Government could then forbid the graphic or visceral or emotionally
charged expression of any opinion or conviction that might reasonably
offend a disadvantaged group. It could outlaw performances of *The Mer-
chant of Venice,* or films about professional women who neglect their
children, or caricatures or parodies of homosexuals in nightclub routines.
Courts would have to balance the value of such expression, as a contribution to public debate or learning, against the damage it might cause to the
standing or sensibilities of its targets. MacKinnon thinks that pornography
is different from other forms of discriminatory or hostile speech. But the
argument she makes for banning it would apply to much else. She point-
edly declares that freedom of speech is respected too much by Americans
and that the Supreme Court was right in 1952 when it sustained a prosecution of anti-Semitic literature—a decision it has since abandoned[14]—and
wrong in 1978 when it struck down an ordinance banning a Nazi march
in Illinois.[15]

So if we must make the choice between liberty and equality that Mac-
Kinnon envisages—if the two constitutional values really are on a collision
course—we should have to choose liberty because the alternative would be
the despotism of thought-police.

But is she right that the two values do conflict in this way? Can we
escape despotism only by cheating on the equality the Constitution also
guarantees? The most fundamental egalitarian command of the Constitution is for equality throughout the political process. We can imagine some
compromises of political equality that would plainly aid disadvantaged
groups—it would undoubtedly aid blacks and women, for example, if
citizens who have repeatedly expressed racist or sexist or bigoted views
were denied the vote altogether. That would be unconstitutional, of
course; the Constitution demands that everyone be permitted to play an
equal part in the formal process of choosing a President, a Congress, and
other officials, that no one be excluded on the ground that his opinions or
tastes are too offensive or unreasonable or despicable to count.

Elections are not all there is to politics, however. Citizens play a continuing part in politics between elections, because informal public debate and
argument influences what responsible officials—and officials anxious for
reelection—will do. So the First Amendment contributes a great deal to
political equality: it insists that just as no one may be excluded from the
vote because his opinions are despicable, so no one may be denied the right

to speak or write or broadcast because what he will say is too offensive to be heard.

That amendment serves other goals as well, of course: free speech helps to expose official stupidity and corruption, and it allows vigorous public debate that sometimes generates new ideas and refutes old ones. But the First Amendment's egalitarian role is independent of these other goals: it forbids censoring cranks or neo-Nazis not because anyone thinks that their contributions will prevent corruption or improve public debate, but just because equality demands that everyone, no matter how eccentric or despicable, have a chance to influence policies as well as elections. Of course it does not follow that government will in the end respect everyone's opinion equally, or that official decisions will be equally congenial to all groups. Equality demands that everyone's opinion be given a chance for influence, not that anyone's opinion will triumph or even be represented in what government eventually does.

The First Amendment's egalitarian role is not confined, however, to political speech. People's lives are affected not just by their political environment—not just by what their Presidents and legislators and other public officials do—but even more comprehensively by what we might call their moral environment. How others treat me—and my own sense of identity and self-respect—are determined in part by the mix of social conventions, opinions, tastes, convictions, prejudices, life styles, and cultures that flourish in the community in which I live. Liberals are sometimes accused of thinking that what people say or do or think in private has no impact on anyone except themselves, and that is plainly wrong. Someone to whom religion is of fundamental importance, for example, will obviously lead a very different and perhaps more satisfying life in a community in which most other people share his convictions than in a dominantly secular society of atheists for whom his beliefs are laughable superstitions. A woman who believes that explicit sexual material degrades her will likely lead a very different, and no doubt more satisfying, life among people who also despise pornography than in a community where others, including other women, think it liberating and fun.

Exactly because the moral environment in which we all live is in good part created by others, however, the question of who shall have the power to help shape that environment, and how, is of fundamental importance, though it is often neglected in political theory. Only one answer is consistent with the ideals of political equality: that no one may be prevented from influencing the shared moral environment, through his own private choices, tastes, opinions, and example, just because these tastes or opinions disgust those who have the power to shut him up or lock him up. Of course, the ways in which anyone may exercise that influence must be limited in order to protect the security and interests of others. People may not try to mold the moral climate by intimidating women with sexual demands or by burning a cross on a black family's lawn, or by refusing to hire women or blacks at all, or by making their working conditions so humiliating as to be intolerable.

But we cannot count, among the kinds of interests that may be protected in this way, a right not to be insulted or damaged just by the fact that others have hostile or uncongenial tastes, or that they are free to express or indulge them in private. Recognizing that right would mean denying that some people—those whose tastes these are—have any right to participate in forming the moral environment at all. Of course it should go without saying that no one has a right to *succeed* in influencing others through his own private choices and tastes. Sexists and bigots have no right to live in a community whose ideology or culture is even partially sexist or bigoted: they have no right to any proportional representation for their odious views. In a genuinely egalitarian society, however, those views cannot be locked out, in advance, by criminal or civil law: they must instead be discredited by the disgust, outrage, and ridicule of other people.

MacKinnon's "egalitarian" argument for censorship is important mainly because it reveals the most important reason for resisting her suggestions, and also because it allows us to answer her charge that liberals who oppose her are crypto-pornographers themselves. She thinks that people who defend the right to pornography are acting out of self-interest, not principle—she says she has been driven to the conclusion that "speech *will* be defined so that men can have their pornography." That charge is based on the inadequacy of the conventional explanation, deriving from John Stuart Mill, that pornography must be protected so that truth may emerge. What is actually at stake in the argument about pornography, however, is not society's chance to discover truth, but its commitment to the very ideal of equality that MacKinnon thinks underrated in the American community. Liberals defend pornography, though most of them despise it, in order to defend a conception of the First Amendment that includes, as at least one of its purposes, protecting equality in the processes through which the moral as well as the political environment is formed. First Amendment liberty is not equality's enemy, but the other side of equality's coin.

MacKinnon is right to emphasize the connection between the fight over pornography and the larger, more general and important, argument about the freedom of Americans to say and teach what others think politically incorrect. She and her followers regard freedom of speech and thought as an elitist, inegalitarian ideal that has been of almost no value to women, blacks, and others without power; they say America would be better off if it demoted that ideal as many other nations have. But most of her constituents would be appalled if this denigration of freedom should escape from universities and other communities where their own values about political correctness are now popular and take root in the more general political culture. Local majorities may find homosexual art or feminist theater just as degrading to women as the kind of pornography MacKinnon hates, or radical or separatist black opinion just as inimical to racial justice as crude racist epithets.

That is an old liberal warning—as old as Voltaire—and many people have grown impatient with it. They are willing to take that chance, they say, to advance a program that seems overwhelmingly important now. Their impatience may prove fatal for that program rather than essential to it, however. If we abandon our traditional understanding of equality for a different one that allows a majority to define some people as too corrupt or offensive or radical to join in the informal moral life of the nation, we will have begun a process that ends, as it has in so many other parts of the world, in making equality something to be feared rather than celebrated, a mocking, "correct" euphemism for tyranny.

ADDENDUM:
A Response to MacKinnon's Reply

Professor MacKinnon says that my review of her book is incompetent, inconsistent, ignorant, appalling, shocking, rock-throwing junk, and that there is next to no difference between me and "kept writers in pornography magazines." This carpet bombing is aimed mainly at my two-sentence discussion, in a note, of the Seventh Circuit Court of Appeals decision in the *Hudnut* case, which declared unconstitutional an antipornography statute MacKinnon and Andrea Dworkin had drafted. I said that that court "assumed that pornography is a significant cause of sexual crime only for the sake of the argument it made," and that it in fact denied that any such significant causal connection had been "demonstrated." Mac-Kinnon sets out three paragraphs of Judge Easterbrook's opinion to show how inaccurate my report is, and adds that her quotation is "unedited." In fact, however, she omitted a crucial footnote, which he attached to the third sentence of the third paragraph she cites, qualifying particularly his remarks about the effect of pornography on sexual violence. Though she mentions the footnote later in her letter, she gives no sense of what it actually contains. Here is the omitted footnote in full (with emphasis added).

> MacKinnon's article collects empirical work that supports this proposition. The social science studies are very difficult to interpret, however, and they conflict. Because much of the effect of speech comes through a process of socialization, it is difficult to measure incremental benefits and injuries caused by particular speech. Several psychologists have found, for example, that those who see violent, sexually explicit films tend to have more violent thoughts. But how often does this lead to actual violence? National commissions on obscenity here, in the United Kingdom, and in Canada have found that it is not possible to demonstrate a direct link between obscenity and rape or exhibitionism. The several opinions in Miller v. California discuss the U.S. commission. See also Report of the Committee on Obscenity and Film Censorship 61–95 (Home Office, Her Majesty's Stationary Office, 1979); Special Committee on Pornography and Prostitution, 1 Pornography and Prostitution in Canada 71–73, 95–103 (Canadian Government Publishing Centre 1985). In saying that we accept the finding that pornography as the ordinance defines it leads to unhappy consequences, we mean only that there is evidence to this effect, that this evidence is consistent with much human experience, and that as judges we must accept the legislative resolution of such disputed empirical questions. See Gregg v. Georgia, 428 U.S. 153, 184–87, 49 L. Ed. 2d. 859, 96 S. Ct. 2909 (1976) (opinion of Stewart, Powell, and Stevens, JJ.).

When a court is asked to declare a statute unconstitutional, it defers to the findings of fact on which the legislature based the statute if the court thinks there is any evidence supporting those findings, even if in its view that evidence is inconclusive. The court is particularly likely to give the legislature the benefit of the doubt about the facts, in that way, when it decides that the statute would be unconstitutional even if the facts were as the legislature supposed. That is what Judge Easterbrook decided in the *Hudnut* case: he held that even if pornography does cause violence, it could do so only through "mental intermediation," and the First Amendment, he said, forbids banning material because it might produce dangerous effects that way. His footnote is explicit in stating that he "accepts" the legislature's findings out of deference, for the sake of the constitutional argument. But he says more: he questions the probative force of the only evidence for the finding that he mentions, and he cites a variety of prestigious reports to the contrary, all claiming that it is impossible to show a causal connection between obscenity and rape. It seems an understatement to conclude that he did not believe that such a connection had been "demonstrated."

MacKinnon also refers to the later *Schiro* case, in which the Seventh Circuit allowed Indiana to reject a killer's defense that he had been rendered insane by reading pornography. The *Schiro* court said that it would be inconsistent for the Seventh Circuit to insist, as it had in the *Hudnut* decision, that Indiana could not ban pornography even if pornography did lead to violence, on the ground that such violence would be mediated by intellectual processes, and then to forbid Indiana to convict a killer who said that his intellectual processes had been destroyed by pornography. That argument, like the earlier *Hudnut* decision it described, "recognizes" that pornography leads to violence only in the hypothetical sense made explicit in the footnote MacKinnon omitted.

She has other complaints: she is angry that I called one of the arguments in her new book a new one. I did not mean, however, the very general argument she now mentions: that pornography should be banned because "every harm pornography does is a harm of inequality." It is indeed a familiar argument that pornography offends sexual equality by contributing to women's social, economic, and political subordination, and though MacKinnon says she is appalled that I have been unaware of that argument—she offers my failure to hear it as evidence that she herself has been "silenced"—I in fact discussed it in the essays reprinted as Chapters 9 and 10 of this book.

The argument I said I had not discussed is a much more specific constitutional thesis: that even if antipornography laws do offend the First Amendment's guarantee of free speech taken on its own, such laws should nevertheless be sustained because they protect rights that the Constitution also guarantees, through the equal protection clause of its Fourteenth Amendment. MacKinnon may mean that she has made that specific argument before; if so, I am sorry that I did not notice and consider it in an earlier article. But since I think, as I said, that the argument is a particularly bad one, I am unclear why she should be so upset that I did not. In any case, the *Hudnut* court seems to have been unaware of the constitutional argument as well: though Easterbrook referred to and discussed a wide range of both her and Andrea Dworkin's arguments, he neither mentioned nor addressed that one. I have no memory whatever, finally, of any such argument arising in the public discussion between Andrea Dworkin and myself.

It is more important that MacKinnon thinks I ignored the real point of her book, which, she says, is that pornography is not "speech" because "pornography is what it does, not what it says." I did not ignore that claim. I did say that I could find no genuine argument in it—I still can't—but I tried. I reported her suggestion that a pornographic description of a rape is itself a kind of rape, which I said is silly, and her claim that pornography is "reality" rather than speech because it produces erections and aids masturbation, which, as I said, seems an unsatisfactory basis on which to deny First Amendment protection.

She also demands that I defend my view that "being discriminated against on the basis of sex is just being 'offended.'" But I said nothing even close to that: on the contrary, I said that distributing pornography, as distinct from using it to sexually harass, does not constitute sexual discrimination. She also demands that I defend the view that pornography is about "ideas." In fact, I took care explicitly to reject that view: I said that much pornography offers no ideas at all, and that it would be wrong to base a First Amendment claim on the view that it does. I added, however, that everyone has an equal right to contribute to what I called the "moral environment"—even people whose tastes reflect no "ideas" but only very offensive "prejudices, life styles, and cultures."

Her reaction to that claim is the most disturbing part of her letter. She refers to my statement that sexists and bigots have no right that laws and institutions be sexist or bigoted, even partially, in proportion to their numbers. She is astonished ("Search me!") that, in that case, I can think that no one has a right to "stop them." I added, just after the passage she quotes, that "in a genuinely egalitarian society, however, those views cannot be locked out, in advance, by criminal or civil law: they must instead be discredited by the disgust, outrage, and ridicule of other people." MacKinnon is not satisfied: she has in mind a quicker, more chilling way of "stopping them" than that.

She ends her letter, characteristically, by picturing me and her other critics as indifferent to the suffering of women. But many feminists, including several who wrote or spoke to me about my review, regret her single-minded concentration on lurid sex. They think that though it has predictably attracted much publicity, it tends to stereotype women as victims, and takes attention from still urgent questions of economic, political, and professional equality. They deplore her alliances with right-wing groups that have produced, for example, a Canadian censorship law that, as many had warned, has been used by conservative moralists to ban gay and lesbian literature by well-known authors, a book on racial injustice by the black feminist scholar bell hooks, and, for a time, Andrea Dworkin's own feminist writing as well. MacKinnon should reflect on these suggestions that the censorship issue is not so simple-minded, so transparently gender-against-gender, as she insists. She should stop calling names long enough to ask whether personal sensationalism, hyperbole, and bad arguments are really what the cause of sexual equality now needs.

October 21, 1993
Addendum, March 3, 1994

11

▼

Why Academic Freedom?

*T*he phrase "academic freedom" collects different images and associations now than it did thirty, or maybe even ten, years ago. We thought, then, about leftist teachers and McCarthyite legislators and loyalty oaths and courageous and cowardly university presidents. Liberals and radicals were all for academic freedom. Many conservatives thought it overrated or even part of the conspiracy to paint America red. Now it is the party of reform that talks down academic freedom and conservatives who call it a bulwark of Western civilization. Now the phrase makes us think of insensitive professors and of speech codes that might protect students from their insensitivity. We wonder whether academic freedom forbids such protection, and, if so, whether academic freedom is as important as liberals once thought.

Some examples will be useful to bear in mind. I do not mean that incidents like these are everyday occurrences on American campuses, as some right-wing critics of universities suggest, or even that they have actually occurred as I describe them; I cite them because they are the kinds of events, real or exaggerated, that have generated new suspicion about and new enthusiasm for academic freedom. A professor is disciplined because he teaches that blacks are inferior to whites. Another is punished because he teaches that Jews are the enemy of blacks. A professor is severely criticized because he assigns the journals of slave-owning plantation managers as reading in a course on American history, and he does not receive what many of his colleagues consider appropriate support from university officials when students complain. Another professor is disciplined because, to illustrate a complex point in contract law, he quotes Byron's line in *Don Juan* about the woman who, whispering "I shall ne'er consent," consented, and another because he describes belly dancing as like holding a vibrator under a plate of Jell-O. The University of Michigan adopts a speech code which prohibits "any behavior, verbal or physical, that stigmatizes or victimizes an individual on the basis of race, ethnicity, religion, sex, sexual orientation, creed, national origin, ancestry, age, marital status, handicap, or Vietnam-era veteran status, and that . . . creates an intimidating, hostile or demeaning environment for educational purposes." Stanford University adopts a different speech code, which forbids speech if it "(1) is intended to insult or stigmatize an individual or a small number of individuals on the basis of their sex, race, color, handicap, religion, sexual orientation, or national and ethnic origin, (2) is addressed directly to the individual or individuals whom it insults or stigmatizes, and (3) makes use of insulting or 'fighting' words or nonverbal symbols." Each of these various events is widely deplored, and is said to constitute a violation of academic freedom.

This shift in causes célèbres has produced a new uncertainty about what academic freedom actually is. This is not surprising. Political values take their meaning from paradigms of their application, and when these shift, values that seemed obvious suddenly resist clear statement. But if the dimensions and goals of academic freedom are now uncertain, it is important that we attempt to redefine them. We must construct a fresh account of academic freedom that meets two tests. First, it must fit well enough with general understandings of what academic freedom does and does not require so that it can provide a new interpretation of an established value, not a new value altogether. Second, it must justify those general understandings as well as they can be justified; it must show why academic freedom *is* a value, so that we can judge how important it is, and whether and when it should yield to other, competing values.[1]

This interpretive project seems particularly timely when we consider the emotional dimension of the contemporary controversies. According to the most popular view of the matter, these disputes force us to choose between two values: equality—in particular, racial and gender equality—on the one hand and academic freedom on the other. This seems an emotional mismatch. Racial injustice and gender stereotyping have done terrible harm, and many American institutions rightly think it imperative to try to eradicate at least their worst consequences. These efforts, particularly in universities, make great demands on many students. Blacks, for example, are expected to compete in universities from which members of their race were largely excluded, and to pursue studies centered on cultures that they had long been taught owed nothing to and offered nothing for them. We know how raw the sensibilities of some such students must be, and we think it only right to do whatever we can to make their situation less difficult. Academic freedom, in contrast, seems an abstract and bloodless value, something to worry about, if at all, only in the long term, after these more urgent problems have been resolved.

Academic freedom has another, different, disadvantage in this supposed encounter. It is often defended on the ground that scholars must be free if they are to discover objective truth. But the very possibility of objective truth is now itself under challenge from an anti–truth-squad of relativists, subjectivists, neo-pragmatists, post-modernists, and similar critics now powerful in the unconfident departments of American universities. According to these critics academic freedom is not just bloodless but fraudulent. This relativist challenge is deeply confused. But its popularity contributes to—and is yet more evidence of—the weakness of the grip that academic freedom now has on the sentiments even of many academics.

We begin reinterpreting academic freedom by reminding ourselves of what, historically, it has been understood to require and not to require. It imposes two levels of insulation. First, it insulates universities, colleges, and other institutions of higher education from political institutions like legislatures and courts and from economic powers like large corporations. A state legislature has, of course, the right to decide which state universities to establish—whether, for example, to add an agricultural or a liberal arts college to the existing university structure. But once political officials have established such an institution, fixed its academic character and its budget, and appointed its officials, they may not dictate how those they have appointed should interpret that character or who should teach what is to be taught, or how. Second, academic freedom insulates scholars from the administrators of their universities: university officials can appoint faculty, allocate budgets to departments, and in that way decide, within limits, what curriculum will be offered. But they cannot dictate how those who have been appointed will teach what has been decided will be taught.

These might seem odd lines to draw. If a legislature may decide that a liberal arts college is what the community needs, and what budget it should have, why should it not also decide what, in detail, should be taught there, and how? Why is the latter decision not simply a continuation and elaboration of the former ones? But academic freedom makes distinctions like these—distinctions between what academic posts should be created and who should fill them, on the one hand, and how those appointed to those posts should acquit their responsibilities, on the other—critically important, and any competent interpretation must explain and justify those distinctions.

Academic freedom is plainly related to a more general and better-known political value, which is freedom of speech, and various American courts have held that central forms of academic freedom are protected by the Constitution's First Amendment. It might therefore seem natural to treat academic freedom as just the application of that more general right to the special case of academic institutions. But that would obscure much that is special about academic freedom. Free speech is a moral right—and in America a legal right, as well—for everyone. But it doesn't provide for everyone what academic freedom provides for scholars. Free speech is not, except in very special circumstances, a right to speak one's mind in a position maintained and supported by others. Legally, of course, the First Amendment applies only against government: it is not violated when private institutions impose speech restrictions as a condition of employment. Even the moral right of free speech is not normally violated by such conditions—it is not violated, for example, when a department store fires someone for denigrating its products, or when a church does not allow one of its priests to preach a rival faith from its pulpit. Free speech, at its core, is the right not to be altogether prevented from saying something, not the right to continue to be supported and aided while saying it by those who think it false or undesirable.

In that respect, academic freedom, which does require certain institutions to support and help people no matter what they write or say or teach, is stronger than the more general right of free speech. In other respects, however, it is less clearly a right, because no one is morally entitled to the status which brings that extra protection. No one is entitled to demand that a particular form of college or university be founded or remain in business. Nor is anyone entitled to an academic or administrative office within those that do exist. Indeed, apart from tenure, which is held only by some, no one is entitled to remain in such an office, even once appointed, beyond the length of a stipulated term. It seems better, therefore, not to count academic freedom as derivative from a more general right to free speech, or, indeed, to count it as involving a right at all. I shall try to show, however, that the two institutions—academic freedom and a right to free speech—are closely connected in a different way: they form important parts of a system of ideas and institutions that creates a culture of individual intellectual responsibility, and that protects it from disintegrating into a culture of intellectual conformity.

We must construct an interpretation of academic freedom that fits these general contours, and justifies the ideal they presuppose. The conventional justification of academic freedom treats it as instrumental in the discovery of truth. According to this view, a system of independent academic institutions and scholars who are independent within them provides the best chance of collectively reaching the truth about a wide range of matters, from science to art to politics. We have a better chance of discovering what is true, it declares, if we leave our academics and their institutions free from external control to the greatest degree possible.

This conventional defense of academic freedom echoes John Stuart Mill's famous defense of freedom of speech. Mill argued that truth emerges best from a marketplace of ideas from which no opinion is excluded. Though most American lawyers accept Mill's argument as the best justification for the First Amendment, that argument does not provide a convincing defense of much of the protection that the First Amendment in fact offers and that partisans of freedom of speech think right.[2] It does not adequately explain why we permit pornography, or even why we tolerate Nazis or certain fundamentalists who, if they did persuade a sufficient number of people to join their terrorism, would destroy liberty thereafter. Mill's kind of defense does seem stronger when it is applied to academic freedom than to free speech generally, however, because those whom academic freedom insulates are less likely to act from nakedly political or ideological motives than are those whose power it insulates them from. Certainly science and probably every other study in the university is more successful, judged in purely academic terms, when it is free from either political control or the dominion of commerce.

But we must nevertheless concede that on many occasions certain compromises of academic freedom might well provide even more efficient truth-seeking strategies, particularly if we want to discover not just what is true but also what is useful or important. Universities do well not to hire scholars, no matter how clever or persuasive, who are committed to ideas their colleagues think patently wrong, or trivial, or of no intellectual importance. It is unobjectionable for a biology department not to hire a creationist, or a history department someone who denies the Holocaust, or an economics department someone who will devote his career only to the special economics of the baseball card market. University resources are limited, and should not be spent on those who will occupy their time developing arguments for what is plainly false or researching what is obviously of no serious interest. Of course we know that sometimes a theory or program now dismissed as wrong or trivial will turn out to be true or crucial. But overall, given that academic resources are limited, it is better that they be allocated to scholars whose work strikes other academics as promising, rather than only on the basis of, say, the raw intelligence of researchers. This argument would not justify forbidding creationists or negationists or baseball card economists to publish their views or to roar them out at Hyde Park Corner. But it does justify university officials deciding to hire other scholars in their place. If that is so, however—if we advance truth and useful discussion by not wasting scarce academic resources on plainly false opinions or trivial projects—then why would we not advance truth even more securely by preventing scholars already in place from teaching those opinions or pursuing those projects if they were converted to them after their appointment? Academic freedom forbids this, but the Millian explanation does not seem to show why.

There is a standard reply to these worries. It is said that even if on some occasions protecting academic freedom does inhibit the search for truth, it would be worse for truth in the long run to allow any exceptions, because we could not be sure that these would be made wisely or that their effects would be limited. The only safe conditions for academic research, according to this view, are those in which academic freedom is protected without exception and with passionate commitment. That might be right, but it does involve a leap of faith. Of course some useful research would be lost if university officials had more power to direct the work of academic faculty, but some useful research would also be gained, and we cannot have any great confidence that the balance would be negative. We think the balance positive when hiring or promotion decisions must be made against scarce resources, even though we know, as I said, that officials will sometimes make mistakes. Dictating to those already on staff is different in various ways, but not so different as to make the opposite judgment compelling.

Even if we were to accept this familiar argument, and suppose that complete academic freedom will advance truth in the long run if the run is long enough, that instrumental assumption does not seem strong enough, on its own, to justify the emotional power that many of us feel academic freedom has, and that it must have if it is to hold its own now, against the moral urgency of the competing goals and ideals I mentioned. Why is it not worth some speculative loss of knowledge, at the margin of research, in order to protect people who have been victims of great social injustice from further insult, or to make their opportunity to help themselves and other members of their race or gender more genuine and effective? In a cosmic instant or two our sun will explode and all our libraries, museums, and palaces will be intergalactic ash. By then human beings and any other intelligent species that have joined us will have come to know only a tiny fraction of what might be known. How can it matter so much if we allow that fraction to be just a little tinier in order to protect some people from injury? If we want to defend academic freedom, we need a ground that better matches its emotional importance for us, and the outrage we feel when it is violated, even in the name of causes we share.

So though the conventional, instrumental defense of academic freedom is important, and at least in general valid, it is not enough. We must connect that defense to something deeper, less contingent and speculative, and more personal. I shall now argue that academic freedom plays an important *ethical* role not just in the lives of the few people it protects, but in the life of the community more generally. It is an important, structural part of the culture of independence that we need in order to lead the kind of lives that we should. An invasion of academic freedom is insulting and harmful for some because it frustrates satisfying important responsibilities, and dangerous for everyone because it weakens the culture of independence and cheapens the ideal that culture protects.

I mean the ideal of ethical individualism.[3] This insists, among its other components, that we each have responsibility for making as much of a success of our lives as we can, and that this responsibility is personal, in the sense that each of us must make up his own mind, as a matter of felt personal conviction, about what a successful life would be. Ethical individualism is the inspiration behind the institutions and attitudes of political liberalism. It supports the central core of liberal ideas that includes both freedom of speech and academic freedom, not just as a wise environment for academic discovery, but as encouragement of and protection for the primacy of individual conviction.

People who accept ethical individualism accept consequent responsibilities. The first is the responsibility not to profess what one believes to be false. This duty is protected, in liberal societies, by a right of conscience that forbids forcing people to religious or moral or political declaration against their will. The second is a more positive responsibility of affirmation: it is a duty to speak out for what one believes to be true. According to ethical individualism, we all have that duty as citizens: it is wrong to remain silent when our society must make a collective decision and we believe we have information or opinion it should take into account. We have that responsibility even when we know that our opinion will not be heeded—when the state acts unjustly, for example, and we know we can only bear witness to our anger at what it does in our name. That sense of responsibility, and of the moral damage done when we are prevented from exercising it, is part of the medley of reasons that together make it so important to us, as individuals, that we have a general right of free speech on political matters.

Some social roles and professions incorporate heightened versions of this personal responsibility. The character of that special responsibility varies. Salesmen should not lie, but need not give their customers commercially neutral advice. Priests are responsible for the whole truth, but need not remain in the pulpit, after they have lost their faith, to explain why their parishioners should abandon that faith as well. Doctors' duties are more inalienable: they must tell their patients what they believe it is in the patient's best interests to hear, and must not accept any external limit on that responsibility. That is one reason why the Reagan administration's order forbidding federally financed doctors from even discussing abortion with their patients was so outrageous. The Supreme Court, in a widely criticized decision, upheld that regulation, on the ground that it is no invasion of the First Amendment to condition the receipt of federal funds on not speaking in defined ways.[4] That was a mistake in law, I believe, but the administration's order was a disgrace in any case, because it ignored the deep responsibility of the moral role of a physician, and the moral harm that follows from frustrating it.[5] The regulation forced doctors to choose between ignoring one of two responsibilities, each cardinal to their professional ethics: not to abandon patients, and to care for them in the way that they, the doctors, think best. So the administrative order, which was withdrawn as one of the first acts of the Clinton administration, violated the principle we might call medical freedom.

Professors and others who teach and study in universities have an even more general and uncompromising responsibility. They have a paradigmatic duty to discover and teach what they find important and true, and this duty is not, even to the degree that medical responsibility may be, subject to any qualification about the best interests of those to whom they speak. It is an undiluted responsibility to the truth, and it is, in that way, the closest a professional responsibility can come to the fundamental ethical responsibility each of us has, according to the ideals of ethical individualism, to live his life in accordance with his own felt convictions.

We have just noticed part of the ethical justification for academic freedom: the institution protects people in a particular role—students and scholars—from the moral damage of frustration in their special responsibilities. But those responsibilities are imposed by conventional understandings—by institutional assignments that might have been different—so we must now consider whether they serve an important purpose and so should be maintained and protected. Why should we have academic institutions whose professors and students and officials are dedicated to discovering and transmitting truth as they individually, one by one, see it?

Ethical individualism needs a particular kind of culture—a culture of independence—in which to flourish. Its enemy is the opposite culture—the culture of conformity, of Khoumeni's Iran, Torquemada's Spain, and Joe McCarthy's America—in which truth is collected not person by person, in acts of independent conviction, but is embedded in monolithic traditions or the fiats of priesthood or junta or majority vote, and dissent from that truth is treason. That totalitarian epistemology—searingly identified in the finally successful campaign of Orwell's dictator to make his victim believe, through torture, that two and two is five—is tyranny's most frightening feature.

Liberal public education, freedom of speech, conscience, and religion, and academic freedom are all parts of our society's support for a culture of independence and of its defense against a culture of conformity. Academic freedom plays a special role because educational institutions are pivotal to those efforts. They are pivotal, first, because they can so easily become engines of conformity, as every totalitarian regime has realized, and, second, because they can provide important encouragement and skills for a life of personal conviction. Part of the point of education, in a liberal society, is learning the importance and depth of an allegiance to personal rather than collective truth. Academic freedom is also important symbolically, because in a free academy the example and virtues of ethical individualism are so patently on display. In no other occupation is it so plainly and evidently the responsibility of professionals to find and tell and teach the truth as they see it. Scholars exist for that, and only for that. A culture of independence values learning "for its own sake" because such learning is also, in that way, for that culture's sake as well.

I should summarize this part of the argument. Academic freedom represents and reinforces the ideals of ethical individualism. It exhibits those ideals in the most appropriate context by creating a theater in which personal conviction about truth and value is all that matters, and it trains scholars and students alike in the skills and attitudes essential to a culture of independence. So any violation of academic freedom is damaging in manifold ways. It is morally harmful to those whose freedom to speak or write or teach is restricted, because a deep responsibility is thereby thwarted. It is morally harmful to those whose learning is corrupted by the same restriction. It damages the general culture of independence that academic freedom nourishes, because any invasion of academic freedom is not only harmful in itself but makes future invasions more likely. And it insults, for everyone, the ideals of ethical individualism, because the scholar serving only his own vision of the truth is a crucial symbol as well as an important progenitor of that ethical ideal. All this is at stake and put in jeopardy every time a teacher is told what or what not to teach or how to teach it.

That is the ethical justification of academic freedom, and it provides a complementary and more comprehensive justification than the conventional, explicitly instrumental, Millian justification. The ethical justification supplies the emotional weight that the instrumental argument cannot. It may now be said that the symbolic and other roles I just claimed for academic freedom are real for only a small fraction of the population— only, perhaps, for a minority even of those who have been university students. I suspect, to the contrary, that the pride that people with no higher education take in local and national universities indicates that a much wider community shares the values I am trying to describe. But if I am wrong, and only a minority now believes that academic freedom has ethical importance, that argues for more rather than less attention to the ethical argument. We hope, after all, that the best forms of education will be available to an ever-growing share of the community, and the ideals of personal conviction, intellectual integrity, and ethical independence are essential to that goal.

We may now return to the crucial test that I said any competent interpretation of academic freedom must meet. That ideal insists on distinctions that, as I said, might seem bizarre at first sight. The key distinction, as I stated it, is between the power of politicians and university officials and colleagues to design institutions and appoint scholars, which academic freedom allows, and their power to control what those scholars do once appointed, which academic freedom prohibits. That distinction might indeed seem odd if we thought that academic freedom served only the instrumental goal of encouraging discovery. Then we might have to concede, as I said, that if it is wise to let officials appoint on the basis of their own judgment about the importance of what a scholar is likely to do, it must also be wise to allow them to correct for mistakes, so far as possible, by disciplining someone already appointed. But from the different ethical perspective we have now developed, the distinction is not only sensible but central. The principle of individual responsibility is not violated when politicians choose university presidents or presidents choose professors on the basis of some collective or institutional opinion about where truth lies. But it is violated when they dictate to faculty after appointment, because then people whose responsibility is to speak and write and teach truth as they see it are prevented from doing so. It is the frustration of responsibility in place that seems so outrageous and so offensive to the ethical ideals we ought to cherish.

Though academic freedom is a profound value, for all the reasons we have now noticed, it is nevertheless only one value among many. We wanted a new interpretation of academic freedom in order to respond to new challenges to that old ideal. How do we choose when academic freedom conflicts with something else that is also important, like equality or decency? We should notice, first, an important distinction between two different kinds of argument for resisting the claim of a conceded value. The first argues for a limit to that value: it suggests that on the best interpretation its point or underlying justification has no application in the case at hand. That is the claim someone makes, for example, when he insists that the sanctity of human life, which is normally outraged by any deliberate killing, is not outraged when a doctor administers a lethal injection to a terminally ill patient who genuinely wants to die. On this view, the conflict is illusory, because the sanctity of life, properly understood, is not violated by such a killing.[6] The second is an argument not for recognizing the limits of a value, but for accepting a compromise of it because though the point of the value does extend to the case in question, its force is nevertheless overridden by a competing value. That is the claim of those who accept free speech as an important value, but nevertheless endorse censorship when it is necessary to protect national security. The distinction is important in the present context, because many of the cases in which people feel strongly that academic freedom must yield to a competing value are actually cases in which the rationale for academic freedom does not apply: they are cases defining the limits of that rationale, not cases suggesting any degraded importance when it really is at stake.

Deliberate insults—by which I mean statements or displays whose principal motive is to cause injury or distress or some other kind of harm—are not even in principle covered by the idea of academic freedom, on either the instrumental or ethical understandings of that value. So when a university prohibits or discourages such insult, it is recognizing the limits of the doctrine, not compromising it. But we must take very great care to distinguish cases when the insult is intentional from cases in which it is not, though the wound may be as great. Intentional harm is generally graver than nonintentional harm; as Oliver Wendell Holmes once said, even a dog knows the difference between being kicked and being stumbled over. But the distinction is important now not for that reason but because though intentional insult is not covered by academic freedom, negligent insult must be.

The distinction between the two is often hard to draw in practice, not only because motives are often obscure and hidden even from the agent whose motives they are, but because people often act with mixed motives: someone who declares that women are weak in abstract reasoning may at once express a biological opinion he sincerely believes and at the same time hope to outrage and insult part of his audience. But since we are describing a limit to an important protection, we should define intentional insult narrowly. We should use the counter-factual test: Would the speaker have said what he did if he did not believe it would cause distress? It is easy to answer that question in some contexts. Few people would bother to burn crosses if they believed that blacks would simply be amused at the sight; few people would shout "nigger" or "kike" at someone they thought would be charmed by the sound of the word. The person who nailed a laundry list to the door of a Chinese-American student at Stanford was not indifferent to whether seeing it there would cause her pain. I am not, of course, urging this test as a limit to the general right of free speech, or to the legal protection of the First Amendment. It would be a clear violation of that right for the legislature to outlaw all speech designed to wound. But the distinct point and virtues of academic freedom would not then be in play. A university may properly demand an atmosphere of decency in which neither faculty nor groups of students act with the intention of intimidating or embarrassing or hurting anyone in the community, and insofar as speech codes banned only such behavior they would be consistent with academic freedom even when (because the university in question was a public institution) they violated the First Amendment. We can safely extend this limit to academic freedom to include language or display that might be called insulting per se, because its meaning in contemporary diction includes insult. Addressing a black student as "boy" or "girl," or wearing a white hood to class, or blazoning a swastika or a *Playboy* centerfold on the wall of an office which students are invited or expected to visit is in itself an insult, and a university can reasonably demand, consistently with academic freedom, that its students and faculty express their opinions in other ways.

Most of the cases that have attracted recent attention, however, are cases in which a student or professor is accused not of wounding some student or group of students intentionally, in the strong sense that the counter-factual test picks out, or of using language that is insulting per se, but of acting with what has come to be called, in a new runic phrase, "insensitivity"—acting, that is, without due consideration of the injury his remarks are likely to cause. The examples of allegedly offensive remarks I cited earlier all fall into that category. The professors who assigned slave-owners' journals or quoted Byron or talked about vibrators were accused of insensitivity, and it is unlikely that any of them even expected, let alone intended, to injure. In other cases, though a teacher with any sense would indeed expect to injure or offend by defending some thesis—that women are not as good at abstract reasoning as men, for example—he would probably not intend that harm either. He would prefer, however unreasonable or silly or unlikely this might be, that women not be offended by his remarks, but take them in a constructive spirit. So the exception for remarks intended to wound, while important, does not reach the cases that have provoked the greatest controversy and pose the most important threats to academic freedom.

So we come, finally, to what is undoubtedly the crucial question. What should academic officials do about culpable insensitivity? Compare the "hate speech" code that Stanford University adopted with that of the University of Michigan, which was held unconstitutional. The former forbids speech if it "(1) is intended to insult or stigmatize an individual or a small number of individuals on the basis of their sex, race, color, handicap, religion, sexual orientation, or national and ethnic origin, (2) is addressed directly to the individual or individuals whom it insults or stigmatizes, and (3) makes use of insulting or 'fighting' words or nonverbal symbols." If "intended to insult or stigmatize" is given the strong sense I described—if no one intends to insult or stigmatize unless he would not have spoken as he did if he did not think the target of his remarks would feel insulted or stigmatized—then the Stanford code does not offend against academic freedom, though, as I said, it is a different question whether it violates the broader and more general moral right of free speech.[7] Michigan, on the other hand, forbade "any behavior, verbal or physical, that stigmatizes or victimizes an individual on the basis of race, ethnicity, religion, sex, sexual orientation, creed, national origin, ancestry, age, marital status, handicap, or Vietnam-era veteran status, and that . . . creates an intimidating, hostile or demeaning environment for educational purposes." There is no requirement of intention in the strict sense I described, so Michigan's code would presumably have allowed the university to punish a lecturer on American history who defended the motives of plantation owners or a student's honest statement that he could not help thinking that homosexuals defy nature's laws. The unvarnished expression of either of these opinions in a classroom might well be felt as insulting and stigmatizing, and might well create a hostile and demeaning environment for some and perhaps many students. Nevertheless, their expression falls within the protection of academic freedom. Prohibiting or punishing such opinions would violate the principle that people must be free to state what they believe to be important and true, in language they believe most precise and apt.

But that is not the end of the story. For academic freedom is, as I said, only one value among many, and we can recognize and honor it while nevertheless insisting that it must sometimes be compromised to protect what is, in context, a more important or urgent one. The argument that it should be compromised now, to protect students from racial or gender insensitivity, can take two very different forms. The first is an argument of policy. Our political, civil, and commercial societies still suffer from the effects of racism and sexism. In some ways the situation is worse than ever: the gap between white and black income and share of wealth continues to increase, for example. Universities have a critical role in helping to reduce the injustice: many of them have changed their admissions policies and their curricula to admit and welcome students who would formerly have been excluded, and to increase the awareness in all students of problems, contributions, and cultures that were formerly virtually ignored. But the insensitivity of some professors and fellow students undermines these important goals. It makes students who should be welcomed feel unwelcome, and it reinforces racist and sexist attitudes that universities aim to marginalize. So, according to this argument of policy, it is irrational to tolerate academic insensitivity, because that is arming the enemy we mean to fight.

Ethical values like academic freedom should yield to public policy only when the need for them to yield is both great and evident, and we do not have clear enough ground for thinking that speech codes or other weapons of censorship would do much to help reduce prejudice. There is no real evidence either way, but it seems equally likely that such measures exacerbate prejudice by allowing its more subtle forms to wear masks of outrage against censorship. In any case, censorship plainly is the enemy, not the friend, of equality in the long run. For as far back as we care to inspect, intellectuals and academics have crowded the bow of the egalitarian movement, and those who hate equality have made it a priority to try to silence them. Times change, of course, but not in that respect. If critics of academic freedom succeed in teaching the public at large that that ideal is overrated, and may be set aside in the interests of attractive social goals, the lesson will be studied in other than egalitarian constituencies. If some people think racial and gender equality are urgent goals, others—and there may well be more of them—think it more urgent that the decline in family values and traditional virtues be halted, and they will be glad of a chance to dictate that university curricula emphasize those virtues and avoid texts that question them, particularly those in which homosexuality and other "different" styles of life are celebrated. I am only repeating an old liberal warning. But it is a warning that cannot be repeated often enough. Censorship will always prove a traitor to justice.

The second version of the argument for compromising academic freedom is very different. It is not an argument of policy, which can only trump an important value if the beneficial results are crucial and evident, but an argument of principle, which, if it is sound, has much greater imperative force. People in a pluralistic society have a right, this argument of principle insists, to work and study and live in an environment that is free from statements or displays they reasonably take to be denigrating or humiliating. On this view, whatever compromises in academic freedom are required to prevent insensitive insults are not limited and temporary adjustments to a special and urgent need, as they are according to the argument of policy. They are rather permanent, structural features of any just community.

This argument of principle has an impressive shape, because it appeals to a competing right rather than an overriding policy, and we know that the closely related value of free speech is sometimes properly compromised out of concern for competing rights. A great volume of literature, it is true, attempts to treat cases in which freedom of speech is set aside as cases of limit rather than compromise. It attempts, for example, to define "speech" so that occasions when censorship is permissible can be treated as cases in which free speech has not been denied. Someone who uses "fighting words" that are very likely to produce immediate violence, for example, is not protected by the First Amendment, and it is often said, by way of justifying that exemption, that he has crossed the line that separates "speech" from "action." But the most energetic constitutional scholarship has not been able to clarify this distinction; in fact, these and similar examples are better understood as cases of compromise of the right of free speech in deference to other rights that are, in context, more urgently or centrally at stake. We have a right to physical security, for example, and it is that right, rather than any mysterious infusion of "action" into "speech" that best explains why shouting "lynch him!" to a mob with a rope, or putting out a Mafia contract, or falsely shouting fire in a crowded theater cannot be protected.

The argument of principle I just described, however, goes far beyond justifying limited constraints on speech like that one. It demands prohibiting any expression or display that might reasonably be thought to embarrass anyone or lower others' esteem for them or their own self-respect. The idea that people have *that* right is absurd. Of course it would be good if everyone liked and respected everyone else who merited that response. But we cannot recognize a right to respect, or a right to be free from the effects of speech that makes respect less likely, without wholly subverting the central ideals of the culture of independence and denying the ethical individualism that that culture protects. Popular opinions and prejudices of any society will always be hurtful to some of its members. Terrible insults are offered every day, in some American community or other, to creationists and religious fundamentalists, to people who believe that homosexuality is deeply sinful or that sex is proper only within marriage, to those who think that God forbids surgery or penicillin or demands holy wars, to people who think that Norman Rockwell was the only great artist of the century, or that Hallmark cards are moving or that Sousa marches are great music, to people who are short or fat or just plain slow. People of a thousand different convictions or shapes or tastes understandably feel ridiculed or insulted by every level of speech and publication in every decent democracy in the world.

A culture of independence almost guarantees that this will be so. Certainly, we should be decent to one another, and bigotry is despicable. But if we really came to think that we violated other people's rights whenever we reported sincere views that denigrated them in their own or others' eyes, we would have compromised our own sense of what it is to live honestly. We must find other, less suicidal, weapons against racism and sexism. We must, as always, put our faith in freedom, not repression.[8]

I will attempt no new summary of my argument, but offer a short exhortation instead. I have been guilty of what must seem an absurd degree of professional hubris and cheerleading. I claim that my own profession—the weak battalions of university teachers—carries much of the responsibility for maintaining a magnificent ethical tradition, and that we must defend our freedom, with passion and whatever strength we all together have, on that ground. We have lately become less confident of our importance, and less ready to insist on our independence. We have allowed academic freedom to seem pale and abstract and even fraudulent. But we must now remember how easy it has proved, elsewhere, for that freedom to be lost, and how hard it is to regain once lost. We do carry a great responsibility, and it is time we carried it once again with pride.

June 1995

III

JUDGES

THERE MAY BE NATIONS where people think it doesn't matter who the judges are, that the law is a mechanical system like a calculator that anyone with the proper training can and will manipulate to the same result. But no one thinks that in America. On the contrary, it is a common objection against the American constitutional tradition, which gives courts power to invalidate acts of Congress and the state legislatures, that when that power is exercised depends not on fixed law but on who the judges— particularly the justices of the Supreme Court—happen to be. The moral reading acknowledges this to be inevitable: the abstract moral proposi- tions of the Bill of Rights do not enforce themselves, and though the interpretive latitude open to any judge on any constitutional occasion is limited by history and integrity, in the ways I tried to describe in the Introduction and in Chapter 2, a judge's political convictions will in many cases figure in his or her account of which interpretation is the most accurate.

The chapters of this part discuss the constitutional convictions of three important judges, whose political convictions have all influenced Ameri- can law, though in very different ways. Robert Bork's greatest contribu- tion to constitutional jurisprudence lay in a failure—in his unsuccessful attempt to be confirmed, after his nomination by President Reagan, as a Supreme Court justice. Three chapters are devoted to this important story. Chapter 12 was written after Reagan nominated Bork, but before the Senate hearings had begun. I argued that it was proper to inspect a prospective justice's constitutional philosophy to decide whether his ap- pointment should be confirmed, and I suggested, on that basis, that Bork's should not be. Chapter 13 was written after the Senate had finally defeated the nomination; I considered what lesson should be drawn from that event. Bork wrote a book offering his own answer to that question, and in Chapter 14 I assessed and rejected his answer. It might seem odd to devote three chapters to a single event in constitutional history, and, in retrospect, I am surprised at the depth of the indignation I expressed over Bork's views. But, as I argue in these chapters, his defeat was a decisive test for the moral reading, because he was throughout his career a declared if inconsis- tent opponent of it, and his nomination provided the most explicit public discussion in history of its role in constitutional interpretation.

Justice Thomas has also become a declared opponent of the moral reading, though, as I argue in Chapter 15, he was once a conservative advocate of it. That chapter was published after Bush had nominated Thomas to the Supreme Court, and immediately after public attention had been diverted from the important issue of his qualifications to the much more sensational issues raised by the charge of his one-time assistant, Professor Anita Hill, that he had sexually harassed her. I tried to direct readers' attention to what I believed to be Thomas's serious deficiencies as a potential Supreme Court justice. He was, in the end, confirmed, and we and our children will continue to face the consequences, for better or worse, for a long time. Chapter 16 is mainly concerned with Hill's charges, the Senate Judiciary Committee's lamentable investigation of them, and the black community's responses to them. None of that has much to do with the moral reading, but it is instructive in many other ways about the judge, race relations, and the nation.

Chapter 17 is about a great judge who, as I said in the Introduction, accepted the moral reading but drew from it the radical view that the Supreme Court should not be the ultimate arbiter of what the Constitution means. The chapter is more personal than the others, because Judge Hand was my boss and my friend. I do not include it for that reason, but I am happy that I have a better one.

12

▼

Bork: The Senate's Responsibility

*P*resident Reagan's nomination of Judge Robert Bork to succeed Justice Lewis Powell on the Supreme Court presents the Senate with an unusual problem. For Bork's views do not lie within the scope of the longstanding debate between liberals and conservatives about the proper role of the Supreme Court. Bork is a constitutional radical who rejects a requirement of the rule of law that all sides in that debate had previously accepted. He rejects the view that the Supreme Court must test its interpretations of the Constitution against the principles latent in its own past decisions as well as other aspects of the nation's constitutional history. He regards central parts of settled constitutional doctrine as mistakes now open to repeal by a right-wing court; and conservative as well as liberal senators should be troubled by the fact that, as I shall argue here, he has so far offered no coherent justifications for this radical, antilegal position.

It would be improper for senators to reject a prospective justice just because they disagreed with his or her detailed views about constitutional issues. But the Senate does have a constitutional responsibility in the process of Supreme Court appointments, beyond ensuring that a nominee is not a crook or a fool. The Constitution is a tradition as well as a document, and the Senate must satisfy itself that a nominee intends in good faith to join and help to interpret that tradition in a lawyerlike way, not to challenge and replace it out of some radical political vision that legal argument can never touch.

The Senate's responsibility is particularly great in the circumstances of the Bork nomination. Bork is the third justice added to the Court by an administration that has for seven years conducted an open and inflexible campaign of ideological appointments on all levels of the federal courts, hoping to make them a seat of right-wing power long after the administration ends. Reagan made no effort to disguise the political character of Bork's appointment: he said that Bork is "widely regarded as the most prominent and intellectually powerful advocate of judicial restraint," and that he "shares my view" of the proper role of the Court. Conservative pressure groups are already raising money to support the nomination, and the right-wing *New York Post* has challenged liberals to "make our day" by opposing it.

Bork's appointment, if confirmed, promises to achieve the dominance of the right on the Supreme Court that Reagan's previous appointments failed to secure. For Justice Powell has been a swing vote, siding mainly with the right on issues of criminal law but with more liberal justices on other issues of individual rights, and he has provided the fifth and conclusive vote, one way or the other, on many occasions. If Bork votes as those who support him have every reason to expect he will, the Court will have lost the balance that Powell provided, and it will have lost the opportunity for cases to be decided one by one on the issues, rather than on some simple ideological test. So the Senate should not apply the relaxed standards it does when a President seeks merely to have his own constitutional philosophy represented on the Supreme Court. The Bork nomination is the climactic stage of a very different presidential ambition: to freeze that institution, for as long as possible, into an orthodoxy of the President's own design.

Few nominees, moreover, have so clearly and definitively announced their positions on matters they are likely to face if confirmed. Bork has declared, for example, that the Supreme Court's decision in *Roe v. Wade,* which limited a state's power to make abortion criminal, was itself "unconstitutional," that the Constitution plainly recognizes the propriety of the death penalty, and that the Court's long string of decisions implementing the "one man, one vote" principle in national and local elections was seriously mistaken. He has called the suggestion that moral minorities such as homosexuals might have constitutional rights against discrimination legally absurd, and has doubted the wisdom of the constitutional rule that the police may not use illegally obtained evidence in a criminal trial. In a dissenting opinion on the circuit court, which the majority said contradicted strong Supreme Court precedent, he said that Congress cannot challenge in court the constitutionality of the President's acts.

The *New York Times* reports White House officials as confident, moreover, that Bork will support the administration's extreme position against affirmative action, which the Supreme Court has rejected in several close votes. And Bork has strongly suggested that he would be ready, as a justice, to reverse past Supreme Court decisions he disapproved of. ("The Court," he said, "ought to be always open to rethinking constitutional problems.") Nominees often decline to answer senators' detailed questions about their views on particular issues, out of a fear that public announcement would jeopardize their freedom of decision later. But Bork has given his own extreme views such publicity that senators need not scruple to ask him to defend them.

Most commentators have assumed that Bork has a well-worked-out constitutional theory, one that is evident and straightforward, though very conservative. The Constitution has nothing in it, Bork says, except what the "framers"—"those who drafted, proposed and ratified its provisions and various amendments"—put there. When a case requires the justices to fix the meaning of an abstract constitutional proposition, such as the requirement of the Fourteenth Amendment that government not deny any person "equal protection" of the law, they should, according to Bork, be guided by the intention of the framers, and nothing more. If they go beyond what the framers intended, then they are relying on "moral precepts" and "abstract philosophy," and therefore are acting as judicial tyrants, usurping authority that belongs to the people. That, Bork believes, is exactly what the Supreme Court did when it decided the abortion case, the one-man-one-vote cases, the death penalty and affirmative action cases, and the other cases of which he disapproves.

Is that an adequate theoretical explanation of his radical constitutional positions? The idea that the Constitution should be limited to the intentions of the framers has been very popular among right-wing lawyers since Attorney General Meese proclaimed it the official jurisprudence of the Reagan administration. It has been widely criticized, in familiar arguments that neither Bork nor any member of the administration has answered.[1] I shall not pursue those arguments here, however, because I am interested, as I said, in a different issue: not whether Bork has a persuasive or plausible constitutional philosophy, but whether he has any constitutional philosophy at all.

In order to explain my doubts I must describe, in some detail, the way Bork actually uses the idea of original intention in his legal arguments. He offered his most elaborate account of that idea in an article written many years ago, discussing the Supreme Court's famous decision in *Brown v. Board of Education,* which used the equal protection clause to declare racial segregation of public schools unconstitutional.[2] The *Brown* case is a potential embarrassment to any theory that emphasizes the importance of the framers' intentions. For there is no evidence that any substantial number of the congressmen who proposed the Fourteenth Amendment thought or hoped that it would be understood as making racially segregated education illegal. In fact, there is the strongest possible evidence to the contrary. The floor manager of the bill that preceded the amendment told the House of Representatives that "civil rights do not mean that all children shall attend the same school," and the same Congress continued the racial segregation of the schools of the District of Columbia, which it then administered.[3]

When the Supreme Court nevertheless decided, in 1954, that the Fourteenth Amendment forbids such segregation, many distinguished constitutional scholars, including the eminent judge Learned Hand and a distinguished law professor, Herbert Wechsler, had serious misgivings. But the decision has by now become so firmly accepted, and so widely hailed as a paradigm of constitutional statesmanship, that it acts as an informal test of constitutional theories. No theory seems acceptable that condemns that decision as a mistake. (I doubt that any Supreme Court nominee would be confirmed if he now said that he thought it wrongly decided.) So Bork's discussion of *Brown v. Board of Education* provides a useful test of what he actually means when he says that the Supreme Court must never depart from the original intention of the framers.

Bork says that the *Brown* case was rightly decided because the original intention that judges should consult is not some set of very concrete opinions the framers might have had, about what would or would not fall within the scope of the general principle they meant to lay down, but the general principle itself. Once judges have identified the principle the framers enacted, then they must enforce it *as* a principle, according to their *own* judgment about what it requires in particular cases, even if that means applying it not only in circumstances the framers did not contemplate, but in ways they would not have approved had they been asked.

Since the framers of the Fourteenth Amendment did not believe they were making segregated schools unconstitutional, nothing less than that expansive interpretation of "original intention" could justify *Brown* as a decision faithful to their intent. And Bork has made it plain on many other occasions that the expansive interpretation is what he has in mind. In a recent case in the District of Columbia Circuit Court of Appeals, for example, he joined a majority decision declaring that the First Amendment protected newspaper columnists from a libel suit brought by a Marxist political scientist after they had reported that he had no standing in his profession.[4] Bork's then colleague on that court, Antonin Scalia, who has since been promoted by Reagan to the Supreme Court, dissented, and chided Bork and the other members of the majority as being faithless to the intention of the framers of the First Amendment, who plainly did not suppose that they were changing the law of libel in the way the majority decision assumed. Bork replied, once again, by insisting that a judge's responsibility is not to the particular concrete opinions the framers might or might not have had about the scope of the First Amendment principle they created, but to that principle itself, which, in his view, required that the press be protected from libel suits in ways the framers would not have anticipated.

That seems right. If we are to accept the thesis that the Constitution is limited to what the framers intended it to be, then we must understand their intentions as large and abstract convictions of principle, not narrow opinions about particular issues. But understanding their intentions that way gives a much greater responsibility to judges than Bork's repeated claims about judicial restraint suggest. For then any description of original intention is a conclusion that must be justified not by history alone, but by some very different form of argument.

History alone might be able to show that some particular concrete opinion, like the opinion that school segregation was not unconstitutional, was widely shared within the group of legislators and others mainly responsible for a constitutional amendment. But it can never determine precisely which general principle or value it would be right to attribute to them. This is so not because we might fail to gather enough evidence, but for the more fundamental reason that people's convictions do not divide themselves neatly into general principles and concrete applications. Rather they take the form of a more complex structure of layers of generality, so that people regard most of their convictions as applications of further principles or values more general still. That means that a judge will have a choice among more or less abstract descriptions of the principle that he regards the framers as having entrusted to his safekeeping, and the actual decisions he makes, in the exercise of that responsibility, will critically depend upon which description he chooses.

I must illustrate that point in order to explain it, and again I can draw on Bork's own arguments to do so.[5] In his discussion of the *Brown* case, he proposed a particular principle of equality as the general principle judges should assign to the framers: the principle that government may not discriminate on grounds of race. But he might just as well have assigned them a more abstract and general principle still: that government ought not to discriminate against any minority when the discrimination reflects only prejudice. The equal protection clause of the Fourteenth Amendment does not, after all, mention race. It says only that government must not deny any person equal protection of the law. The Fourteenth Amendment was, of course, adopted after and in consequence of the Civil War, which was fought over slavery. But Lincoln said the war was fought to test the proposition that *all* men are created equal, and of course he meant women as well. In any case it would be preposterous to think that the statesmen who created the equal protection clause thought that official prejudice was offensive only in the case of race. They thought that official racial discrimination was outrageous because they held some more general principle condemning all forms of official prejudice. Indeed, their views about race would not have been *moral* views, which they plainly were, unless they held them in virtue of some more general principle of that sort.

Then why should judges not attempt to define and enforce that more general principle? Why should they not say that the framers enacted a principle that outlaws any form of official discrimination based on prejudice? It would follow that the equal protection clause protects women, for example, as well as blacks from discriminatory legislation. The framers apparently did not think that their principle had that range; they did not think that gender distinctions reflected stereotype or prejudice. (It took a later constitutional amendment, after all, to give women the vote.) But once we have defined the principle we attribute to the framers in the more abstract way, we must treat their views about women as misunderstandings of the force of their own principle, which time has given us the vision to correct, just as we treat their views about racially segregated education. That, in effect, is what the Supreme Court has done.[6] But now consider the case of homosexuals. Bork called the suggestion that homosexuals are protected by the Constitution a blatant example of trying to amend that document by illegitimate fiat. But once we have stated the framers' intention as a general principle condemning all discrimination based on prejudice, then a strong case can be made that we must recognize homosexual rights against such discrimination in order to be faithful to that intention.

The framers might not have agreed, even if they had examined the question. But once again a judge might well think himself forced, in all intellectual honesty, to regard that as another mistake they would have made, comparable to their mistakes about school segregation and women. Once again, as in those cases, time has given us the information and understanding that they lacked. Superstitions about homosexuality have been exposed and disproved, many states have repealed laws making homosexual acts criminal, and those laws that remain are very widely regarded as now based on nothing but prejudice. I do not mean to claim that the argument in favor of homosexual rights would be irresistible if we accepted the broader reading of original intention that I described. But the argument would state a strong case that any opponent would have to answer in detail, not simply brush aside as Bork did.[7]

An appeal to the framers' intention, in other words, decides nothing until some choice is made about the right way to formulate that intention on any particular issue. If we choose the narrowest, most concrete formulation of original intention, which fixes on the discrete expressed opinions of the framers and ignores the more general moral vision they were trying to serve, then we must regard *Brown* as unfaithful to the framers' will; and that conclusion will seem to most people ample evidence that the most concrete formulation is the wrong one. If we assign to the framers a principle that is sufficiently general not to seem arbitrary and ad hoc, on the other hand, like the principle that government must not discriminate on grounds of prejudice, then many of the decisions Bork castigates as illegitimate become proper according to the standards Bork himself claims to endorse.

So everything depends on the level of generality a judge chooses as the appropriate one, and he must have some reason for his choice. Bork chooses a level intermediate between the two I just described.[8] He says that judges should assign the framers a principle limited to the groups or topics they actually discussed. If race was discussed during the debate over the equal protection clause, but neither gender nor sexual behavior was "under discussion," then the original intention includes the principle that government should not discriminate racially. It does not include the more general principle that the government should not act out of prejudice against any group of citizens, because that more general principle would apply to women and homosexuals, who were not discussed. The odd suggestion that we can assign no general principle to the framers whose application would extend to any group or topic not "under discussion" would of course sharply limit the individual rights the Constitution would protect. But it is flatly inconsistent with Bork's other opinions—the framers of the First Amendment did not discuss the law of libel, for example. And it has no jurisprudential or historical merit at all.

There is no more sense in assigning the framers an intention to protect only the groups they actually mentioned than in assigning them an intention limited to the concrete applications they actually envisioned, which Bork agrees would be absurd. The framers meant to enact a moral principle of constitutional dimensions, and they used broad and abstract language appropriate to that aim. Of course they discussed only the applications of the principle that were most on their minds, but they intended their discussion to draw on the more general principle, not eviscerate it. Perhaps they disagreed among themselves about what their principle would require, beyond the issues they discussed. And contemporary judges, with more information, may think it requires legal decisions few if any of the framers anticipated, as in the case of segregated schools and gender discrimination. But Bork's suggestion insults the framers rather than respects them, because it denies that they were acting on principle at all. It reduces a constitutional vision to a set of arbitrary and isolated decrees.

Bork defends this truncated view of original intention only by appealing to the platitude that judges must choose "no level of generality higher than that which interpretation of the words, structure, and history of the Constitution fairly supports." That is certainly true, but unhelpful, unless Bork can produce an argument that his own, truncated conception meets that test; and he has not, so far as I am aware, produced even the beginning of such an argument. His conception yields narrow constitutional rules that protect only a few groups while excluding others in the same moral position. How can a discriminatory rule of that sort count as a fair interpretation of the wholly general and abstract language that the framers actually used when they referred to equal protection for all persons? Most lawyers think that the ideal of integrity of principle—that fundamental rights recognized for one group extend to all—is central to the Constitution's structure. How, then, can Bork's narrow rules be recommended by any fair interpretation of that structure? Unless he can produce some genuine argument for his curtailed view of original intention, beyond the fact that it produces decisions he and his supporters approve, his constitutional philosophy is empty: not just impoverished and unattractive but no philosophy at all.

Judges in the mainstream of our constitutional practice are much more respectful of the framers' intentions, understood as a matter of principle, than Bork is. They accept the responsibility the framers imposed on them, to develop legal principles of moral breadth to protect the rights of individuals against the majority. That responsibility requires judgment and skill, but it does not give judges political license. They test competing principles in the interpretative, legal manner, by asking how far each fits the framers' decisions and helps to make sense of them, not as isolated historical events but as part of a constitutional tradition that includes the general structure of the Constitution as well as past Supreme Court and other judicial decisions. Of course competent and responsible judges disagree about the results of that exercise. Some reach mainly conservative results and others mainly liberal ones. Some, like Justice Powell, resist classification because their views are particularly sensitive to differences between different kinds of issues. Disagreement is inevitable, but the responsibility each judge accepts, of testing the principles he or she proposes in that way, disciplines each judge's work, and concentrates and deepens constitutional debate.

Bork, however, disdains these familiar methods of legal argument and analysis; he believes he has no responsibility to treat the Constitution as an integrated structure of moral and political principles, and no responsibility to respect the principles latent in past Supreme Court decisions he regrets were made.[9] In 1971 he subscribed to an alarming moral theory in an effort to explain why.[10] He said that moral opinions were simply sources of what he called "gratification," and that "there is no principled way to decide that one man's gratifications are more deserving of respect than another's, or that one form of gratification is more worthy than another." Taken at face value, that means that no one could have a principled reason for preferring the satisfactions of charity or justice, for example, to those of racism or rape.

A crude moral skeptic is an odd person to carry the colors of the moral fundamentalists. Nevertheless, if Bork is still that kind of skeptic, this would explain his legal cynicism, his indifference to whether constitutional law is coherent in principle. If not, we must look elsewhere to find political convictions that might explain his contempt for the integrity of law. His writings show no developed political philosophy, however, beyond frequent appeals to the truism that elected legislators, not judges, ought to make law when the Constitution is silent. No one disputes that, of course; people disagree only about when the Constitution *is* silent. Bork says it is

silent about gender discrimination and homosexual rights, even though it
declares that everyone must have equal protection of the law. But he offers,
as I have said, no argument for that surprising view.

He does suggest, from time to time, a more worrying explanation of his
narrow reading of the Constitution, because he flirts with the radical
populist thesis that minorities in fact have no moral rights against the
majority at all. That thesis does recommend giving as little force to the
framers' intentions as possible, by treating the Constitution as a collection
of isolated rules, each strictly limited to matters that the framers discussed.
But populism of that form is so plainly inconsistent with the text and spirit
of the Constitution, and with the most apparent and fundamental convictions of the framers, that anyone who endorses it seems unqualified, for
that reason alone, for a place on the Court.

There is very little else about political morality to be found in Bork's
writings. He did declare an amazing political position long ago, in 1963.[11]
He opposed the Civil Rights Acts on the ground that forbidding people
who own restaurants and hotels to discriminate against blacks would
infringe their rights to liberty. He tried to defend that position by appealing
to John Stuart Mill's liberal principle that the law should not enforce
morality for the sake of morality alone. He called the idea that people's
liberty can be restricted just because the majority disapproves of their
behavior an idea of "unsurpassed ugliness."

His analysis of the connection between liberty and civil rights was
confused. The Civil Rights Acts do not violate Mill's principle. They forbid
racial discrimination not just on the ground that the majority dislikes
racists, but because discrimination is a profound harm and insult to its
victims. Perhaps Bork realized this mistake, because in 1973 he declared,
in hearings confirming his appointment as Nixon's solicitor general, that
he had come to approve of the Civil Rights Acts. But in 1984, without
acknowledging any change in view, he disavowed Mill's principle entirely,
and embraced what he had formerly called an idea of unsurpassed ugliness, the idea that the majority has a right to forbid behavior just because
it thinks it morally wrong.[12] In a lecture before the American Enterprise
Institute, in which he was discussing the liberty not of racists but of sexual
minorities, he dismissed the idea that "moral harm is not harm legislators
are entitled to consider," and accepted Lord Devlin's view that a community is entitled to legislate about sexual and other aspects of morality
because "what makes a society is a community of ideas, not political ideas
alone but also ideas about the way its members should behave and govern

their lives."[13] Perhaps Bork's convictions did shift so dramatically over time. But it is hard to resist a less attractive conclusion: that his principles adjust themselves to the prejudices of the right, however inconsistent these might be.

In any case, the Senate Judiciary Committee should try to discover, if it can, the true grounds of Bork's hostility to ordinary legal argument in constitutional law. It should not be satisfied if he defends his announced positions by appealing only and vaguely to the original intention of the framers. Or denounces past decisions he might vote to repeal by saying that the judges who decided them invented new rights when the Constitution was silent. For these claims, as I have tried to show, are empty in themselves, and his attempts to make them more substantial show only that he uses original intention as alchemists once used phlogiston, to hide the fact that he has no theory at all, no conservative jurisprudence, but only right-wing dogma to guide his decisions. Will the Senate allow the Supreme Court to become the fortress of a reactionary antilegal ideology with so meager and shabby an intellectual base?

August 13, 1987

13

▼

What Bork's Defeat Meant

Judge Bork's defeat is already history; we have since had the farce of Douglas H. Ginsburg's downfall and have now the Anthony Kennedy nomination to worry about. But a second battle over Bork is under way—the battle over the best explanation of his defeat—and though I shall have to consider whether and why Judge Kennedy is a more attractive nominee than Bork was, the meaning of Bork's loss is my central concern here. Judge Ginsburg's destruction was sad, but it raised no issues of constitutional dimension. Of course it is absurd and embarrassing that his occasional use of marijuana several years ago while he was a law professor should be thought to have disqualified him. Smoking pot is and was illegal, and law professors should not break the law. But a professor who confessed that he broke the speed limit on occasion, or had once or twice driven after a few drinks, would not have been punished as Ginsburg was.

There were, however, more serious complaints against him. He was only a journeyman academic lawyer and had not shown any particular distinction in his brief career as a judge. He had used bad judgment as a deputy attorney general, moreover, in participating in a matter that might well have substantially affected his own financial interests. He should not have been nominated, but his unfortunate story is of no general importance beyond confirming what we already know about the hypocrisy and incompetence of the Reagan administration.

Bork's defeat is another matter, and the argument about what really happened to him is likely, as I shall try to explain, to have serious consequences for constitutional law. We must distinguish between two aspects

276

of that argument. The first is a question of explanation. What caused Bork's defeat? How important, for example, was the fierce opposition of groups representing black voters? The second is a question of interpretation. What does Bork's defeat mean? Did the American public reject Bork's announced philosophy of original intention? If so, what alternative constitutional philosophy, if any, did the public endorse? These two very different questions are obviously connected, because we cannot intelligently consider the meaning of Bork's defeat until we have some grasp of what factors actually caused it. So though my main interest is in the second, interpretative, question, I shall begin with the first.

When Bork was nominated last in June 1987, most commentators expected that although he would be opposed bitterly by a few liberal Democrats, he would nevertheless be confirmed fairly easily in the end. Relatively few Supreme Court nominees have been rejected, even when the Senate was controlled, as it is now, by a party opposed to the President's. Everyone seemed agreed that a President may name justices to suit his constitutional views, and that the Senate may properly reject his choice only if it is dissatisfied with the nominee's personal integrity or competence.[1] Since no evidence appeared to discredit Bork personally, and since he was plainly an able man, it seemed almost impossible that he would join the small list of defeated nominees. In the end, however, he was defeated by a greater margin than any other Supreme Court nominee in history. What caused that remarkable result?

Any adequate answer must give due weight to many different factors. Reagan's growing political weakness played a part. So did the political skill of the liberal senators opposing Bork. Senator Ted Kennedy, in particular, was extremely effective in persuading other senators who might have been expected to endorse the nomination at once to delay long enough so that arguments might have an impact publicly. Liberal political action groups decided at once to oppose Bork, and they found it surprisingly easy to raise money from public contributions to do so. They organized petitions, bought television advertising, and persuaded other groups to join in their efforts. Black groups were undoubtedly particularly effective, especially in influencing southern senators like Howell Heflin, a key member of the judiciary committee, who had been elected with 80 percent of the black vote. The nomination was lost, in part, in the civil rights marches and voting registration drives of the sixties.

Bork's most extreme supporters argue that the groups opposing him, which they call a "lynch mob" of "special interests," deliberately distorted his views by calling him a racist or a moral bigot and suggesting that he approved of sterilizing women. The political campaign against Bork did indeed include misleading comment. Bork's supporters complain particularly about a sixty-second television spot narrated by Gregory Peck and produced by People for the American Way, a liberal political action fund. Though that organization knew better—it produced an excellent and scrupulously fair scholarly report on Bork's judicial career—the Peck commercial was indeed misleading in several respects.[2] But the unfair advertising against Bork was matched by equally unfair advertising for him. And the advertising on both sides seems unlikely to have had anything like the effect on forming the public's conception of Bork's views that the Senate Judiciary Committee's hearings themselves had.

The hearings lasted nearly three weeks; most were broadcast in full on public service and cable networks, and large portions were replayed on prime-time television news broadcasts. Though Senator Joseph Biden, the committee chairman, had announced his opposition to the nomination when Reagan made it, he conducted the hearings with evident fairness: Bork was not only allowed but encouraged to explain and defend his views in as much detail, and with as much clarification, as he wished. The argument and discussion of the hearings were often of extremely high quality—foreign visitors who tuned in were astounded—and were sometimes, as during a long Saturday morning discussion between Bork and Senator Arlen Specter, of academic depth and rigor.

Those who watched the hearings on television and followed the reports of them in the press seemed fascinated, delighted to join an extended seminar on the Constitution in its bicentennial year. The most damaging views about what Bork thinks—that he rejects a constitutional right to privacy in matters of sexual intimacy, for example—were learned from the judge himself. The right-wing charge, that senators and public alike were gulled by unscrupulous liberal broadcasts, is not only amusing (remember what the right did in Rose Bird's judicial reelection campaign in California in 1986) but insulting, and it has no support in the record. The charge is interesting only because it suggests how fearful right-wing commentators are that Bork's loss will be interpreted as a jurisprudential as well as a political defeat.

Other factors, beyond politics and the argument of the hearings, must have had some influence on the result. In the early days of the hearings, for example, a new issue emerged which, while not exactly a matter of personal integrity, nevertheless approached one: the issue of what was immediately called the "confirmation conversion." Bork appeared suddenly to have changed his mind about some of his fiercest and longest-held opinions on constitutional law and theory, many of which he had repeated in speeches as recently as January 1987.[3] To some it seemed that he was jettisoning the views that had earned him right-wing support for the nomination in order to make confirmation by a Senate controlled by Democrats more likely; and some senators speculated that this kind of flexibility might be undesirable in a justice.

Bork's performance as a witness was in other ways not as impressive as it was expected to be. Though the White House had predicted he would prove a second Ollie North, he did not capture public sympathy, perhaps in part because he was shifting as well as defending ground, perhaps in part for the much worse reason that he seemed too dry and academic and lacking in charm.

The opinions of Bork's peers must also have contributed to his defeat. In early September, before the hearings began, the American Bar Association's prestigious committee which rates judicial nominees reported a split vote about Bork's qualifications: while eight members found him very well qualified, three found him unqualified, and one was willing to vote only "not opposed." Though more witnesses supported the nomination at the hearings than opposed it, and though Bork's supporters included a former President (Ford) and Chief Justice (Burger), and three former attorneys general (William Rogers, Griffin Bell, and Edward Levi), as well as hosts of distinguished law professors and lawyers, the opposing witnesses seemed to have the better of the argument, mainly because they talked about the substance of Bork's announced views while his supporters mainly praised his character and mental ability. But the most extraordinary and devastating judgment was delivered by Bork's former academic colleagues: 40 percent of the faculty members of all accredited law schools in the United States signed petitions calling on the Senate to reject him.

Liberal commentators and politicians insist that the Bork episode settled something larger than whether he should be promoted to the Supreme Court: that the nation also declared its will on fundamental issues of constitutional jurisprudence. The right wing seems to accept, or at least to fear, that that claim is true; nothing else could explain its savage fury at Bork's defeat.[4] No one thinks, of course, that the nation engaged in an actual referendum, conducted through senators' mailbags and public opinion polls, in which a majority of Americans reported their considered opinions on matters of constitutional jurisprudence. But the public apparently sensed the constitutional importance of the Senate's decision; and it is part of our constitutional tradition, in such circumstances, that the nation as a whole is regarded as more committed than it was before to the principles that provide the most convincing justification for what the Senate did.

We treat other political events in our history as calling for interpretation in the same sense and with the same consequence. Constitutional lawyers say that the history and the outcome of the Civil War showed a national commitment to some form of racial equality, and they mean this not as a historical explanation of the causes of the war—that would be too crude and misleading a claim—but as a principle essential to any justification of the slaughter. There are less dramatic examples. When Franklin Roosevelt was forced to abandon his court-packing plan at the height of his political popularity, for example, lawyers offered an interpretive account of his failure: they said that the country rejected the plan in defense of the principle of judicial independence. The debate over Bork, like the debate over Roosevelt's plan, left the public in no doubt that the issue was one of constitutional principles, and no senator could have justified his vote on any other grounds. So it is inevitable that the result, the first Court nomination defeat over a question of constitutional principle in half a century, will be treated as an event of constitutional dimensions, and that explains why it seems natural to everyone, Bork's opponents and supporters alike, to claim or fear that the defeat will be treated as having settled something, at least for a time, about our fundamental law.

Part of what was settled seems plain enough: the country rejected the crude jurisprudence of Reagan and Meese, the philosophy Bork was nominated to embody and defend. Since the mid-1950s, when bumper stickers called for Chief Justice Earl Warren's impeachment and Nixon began running against the Supreme Court as against a political enemy, right-wing politicians have assumed that most Americans resent the Court's landmark decisions about race, school prayer, abortion, and the rights of accused criminals, and deny the Court's authority to make such decisions. But when Bork denounced the Court for ignoring original intention, the people—the supposed victims of judicial tyranny—did not rush to his side. On the contrary, many of the positions he justified by appealing to original intention—that the equal protection clause specially condemns only racial discrimination, for example, and that the Constitution, in spite of what the Supreme Court has said, contains no general right of privacy—were so thoroughly discredited in the hearings, and proved so generally unpopular, that I doubt that they will any longer be advanced even by lawyers and judges who found them congenial before. That, in itself, may significantly affect the course of constitutional law. The standard of "original intention," as a strict and exclusive limit on the grounds of legitimate Supreme Court decisions, is probably dead.

But we must now confront a much more difficult issue of interpretation: in what *way* has Bork's crude historicism been rejected? Bork's announced philosophy, after all, has two parts. The first is jurisprudential: it takes a narrow, positivistic view of the limits of the Constitution as law. It insists that the Constitution creates no rights except those explicit in the text of the document, interpreted to express some pertinent expectation of the framers.[5] The second part is judicial: it insists that judges must stick to the Constitution as law, that they must never invent new rights to make the Constitution better. So it is not enough to say that we have rejected Bork's historicism. Have we rejected both parts of his philosophy? If only one, which one? It makes a great difference how these questions are answered.

Many politicians and commentators seem to accept Bork's first, jurisprudential, thesis about what the law is, but reject his second, judicial, thesis that judges should always, and strictly, enforce the law so understood. The *Washington Post,* for example, in a curious editorial explaining its reluctant opposition, said that Bork pushed his wholly admirable concern for the law too far, that law and justice "are not always the same," that the Constitution has "elasticity," and that Bork had not shown that he was willing to use a judge's discretion to exploit that elasticity generously. On this view, even if Bork was right in thinking that the Supreme Court had no warrant in strict constitutional law when it decided, in *Griswold v. Connecticut,* to strike down laws prohibiting contraceptives, he might nevertheless be wrong in objecting to that decision, because such laws are so silly, and their injustice so apparent, that any justice of the right sensitivity would exercise discretion and declare them unconstitutional anyway. This also seemed to be the view of several senators who, one by one, as the nomination was dying, announced their decision to vote against it. They said they were troubled that the candidate showed too little evidence of the discretion and humanity they thought appropriate to a Supreme Court justice. They thought he was too zealous in his determination to apply the law in a rigid manner.

We can reject Bork's philosophy in a very different, indeed the opposite, way, however, by accepting his second, judicial, claim that judges have an

overriding and exclusive obligation to respect the Constitution, but denying his first, jurisprudential, claim about what kind of a Constitution we
have. We can insist, that is, that our fundamental law consists not simply
of a collection of rules read in the light of what their authors expected but
also of the principles necessary to explain and justify the two centuries of
official practice and judicial decisions that form our larger constitutional
history.

This view replaces Bork's historicism with a jurisprudence not of discretion but of principle. His mistake in rejecting *Griswold,* on this argument,
was not the mistake of pressing the law too far but of misunderstanding
what the law is. The Supreme Court argued, in that case, that people have
a constitutional right to privacy because we cannot explain and justify our
constitutional history as a whole without supposing that individuals have
a right to make their own decisions about matters of personal and intimate
concern to them, free from the surveillance and moral demands of their
fellow citizens. Bork's historicism is defective, on this view, because it
cannot even comprehend that kind of argument. Anthony Lewis had in
mind this way of rejecting Bork's philosophy when he said that the Bork
decision showed that the American people declined to take a "wizened"
view of what their Constitution is.

That controversy is the nerve of the problem of interpreting Judge
Bork's defeat. Does the best justification of that event rest on a commitment to a jurisprudence of discretion or of principle? It matters whether
the legal profession settles on one rather than the other answer. Discretion
treats decisions like *Griswold,* even when it approves those decisions, as
special and limited exceptions to the general rule that only rights explicit in
the Constitution should be recognized. If we understand *Griswold* in that
way, then the decision offers only a fragile hope to other groups who want
their privacy protected: the hope that later judges will think common sense
or compassion demands that elasticity be exploited in their favor as well.

If we understand *Griswold* as an exercise in principle, however, then the
promise of the decision is more robust: that other groups will have the
benefit of whatever principle the decision presupposes, limited and circum-
scribed only in ways that protect its character as a genuine, nonarbitrary
moral principle. In *Bowers v. Hardwick,*[6] the Court refused to extend to
homosexuals the principle of privacy it had recognized in *Griswold.* The
contrast between the two approaches we are considering, discretion and
principle, is evident in the difference between the two main opinions in the
case. Justice White, writing for the majority, suggested that *Griswold* and

the earlier privacy cases be treated as not "much more than the imposition of the Justices' own choice of values," and therefore that these decisions be limited strictly to the particular beneficiaries of privacy, like users of contraceptives, that they discussed. Justice Blackmun's dissenting opinion, on the contrary, insisted on treating those cases as decided on a more general principle that future judges should try to identify and respect, and therefore as extending to other groups, including homosexuals, beyond the immediate beneficiaries of the decisions.[7]

I have no doubt which is the better answer to the interpretive question I posed. Though several senators explained their votes, outside the hearings, by objecting to Bork's rigidity and his apparent lack of humanity, the argument in the committee room was devoted almost exclusively to the first part of his historicism, to the question of whether his original intention view of the Constitution as law is coherent and persuasive. I cannot recall any challenge to the second part of his historicism—to his claim, which seems absolutely right, that a justice's overriding responsibility in constitutional cases is to what he or she thinks that the Constitution, as it stands, actually requires. A jurisprudence of principle is, moreover, in every way more attractive than one of discretion. And it is safer: if we face another threat to our liberty comparable to the McCarthyite threat of the fifties, we will not be well served by a Court grown used to the idea of an elastic Constitution, the idea that principle should be tempered with what then passes for common sense.

So the best interpretation of Bork's defeat is not that he is too rigidly devoted to the rule of law but that his jurisprudence—his vision of what the rule of law requires—is superficial and inadequate. My main concern, however, is not to defend that answer to the interpretive question but to urge the importance of the question itself. Constitutional lawyers and historians may debate the meaning of the Senate's decision for some time to come. But our Constitution will be affected by any answer judges and scholars settle on even temporarily. A critical part of the Bork story has only now begun.

Will future Supreme Court appointments provoke the political wars Bork's nomination did? Will political action groups take sides and do battle as a matter of course? Will public opinion polls become an ordinary feature of confirmation proceedings? Everyone hopes not, but many commentators have been pessimistic. The Supreme Court's decisions are so important to so many people, they say, that some political group or other will be moved by the Bork precedent to try to defeat any appointment a President makes.

That view seems premature. Reagan chose to make the Bork nomination political. During the 1986 midterm elections he asked the voters to elect Republican senators so that they could vote for his nominees (he expressed shock when the Democrats elected against that advice opposed his nominee). He chose Bork in spite of Senator Robert Byrd's prescient opinion that Bork alone, of all the candidates on the short list, would be regarded as a political appointment, and he offered Bork to the nation not simply as a distinguished jurist but as a lawyer representing his own radical view of the law. When Bork was defeated Reagan called the opposition a lynch mob and promised a new nominee—it turned out to be Ginsburg— who would upset the liberals just as much. If future Presidents behave like that, their nominees will almost certainly face political opposition, particularly when the Senate is controlled by an opposition party. But that lesson may itself lead future Presidents toward less confrontational appointments; and the shared sense of the danger that Supreme Court appointments have already become too political may encourage consensus rather than controversy.

It may already have done so. When Reagan nominated Kennedy he apologized for his political presentations of Bork and Ginsburg: he said he had become wiser in the last few months. And the far right's hostility to Kennedy had been widely reported when Ginsburg was chosen before him, so that Kennedy appeared more moderate for that reason. In further statements Reagan stressed not Kennedy's ideological purity but his so far favorable reception by liberals, and that favorable reception itself reflects the concern of the liberals not to be seen this time as the group first bringing politics into the story. So a wary, unspoken bargain seems to have been struck, allowing all groups to walk back from the brink together. Have the liberals been tricked, in this way, into accepting someone they should oppose? Is Kennedy only a Bork dressed up in the clothes of moderation?

A judge's political and moral convictions must inevitably affect his judicial decisions, and Kennedy's many opinions as a circuit court judge suggest that his convictions are on the whole decidedly conservative. He has refused invitations to set aside death sentences when other judges might have done so,[8] accepted fresh exceptions to the exclusionary rule, which forbids using evidence in a criminal trial that the police obtained illegally,[9] and rejected arguments, which more liberal judges might have approved, urging him to strike down legal or institutional arrangements as discriminatory against blacks or women.[10] But he did not appeal to any historicist, "original intention" theory of the Constitution, or any other theory suggesting a general hostility to the idea of individual constitutional rights against government power, to justify these decisions. On the contrary he appears to accept the idea central to what I called a jurisprudence of principle: that courts must try to discover principles justifying not only the text of the Constitution but the traditions and practices, including past Supreme Court decisions, that are also part of our constitutional record.

In a speech to a judicial conference in August 1987 Kennedy insisted that Court decisions must be based on "some demonstrated historical link between the rule being advanced in court and the announced declarations and language of the framers." This falls far short of supposing that abstract constitutional language must be applied only in ways the framers anticipated. And he added that the courts must also respect what he called an "unwritten constitution," which "consists of our ethical culture, our shared beliefs, our common vision," and which, he added significantly, acts as "an additional brake, an additional restraint" on the power of the government.

The force of this concern for principles that constrain government is evident in at least some of Kennedy's judicial opinions. Bork's decision in *Dronenberg,* that the Navy's policy of dismissing homosexuals did not violate the Constitution, figured prominently in his hearings because in that opinion he refused even to try to find any general principle behind the Supreme Court's decision in *Griswold* and other privacy cases. He argued that since these decisions were wrong because unfaithful to original intention he had no duty to treat them as standing for any general principle at all. Kennedy reached the same conclusion about the Navy's policy, in a separate case, but his opinion was very different.[11] He assumed that he had the duty that Bork rejected; and he even assumed, for the sake of the argument, that the principle to be found in the privacy decisions extended to homosexuals. He said that the military's special needs for disciplined and unquestioned authority were strong enough to override that principle in the present case; but he was careful to point out that these needs were exceptional and that his argument justified no larger conclusion denying homosexuals rights in other contexts.

Kennedy's attraction to principle was equally evident in another opinion. He dissented from a decision of his entire court, *en banc,* which accepted as evidence heroin that the police had discovered by offering the five-year-old son of a defendant five dollars to tell them where it was hidden.[12] He did not rely, as had the trial judge, on any simple, discretion-like judgment that the police had behaved in a repulsive way. He found a principle protecting the relationship between mother and child from such assaults latent in a string of constitutional cases, including one well-known Supreme Court decision that Bork had denounced as plainly wrong.[13] And Kennedy's best-known opinion, in which he declared unconstitutional a procedure authorizing one house of Congress to set aside a deportation order on hardship grounds, contains an extended discussion of the principle of separation of powers which, although it draws extensively on the views of Jefferson and his contemporaries, aims to construct an interpretation of that principle faithful to our entire constitutional record.[14]

The hearings may reveal strains of narrow historicism in Kennedy's jurisprudence that I did not find in his opinions. And he is almost certain to reach conclusions that a more liberal judge would reject. But the danger Bork posed to the ideal of constitutional integrity was not simply the threat of conservative results. Bork is a radical because he opposes that ideal itself; Kennedy, on the record so far, seems to accept it. Bork always has available a mechanical, unreflective way to choke off arguments of principle; he claims that these arguments are preempted by purportedly historical claims about what the framers had in mind.

Kennedy seems likely to accept more intellectual discipline, to insist on more lawyerlike, principled support of his own conservative inclinations; and conservative principles, fairly applied, protect minorities better than does the raw majoritarianism of strict historicism. So Kennedy's appointment, if he is confirmed, would not show the fight against Bork to have been pointless. His grudging nomination might prove, on the contrary, to be an early confirmation that, in rejecting Bork, the Senate succeeded in putting an alien and unattractive theory of our Constitution to rest.

December 17, 1987

14

▼

Bork's Own Postmortem

Although I have written about Robert Bork's constitutional theories elsewhere,[1] I agreed to review *The Tempting of America*[2] because he there sets out what he calls the "original understanding" thesis in a more complete and revealing form than he has attempted before. That thesis is unlikely to recover from his new defense of it, and his book may prove an important event for that reason. Bork also argues that law must be a matter of common sense, and that the flourishing of academic legal theory, far from a sign of law's health and liveliness, is rather a symptom of its decadence. That is a claim of independent importance, and I shall comment on it briefly.

I want first to make an overdue protest. Bork intends his book, among other things, to persuade the American public that the negative opinion many people formed of him during his unsuccessful nomination hearings was the result of deliberate lies and outrageous and crude simplifications, and that he is not, as some of those who campaigned against him claimed, a racist or a bigot or a madman. I hope that the book's popularity signals his success in that aim. No doubt Bork was the victim of outrageous distortions and fallacious, question-begging arguments. I do not think these misrepresentations played anything like as important a role in his defeat as he believes they did. Bork was defeated mainly because he challenged a style of interpreting the Constitution that has become part of the American political tradition, and that the public, much to his surprise, largely supports. But in any case he is surely justified in trying to redeem his public reputation.

Bork himself, however, has made a career of grossly unfair charges against those who disagree with his views, and in this book his charges become even more shrill and mendacious. He wants to persuade the public that he is not just an unsuccessful Supreme Court nominee, but a martyr in a patriotic war against scheming and powerful enemies of democracy. These well-disguised enemies are professors of law who, knowing that the Constitution does not support their egalitarian designs for America, produce insidious theories to trick judges into abandoning the real Constitution and replacing it with a different one the professors have invented.[3]

It is depressing that Bork is so anxious for martyrdom that he is willing to invent fantasies to achieve it. But it is simply intolerable that in his quest for redemption he should accuse a significant portion of the academic legal profession of being tricksters and cynics who care only for results at whatever cost. "Professions and academic disciplines that once possessed a life and structure of their own have steadily succumbed," he tells us, "in some cases almost entirely, to the belief that nothing matters beyond politically desirable results, however achieved . . . It is coming to be denied that anything counts, not logic, not objectivity, not even intellectual honesty, that stands in the way of the 'correct' political outcome" (p. 1).

He continues: "The clash over my nomination was simply one battle in this long-running war for control of our legal culture" (p. 2). "The forces that would break law to a tame instrument of a particular political thrust are past midway in a long march through our institutions. They have overrun a number of law schools, including a large majority of America's most prestigious" (p. 3). Decades of liberal political influence have imposed on constitutional law an "intellectual class moral relativism" (p. 247). "The point of the academic exercise is to be free of democracy in order to impose the values of an elite upon the rest of us" (p. 145).

"[Alexander Bickel, John Hart Ely, and Laurence Tribe] typify today's American professoriate," Bork reports, in "that they would depart, in varying degrees, from the actual Constitution of the United States . . . What follows is a demonstration of that truth by sampling the views of other academic constitutional theorists" (p. 207). These co-conspirators include, for example, Frank Michelman, Thomas Grey, David Richards, and myself (pp. 207, 209, 210, and 213, respectively).

Those several scholars, whom Bork singles out to "demonstrate" his "truth," hold different views. But of none of them is it remotely true, nor does Bork offer any shred of evidence to support the claim, that he "would depart . . . from the actual Constitution." Or that he believes "nothing matters beyond politically desirable results, however achieved." Or that he urges judges to decline to "abid[e] by the American form of government" (p. 1). Or that he thinks the Constitution and statutes "are malleable texts that judges may rewrite to see that particular groups or political causes win" (p. 2). Or that he is a moral relativist, a philosophical position Bork seems hardly to understand.[4]

Bork deploys these wild charges almost randomly throughout his book. They are irresponsibly false. Nearly all the constitutional lawyers and legal philosophers who disagree with him disagree not about whether the Constitution should be obeyed but about the proper way to decide what its various provisions actually require. That conflict is part of a larger and older dispute among lawyers about what any statute is, that is, about the most accurate way of fixing the legal impact of any piece of legislation. (And that dispute is itself part of an even wider debate, which spans a variety of disciplines, about the character and proper standards of interpretation in general.) Bork subscribes to one answer to the question of what the Constitution is, which is also the answer conservative Presidents and politicians have embraced in recent decades. Bork says that the Constitution should be interpreted in accordance with what he calls the "original understanding": it should be thought to have only the force it was assumed to have by those who enacted and ratified it (pp. 143–146).

It is true that this view, however popular among politicians, is not much in favor in law schools, where it is generally regarded as confused and unhelpful.[5] Some law professors believe that the Constitution is incomplete or open-ended, so that judges have no choice but to expand its provisions to meet new cases. Others believe that the Constitution, properly understood, is not so much open-ended as structural: that on the best interpretation it itself requires that judges serve something of the role Alexander Bickel described, as guardians of moral principles inherent in the national tradition. Others think the Constitution, on the best interpretation, is abstract: that it lays down general moral principles that contemporary lawyers, judges, and citizens must apply by finding the best answers to the moral questions these abstract principles pose. Some of those who take this last view think that the work of moral philosophers, even when philosophers disagree, provides a useful source, among others, of suggestions and argument.

These different positions all contemplate judges exercising a more judgmental and less mechanical role in interpreting the Constitution than Bork sometimes suggests his original understanding view allows them. Scholars insist on a more active judicial role, however, not because they want to subvert the Constitution, but because they believe a more active role is essential to respecting the Constitution, to enforcing the American form of government. It certainly does not follow—it seems a crude misunderstanding to say—that people who hold these views put politics before the Constitution, or would depart from the Constitution in the name of equality, or are guilty of the other sins Bork attributes to them.

If Bork's version of what the Constitution requires is in fact the right view, then the effect of judges following a different view would indeed be a departure from the actual Constitution. But that hardly means that scholars who disagree with Bork intend or advocate that result. For they have the same view about the effects of Bork's views: I myself think that the effect of following his version of original understanding would be—indeed, in recent years has been—a departure from the actual Constitution. But I do not accuse him of bad faith, or of wanting to subvert the American form of government.

Bork's caustic jurisprudence debases the quality of the debate. He coarsens the public argument by reducing it to a stock Western drama, heroes against horse thieves. He may find the real argument too complex for his polemical purposes. But he should not stoop to tactics he rightly deplores when they are aimed against him.

Bork was stung by the popular perception that he did not distinguish himself intellectually in the hearings. He grumbles, for example, that the public mistook his extended exchange with Senator Arlen Specter about constitutional theory, in which Bork claims Specter failed to grasp his views on the Constitution, for a serious jurisprudential discussion (pp. 301–306). He hopes to repair the public misunderstanding in this book by offering an intellectual defense of the original understanding method in constitutional analysis, to show the public that it should now reject the constitutional style it has been seduced into approving. In fact his book, if carefully read, may achieve exactly the opposite of its intended effect. The arguments are so weak, and Bork's apparent concessions to his critics so comprehensive, that his book might mark the end of the original understanding thesis as a serious constitutional philosophy.

Bork claims that the prestigious law schools reject originalism because it produces a Constitution too conservative for most professors' liberal and egalitarian tastes (pp. 134–138). Law school professors differ too much in their own political views to make that a plausible explanation, however.

They reject Bork's thesis primarily on conceptual rather than political grounds. These professors regard the idea of an original understanding as radically ambiguous and incomplete, almost empty, until the concept is supplemented by the contemporary political judgment that Bork says it rules out.

It is worth explaining this objection in some detail to see how thoroughly Bork now capitulates to it.[6] I must begin by emphasizing a distinction which is rarely explicit in discussions of the original understanding thesis, but which is, I think, essential to understanding its vulnerability to the objection I shall describe. The thesis insists that judges should interpret the Constitution to mean only what the framers intended it to mean. But the framers had two very different kinds of intention that, in very different senses, constituted what they meant. They had linguistic intentions, that is, intentions that the Constitution contain particular statements. They also had legal intentions, that is, intentions about what the law would be in virtue of these statements.

We make constant assumptions about the framers' linguistic intentions, and we never contradict these in our views about what the Constitution says. We assume, for example, that the framers of the Eighth Amendment meant by "cruel" roughly what we mean by "cruel," and that they followed roughly the same linguistic practices we do in forming statements out of words. We therefore assume that they intended the Constitution to say that cruel and unusual punishments are forbidden rather than, for example, that expensive and unusual punishments are forbidden. (We would give up that assumption, however, if, incredibly, we learned that "cruel" was invariably used to mean expensive in the eighteenth century.) We also assume that they intended to say something as abstract as we would intend to say if we said, "Cruel and unusual punishments are forbidden." Suppose we discover that they expected that the bastinado would be forbidden by the Eighth Amendment, but not solitary confinement. We would not then think that they intended to say that the bastinado but not solitary confinement was forbidden. We would have no justification for attributing to them that degree of linguistic incompetence. We would instead classify their opinions about these punishments as part of their legal rather than linguistic intentions. We would say that they thought they were outlawing the bastinado but not solitary confinement, or that that is what they hoped they were doing.

The original understanding asks judges not merely to make the framers' linguistic intentions decisive over what they said, which is innocuous, but to make their legal intentions decisive over what they did, that is, over what effect their statements had on constitutional law. The difference is evident. Suppose I say to my real estate agent, "Do whatever possible to sell my house at the highest price you can, but do nothing unfair." She would of course make assumptions about my linguistic intentions in deciding what I said. If my tone of voice suggested quotation marks around "unfair," she might decide that I had not, in fact, told her to avoid unfair means. Assume, however, there is no question of what I meant to say. She rightly thinks that I intended to say, and did say, that she should avoid unfair means. Nevertheless, it may be problematic what responsibilities I had actually imposed on her. Suppose she thinks that a particular negotiating strategy—bluffing—is unfair, but she knows that I disagree. She might well think that I had ruled out bluffing even though I did not intend to do so.

So even though the framers' linguistic intentions fix what they said, it does not follow that their legal intentions fix what they did. We need an independent argument for the original understanding thesis. The agency example suggests what kind of argument might be proposed. Someone might say, about the agency case, that agents have a responsibility to carry out their clients' wishes, and should therefore defer to their convictions. And someone might say, about the constitutional case, that since the framers were the people whose decision made the Constitution our fundamental law, their convictions should be respected.

We must recognize three points about that kind of argument, however. First, the argument necessarily draws on normative rather than semantic or logical assumptions. It draws, in the former case, on normative assumptions about the proper relations between clients and agents and, in the latter, on normative assumptions about the proper balance of authority, in a democracy, between remote constitutional architects, contemporary legislators, and judges. Second, these normative assumptions cannot be justified, without the most blatant and absurd circularity, by appealing to the intentions or wishes or decisions of the people whose authority they propose to describe. It would be absurd to argue that agents should defer to the wishes of clients because that is what clients wish, or that judges should respect particular convictions or expectations of the framers because the framers expected that they would or believed or decided that they should.

The third point forms the objection before which, as I shall try to show, Bork capitulates. It is that these arguments, even if supported by independent normative claims, are radically incomplete if they purport to establish only that agents or judges should respect clients' or framers' wishes or intentions or convictions or expectations. In most pertinent cases the question at issue is not whether the convictions, expectations, and beliefs of those in authority count, but which of these mental states count and how. In the agency example, for instance, on the assumption that my instruction was not cynical or manipulative or only for effect, I had at least two relevant convictions. The first is that nothing that is unfair should be done on my behalf. The second is that bluffing is not unfair. My agent believes that these convictions are in conflict, and so she cannot decide what her instructions require just by resolving to follow my convictions. She must decide which of my convictions—the more abstract or the more concrete—to enforce.

This is not, of course, a problem of discovering what my "true" intentions or convictions or beliefs are. Both the convictions I described are genuine. Nor is it a problem of discovering which is more important to me, which, as someone might put it, I would abandon first. For I do not hold them as even potentially conflicting convictions—I hold the more concrete as part of the more abstract—and any idea of my choosing between them is incoherent. Since it is the agent, not I, who sees the convictions as inconsistent, it is she who must make the selection. She must elaborate whatever normative argument she had for deferring to my convictions in the first place so that these now provide a reason for selecting one type or level of my convictions as the appropriate type or level.

Suppose she tries to avoid that responsibility by, in effect, passing it on to me. Suppose she tries to discover, not merely my opinions about fair play in negotiating, but also my second-order opinions about how my opinions about fair play should figure in determining the responsibilities of agents I instruct. Her problem will remain, even if she does discover that I have such second-order opinions, because she needs a reason why she should treat those opinons as decisive. Suppose I myself think that, on the best theory of agency, an agent should apply her own convictions in applying a client's abstract instructions. If she thinks the contrary, why should she not follow her own convictions on that matter rather than my (as she thinks mistaken) views? There may be a good answer. But it will take the form of an even more complex normative theory of agency than the one she first used, and, unless she has a taste for infinite regress, she must decide on her own about the merits of that theory.

Exactly the same is true of constitutional interpretation. We must assume that the legal intentions of the framers were honorable rather than cynical. They intended to commit the nation to abstract principles of political morality about speech and punishment and equality, for example. They also had a variety of more concrete convictions about the correct application of these abstract principles to particular issues. If contemporary judges think that their concrete convictions were in conflict with their abstract ones, because they did not reach the correct conclusions about the effect of their own principles, then the judges have a choice to make. It is unhelpful to tell them to follow the framers' legal intentions. They need to know which legal intentions—at how general a level of abstraction—and why. So Bork and others who support the original understanding thesis must supply an independent normative theory—a particular political conception of constitutional democracy—to answer that need. That normative theory must justify not only a general attitude of deference, but also what I shall call an interpretive schema: a particular account of how different levels of the framers' convictions and expectations contribute to concrete judicial decisions.

An example Bork himself discusses—the equal protection clause of the Fourteenth Amendment—reveals the character of the political theory that is needed. Suppose we provisionally accept the original understanding thesis, as a guide to deciding equal protection cases, and therefore set out to collect all the historical information we can about the mental states of the framers of that clause. Suppose we discover the following. All the framers of the equal protection clause believed, as a matter of political conviction, that people should all be equal in the eyes of the law and the state. They were convinced that certain specific forms of official discrimination against blacks were morally wrong for that reason, and they adopted the amendment mainly to prevent states from discriminating against blacks in those ways. They agreed, for example, that it would be morally wrong for a state to create certain special remedies for breach of contract and make these remedies available to white plaintiffs but not black ones. The framers assumed that the clause they were adopting would prohibit that form of discrimination.

They also shared certain opinions about which forms of official discrimination were not wrong and would not be prohibited by the clause. They shared the view, for example, that racial segregation of public schools did not violate the clause. (Many of them, in fact, themselves voted to segregate schools.) None of them even considered the possibility that state institutions would one day adopt affirmative action racial quotas designed to repair the damages of past segregation; therefore, none of them had any opinion about whether such quotas would violate the clause. Some of them thought that women were unjustly treated by laws that discriminated in favor of men. Most did not, and assumed that the gender-based distinctions then common were not outlawed by the clause. Most thought that homosexual acts were grossly immoral, and would have been mystified by the suggestion that laws prohibiting such acts constituted an unjustified form of discrimination.

Bork himself distinguishes four different statements of the legal effect of the equal protection clause, each of which treats the catalogue of information I just listed differently.

1. The clause has the effect of condemning not all cases of discrimination, but only those cases that the framers collectively expected it to condemn. So understood, the clause forbids discrimination against blacks in legal remedies for breach of contract, but it does not forbid racially segregated schools, or affirmative action quotas that disadvantage whites, or discrimination against women or homosexuals.

2. The clause has the effect of establishing what Bork calls the principle of "black equality," which holds that blacks must be treated in whatever way the ideal of equal citizenship, correctly understood, actually requires. Judges must therefore decide for themselves whether school desegregation violates black equality. Since the clause establishes black equality, however, judges may not use it to strike down affirmative action quotas or discrimination against women or homosexuals.

3. The clause has the effect of establishing a principle of racial rather than just black equality. So, even though the framers of the equal protection clause did not contemplate affirmative action, the clause they adopted might, on the right understanding of racial equality, nevertheless condemn affirmative action, and judges have the responsibility to decide for themselves whether it does, but judges could not properly maintain that the clause protects women or homosexuals, because that is a matter of gender or sexual orientation, not racial equality.

4. The clause has the effect of establishing a general principle of equality, which requires for all Americans what equal citizenship, properly understood, demands. So, if we assume that the best conception of equality is in fact denied by school segregation, quota systems, and laws that disadvantage people on the basis of sex or sexual orientation, the clause condemns these discriminations, in spite of what the framers themselves thought or would have approved.

These four accounts are all consistent with the full set of convictions, beliefs, and expectations I assumed the ratifiers had. The four accounts represent not different hypotheses about the framers' mental states, but different ways of structuring the same assumptions about what their mental states were. Each account states a genuine original understanding, but of a different kind or at a different level, and with very different consequences. It is, of course, possible that some of the framers had second-order opinions about the right way to take their own convictions and expectations into account in deciding what the clause they enacted does. It is unlikely that many of them had opinions about that jurisprudential question, however, and vanishingly unlikely that a majority of them had the same opinion about it. But even if they were all united in the same opinion, that would simply add one more piece of mental furniture to the inventory we had to consult. We should still have to decide whether and how to take that conviction into account in deciding on the legal consequences of their enacting the propositions they did.[7]

In the last analysis it is we—people who in different roles must now decide what the Constitution does—who must decide how the various convictions and expectations of the framers figure in an account of that document's legal effect. We need a normative political theory—a particular conception of constitutional democracy—to justify our choice, and that theory must justify a particular interpretive schema for deciding which of the various mental states I described count and how. It is easy enough to formulate a reductive schema that would pick out the first of the four accounts I just listed as a correct account of the force of the equal protection clause. This reductive schema holds that the impact of a constitutional provision is fixed, in an exhaustive way, by the widely shared concrete expectations of the framers, so that the equal protection clause has only the specific consequences they expected it would. If we adopt that schema, then on the assumptions I described school segregation is not unconstitutional, and the Supreme Court's decision in *Brown* was a flat mistake.

We might compose a political argument, of sorts, for adopting the reductive schema. We might say, for example, that it is crucially important that Supreme Court decisions not depend on the political opinions of particular judges, and that judges should be guided by the framers' concrete convictions, not because judges have any other or better reason for deferring to the framers, but just to prevent them from relying on their own beliefs. That is a possible justification, though it is hardly compelling and is certainly controversial. Suppose we reject the reductive schema, however. Then we would need some other interpretive schema to decide which of the four accounts of the meaning of the equal protection clause is the best or most sound one, and we should need to deploy a political theory purporting to justify that other schema as the best one available.[8]

What choice does Bork make? His explicit remarks are wholly unhelpful. He says, for example, that we learn the correct way to choose among different accounts of a constitutional provision's force by discovering what the Constitution, properly interpreted, means.[9]

He adds that we find out what the Constitution means by studying its "text, structure, and history" (p. 162) or by divining the principles its framers wanted it to embody. Presumably he has in mind, when he says we must discover what a clause means, discovering its legal impact, rather than just what it says. But then he begs the question by saying we must consult text, history, and structure. We need to know which of the numberless facts about text, history, and structure contribute to fixing a clause's impact and how. Sometimes Bork's question-begging is spectacular. Here is his reply, for example, to the suggestion I just made, that we must rely on a theory of democracy, or some other controversial political theory, in justifying any particular interpretive schema: "It has been argued . . . that the claim of proponents of original understanding to political neutrality is a pretense since the choice of that philosophy is itself a political decision. It certainly is, but the political content of that choice is not made by the judge; it was made long ago by those who designed and enacted the Constitution" (pp. 176–177).

That statement shows the confusion I warned against earlier. We cannot justify appealing to a particular set of convictions on the ground that those convictions support that appeal. We must decide to give effect to the framers' intention before we can be guided by "the political content" of the choice they "made long ago." And we must decide how to disentangle the principle they enacted from their convictions about its proper application in order to discover the political content of their decision. We cannot coherently assign these decisions back to the framers; we must make them, on grounds of political morality, for ourselves.

So we need to turn to Bork's more detailed discussions of particular cases and problems to discover the interpretive schema he himself uses. On occasion he seems to adopt what I called the reductive schema. He asserts, for example, that the cruel and unusual punishment clause of the Eighth Amendment cannot be understood as outlawing capital punishment because other parts of the Constitution make no sense except on the assumption that the framers thought that capital punishment was permitted (p. 9).

(I return to this issue later.) But he implicitly rejects the reductive schema when he explains that the original understanding method would not condemn the Supreme Court's decision in *Brown* (pp. 81–83). According to Bork, the framers intended to establish a principle of equality, and they simply erred in thinking that equality would not condemn racial segregation. They had inconsistent views, and judges must follow the more abstract of these—the principle they enacted—rather than their own specific views about what that principle required.

Bork rejects the reductive schema explicitly in another discussion intended to show that it is no objection to the original understanding view that the specific opinions of the framers are often unknown (pp. 161–162). He writes that in many cases their collective opinions are not only unknown but nonexistent—that often the framers, as a group, had no concrete opinions at all. "Indeed," he states, "the various ratifying conventions would surely have split within themselves and with one another in the application of the principles they adopted to particular fact situations. That tells us nothing other than that the ratifiers were like other legislators" (p. 163). He does not say that therefore judges have a duty to try, as best they can, to discover the concrete views of the majority of ratifiers. That would be silly, and in any case insufficient, because Bork qualifies his original understanding thesis in another pertinent way. "Though I have written of the understanding of the ratifiers of the Constitution," he says, "since they enacted it and made it law, that is actually a shorthand formulation, because what the ratifiers understood themselves to be enacting must be taken to be what the public of that time would have understood the words to mean" (p. 144). Presumably "the public of that time" would have been at least as divided about the specific consequences of constitutional principles as were the framers, and it would be preposterous to think that the meaning of the Constitution depends on which concrete view about application, if only we knew it, was the most popular then.

Uncertainty about what the framers thought, or the fact that they likely disagreed, does not matter, Bork says, because a judge is concerned with principles and not with specific intentions:

> In short, all that a judge committed to original understanding requires is
> that the text, structure, and history of the Constitution provide him not
> with a conclusion but with a major premise. That major premise is a
> principle or stated value that the ratifiers wanted to protect against hostile

legislation or executive action. The judge must then see whether that principle or value is threatened by the statute or action challenged in the case before him. The answer to that question provides his minor premise, and the conclusion follows. It does not follow without difficulty, and two judges equally devoted to the original purpose may disagree about the reach or application of the principle at stake and so arrive at different results, but that in no way distinguishes the task from the difficulties of applying any other legal writing (pp. 162–163).

We should pause to notice what an amazing passage this is. It could have been written by almost any of the people Bork takes to be members of the academic conspiracy against him and the nation. For Bork's analysis is entirely consistent with the view—indeed it seems to be the view—I described above, which holds that the Constitution enacts abstract principles that judges must interpret, as best they can, according to their own lights. Bork does say that the principle the judge applies must be one that the framers "wanted." But once he abandons the reductive interpretation of what they wanted—that they wanted their own specific views realized—once he accepts that the principle they wanted might have condemned their own specific views, as in the case of segregation, then he has nothing left to which he can tether an opinion of what they wanted, except the exceedingly abstract language they used.

In any case this passage plainly rejects the reductive schema, and Bork emphatically rejects the first account of the meaning of the equal protection clause under the historical assumptions I described. In another discussion he insists that under those assumptions the second account would be the correct one, and that the third or fourth would be inappropriate. If there is no evidence that the framers intended to protect whites or women from discrimination, Bork asserts, then although the Constitution contains a principle requiring "black equality," it does not contain one requiring "the next higher level of generality above black equality, which is racial equality" (p. 149). We therefore could not say that quotas were unconstitutional.[10]

Bork never identifies the interpretive schema he relies on in choosing the second and rejecting the third account in this discussion. If it does not matter that the framers and their public thought segregation was constitutional, then why should it matter whether they also thought affirmative action quotas were constitutional? And if that wouldn't matter, then how could it possibly matter that we have no evidence of what they thought about quotas or even that they thought about them at all? Why should we not say that the principle the framers "wanted" was a principle of racial equality and that therefore (if this is what we think follows from a principle of racial equality) quotas are unconstitutional? What in the history, except for concerns that Bork has now declared irrelevant, prevents us from taking that line?

Apparently nothing, because in yet a different part of the book Bork adopts exactly this line, without noticing, or at any rate without identifying, the contradiction with his earlier remarks. He endorses the recent affirmative action decision in *Richmond v. J. A. Croson Co.*[11] on the ground that the equal protection clause does protect whites as well as blacks; he assumes, then, that the third rather than the second account of what the equal protection clause means is correct despite the absence of evidence that the framers had any opinions about quotas (pp. 107–109). Even on that assumption, he thinks it correct to interpret what they did as enacting a principle of racial and not merely black equality.

Bork never adopts the fourth summary. That is hardly surprising, for he thinks that the equal protection clause does not apply to gender discrimination (p. 329), or to discrimination against homosexuals (pp. 117–126, 250). But once he abandons the reductive interpretive strategy, which limits the force of the clause to the framers' own specific convictions about what forms of discrimination are incompatible with equal citizenship, then he has no other means of checking the abstract language solely by reference to those convictions. He is in a kind of free fall in which the original understanding can be anything, and the only check on his judgment is his own political instincts. That fact explains why he adopts the third account of the original understanding when he explains that the Constitution outlaws racial quotas, the first when he explains that it does not outlaw capital punishment, the second when he tries to show that *Brown* is compatible with this approach (a test any constitutional theory must now pass), and the fourth never—in spite of the fact that he has no independent way to distinguish the fourth from the others. Bork's abandonment of the reductive schema also explains the often circular and opaque nature of his theoretical discussion; where he rejects the reductive schema, Bork has nothing to say.

Consider, in more detail, his argument about capital punishment. Bork claims that we know that the Eighth Amendment does not forbid capital punishment because the Fifth Amendment contemplates the death penalty when it forbids that anyone should be "twice put in jeopardy of life" for the same offense, or be deprived of life without due process of law (pp. 213–214). That language does suggest that most of the framers thought it at least an open question whether capital punishment is outlawed by the Eighth Amendment. But we do not need that evidence: it seems incredible, quite apart from the language of the Fifth Amendment, that any substantial number of the framers of the Eighth Amendment thought it outlawed capital punishment, which was then a familiar part of criminal process almost everywhere. If we adopted the reductive schema, therefore, Bork would be right that capital punishment is unquestionably constitutional. But once we abandon that schema, as Bork has elsewhere, his argument collapses. For only that schema makes the framers' concrete opinions decisive in the way the argument assumes.

When we abandon the reductive schema, we may develop the following kind of argument, which I shall state in Bork's own vocabulary. The Eighth Amendment enacts the following major premise: punishments inherently cruel and unusual in the practices of civilized nations must not be inflicted. The framers did not think the death penalty failed those two tests; in fact, it plainly did not fail the second when the amendment was adopted, though it probably does now. Whether it also fails the first test now becomes a matter of minor premise that judges applying the clause must inescapably decide for themselves. On that interpretation, the Fifth Amendment language, which merely confirms what the framers themselves thought, cannot assist judges any more than the fact that the framers of the Fourteenth Amendment accepted segregated schools assists in understanding the equal protection clause.

Holding that the Eighth Amendment forbids capital punishment does not produce any contradiction with the Constitution as a whole. The argument I just described is not that the Eighth Amendment expressly or automatically forbids capital punishment, but rather that the amendment establishes a principle that under certain circumstances, or connected to certain "minor premises," would have that result. It is perfectly consistent both to adopt such a principle, in its abstract form, and to insist that if (or so long as) the principle is understood to permit capital punishment, the process through which the penalty is inflicted must meet the independent requirements of the Fifth Amendment.

I should now take note of Bork's surprising announcement that he can prove that any method of constitutional interpretation other than the original understanding thesis is "impossible" in the same way that a perpetual motion machine is impossible (pp. 251–253). His "proof" has these steps. First, any method not based on original understanding requires judges to make "major moral choices." Second, judges cannot show that they have legitimate authority to make major moral choices for the rest of the community. Third, in the absence of such authority, judges must only make decisions based on a moral theory the public would accept. Fourth, since people disagree deeply on matters of morality, no such moral theory exists, and judges therefore must not make moral choices (pp. 251–253).

The key step is the second. Bork rejects the position that judges have legitimate authority under our system of government to make controversial and important moral judgments in the course of a good faith interpretation of the Constitution (pp. 176–178, 252–253). But that view—that under the best understanding of our constitutional democracy judges do have such authority, legitimately—is very widely accepted. Bork says his view is correct and that the contrary view is therefore wrong. But his "impossibility" claim suggests he can prove that his view is the right one, which of course, since his view itself depends on a moral theory many people would reject, he cannot. The only impossibility in this story, in other words, is the impossibility of Bork's rescuing his argument from self-contradiction.

Bork seems to forget, moreover, that on his own account the method of original understanding also requires judges to make controversial moral choices in applying abstract constitutional principles. Bork says these are matters of "minor premise," perhaps intending to distinguish them from the "major" choices he insists other theories require (pp. 162–163). But the examples he offers—the question whether school segregation denies equal protection, for example—show that these choices are sufficiently "major" to cause great concern if judges really have no legitimate authority to make them.

I conclude that Bork's defense of the original understanding thesis is a complete failure. The right-wing lawyers and politicians who have embraced the thesis with such passion and delight have always assumed—indeed they must assume—that it includes what I have called the reductive schema, according to which the Constitution imposes no limit on majority will beyond what the framers themselves would have expected. But Bork's confirmation hearings made plain that he had to abandon that reductive schema, because it would condemn *Brown* (despite Bork's assertions to the contrary) and other constitutional principles America would not now give up. He can offer nothing in its place except unelaborated, dead-end claims about the "meaning" of the "text, structure, and history" of the Constitution. He has transformed the original understanding thesis into a platitude anyone can accept and use to justify almost any result. Some other conservative legal scholar might succeed further with the idea of an original understanding than Bork has. But until someone does we are entitled, on the evidence of this book, to store the theory away with phlogistonism and the bogeyman.

Bork wants his public to regard constitutional law as a simple matter, to accept that a good lawyer needs only plain common sense, innocent of any complicated theorizing, to know what the Constitution requires. Here is a sample: "Of course the judge is bound to apply the law as those who made the law wanted him to. That is the common, everyday view of what law is. I stress the point only because that commonsense view is hotly, extensively, and eruditely denied by constitutional sophisticates, particularly those who teach the subject in the law schools" (p. 5).

"Sophistication" and "philosophy" are often mentioned in *The Tempting of America*, but never with approval. Law professors who appeal to philosophy, literary theory, or other complicated disciplines are treated as charlatans. They write in pretentious and mystifying jargon, and they often refer to foreign, and sometimes Marxist, writers. Gullible judges pretend to understand. But Bork knows that the academic emperors have no clothes; he assures his audience that their theories are nonsense and can safely be ignored. He regards with hilarity the suggestion various professors make, that the work of Foucault or Rawls or Habermas or some other philosopher has a bearing on constitutional law. He argues, as I noted earlier, that the complexity of contemporary constitutional theory, and its attempt to find connections with areas of knowledge outside law, are a sign that constitutional law is sick.

One is tempted to dismiss these statements as mere crowd-pleasing anti-intellectualism with perhaps a tinge of personal Luddite smugness. Even Bork's own discussion of constitutional issues betrays much more "sophistication" than his imitation of Dr. Johnson kicking a stone to refute Berkeley's idealism suggests. But from Bork's tone of voice as well as his explicit claims, we can construct a further, unstated but implicit, argument for his constitutional views. In a decent society (one might say) the public as a whole understands and accepts the basic principles of government. So the standards judges apply to decide what the Constitution means should be those the public as a whole can easily grasp. The original understanding thesis, Bork claims, is a simple matter of common sense. More complicated theories—that the Constitution enacts concepts not conceptions, for example, or that understanding it requires constructive interpretation in which moral argument figures—draw on ideas, distinctions, and experiences that are not common stock in the republic. This observation explains why constitutional law really is in a healthier state—better suited to ideals of participation and shared understanding—when it is simpler, less dependent on febrile academic argument. On this account, the death of complex constitutional theory would be a tribute to the rule of the people (pp. 134–138).

But this argument misunderstands the academic critique of the original understanding doctrine. The law professors Bork distrusts do not argue that the original understanding thesis, though simple, easily grasped, and widely appealing, should defer to some exotic metaphysics. They point out, as I did in the last section, that the idea of an original understanding is much more complex than it first appears, that no single understanding exists, and that the idea, when treated as simple, serves only to allow judges to treat their personal political convictions as neutral constitutional law. If an attractive and coherent political morality is also simple and easily understood by a wide public, that accessibility is a strong, though not necessarily decisive, argument in its favor. It does not follow that a bogus theory should survive just because it seems simple.

Nor can we put limits in advance on the depth and complexity of philosophical discussion in legal writing. Of course, academic lawyers should not set out (as I fear some do) to parade their knowledge as if it were part of law's business to provide theaters for interdisciplinary performances. But legal doctrine is inevitably philosophically exposed. Its proper business forces it to use the concepts of will, intention, meaning, responsibility, justice, and other ideas that are frequent sources of philosophical complexity and confusion. Academic lawyers cannot avoid philosophy—it goes with the territory—though of course they can do it badly and ignorantly. It is irresponsible for a lawyer to insist that the concepts of meaning and original intention should occupy the center of constitutional practice and then ignore the revolution in our understanding of those concepts in this century. He cannot pretend that Wittgenstein or Donald Davidson, for instance, had never written about mental events.

I know that these remarks raise many problems for and about both legal practice and academic law. It seems irresponsible, as I just said, for lawyers to ignore philosophical discussion of the concepts they treat as central to their work. But it is also true that most lawyers and judges, and indeed most legal scholars, have no time for serious study of technical philosophy. I hope to take up that dilemma on another occasion. I want now, however, to contest the assumption on which Bork's view, reconstructed above, rests: that the general public cannot understand a basic structure of government within which lawyers argue and judges decide issues of philosophical depth. There is nothing abstruse or even unfamiliar in the notion that the Constitution lays down abstract principles whose dimensions and application are inherently controversial, that judges have the responsibility to interpret those abstract principles in a way that fits, dignifies, and improves our political history, and that judges with that arduous responsibility should be encouraged to take account of and reflect on the work of others who have thought and written about those difficult matters.

It is of course a further, difficult and complex question what counts as the correct way for judges to exercise their great responsibility. That further, difficult question is what the real academic debate is now about. The debate is not, contrary to Bork's suggestion, mainly conducted in arcane jargon, and it only occasionally draws explicitly on technical philosophical argument. It is true that not as many people can follow this debate as can understand the more general view of judicial responsibility that sponsors it. But that fact is hardly surprising or disturbing. Not as many people can follow intricate discussions of tax economics as can understand that Congress has the responsibility to set tax policy and to consult and listen to experts when it does.

The constitutional debate in the law schools and in the political community as a whole would cease, or become much less lively, if people came no longer to think of the Constitution as an abstract commitment to political ideals, if they did settle into some deadening illusion of an original understanding in which the major questions were all answered. That would certainly make constitutional law less democratic, in the sense of less participatory. Bork's odd thesis that controversy reflects the decay of constitutional theory is another product of his rigid, parochial, and depressing account of the proper nature of law.

Spring 1990

15

▼

The Thomas Nomination

As of this moment, the nomination of Judge Clarence Thomas to the
Supreme Court apparently hinges on how many senators accept the
charges made by Professor Anita Hill, of the University of Oklahoma Law
School, that Thomas sexually harassed her when she was his assistant at
the Department of Education and the Equal Employment Opportunity
Commission. Though the Senate Judiciary Committee knew of the accusation before it voted on the nomination, no member of that committee
mentioned it publicly until it was leaked to the press only two days before
the whole Senate was scheduled to vote on the nomination. Thomas's
supporters were ready to insist on a vote as scheduled, but so much of the
public was outraged at the nearly all-male Senate's seeming indifference to
a charge of sexual harassment, and so many senators who had planned to
vote for him were reluctant to do so without further investigation, that the
supporters agreed to a one-week postponement, and the Judiciary Committee undertook to hold further hearings, restricted to investigating these
and perhaps other charges of similar misconduct, at which Thomas and
Hill agreed to appear.

The Senate plainly mismanaged the matter, and the reputation of the
Judiciary Committee and of senators who opposed a delay has been
damaged. But it would be very unfortunate if these serious failings ob-
scured other, more structural and pervasive, defects in the nomination
process that the hearings had already revealed. Before Hill's allegations
were made public, even Thomas's opponents predicted that he would be
confirmed by a comfortable if not great margin. The Senate was ready to

overlook doubts about his qualifications that are in the long run more consequential for constitutional law than those on which the public's attention became concentrated after Professor Hill's charges became known.

When the Judiciary Committee began its hearings, Senator Herbert Kohl of Wisconsin laid down a test he said the nominee must meet. Thomas had said in 1990, when the committee was considering his appointment to the District of Columbia Circuit Court, that he did not then have "a fully developed constitutional philosophy." Kohl said that though the lack of such a philosophy did not disqualify a candidate for the circuit court, the Supreme Court was different. "In my judgment," he said, "if you cannot articulate a constitutional philosophy, one that includes full safeguards for individuals and minorities and that also squares with your past statements, then in my opinion you are not qualified to sit on the Supreme Court."

Thomas flunked that test in a spectacular way, as even some of the senators who in the end voted to confirm him conceded. He spent his five days of testimony, in fact, denying having any "constitutional philosophy" at all, and trying to explain away the past statements Kohl had in mind. Presumably his White House coaches urged him to adopt that know-nothing strategy. Robert Bork had published radical and highly controversial opinions about constitutional law before his nomination, and these caused his ultimate defeat. Justices Kennedy and Souter, on the other hand, had published almost nothing about constitutional theory; they were easily confirmed, though their votes on the Court, so far, have justified the trust conservatives placed in them.

Thomas is in some ways an exceptionally appealing candidate for the Supreme Court. He is a black man born into poverty and racial disadvantage who nevertheless achieved considerable success, and some of his supporters believe that a justice from that background will eventually raise the level of the Court's compassion for the unfortunate. But his record is much more like Bork's than like that of either of the two other successful nominees. Thomas was chairman of the Equal Employment Opportunity Commission in the Reagan administration, and, as one of the few blacks in that administration, he delivered several speeches to conservative groups. He was on the board of advisers of a conservative black journal, and signed an important report on family policy which called, among other things, for the appointment of justices to the Supreme Court who would vote to overrule *Roe v. Wade.* On several occasions he denounced affirmative action programs for blacks and other minorities, in spite of having himself been admitted to Yale Law School through such a program, and he has shown strange insensitivity to the problems of blacks less successful than himself, even suggesting that his own sister was a welfare scrounger. He condemned the Supreme Court's decision upholding the law under which independent prosecutors can be appointed to investigate officers of the executive branch, and complained that even Chief Justice Rehnquist had voted to uphold that law, remarking that "we can no longer rely on conservative figures to advance our cause."

Two of his published views were particularly frightening to constitutional lawyers: they were, in fact, far more extreme than anything Bork has written. In 1987, in a lecture to The Heritage Foundation, Thomas enthusiastically endorsed an article by Lewis Lehrman, a trustee of the foundation, in which Lehrman had declared that according to the "natural law" a fetus has an inalienable right to life, and that *Roe v. Wade* was therefore a terrible mistake. Thomas said that Lehrman's article "on the Declaration of Independence and the meaning of the right to life is a splendid example of applying natural law."[1] But if Lehrman is right, then it follows not just that states must be permitted to make abortion criminal if a majority of their voters so wish, but that all states must be required to make abortion a crime from the moment of conception, whatever their voters think. No past nominee, including Bork, has ever offered any such view, and none of the present justices, or any prominent politician, has come close to proposing it.

In 1987, moreover, Thomas also suggested, in a speech to the Pacific Research Institute, that he supported a much more active role for the Supreme Court in protecting businesses from regulation for safety or conservation or other purposes. "I find attractive," he said, "the arguments of scholars such as Stephen Macedo, who defend an activist Supreme Court that would strike down laws restricting property rights." Some background is necessary to understand why that statement alarmed constitutional lawyers. In 1905, in the famous case of *Lochner v. New York,* the Supreme Court held that New York's law forbidding bakeries to hire bakers to work more than ten hours a day was unconstitutional because it violated the command of the Fourteenth Amendment that "liberty" not be infringed without due process of law. The Court used similar arguments in later cases, including cases that struck down early New Deal economic regulation.

Almost all constitutional lawyers now regard the *Lochner* decision, and the decisions that followed in its spirit, as disastrous mistakes. By the

1950s it was orthodox opinion that the due process and equal protection clauses leave state and national governments almost wholly free to balance competing interests of liberty, safety, equality, conservation, economic policy, and social justice in deciding how to regulate business practice. In 1955, for example, in the well-known case of *Williams v. Lee Optical*, the Court held that Oklahoma was permitted to impose restrictions on opticians that it did not impose on sellers of ready-made glasses, because there might well be some rational basis for that distinction even though Oklahoma had not provided one. The Court's hands-off attitude on economic matters is now thought necessary to allow government to regulate the economy effectively.

Stephen Macedo, who is a professor of government at Harvard, and some other constitutional scholars, including Richard Epstein of the University of Chicago Law School, have argued that the Court should reverse that practice and apply a stricter test to protect businesses, a test much closer to the strict test it uses to protect individuals from racial and other forms of discrimination. Macedo argues, for example, that the Court's decision in the optician case should now be overruled, and that the natural rights the Constitution protects should be understood to include economic as well as personal rights.[2] Bork, on the contrary, had emphasized his own firm opposition to any return to the spirit of the *Lochner* case; he supported the orthodox view that businesses do not have any substantial constitutional rights that restrict what government can do by way of safety or redistributive programs, beyond the right to be compensated when government directly confiscates their property.

It is extremely doubtful that Thomas could have been confirmed if he had remained loyal to his extreme position about abortion and his support for strengthened economic constitutional rights. He might simply have told the committee that he had changed his mind on these matters. But Bork had announced similar important changes in his views, and was savaged for what his critics then called, skeptically, a "confirmation conversion." So Thomas's advisers counseled a different strategy: they doubtless told him simply to disown ever having held the views his past statements seemed to announce.

Thomas explained his endorsement of the Lehrman article by saying he wanted to interest a conservative audience in civil rights, and thought that introducing them to the idea of natural law would be helpful to that end. He had, he said, chosen the Lehrman article to praise because his lecture was in the Lehrman auditorium, and he thought the choice of Lehrman would please his right-wing audience. He had only skimmed the article, and did not know that the only example of natural law thinking it contained was Lehrman's argument about abortion, in spite of the fact that Lehrman's article was titled "The Declaration of Independence and the Right to Life."

He took the same line about his reference to Macedo. He could not recall Macedo's arguments; he could only remember that he found them interesting. He meant merely to endorse the general idea that people have rights under natural law, not to endorse the particular use that Macedo actually made of the idea. Nor did he think that "natural law" or "natural rights" really had any connection with constitutional law at all. He had meant to say, in praising Lehrman's and Macedo's arguments about how the Court should decide cases, only that he found the idea of natural law interesting in some contexts, as an idea to "play around with," not that judges should use natural law to decide cases.

Several senators expressed dissatisfaction with these unpersuasive disavowals, but they were unable to coax any better explanation from him of what he had meant. Some senators attempted to discover his present views. They asked whether he accepted that the Constitution contains a right to privacy. Bork had denied any general right to privacy—he criticized the idea as something liberal judges had invented. But Kennedy and Souter had both said the Constitution does include such a right, and they had been easily confirmed. Thomas said he now agreed with them. But when he was asked the obvious next question—whether he thought the right to privacy includes a woman's right to control her own reproduction, as the Court had held it does in Roe v. Wade—he declined to answer on the ground that disclosing his opinion about that case would compromise his independence when the Court was asked to overrule it.

That is absurd. Judicial independence does not consist in justices having no previous opinions about the issues that come before them but in their willingness to attend carefully and honestly to arguments on both sides, and to be ready to change their minds if convinced. The majority of the present justices have made their opinions about Roe v. Wade plain, and no one doubts, for that reason, that they can fairly decide whether it should be reversed.[3] There are, I believe, sound reasons why nominees should in principle be reluctant to disclose their views about pending or imminent cases. The Constitution is designed to protect minority rights from violation by majoritarian authority, and it would undermine that function if senators could veto nominees who admitted an intention to vote for a politically unpopular minority in a pending case. But in this case there were important countervailing reasons for candor. Thomas was nominated by the leader of a party whose platform promised to appoint judges who would overrule *Roe v. Wade,* a fact that raised at least a suspicion that the administration knew how he intended to vote. In any case, as Senator Howard Metzenbaum pointed out with some annoyance, Thomas's scruples about discussing potential cases were highly selective: he had no compunctions about announcing his views on a number of other highly controversial constitutional issues that might well come before the Court, including not only the question of independent prosecutors, which I have mentioned, but the constitutionality of criminal sentencing guidelines and sensitive First Amendment issues about the establishment of religion.

Thomas could, moreover, have discussed the central jurisprudential issues involved in the abortion controversy—whether the right to privacy extends to procreative autonomy in principle, and what legitimate interests a state has in protecting fetal life—without having to indicate how he would resolve any conflict between that right and that interest in the circumstances of any particular case. That discussion might have given shrewd observers a good sense of his likely vote, but it would fall short of committing him to a concrete position.

Thomas would not be drawn into any discussion which bore on abortion at all, however, and some of the statements he made to suggest his openness of mind on the subject were breathtaking. Though he was at Yale Law School when *Roe v. Wade* was decided, he said he could not remember any discussion of the decision either in class or among fellow students. He had never since discussed the issue with anyone else, he said, and in fact had no opinion about *Roe v. Wade* himself, in spite of his unstinting endorsement of Lehrman's claim that that decision was judicial murder. He said he had signed the report on family policy, which recommended that justices be appointed who would overrule that decision, without reading the report, and did not know that it expressed that view.

So Thomas's five days of testimony left senators with the following choice. If they did not believe his disavowals of his past statements, or his claim never to have discussed abortion with others or come to any view himself, then he had lied to them, deliberately covering up his record and opinions because he knew the American public would not wish him confirmed if it knew the truth. If they did believe him, then, by his own admission, his many speeches had been made in complete ignorance of or indifference to the most important constitutional issues of his time. He had

praised books and articles he had not read or had only skimmed, strongly
endorsing ideas he either did not understand or rejected, just to impress
particular right-wing audiences he was addressing, to get them to support
his views on other matters, and, perhaps, to advance his own career in a
right-wing administration. How could a senator vote for Thomas on either
assumption?

But the Judiciary Committee split seven to seven on the nomination,
and, as I have said, the full Senate would apparently have confirmed him if
the allegations of sexual harassment had not been publicized. No doubt
President Bush selected Thomas to succeed the only black justice ever
previously appointed to the Court, Thurgood Marshall, exactly because it
was so difficult for politicians to oppose a black nominee for that position.
(Bush, of course, cynically claimed that race played no part in Thomas's
selection.) In any case, the liberal senators who voted for him stressed his
background as their reason: Senator Arlen Specter of Pennsylvania, the
only Republican on the Judiciary Committee who had voted against Bork,
said he voted for Thomas by paying more attention to his "roots" than to
his writing, and others suggested, as Dean Guido Calabresi of the Yale
Law School had argued in his testimony before the committee, that
Thomas would add diversity to the Court, and might "grow" in office. If
Thomas is confirmed, we must hope that these predictions are justified,
that he develops an independent position that reflects rather than denies
his distinct background, and that he does not become just one more willing
corporal in Rehnquist's campaign to reverse the main achievements of
constitutional law of the last four decades. Nevertheless, the manner of
Thomas's appointment—the mockery it made of the Senate's constitutional duty to pass on judicial qualification—has damaged the nomination
process no matter how good or bad a justice he might become.

When the hearings closed, the Judiciary Committee's chairman, Joseph
Biden, announced that he would be considering revisions in the committee's procedures for future Supreme Court nominations. He might recommend, as Anthony Lewis suggested in the *New York Times,* that special
counsel for each side, rather than committee members themselves, should
carry the main burden of questioning a nominee, as such counsel do in
other committee hearings. The main flaw in the Thomas hearings was not
procedural, however, but jurisprudential. No change in procedures can
protect the committee from a future stonewalling nominee—particularly
one who has published very little, as Kennedy and Souter had—unless at

least a substantial number of its members are willing, in public, to abandon a thesis which no one with any experience in constitutional law really believes but which most senators apparently think the public cherishes.

This could be called "the neutrality thesis": that a Supreme Court justice can reach a decision in a difficult constitutional case by some technical legal method that wholly insulates his decision from his own most basic convictions about political fairness and social justice. The thesis does not insist only that a justice can set aside his own party or sectional allegiances, or his own self-interest, in reaching decisions, as of course he can and must. It also insists that justices can reach decisions uninfluenced by their own convictions about fundamental issues of political and constitutional philosophy. Political theorists and legal philosophers disagree about such fundamental issues: they disagree, for example, over whether an ideal democracy is one in which the constitutional rights individual citizens have against the majority are limited to detailed rights codified in explicit texts, so that contemporary majorities are free themselves to decide whether any further or more generous rights should be accorded, or whether, on the contrary, a true democracy accepts that constitutional rights should be understood as reflecting some overall, coherent conception of free and equal citizenship, understood as a national moral ideal, so that individual citizens must have the power to argue, before courts charged with enforcing that national commitment, that the ideal grants them rights not previously recognized.

They disagree about more substantive issues as well; they disagree, for example, over whether the liberty of individuals to make personal ethical choices for themselves—about religious observance or sexual behavior, for instance—is only a liberty some people, including liberals, particularly value although others do not, or whether that liberty is, on the other hand, so fundamental to the very idea of a free society that no community that abridges it can be called truly free. They disagree about philosophical issues that cut across the other differences of opinion I have mentioned: they disagree, for example, about whether fundamental political principles, including ideals of democracy and principles affirming basic liberties, have some objective moral standing, or whether any such principles derive only from subjective preferences, so that democratic politics can be only a matter of satisfying whatever preferences or prejudices the public happens to have.

The neutrality thesis holds that an honest justice's opinions on issues like these need not, and should not, make a difference to his decisions in constitutional cases. That is preposterous. The crucial clauses of the Constitution are drafted in very abstract moral language: they command "due process," for example, and "equal protection of the laws." It is true, and important, that any judge's opinions about the correct application of these abstract clauses to particular cases must respect the Constitution's text and the history of its enactment and interpretation. But, as almost every controversial Supreme Court decision demonstrates, these can often be read in different ways, and any particular justice's interpretation will be dominated by his convictions about what an ideal democracy would be like, or what rights are really fundamental, or whether ideas about the character of ideal democracy and fundamental rights have an objective basis or are only subjective preferences.

It is important to see, however, that if the neutrality thesis were true, then Senator Kohl's test would be inappropriate: the committee would have no need to investigate a judge's own "constitutional philosophy" because that philosophy would not figure in his constitutional decisions. So different Republican senators repeatedly endorsed the neutrality thesis throughout the hearings. Senator Charles Grassley of Iowa asked Thomas, for example, whether he agreed that judges should decide neutrally, applying the Constitution as it really is, not reading their own philosophy into it, as in Grassley's view too many justices have done in recent years. Thomas solemnly said that he did agree. Some senators expressed disquiet about the neutrality thesis, and Senator Paul Simon of Illinois said that Thomas's claim that he had no agenda was unrealistic because "the reality is that you become a policy maker on the United States Supreme Court." But Simon did not press the point, and no senator asked Thomas how judges could be neutral in constitutional matters.

Thomas himself expressly relied at several points on the neutrality thesis as a justification for not responding to the committee's questions. "With respect to my personal views," he told Senator Strom Thurmond of South Carolina, "my personal views have no place in adjudication." Several times he used a peculiar metaphor, which presupposes the neutrality thesis, to explain why his former views were irrelevant. Those views, he said, were appropriate to a politician and a member of the executive, who must sometimes act as a litigator for his administration. But now, as a judge, he had "stripped down like a runner," shedding all past opinions and convictions so that he could just apply strict, neutral legal reasoning the way a good judge does, entirely uninfluenced by any philosophical convictions of his own about the character of democracy or the nature of the Constitution or which rights are fundamental to liberty.

The myth of judicial neutrality has been a favorite Republican dogma for decades: Nixon, Reagan, and Bush all condemned liberal justices for "inventing" rights based on their own personal moral views, and promised to appoint justices who would decide constitutional cases in a neutral way, so that their decisions would be based only on the law and in no way on their own moral views. They and their nominees, including Bork, appealed to the idea of an "original intention" to explain how constitutional decisions could be neutral. Justices can decide even very hard constitutional cases, they said, by discovering and applying the intentions of the constitutional "framers"—the statesmen who enacted the particular constitutional clauses in question. But Bork's conspicuous failure to provide a coherent defense of that view, in his own Senate confirmation hearings and in his later book, has exposed the view's central failure.[4] We must understand the intentions of the framers of the equal protection clause, for instance, to be abstract rather than concrete: they intended to say what they did say, that the law should treat people as equals, not that it should treat people in the way they themselves happened to think amounted to treating them as equals. So even judges who accept the responsibility of respecting the framers' intentions must still decide for themselves what treating people as equals requires in the circumstances of contemporary society.[5]

If the senators had read Thomas's past writings carefully, they would have discovered the important fact that he himself had rejected the neutrality thesis, and had been preaching against it for many years. He rejected "original intention" jurisprudence as it had been understood by other conservative lawyers, which, he said, "readily lapses into a Holmesian indifference toward or even contempt of 'values.'" "I would advocate instead," he said, "a true jurisprudence of original intent" in which "morality and political judgment are understood in objective terms."[6] Conservatives should argue, he said, not that judges can discover some "original intention" of the founders that is sufficiently detailed and concrete to decide all constitutional cases, but that the best substantive political morality, and therefore the best interpretation of the abstract clauses of the Constitution, is a conservative one. That is, that the best contemporary understanding of the abstract ideals declared not only in the Constitution, but in the Declaration of Independence and the *Federalist Papers* as well, justifies conservative views about abortion and economic rights and the injustice of affirmative action. "The higher law background," he said, ". . . provides the only firm basis for just, wise, and constitutional decisions."[7]

That was the real—but unfortunately misunderstood—point of Thomas's repeated discussions of "natural law" in his speeches and articles. Several senators questioned him about natural law in the hearings, and the press devoted much time and space to discussions of the subject. But the committee exchanges, and most of the press reports, were deeply confused. The phrase "natural law" refers to an objective moral reality which endows people with fundamental moral rights that are not created by custom or convention or legislation, but rather exist as an independent body of moral principle.[8] As Thomas pointed out, most of the eighteenth-century statesmen who drafted and argued for the Constitution believed in natural law. So, I think, do most Americans now: most of us think that apartheid, or torture, or other forms of brutal repression, for example, are morally wrong, according to objective principles, even when condoned by the laws in force where they occur.

The idea of natural law has figured in two very different, though both controversial, claims that legal philosophers have debated over the last several centuries. The first is an absolute claim about the ultimate test of what the law actually is in any political community. Some philosophers, including Saint Thomas Aquinas, insisted that natural law must be treated as the ultimate law of any human society, so that laws made by human legislators, including statesmen who frame constitutions, are invalid—no law at all—if they contradict that fundamental moral or divine law.

Some of the American abolitionists were advocates of natural law in that absolute sense: they argued that the Constitution itself was legally invalid because it embodied an unjust compromise that permitted slavery to continue, a compromise that was contrary to natural law. Some twentieth-century legal philosophers, including Lon Fuller of the Harvard Law School, took the same view of the Nazi legal system: they argued that Nazi laws were invalid because they were too immoral to count as law at all. I know of no constitutional scholar who applies that view to the American Constitution now, however: no scholar claims that part of what the Constitution plainly says is not binding on judges because it is too immoral to be law.

The second claim in which the idea of natural law figures is a very different and much more popular one. It is interpretive rather than absolute: it holds not that immoral laws are invalid but that abstract or vague or otherwise unclear laws, including the abstract clauses of the Constitution, should be interpreted, so far as their language permits, to conform to the objective moral rights the natural law doctrine assumes people to have.[9] The interpretive view holds that when judges must decide, for example, whether some punishment offends the Eighth Amendment's condemnation of "cruel and unusual" punishments, they should decide by asking which punishments are, as a matter of objective moral fact, really cruel; and when they must decide whether some law offends the due process clause of the Fourteenth Amendment, they should decide by asking whether the law violates an important objective moral right.

Thomas's writings make plain that he had the interpretive not the absolute natural law claim in mind. The interpretive claim does not imply, as the absolute one does, that Supreme Court justices have the authority to override the clear terms of the Constitution when they believe morality would dictate what they know the Constitution does not. But the interpretive claim plainly rejects the ideal of neutral adjudication that Thomas claimed to hold when he spoke in the hearings about stripping down like a runner. Two judges each of whom accepts the interpretive claim will produce dramatically different decisions if they disagree about what objective moral rights people actually have. Thomas said, in his speeches, that liberals had been using the interpretive natural law method to support liberal decisions, and he encouraged conservatives to use the same method in a radically different direction: to emphasize the moral rights of a fetus rather than of a pregnant woman, and the moral dignity of individuals disadvantaged or insulted by affirmative action rather than of groups benefited by it. Objective morality, he said, as conservatives understand it, provides the best understanding of the Constitution, and is therefore the best protection against not only what he called "run-amok judges" but also "run-amok majorities"— majorities who might vote for permissive abortion laws or affirmative action "set-aside" programs or restrictive economic regulation.[10]

Senator Biden and other senators for some reason assumed that Thomas's earlier endorsements of natural law were meant as endorsements of the absolute, now almost unanimously rejected, claim. They asked him whether he really thought that Supreme Court justices could "override" the Constitution in the name of ultimate moral principles. Thomas accepted that mistaken characterization of his earlier statements, and said that his interest in natural law was only theoretical—he was interested in how Lincoln, as a statesman, could have thought the Constitution invalid on the question of slavery—and that he obviously did not think that judges had the power to declare the Constitution invalid. That seemed evasive, because, as Biden pointed out, his earlier statements were plainly about what judges, not statesmen, should do. But if he had corrected the senators' mistake, and insisted that he had in mind the interpretive claim of natural law, which obviously includes a view of how judges should decide cases, he could not have maintained his pretense of believing that judges could decide constitutional cases in a neutral, stripped-down, way. He would have opened himself to exactly the discussion of his substantive views of moral principle he was so anxious to avoid, presumably because he knew how unpopular his views would be with the senators and their constituents.

The senators' confusion over natural law made it easier, therefore, for Thomas to dissociate himself from his own jurisprudence. If the committee had correctly identified his past view as rejecting the myth of neutral adjudication, and as urging judges to take objective morality into account in deciding what the Constitution means, then the senators could more easily have pressed him to discuss his own moral beliefs. He could then have been asked, for example, how judges should reach and test their moral convictions. He sometimes flirted with an explicitly theological explanation of the source of the conservative view of moral rights. "As John Quincy Adams put it," he said, "'Our political way of life is by the laws of nature of nature's God.'"[11] But for the most part he rested his argument on the Declaration of Independence and on the fact that the founders believed in an objective moral order, as the *Federalist Papers,* among other sources he cited, amply demonstrate.

None of these sources, of course, is an authority for the view that the objective moral order is a distinctly conservative rather than a liberal one. The proposition that all men are created equal, and are endowed with inalienable individual rights, leaves entirely open what equal citizenship consists in, and which moral rights people actually have. Thomas simply assumed—as he expected his conservative audiences would—that these natural rights were inconsistent with abortion, affirmative action, and burdensome regulation of business. Once he had acknowledged the dominant role of moral conviction in constitutional adjudication, however, he would have had no ground on which to refuse to defend his own opinions on these and other issues. He might have declined to say how he would decide particular pending Supreme Court cases. But he could not have avoided discussing the general moral issues he had himself raised as central to large numbers of cases. The resulting discussion would have been fascinating, not only for its impact on his nomination, but as a rare opportunity for a public discussion of moral issues about which the nation is now very deeply divided.

Of course since Thomas had presumably been coached to say as little as possible, he might have disowned the second as well as the first claim of natural law, even if these had been carefully distinguished. He might well have insisted that, contrary to what he had said so often before, judges really can decide great constitutional cases in a morally neutral way. But if any member of the committee had been ready to challenge that myth, he could have pressed Thomas to defend it against Thomas's own earlier objections. In his speeches Thomas had ridiculed the idea that "original intention" can provide clear results in all or even the most difficult cases. Did he now mean to endorse that method? If so, how would he answer his own powerful objections to it, as well as the objections others have raised?

What other neutral method could he describe? The main academic opponents of the idea that moral principle should play a role in legal interpretation are skeptics, who claim that the very idea of objective moral principle is an illusion. They advocate not that judges decide cases neutrally, which they rightly regard as impossible, but that judges should enforce their own personal preferences, just because they are in power and therefore in a position to make their own preferences into law. We have good reason to fear, as I have argued elsewhere, that Chief Justice Rehnquist and some of his supporters on the court actually embrace that cynical form of skepticism.[12] But Thomas could hardly have publicly endorsed it.

In the end, however, Thomas was allowed to hide behind the standard Republican myth, the myth he had himself so often denounced, because none of the senators insisted on what is obvious: that the Supreme Court is necessarily a forum of principle where the justices' own convictions about the most fundamental issues of democracy and justice will often be decisive of what the Court decides. I do not mean to endorse Thomas's own interpretive natural law view, which, as he explained it in his articles, makes only the justices' opinions about objective moral reality pertinent to their decisions.

He ignored a crucial requirement of constitutional adjudication: Supreme Court justices, like all judges, must always respect the integrity of the law, which means that they must not deploy moral principles, no matter how much they are personally committed to such principles, that cannot be defended as consistent with the general history of past Supreme Court decisions and the general structure of American political practice.[13] But very often sharply different political principles, which recommend very different results in a new case, can be seen as consistent with the past, and justices then have no choice but to decide for themselves which to prefer on general grounds of political morality.

In the *Griswold* case, for example, in which the Supreme Court announced the right to privacy which figures so prominently in the abortion controversy, both the principle that individuals have a right to be sovereign over personal decisions central to their moral personality, and the principle that they do not, had support in different parts of constitutional history. The Court's decision, in favor of some form of that right, was necessarily based on the justices' own sense that the right of privacy is not simply something some citizens are anxious to have but is rather a central feature of any genuinely free society.

No doubt many people, perhaps including many senators, prefer the myth of morally neutral adjudication to that more complex but more accurate description of how justices interpret the Constitution. But we can no longer afford whatever comfort the myth may give us. Successive Republican administrations have campaigned to capture the Supreme Court for their right-wing constituencies for the next generation. Conservatives used to say that they were taking the Supreme Court away from the elitist liberals and handing it back to the people. But the Bork defeat showed that they were wrong about the kind of Constitution the people actually want.

If Thomas is confirmed, it will make plain what the Kennedy and Souter appointments suggested—that further right-wing appointments to the Court are much more likely to succeed if the nominees' convictions and intentions are kept hidden from the public. The Senate's constitutional role requires it to combat that unattractive strategy by refusing to let nominees picked for their politics hide behind the myth that politics never matters. Next time the myth should be attacked directly, by senators or committee counsel who can explain to the public why constitutional philosophy matters very much, and why nominees who say they have none are unfit for the job they want.

November 7, 1991

16

▼

Anita Hill and
Clarence Thomas

We knew, as we watched the Clarence Thomas hearings in the Senate Judiciary Committee, that they were an important event in American legal and social history, that they were as revealing as they were disgraceful. But we disagreed sharply about what it was they revealed, and how similar disgraces might be avoided in the future. The anniversary of the hearings is an occasion for another, more considered look, aided by four important and diverse new books about the Thomas nomination.

Senator Paul Simon, Democrat of Illinois, is a member of the Senate Judiciary Committee who voted against Judge Thomas. In his book *Advise and Consent*, he offers a thoughtful, modest, and shrewd appraisal of his and the Senate's performance, not just in the Thomas hearings, but also in the equally embattled nomination hearings four years earlier that led to the rejection of Robert Bork as a Supreme Court justice. And he adds an instructive history of other important confirmation struggles in American history and makes helpful suggestions about reforming the confirmation process.

Simon observes that in the second round of hearings (which explored charges by Anita F. Hill, an Oklahoma law professor, that Judge Thomas had sexually harassed her when she worked for him years earlier), the Republican senators on the committee, especially Orrin G. Hatch of Utah, Alan Simpson of Wyoming, and Arlen Specter of Pennsylvania, acted as partisans eager to destroy Hill. Simon concedes that the Democrats, attempting a more judicious demeanor, made several mistakes, and he suggests that Judge Thomas would not have been confirmed—the eventual vote for him in the Senate was fifty-two to forty-eight, the smallest winning margin for a Supreme Court appointment in history—if they had not. He thinks, for example, that they were wrong in not insisting that Angela Wright testify. Wright, another former employee who worked for Judge Thomas on the Equal Employment Opportunity Commission in 1984 and 1985, swore under oath that he had behaved toward her in much the same sexually offensive way that he was alleged to have treated Hill. Judge Thomas testified that he had fired her because she had called a fellow employee a "faggot." But she had denied that, and Simon points out that Judge Thomas had given her a glowing testimonial after she left his employ. Angela Wright's affidavit was included in the committee's final report, but after much discussion on both sides, it was decided not to ask her to testify on television. The impact of her story would have been much greater if she had done so.

Simon also believes it was a mistake to propose (as did Senator Joseph Biden of Delaware, the Democratic chairman of the committee) that Judge Thomas should have the benefit of the doubt about Anita Hill's charges, which meant that senators unpersuaded either way should decide on the assumption that Judge Thomas, not Hill, was telling the truth. The hearings were not a criminal trial, where the defendant should have the benefit of that kind of doubt, but an attempt to discover whether it was in the country's best interests that Judge Thomas be confirmed in spite of Hill's charges. Many senators said they were voting for Judge Thomas because they didn't know whom to believe; that argument, which Simon calls the weakest one for the nomination, allowed them to avoid deciding the crucial question of whether it was right to confirm Judge Thomas's nomination.

Many critics of the Democrats' performance also thought they should have asked Judge Thomas whether he had ever seen pornographic films of the kind Anita Hill claimed he had insisted on describing to her. *Newsweek* reported that a newspaper had found records of Judge Thomas's renting such films. Simon insists, however, that the Democrats were right not to enter that territory; Supreme Court nominees should not be expected to discuss their sexual activities and preferences, and it might have set a precedent if Judge Thomas had been asked to do so even in his special circumstances.

Timothy M. Phelps and Helen Winternitz are political journalists (he is a *Newsday* reporter who, along with Nina Totenberg of National Public Radio, first broke the story of Anita Hill's charges). Their book, *Capitol*

Games, is a comprehensive, beautifully written, and insightful overview of the whole Clarence Thomas story, from his rise from poverty in Pinpoint, Georgia, through his first year of service on the Supreme Court. Much of the account is based on the authors' own research, some of which is published for the first time.

Phelps and Winternitz also believe that the confirmation battle turned on the political effectiveness of the Bush administration and on the ineffectiveness and mistakes of the nomination's opponents. They say that the decision not to solicit Angela Wright's testimony was "probably the most important of the whole hearings," because "the question of whether more than one alleged victim of Thomas's sexual harassment existed was absolutely critical in many senators' minds." The authors say that Wright, like Anita Hill, had told her story years ago, when it happened, to a responsible witness, Rose Jourdain, who was interviewed by the committee staff; Jourdain's confirmation rebutted the Republicans' suggestion that Wright made up her story after she read Anita Hill's account, as vengeance for having been fired. The authors also point out, however, that Hill's own hastily assembled staff of advisers themselves asked that Wright not testify: they were afraid of confusing Hill's solid image with that of the more mercurial Angela Wright.

Phelps and Winternitz also provide a detailed and intriguing account of how Judge Thomas's key supporters in the Bush administration maneuvered to gain him the nomination, and then acted to confuse and delay any opposition by blacks. They report, for instance, that the White House arranged for intermediaries to approach Benjamin Hooks, the executive director of the National Association for the Advancement of Colored People, who informed them before the nomination was announced that he would not oppose Judge Thomas and might even support him. In the end that organization did oppose Judge Thomas, and Hooks himself testified against the nomination. But the NAACP's delay, which the authors say Benjamin Hooks helped to produce, made its opposition much less effective, and many commentators claimed that Judge Thomas would have been defeated if the NAACP and similar organizations had acted earlier. *Capitol Games* reports a good deal of other White House intervention of the same sort. It maintains, for example, that the administration changed its announced position against financial aid to all-black schools to gain the support of an important black Alabama politician who was influential with Richard Shelby, the Democratic senator from Alabama who voted for Judge Thomas.

Two other recent books on these subjects are entirely different in content and scope, and they are even more arresting. *Race-ing Justice, En-gendering Power* is a collection of eighteen essays about the Thomas nomination, written by prominent academics and edited, with an introduction, by the novelist and critic Toni Morrison. *Court of Appeal* is made up of forty-two essays by black writers, teachers, and intellectuals, together with a chronology of the confirmation events and a variety of official statements and position papers. The essays in the first of these collections are, on the whole, more scholarly and analytical. Those in the second are more diverse in length, style, tone, and perspective. But collectively, an extraordinary range of distinguished black intellectuals appears. The fact that so many of them react as passionately and eloquently as they do, yet interpret the events and their importance so differently from one another, is itself an important fact in the history of race and gender in the United States. *Race-ing Justice, En-gendering Power* and *Court of Appeal* are thus among the rare books that are themselves events in the history they interpret.

The Thomas hearings revealed a great deal about the United States, its people, and its politics. It taught us much about the character of some of our most prominent officials, including not only Judge Thomas himself, but also President Bush—whose cynicism has never been more evident than when he claimed that race played no part in his choice of Judge Thomas to replace Justice Thurgood Marshall, and that Judge Thomas, who had never practiced law or produced any legal scholarship at all, was simply "the best man for the job." As for Senators Hatch, Simpson, and Specter, their political careers and those of other politicians may well have been shortened, and will certainly be changed, by what the women of America learned about them in the course of the nomination hearings.

In retrospect, however, two more structural issues that the nomination brought into sharper focus seem more important than the character or the fates of particular politicians. The first is a jurisprudential problem. Though the second round of the Thomas hearings was tawdry, the first round, meant to explore his qualifications, was an even graver disaster. Though some of the senators pressed Judge Thomas to declare his views about *Roe v. Wade* and other specific cases, he was never asked to explain his views about absolutely crucial issues of constitutional theory no Supreme Court nominee should ever be allowed to evade again—like the question, for example, of whether the abstract provisions of the Bill of Rights should be read narrowly, on the ground that any restriction on the majority's power to have what it wants diminishes democracy, or more broadly, on the competing view that guaranteeing basic rights is a precondition of democracy. Judges' convictions about such basic issues inevitably guide their interpretation of the Constitution, no matter how neutral they claim to be or how fervently they promise not to "read their own views" into the text.

Potential justices may properly refuse to declare how they would vote on specific cases. But they should have reflected on these fundamental constitutional issues before appearing before the committee, and should be disqualified if they refuse to explain their views about them, because senators and the public are entitled to know not just the "character" a nominee's handlers have decided to project, but also whether a nominee has a constitutional philosophy, and what it is. The committee might well consider publishing a report, in advance of the next nomination, describing issues candidates should be prepared to discuss. If in the first round of hearings Clarence Thomas had disclosed the philosophical convictions that he subsequently revealed on the Court, another round might never have been necessary.

The second structural issue the hearings brought to the surface is cultural rather than jurisprudential, and it is the main focus of the two collections of essays. For decades it was thought to be a cardinal requirement of black progress toward social and economic justice that blacks work and fight together, for one another and for the race. But particularly since the early 1980s, many blacks have come seriously to doubt the point of that solidarity for themselves and its value for their race. For example, a growing number of educated and prosperous black professionals, many of whom benefited from affirmative action programs in universities and professional schools, now embrace a neo-conservatism that, as Robert Chrisman, an editor of *The Black Scholar,* says, seems more attitudinal than philosophical, but that condemns those same affirmative action programs and other liberal policies.

These blacks say such programs are bad for the race, because they perpetuate feelings of inferiority and limit what the most successful blacks can achieve on their own. Some blacks have been tempted to that view, not only by a genuine belief in its soundness, which some thoughtful and committed black scholars hold, but also because it offers them a career in Republican politics, where conservative blacks enjoy the benefit, as some have put it, of a very short queue. The development constitutes a clear challenge to orthodox black solidarity; at the same time, it makes it unclear what black solidarity now amounts to, since there is no longer a consensus about what blacks anxious to help their race as well as themselves should now do or support.

Clarence Thomas, in his political opinions and career, exemplifies this rejection of old-fashioned black solidarity. But in the end it was old-fashioned solidarity that won him a place on the Supreme Court, and allowed the right wing to secure a justice doctrinaire and young enough to serve their interests for perhaps four decades. In retrospect, Judge Thomas's exploitation of the old ideal, in both phases of the hearings, seems extraordinarily skillful.

Robert Bork was denied confirmation because, among other reasons, his record showed distaste for affirmative action programs and for judicial decisions regarded as essential to the civil rights movement. Southern senators voted against Judge Bork because they worried about losing the crucial black vote in their states. Judge Thomas's record was, if anything, worse than Judge Bork's in that respect. In speeches to right-wing groups over several years, he had attacked conventional ideas about minority rights, made fun of civil rights heroes, including Thurgood Marshall, and ridiculed his own sister for accepting welfare.

He was endorsed by Senator Strom Thurmond of South Carolina, who once had called for segregation forever; by Senator Jesse Helms of North Carolina, whom many blacks have regarded as their enemy for decades; and by the racist from Louisiana, David Duke. But the same southern senators who had voted against Robert Bork out of deference to black constituents supported Clarence Thomas because the polls told them that was what these constituents wanted now. If the Thomas appointment was bad for most American blacks—and most of the contributors to *Race-ing Justice, En-Gendering Power* and *Court of Appeal* think it was—then it was, in part, a self-inflicted wound.

Despite Judge Thomas's own past claims that blacks must think and act as individuals, in the end he appealed directly to the black community, above the heads of the senators he was facing, claiming that community's support just because he was black, just because he was one of them. In the first round of hearings, before Anita Hill's charges had been made public, he steadily refused to discuss constitutional law or theory. He wrote off all the radical speeches that had earned him his nomination with bland confessions that would have shamed most people—he said he hadn't even bothered to read a crucial White House report he had signed, or an extreme anti-abortion pamphlet he had once praised as "splendid," and said he had praised the pamphlet only because he knew his audience admired its author. He said he had never discussed *Roe v. Wade,* and had no view about the case himself, although the decision was handed down while he was at Yale Law School and soon became the most controversial and discussed legal decision of his generation. Though Judge Thomas made this last declaration with a poker face, he could hardly have expected many people to believe it; and, as Senator Simon writes, that statement and others made under oath by Judge Thomas "invited disbelief" and left "some of us on the committee . . . with the feeling that he had not been straight with us."

Clarence Thomas seemed not to care whether any of what he said was actually believed. He emphasized, instead, his background and experience, dwelling on his childhood in poverty, appealing directly to blacks as one of them, telling them that his race was all that mattered. It worked. The first polls reported that blacks supported him by a roughly two-to-one margin, and that fact made it immediately more difficult for liberal senators flatly to declare him incompetent or unqualified.

It was not only unsophisticated blacks, who might have been unaware of Judge Thomas's convictions about race, who supported him on grounds of solidarity. Several contributors to *Race-ing Justice, En-gendering Power* and *Court of Appeal* offered arguments justifying the same support. Some said they supported him because if he failed, President Bush would appoint a hostile conservative anyway, but a white one. Many took the view of Maya Angelou, the prominent black writer, who, in an essay first published before the hearings began, said that though many of Judge Thomas's views were terrible, blacks should support him because he might well change, responding to his black heritage, once on the Court.

These reasons seem rationalizations. Isn't it a worse insult to blacks to have an unqualified and hostile black justice, who can pose as their representative, than it would be to have an equally unqualified and hostile white one? What reason did anyone have to suppose that Justice Thomas would suddenly feel a sympathy for other blacks he had not shown before? Ronald W. Walters, chairman of the Political Science Department at Howard University in Washington, ridicules the hope that once Justice Thomas put on his robe "all the spirits of his black ancestors would rain down upon him and that this divine revelation would cause him to 'do the right thing.'" Justice Thomas's performance on the Court suggests, so far, that Walters was closer to the truth than Angelou. Justice Thomas has voted with Antonin Scalia, the fiercest conservative on the Court, in all but two cases, and his opinions led the *New York Times* to call him, in an editorial, "the youngest and the cruelest" justice. The only major civil rights organization that supported him in the confirmation, the Southern Christian Leadership Conference, has now, with the benefit of hindsight, changed its mind.

It is hard to resist the conclusion that even the black intellectuals who supported Clarence Thomas initially did so because they were emotionally unable to oppose a black man's bid for one of the most elevated positions an American can reach. It is also hard to resist the conclusion of Manning Marable, a professor of history and political science at the University of Colorado, Boulder, in *Race-ing Justice, En-gendering Power,* that in the Thomas case "the majority of the African-American community has supported the wrong person for the wrong position for the wrong reasons"; or Toni Morrison's conclusion, in her elegant introduction to that volume, that "the time for undiscriminating racial unity has passed."

The second round of hearings turned on a very different challenge to old ideals of solidarity, sponsored by black women torn between loyalty to race and a sense of the injustices, like those Anita Hill said she had suffered, that solidarity sometimes keeps hidden. In reply to that different challenge, Clarence Thomas expanded his appeal to solidarity to include one of its less attractive aspects—he sent the message that Anita Hill was a traitor who had dishonored him in front of white people. He found the perfect image for that message in an irresponsible historical distortion: he cried out that he was the victim of a lynching, meaning that Anita Hill had betrayed black men by reinforcing the sexual stereotype that had caused so many of them really to be lynched in the past.

In that explosive moment of self-pity, Clarence Thomas tried to tell blacks, once again, not to listen to the testimony or arguments that were coming, but to support him simply as the archetypal black victim, this time betrayed by one of their own. He announced that he had not even listened to Anita Hill's statement, which astounded even some of his supporters, but brilliantly reinforced, by example, the advice he meant to give: that the details or truth of what she said were beside the point.

Once again the strategy worked. No one produced a respectable argument suggesting a motive for Anita Hill to lie, and the Republicans' lame alternative suggestion, that she was suffering from delusional erotomania, collapsed when their only evidence was the bizarre testimony of a narcissistic witness who, Senator Simon believes, plainly had emotional problems and needed help himself. But most Americans, including most black Americans, nevertheless told polltakers that they thought Judge Thomas was telling the truth, and it gradually became clear that what they really meant was that he should not lose his prize just because he had talked dirty to a black woman a long time ago.

The two collections of essays report a wide variety of explanations for that conviction, and most of these reveal disturbing assumptions: that sex has a different meaning in the black community, that black women are less innocent or need less protection than white ones, and that in any case black women have no right to shame black men by telling sexual tales on the street. As several of the essays argue, white American culture has promoted the first two of those assumptions since slavery, and the polls show how ready most Americans are to accept the third as well.

In *Race-ing Justice, En-gendering Power,* Andrew Ross, who teaches English at Princeton University, suggests that although Senator Hatch claimed to be Judge Thomas's principal defender, his elaborate and re-peated detailing of Anita Hill's embarrassing charges, asking the nominee to deny them one by one after he had already denied them all categorically together, acted to fix the stereotype of black sexuality in people's minds as effectively as anything Hill had said herself. Gayle Pemberton, an associate director of Afro-American Studies at Princeton, reports "much speculation among black women how the hearings might have been transformed had Anita Hill been white." And Toni Morrison, in her introduction, says that "an accusation of such weight as sexual misconduct would probably have disqualified a white candidate on its face."

Anita Hill's testimony failed to stop Clarence Thomas, however, pri-marily because blacks as well as whites supported him against her by about two to one. Several contributors to *Court of Appeal* were themselves in that large majority. Jacquelyne Johnson Jackson, an associate professor of medical sociology at Duke University Medical Center, reports her own reaction: her "first and lasting" impression of Anita Hill, she says, was that "she's 'them against us,'" and must be "a scorned woman" who antici-pated "personal and monetary benefits." Nathan and Julia Hare decided that Hill was the tool of white feminists anxious to deny Judge Thomas the nomination after he had earned it "fair and square," and they express pride that "black people as a whole had stood impressively tall and . . . justice had triumphed in black America."

Other contributors to the two collections report the same reactions among black friends and neighbors. A customer at a candle store told the economist Julianne Malveaux, who came into the shop in the midst of the hearings, "I hate that bitch." Melba Joyce Boyd, the director of African-American Studies at the University of Michigan, Flint, reports the view of her friend's husband and father-in-law that Hill "should never have exposed him in front of white America." "Black women," Boyd says, "are still expected to . . . endure indignities simply because to reveal the truth about the devils in the camp would be an embarrassment for the 'race.'"

In a much-discussed op-ed piece in the *New York Times,* reprinted in *Court of Appeal,* the sociologist Orlando Patterson offered his own version of that point of view. He said that gender relations within the black community are different from the "neo-Puritan and elitist model" promoted by "the dominant school of American feminists," and that while Judge Thomas had "allegedly regaled" Anita Hill with "Rabelaisian" humor, it was perhaps only to reaffirm their common cultural origins. Patterson added that Clarence Thomas was entitled to lie under oath, and deny these conversations even if they had taken place, on what Patterson called the "utilitarian" ground that the punishment Puritan white America would enact if he told the truth was wholly disproportionate to any offense he had committed.

That is preposterous: a judge who would accept that kind of excuse for perjury, let alone one who would commit perjury himself even to save his career, is fit only for impeachment. Patterson's whole argument overlooks, moreover, the crucial fact that Clarence Thomas and Anita Hill were not on equal terms in the workplace that his earthy humor supposedly enlivened. Judge Thomas had power over her future, not just as an employer but because he was the kind of potential sponsor young professionals, and particularly black ones, need and are reluctant to cut off or offend. It is that kind of power that makes sexual harassment so vile: it forces women to choose between humiliation and self-injury, a choice that drove Anita Hill into the hospital with stomach pain ten years ago and left a sense of injustice burning in her for a decade.

Orlando Patterson's essay helps explain, however, the sense many black women have that their problems are special, that they cannot simply merge their interests with those of either black men or white women. In a *New York Times Magazine* article reprinted in *Court of Appeal,* Rosemary L. Bray, an editor of *The New York Times Book Review,* says "black men and white women have often made claims to our loyalty and our solidarity in the service of their respective struggles for recognition and autonomy, understanding only dimly that what might seem like liberty for each is for us only a kind of parole." Several contributors to the two collections suggest that black women therefore need a special, collective sense of their own identity and their own problems; they need, in effect, a new concept of distinctly black feminism.

That concept might well have great sociological value. But it would be dangerous if it became just another form of spurious solidarity, another category that could be used by people with power to claim the automatic allegiance of those without it. Anita Hill acted when she did, and maintained her extraordinary dignity throughout, for only one reason that either research or rationality has yet brought to light. She thought it wrong that someone who abused power and enjoyed other people's suffering should join a court whose members must rely on their own instincts to interpret the most basic rights of American citizens. She acted out of allegiance not to race or class or sex, but only to humanity and the ideals of law.

Many of the black writers point out that Anita Hill had no useful cultural stereotypes available to match those Judge Thomas used to win support for himself: black women, they say, have no stock characters to draw on, other than Mammy or the welfare scrounger or—a particular danger in this case—Jezebel. But Anita Hill did better without stereotypes than she could have done with them. Despite the initial polls that suggested she had failed, she has, in fact, succeeded, as Paul Simon emphasizes with great pleasure, in making Americans much more conscious of sexual harassment and oppression than they have ever been. It was Anita Hill—not Justice Thomas, after all—who was invited to address the American Bar Association and a great variety of other important forums during the year after the hearings. Her evident appeal just to principle, rather than to some image or group whose banner she might have carried into the political wars, may well have been the key to her success. If the senators who tried to humiliate her had been equally committed to principle—if they had tested Clarence Thomas's jurisprudential integrity and commitment instead of his standing in the polls—they would have better served the Constitution, the nation, and the still alarmingly urgent goal of racial justice.

October 25, 1992

17

Learned Hand

After law school, I clerked for a year for Judge Learned Hand, of the United States Court of Appeals for the Second Circuit in Manhattan. One evening I had to drop off a memorandum at his house, and I asked a young woman whom I had just met, and who was having dinner with me, to come along because it would take only a second. But when Hand answered the door, he invited us in, made dry martinis, and talked to my new friend for almost two hours about art history, his old friend Bernard Berenson, the state of Harvard College, New York politics, the Supreme Court, and much more. When we left, walking down the brownstone steps, she asked, "If I see more of you, do I get to see more of him?"

Learned Hand was one of America's greatest judges and now, through Gerald Gunther's brilliant biography, we can all see much more of him. Hand wrote prodigiously—thousands of judicial decisions, and tens of thousands of memoranda to his fellow judges, letters to his legions of friends, academic essays, ceremonial speeches, and philosophical essays—and an enormous volume of material was at Gunther's disposal soon after the judge's death in 1961. Gunther has had a very distinguished academic career in the intervening decades—he is a professor of constitutional law at Stanford Law School, and the author of one of the leading casebooks in that subject. But Hand's family and admirers had been growing impatient for his biography.

It was worth the wait. *Learned Hand,* at over eight hundred pages, is not only comprehensive but penetrating and illuminating as well. Its dust jacket, with the famous brooding photograph of Hand as the Platonic form of a judge, eyes glowing under the famous eyebrows, is a splendid bonus. Gunther's book combines four different stories, each of which would have made a book on its own, and its achievement can best be appreciated by reviewing each of these stories in turn.

The first is a history of America's second century, from the perspective of a public and sensitive man who lived through almost all of it. Hand was born in 1872, a few years after the Civil War ended, and died in 1961, when John Kennedy was President. Describing his life means describing many of the central American institutions, personalities, and movements of those ninety years. At Harvard College in the 1890s Hand studied philosophy with Santayana, Royce, and James; he also made friends with Jews there, which helped to spoil his chances for membership in the exclusive Porcellean Club, which he badly wanted. At Harvard Law School he watched the beginnings of Dean Christopher Columbus Langdell's transformation of American legal education through the case system. His own law practice, first in Albany, where he had been born, and then in New York, was dull, but it was still possible then for a bright, personable young lawyer with a good academic record to know most people who counted at the bar, and he did. In 1909 his friends secured a federal judgeship for him, a job so little desired by promising lawyers, and so badly paid, that his father-in-law thought him a fool for seeking it.

Though Hand's family were Democrats in the Jeffersonian tradition, and were appalled at the "progressive" doctrine that national government should regulate commerce and industry in the interests of justice, he himself was an early convert to the progressive movement. He persuaded Theodore Roosevelt, whom he had met, to read Herbert Croly's progressive manifesto, *The Promise of American Life*, which became Roosevelt's bible. He himself worked with Croly in founding the *New Republic*, for which he wrote unsigned articles. In 1912, he joined Roosevelt's Progressive party, helped draft its platform, and a year later ran unsuccessfully for a seat on the New York Court of Appeals on its ticket.

Thereafter he was more faithful to his own view that judges should not publicly take sides on controversial political issues. But he was outraged, both as a judge and a progressive, by the decisions of the deeply conservative Supreme Court, which declared unconstitutional much of the social legislation that is now considered routine in a just society, including laws stipulating maximum working hours and imposing minimum wages for women. According to the Court of that time, such legislation offended the due process clause of the Fourteenth Amendment by depriving citizens of a fundamental liberty of contract, and this Hand thought preposterous.

He deeply disliked Harding and Coolidge, and was disappointed in Hoover, whom he had admired as an administrator. While he believed FDR to be intellectually shallow, he admired him for his optimism and experimentalism. He had a clearer sense of the coming of World War II than others, particularly his then close friend Walter Lippman, and became a national figure during the war when he gave a widely quoted and reprinted speech about liberty in a patriotic ceremony in Central Park. ("The spirit of liberty," he said, "is the spirit which is not too sure that it is right.") In the postwar period, he was appalled by the sadism and folly of McCarthyism, as well as by the liberal decisions of the Supreme Court under Chief Justice Warren, which he thought just as wrong-headed as the conservative decisions of earlier years.

Gunther discusses Hand's place in and reaction to these great events and periods of American political history, and describes the other political actors Hand knew and corresponded with, all with great verve. *Learned Hand* seems essential material for historians of any part of the judge's long era.

The book's second story provides a psychological portrait of an unusually complex, even paradoxical, person. Hand was funny, spontaneous, and gregarious; he loved practical jokes, classical puns, bawdy stories, and Gilbert and Sullivan arias, which he would suddenly begin to sing, breaking the studious silence of his chambers. His relations with his clerks were unusually close: in my time he and his clerk worked face to face across two pushed-together desks. Though he had himself invented the law clerk system (paying his first clerks out of his own salary), he claimed uncertainty about how to use those assistants. "Most of my colleagues have their clerks look up the law," he told me on my first day. "But I know where the law is better than you do," he said, gesturing toward the books that lined the walls, "because I wrote most of it. Most of my colleagues ask their clerks to write the first draft of opinions. Maybe you write better than I do. But I'm a vain man, and I won't think so. So what shall I do with you? You'd better just read what I write and tell me what's wrong with it. And in our spare time, if we have any, we'll just talk."

But in spite of Hand's charm and playfulness he was amazingly insecure: he thought himself weak and even cowardly—he once compared himself with Casper Milquetoast—and his low view of his own abilities was only sporadically lifted by his growing fame. Gunther suggests many roots and reinforcements of this insecurity. Hand's remote father, a lawyer who was a hero to his family and to the legal community of Victorian Albany, died when Hand was only fourteen, and Hand felt he could not live up to his father's standards. He never forgot being ignored by the "swells" and their clubs at Harvard—he would talk of this social failure, with droll pain, even in his late eighties. And the fact that he was never appointed to the Supreme Court pained him too, much more than he ever let on, except in an extraordinary letter to Felix Frankfurter in 1950 in which Hand admitted that he longed for a place on the Court "beyond all else"; but he despised this weakness, as he saw it, and worried that it was only the "importance, the power, the trappings" of the office he wanted.

His marriage was one few others would have tolerated: his wife, Frances, whom he adored, had a very close friendship for decades with another man, Louis Dow, a Dartmouth professor of French. The Hands had bought a country house in Cornish, New Hampshire, near Dartmouth, and after Dow's own wife entered a mental hospital in 1913, he spent much time there with Frances while Learned stayed in New York. In the 1930s, Frances made several trips to Europe with Dow and without her husband. Gunther tells the story with great tact, and says he has an open mind about whether the relationship between the two friends was ever a "physical" one. In any case, Hand was, Gunther thinks, desperately anxious for a more intimate relationship with his wife, and after Dow died in 1944, their letters do become tender and playful—his seeming almost childlike in their gratitude for her affection.

Learned Hand's third story is a professional, even technical, one. Every American law student learns that Hand was part of a quartet, with Holmes, Brandeis, and Cardozo, of the greatest American judges. Many scholars, in my view plausibly, put Hand at the top of even that exalted list. The other three were on the Supreme Court but, as Gunther makes plain, the reasons Hand was never chosen, during the years when he might have been, were accidents of politics; when Felix Frankfurter was asked to name the greatest jurist on the Supreme Court he said that the greatest jurist was not on the Supreme Court. But few lawyers today (and very few nonlawyers) have any idea why Hand was such a great judge, and in the most impressive pages of the book—particularly in one long chapter entirely devoted to legal analysis—Gunther answers that question, not by abstractions but through an uncompromising and detailed discussion of some of the most arcane matters of federal law: constitutional law and the law of obscenity, as well as apparently much duller matters of admiralty, patent, copyright, and administrative law.

While some readers will be daunted at the prospect of sixty-five pages explaining how Hand practically reinvented each of these fields of law, they will find that Gunther's exposition is remarkably clear and vivid. As Gunther realized, there is no other way to explain what judging is like, and why Hand was so good at it, than to set out, in an uncondescending way, the problems he faced, the methods he used, and the solutions he offered. For it was above all in the details of his daily work that Hand was a genius. When he was asked to give a tribute to Holmes, whom he deeply admired, at the Harvard Law School in 1930, he said that Holmes was president of the "Society of Jobbists," those who belong to a craft that does not seek glamour or attention but "gives good measure for its wages" and "demands right quality, better than the market will pass." In 1958, in his Holmes Lectures at the Harvard Law School, he said that his teachers there had taught him that "it is as craftsmen that we get our satisfactions and our pay."

The Second Circuit, alone among circuit courts, requires its judges to explain their views on each case in written memoranda before the formal conference at which a collective decision is reached. Hand kept his thousands of pre-conference memoranda, and they reveal a jobbist at work. They are full of good and bad jokes, and some wicked, malicious asides, few of which survived in the eventual formal opinions he wrote. But they are also, as Gunther suggests, dense with meticulous hard work, showing not just the imaginative insight that made his opinions so often pathbreaking, but also a staggering degree of industry, day after day, decade after decade, exploring issues well beyond those strictly raised in the case, always in search of a better understanding of the commercial and human problems the law had somehow to solve. In admiralty cases involving collisions between ships, he prepared detailed drawings of how each accident happened until he felt he understood it as well or better than those on board. In patent cases involving inventions of sometimes mind-numbing complexity, when his fellow judges were content with a quick characterization of the issue taken from briefs, Hand made drawings, teaching himself physics or chemistry when necessary, until he understood the technical problem well enough to feel competent to pass on whether a putative invention should be thought to have infringed someone else's patent.

He was a federal judge for fifty-three years; for a great part of that period he was thought to be the best in the business, and by the end he was a legend. But he worked in the same laborious way until he died, as if each case, no matter how complex or trivial, exciting or mundane, was the most important a judge might ever confront.

He did take quiet pleasure in his growing fame. During my clerkship, he once exercised his prerogative to sit as a district judge, trying a new case on his own, instead of acting in his normal role as a circuit court judge hearing appeals, and he chose an admiralty case, because he particularly loved boats. I knew that the lawyers in the case would have no idea that he was sitting before he entered the courtroom, so I ran down to the court to watch that event. "All rise," the clerk said to two startled young lawyers, "Judge Learned Hand, presiding," after which Hand entered, sober and brusque, the great eyebrows knitted in concentration. There was much whispered conference until a young lawyer rose and said, "May it please the court, I request an hour's adjournment so that I can call my office. My senior partner will fire me if I don't give him a chance to argue this case." Hand consented, and both lawyers bolted from the room. An hour later the senior partners of two well-known admiralty firms, neither having the slightest knowledge of the case, were on their feet before the great judge. "Now I can write my memoirs," one of them told me afterward.

The fourth story Gunther tells is the most important though it is the least explicit. America's political system is unique in the extraordinary power it gives judges to declare the acts of legislatures and other officials invalid if the judges believe those acts offend any of the abstract moral standards of the Constitution's Bill of Rights, which include the provision, for example, that government shall not infringe "freedom of speech" or deny "due process of law" or "equal protection of the laws." It is therefore a crucial question how judges should interpret such abstract phrases, and Gunther provides the material we need to study Hand's dramatic answer.

Some judges decide constitutional cases on the assumption that is their duty, so far as the Constitution's text and past decisions permit, to interpret these moral phrases according to their own views about which liberties are necessary in a decent society and which forms of equality are essential to equal citizenship. The conservative judges who invalidated legislation regulating the maximum number of working hours assumed that freedom of contract is so fundamental that "due process" of law requires its protection. The judges who declared racial segregation of schools unconstitutional thought this form of discrimination so invidious that it undermines "equal" protection of law.

But from the beginning of our constitutional history, other lawyers and judges have objected to the assumption that judges should make such decisions; judges should not, they said, have so much power. That was the view of James Bradley Thayer, Hand's favorite teacher at the Harvard Law School, who said, in 1893, that judges should declare statutes unconstitutional only "when those who have the right to make laws have not merely made a mistake, but have made a very clear one,—so clear that it is not open to rational question."[1] Hand was much influenced by Thayer, and when the Supreme Court held unconstitutional the progressive economic and social legislation he himself favored, he became even more distrustful of judicial power.

As a judge, Hand initially made one significant exception to his creed of restraint. In 1917, Congress, in a World War I fervor, adopted the Espionage Act, which made statements critical of the war a crime, and allowed the postmaster general to exclude from the mails periodicals containing antiwar statements. Under that authority, the post office banned an issue of *The Masses,* a radical journal edited by Max Eastman, which contained several cartoons and articles depicting the war as a weapon of big business against the interests of workers. The case came before Hand, who was still a district judge, and who knew he would damage his chances for promotion if he lifted the ban. But he did so in a brilliant decision that remains one of the strongest, and most prophetic, judicial defenses of free speech. He said that the First Amendment's guarantee means that even dangerous speech must not be prohibited or punished unless what is said constitutes a direct incitement to crime, and that the Espionage Act should be interpreted as subject to that limitation.

Hand was promptly overruled, and his reputation did suffer. When he had failed to convert even Holmes to his view, he gave it up—he called it a toy boat that hadn't sailed very far and must be taken out of the water. Holmes's own "clear and present danger" test, which offered less protection because it allowed speech to be punished when a judge or jury thought it was likely to cause imminent harmful acts, whether or not the speaker actually called for them, became the constitutional standard (although the law has now settled, in recent years, into a view closer to Hand's original opinion).

In 1950, in the *Dennis* case, Hand felt himself bound to use Holmes's test in reviewing the conviction of Communist party leaders, under the

Smith Act, for conspiracy to advocate overthrowing the government by force or violence. He said that Congress might well think, in the midst of the cold war, that the threat of Communist violence did present a clear and present danger, and he upheld the conviction in language the Supreme Court adopted in confirming his ruling. Though Gunther defends Hand's decision, as that of a good lower court judge following Supreme Court precedent, the decision can only be explained as showing his increasingly strong view that judges should not overrule political or predictive or moral judgments that other institutions have made. In fact, he himself thought, as he said in a letter to Bernard Berenson shortly after his *Dennis* decision, that the prosecution was a tactical mistake, a statement that is hardly consistent with the judgment that the threat was clear and present. On any reading, Hand's opinion in *Dennis* shows much less concern for court-protected freedom of speech, and much more for judicial restraint, than his radical opinion in *Masses* did.

By 1958, when he gave his long-awaited Holmes Lectures at Harvard, his opposition to judges' second-guessing legislators about moral issues had stiffened into the strongest doctrine of restraint ever defended by a major judicial figure. He said that there was no warrant in the Constitution for judges having any power to invalidate the acts of another "department" of government, and that though he agreed that it was necessary to read such a power into that document, in order to save the nation from the paralysis that would follow if, for example, the President and Congress interpreted the Constitution in different ways, that power should be exercised only when necessary to prevent that paralysis. It was certainly not necessary for judges to remake decisions the legislature had already made, either about the likely results of different economic or other policies or about the best balance of competing moral values. Judges should ask only whether the legislative judgment was honest and impartial—and then he added that even this question was too "political" for judges.

His austere view would deny citizens the protection, in court, of their most important constitutional guarantees: the due process and equal protection clauses of the Fifth and Fourteenth Amendments—and of the First Amendment as well, for Hand had come to think that even Holmes's clear and present danger test gave judges too much power. "For once Homer nodded" he said of Holmes's view, and he ridiculed, as unhelpful, his own formulation of that test in *Dennis*.[2] He did not shrink, moreover, from accepting the most difficult conclusion his view entailed. The Supreme Court had made its famous decision, in *Brown,* four years earlier: it had declared that the long-standing racial segregation of public schools in the South was unconstitutional. Its decision caused immediate controversy, but by 1958 it was widely regarded as among the greatest decisions the Court had ever made. Hand nevertheless told his audience, with evident sadness, that he thought it indefensible.[3] He had hated and opposed prejudice all his life, and yet he insisted, at the end of his career, that the American Constitution, with its enviable Bill of Rights, did not give judges power to outlaw prejudice's worst results. What drove this great judge to that depressing conclusion?

Hand was one of three famous judges whose constitutional philosophy was influenced by Thayer. The others were Oliver Wendell Holmes and Felix Frankfurter, and since Hand's version of judicial restraint was stricter than that of the other two, it may be instructive to compare his reasons with theirs.[4] Frankfurter's grounds for restraint were often practical and political. He remembered the popular outrage that greeted the conservative Supreme Court decisions striking down early New Deal legislation, and cared as much about protecting the Court's reputation from the people as the people from the Court. Though he was on the Court when *Brown* was decided, and joined in its unanimous decision, he thought that the Court's authority would suffer if it opposed popular opinion too forcefully, and sometimes went to what might seem unprincipled lengths to avoid unpopular or divisive decisions—he fought to delay any decision that laws against interracial marriage were unconstitutional, for example.

Holmes's reasons for constitutional restraint were different: they were based not on practical politics but on philosophical skepticism about morality. This was not a matter of personal uncertainty: he had very firm and confident convictions about almost everything. But he said that these were only *his* opinions, only what he, constituted and conditioned as he was, could not help believing. So he called them his "can't helps" and insisted that from an objective point of view there was no more to be said for them than for the opposite opinions. He had no reason, he declared, to think that his "can't helps" were those of the cosmos, and he therefore thought it absurd for him or for any other judge to appeal to moral "truth," which meant nothing more, he said, than the judge's subjective opinion. Instead, he said, echoing Thayer, judges must strike down only legislation that no rational or reasonable person could think proper—only legislation, that is, that offends the "can't helps" of all reasonable people.

Though Holmes's form of moral skepticism reflected much of the pragmatist philosophy of his time, and is now embraced by Richard Rorty and others who deny the possibility of "objective" truth, it is confused. If someone can't help believing something, he can't help *believing* it, and then he contradicts himself if he says that it isn't really true, or no more true than its opposite. It doesn't remove the contradiction for him to say that though he believes some moral claim to be true, he doesn't believe that it is "ultimately" or "objectively" or "foundationally" or "cosmically" true. So far as these odd adverbs make any sense at all, they simply repeat, in a table-thumping way, the original opinion he says he can't help believing. There is no distinct "foundational" truth, no distinct point of view of the cosmos. There is only ordinary truth, and someone's "can't helps" are, among other things, his beliefs about what is, in that ordinary way, true. Holmes recognized this himself in the arguments he gave for his clear and present danger test, which, while not as strong as Hand's view in the *Masses* case, nevertheless justified judges in overruling censorship laws. Holmes said that a free marketplace of ideas is the best way to discover truth, which makes no sense if there are only individual "can't helps," and no real truth for free discussion to discover.

Holmes's philosophical skepticism was too muddled to have any important effect on his own legal arguments, and in fact it didn't. He did dissent from the ultra-conservative due process decisions of the Supreme Court when he was on it, but he did so not in spite of his own moral convictions but because of them. He did not necessarily agree with the economic theories behind the progressive social legislation he voted to uphold, but he plainly did not think that these laws were immoral, or that they violated any important individual rights, as his colleagues who voted to invalidate them did think. According to Louis Brandeis, Holmes's actual working test for unconstitutionality was the question: "Does it make you puke?" which presumably means, in less visceral language, "Does it offend your deepest moral 'can't helps' or convictions?"[5] There was nothing in maximum hour or minimum wage legislation that was capable of making Holmes puke. But if he had still been on the Court in the 1950s, when the war had finally made Jim Crow laws seem intolerable, it might well have made him puke that black children were turned away from white schools. There is no reason to doubt that he would have voted, in *Brown*, the same way Frankfurter did.

Hand was also a skeptic, but his skepticism was very different from Holmes's. Hand's skepticism consisted not in the philosophical view that no moral conviction can be objectively true, but in a disabling uncertainty that he—or anyone else—could discover which convictions were true: he thought moral matters were much too subtle and complex to allow anyone much confidence in his own opinions. He often said that he despised "absolutes." He meant, by that ambiguous phrase, that he distrusted any attempt to resolve the untidy complexity of a moral or legal or political issue in a neat and simple formula. He resisted Frankfurter's heated defense of Sacco and Vanzetti's innocence (until, after their execution, he seemed to regret his failure to study the case more thoroughly) mainly on the ground that the case must be more complex than Frankfurter had allowed. By 1944, as I said, he had come to the remarkable view that the spirit of liberty is essentially the spirit "that is not too sure that it is right," and in his Holmes Lectures he recommended, as a "combination of tolerance and imagination that to me is the epitome of all good government," Benjamin Franklin's plea that people should on occasion "doubt a little of [their] own infallibility."[6]

Hand's personal uncertainty about moral issues, and his sense that moral truth is more complicated than any simple formula can disclose, obviously contributed to his distaste for judicial activism in constitutional matters. But these factors, alone, cannot explain his extreme position—the people's representatives, after all, are as likely to be wrong as judges, and should doubt their own infallibility as much. A different idea, emphasized by his teacher Thayer, had a further and decisive role. Hand believed passionately in the virtues of what is often called civic republicanism: he thought that a political community could not flourish, or its citizens develop and improve their own sense of moral responsibility, unless they participated in the community's deepest and most important decisions about justice. In his Central Park speech he warned that "liberty lies in the hearts of men and women; when it dies there, no constitution, no law, no court can save it; no constitution, no law, no court can even do much to help."[7] (Thayer had written, a half-century earlier, that "under no system can the power of courts save a people from ruin; our chief protection lies elsewhere.")[8] And Hand's most formal statement of his views, in his 1958 Holmes Lectures, culminated in this passage:

> For myself it would be most irksome to be ruled by a bevy of Platonic Guardians, even if I knew how to choose them, which I assuredly do not. If they were in charge, I should miss the stimulus of living in a society where I have, at least theoretically, some part in the direction of public

affairs. Of course I know how illusory would be the belief that my vote determined anything; but nevertheless when I go to the polls I have a satisfaction in the sense that we are all engaged in a common venture. If you retort that a sheep in the flock may feel something like it; I reply, following Saint Francis, "My brother, the Sheep."[9]

Though Hand's views about judicial restraint are not much studied in law schools now, or treated as very important, they in fact made a considerable contribution to the long national debate about constitutional interpretation. Both before his lectures and after, constitutional experts and scholars have tried in various ways to evade the stern question he insisted on facing. When and how far is it right for judges testing statutes against the Bill of Rights to rely on their own moral convictions about which liberties and which forms of equality are fundamental? Many contemporary judges, scholars, and journalists hope for an answer to that question that will enable them to applaud the Supreme Court for its decision in *Brown* and condemn it and Hand for the decision in *Dennis* while nevertheless insisting that judges may not substitute their own moral convictions for those of legislatures.

But all the notable attempts by constitutional scholars and judges to explain how that is possible—from Herbert Wechsler's plea that judges develop "neutral" principles that nevertheless impose serious constraints on legislation to Robert Bork's attempt to show that *Brown* was right while all the other liberal decisions of the last few decades were wrong—fail for a reason Hand saw clearly and most of his critics ignore. The great constitutional clauses set out extremely abstract moral principles that must be interpreted before they can be applied, and any interpretation will commit the interpreter to answers to fundamental questions of political morality and philosophy. As Hand said, any attempt to decide how the original "framers" of these principles would have interpreted them is both hopeless and pointless. It is therefore an inescapable question whether, in the end, the interpretations of the legislatures or those of the judges will prevail, and though lawyers who dislike either answer call for something in between, there is, as Hand pointed out, no logical space for anything in between.

Hand chose the interpretations of the legislators who had been elected by the people, and his argument needs to be answered, not just set aside by pointing out that it entails the judicial abstinence he gloomily conceded it did. I think his argument can be answered. He was right in saying that a nation is sick when its most important collective moral decisions are reserved for specialists who decide in isolation and furnish the public with only Delphic verdicts. But he wrongly rejected an apparently paradoxical possibility that was difficult to see in the years in which his opinions were formed, but is more evident now: that individual citizens can in fact exercise the moral responsibilities of citizenship better when final decisions involving constitutional values are removed from ordinary politics and assigned to courts, whose decisions are meant to turn on principle, not on the weight of numbers or the balance of political influence.

It is true, of course, that when political controversies are decided by legislatures or other elected officials, the decision is likely to be governed by what most people want. That is desirable when an issue turns on the question of what is in the best interests of the community as a whole, and the gains to some groups are balanced against losses to others. In such matters, numbers should count. But they need not count, at least not for that reason, in matters of fundamental principle, when the community must decide, for example, whether blacks have a constitutional right to be protected from discrimination, or atheists from the presence of prayer in public schools, or pregnant women from majoritarian views about how and why life is sacred. In such cases, it is important that the public participate in the decision not because the community should reach the decision most people favor, but for the very different reason that Hand emphasized: that self-respect requires that people participate, as partners in a joint venture, in the moral argument over the rules under which they live. The distinction Hand relied on in the passage I quoted is essential: between a single citizen's *power* over a collective decision, which in a large nation is all but illusory, and that citizen's *role* as a moral agent participating in his own governance, which is sometimes better protected if the mechanisms of decision are not ultimately majoritarian.

For though the public debate that precedes a referendum or a legislative decision about some great issue of principle may be of high quality, emphasizing reasoned debate, it rarely is. Depressingly often—as in arguments over the morality of gun control, for example—the process is dominated by political alliances that are formed around a single issue and use the familiar tactics of pressure groups to bribe or blackmail legislators into voting as they wish. The great moral debate that Hand thought essential to the spirit of liberty never begins. Ordinary politics generally aims, moreover, at a political compromise that gives all powerful groups enough of what they want to prevent their disaffection, and reasoned argument elaborating underlying moral principles is rarely part of or even congenial to such compromises.

When an issue is seen as constitutional, however, and as one that will ultimately be resolved by courts applying general constitutional principles, the quality of public argument is often improved, because the argument concentrates from the start on questions of political morality. Legislators often feel compelled to argue for the constitutionality and not just the popularity of measures they support, and Presidents or governors who veto a law cite constitutional arguments to justify their decision. When a constitutional issue has been decided by the Supreme Court, and is important enough so that it can be expected to be elaborated, expanded, contracted, or even reversed, by future decisions, a sustained national debate begins, in newspapers and other media, in law schools and classrooms, in public meetings and around dinner tables. That debate better matches Hand's conception of republican government, in its emphasis on matters of principle, than almost anything the legislative process on its own is likely to produce.

The great national debates about racial justice that intensified in the 1950s illustrate this claim. So do the arguments about abortion that began two decades later, after the Supreme Court's decision in *Roe v. Wade*. The abortion controversy has been extremely violent and has divided us as few other issues have. (It might very well have been just as violent if the law had been settled, not by a Supreme Court decision, but by political battles, state by state.) But, in spite of all the violence, it is also true that the public discussion of that issue in America has involved many more people, and has been more successful at identifying the complex variety of moral and ethical issues involved, than in other countries where a political compromise was engineered. In France, for example, this was done more in the interest of avoiding intense public discussion than of reflecting it, and in Ireland the dominant political group directly imposed its will, smothering any effective debate. Americans better understand, for instance, the distinction between the question whether abortion is morally or ethically permissible, on the one hand, and the question whether government has the right to prohibit it, on the other; they also better understand the more general and constitutionally crucial idea on which that distinction rests: that individuals have rights that may work against the general will or the collective interest or good.

I must be careful not to overstate my point. Of course I am not arguing that only courts should consider issues of moral principle, or that all issues of moral principle should be regarded as constitutional ones, or that judges should reverse any legislative decision they think morally unsound. There are many arguments for limiting the constitutional power of judges (and many others for expanding those powers) that I have not considered here.[10] I mean only that Hand's main reasons for denying judges any such power at all, in spite of the Constitution's direct instruction that government be limited by moral principle, might actually count against rather than for his conclusions.

In any case, however, the civic benefits of public discussion I described can be realized only when judges and the public cooperate in securing them. When Hand began to worry about the effects of a strong judiciary on the spirit of liberty, many judges treated constitutional issues as more conceptual than moral, and rarely brought moral argument explicitly into their opinions. Constitutional jurisprudence has improved since then, and Supreme Court opinions are more explicitly concerned with moral argument. True, those opinions are not very widely read by the general public. But many of the most important of them are now written in less technical language, so that they are available to journalists as well as professional lawyers, and this change has facilitated—as well as reflected—the steadily growing media attention they receive in the press.[11]

The process of nominating Supreme Court justices and other federal judges is also more open than it once was, and this, too, allows the public to participate more effectively, coming to understand constitutional issues better, and to influence decisions more, through its reaction to and part in those proceedings. The political process that ended in the Senate's rejecting Bork's nomination provided a crucial introduction to constitutional theory for many people, and the verdict the public rendered, though informal, may well have had important consequences for the law. It may have been among the historical causes, for example, of the impressive argument of principle at the center of the Court's 1992 decision in *Planned Parenthood v. Casey*, which confirmed its earlier *Roe v. Wade* decision, but in a way that took account of, and reflected, the long public argument that earlier decision had generated.

So we, Hand's "sheep," do play a part in a common constitutional venture in the United States. It is a different venture, to be sure, from what it would be if all great decisions of principle were taken by majority vote. But it may be a better one—better suited to developing a national sense of justice, and to keeping our spirit of liberty alive—because it engages us as moral deliberators and advocates rather than just as numbers in a political count. I cannot suggest that Hand would have changed his mind had he lived longer and noticed the developments I have been describing. But the structure of his argument—his insistence on the need for a dramatic choice between constitutional philosophies, and his emphasis on the importance of that choice for self-government—are even more important now than when he gave his brave Holmes Lectures, to an admiring but astonished audience, in 1958.

I want to end, however, by turning back from Hand's work and thought to his character, because though he was a great judge, it was the man that I loved. Law clerks then normally received a month's paid vacation at the end of their service. But Hand told me, when I raised the question, that he didn't approve of that practice, and thought it particularly wrong that the public should pay for a vacation for me, since he was technically retired by my time, sitting only when he chose to, and since much of our time together had been spent discussing the Holmes Lectures he was then writing. So, though he regretted it, I would have no paid vacation.

I was only a little surprised: I knew Hand was passionate for public economy, and turned off all the light bulbs at the end of the day, not only in his own chambers but in other judges' chambers as well. A few days after my duties ended, I married the woman who had been so impressed with my boss five months earlier. Hand's wedding present was his personal check for a full month's salary.

August 11, 1994

Notes

Introduction

1. Some branches of legal theory, including the "Realist" and "Critical Legal Studies" movements of recent decades, emphasize the role of politics for a skeptical reason: to suggest that if law depends on political morality, it cannot claim "objective" truth or validity or force. I reject that skeptical claim, and have tried to answer it in other work. See, for example, *Law's Empire* (Harvard University Press, 1986).
2. *Adarand Constructors, Inc. v. Pena,* 115 S. Ct. 2097 (1995).
3. *Texas v. Johnson,* 491 U.S. 397 (1989).
4. See Antonin Scalia, "Originalism: The Lesser Evil," *The University of Cincinati Law Review,* vol. 57 (1989), pp. 849–865.
5. See John Hart Ely, *Democracy and Distrust: A Theory of Judicial Review* (Harvard University Press, 1980). Ely's book has been very influential, not because of his distinction between interpretive and noninterpretive approaches to the Constitution, which is happily not much used now, but because he was a pioneer in understanding that some constitutional constraints can be best understood as facilitating rather than compromising democracy. I believe he was wrong in limiting this account to constitutional rights that can be understood as enhancements of constitutional procedure rather than as more substantive rights. See my article "The Forum of Principle," in *A Matter of Principle* (Harvard University Press, 1985).
6. For a general discussion of integrity in law, see *Law's Empire.*
7. See *Law's Empire,* p. 228.
8. Thomas Babington, Lord Macaulay, letter to H. S. Randall, May 23, 1857.
9. For a valuable discussion of the evolution of the idea of judicial review in

America, see Gordon Wood, "The Origins of Judicial Review," *Suffolk University Law Review,* vol. 22 (1988), p. 1293.

10. Justice Scalia insists that statutes be enforced in accordance with what their words mean rather than with what historical evidence shows the legislators themselves expected or intended would be the concrete legal consequences of their own statute. See Scalia, "Originalism." But he also insists on limiting each of the abstract provisions of the Bill of Rights to the force it would have been thought to have at the time of its enactment, so that, for example, the prohibition against "cruel and unusual punishments" of the Eighth Amendment, properly interpreted, does not forbid public flogging, though everyone is now agreed that it does, because such flogging was practiced when the Eighth Amendment was adopted. Scalia agrees that contemporary judges should not hold flogging constitutional, because that would seem too outrageous now, but he does insist that the due process clauses and equal protection clauses should not be used to strike down laws that were commonplace when these clauses were enacted. His position about constitutional law is consistent with his general account of statutory interpretation only if we suppose that the best contemporary translation of what the people who enacted the Eighth Amendment actually said is not that cruel and unusual punishments are forbidden, which is what the language they used certainly suggests, but that punishments that were then generally regarded as cruel and unusual were forbidden, a reading we have absolutely no reason to accept.

11. Some scholars have tried to define an "intermediate" strategy in a way that, they hope, does not require answers to these questions. They say we should look not to the concrete opinions or expectations of the framers, as originalism does, nor to the very abstract principles to which the moral reading attends, but to something at an intermediate level of abstraction. Judge Bork suggested, for example, in explaining why *Brown* was right after all, that the framers of the equal protection clause embraced a principle general enough to condemn racial school segregation in spite of what the framers themselves thought, but not so general that it would protect homosexuals. But, as I argue in Chapter 14, there is no nonarbitrary way of selecting any particular level of abstraction at which a constitutional principle can be framed except the level at which the text states it. Why, for example, should we choose, as the intermediate principle, one that forbids any discrimination between races rather than one that permits affirmative action in favor of a formerly disadvantaged group? Or vice versa?

12. *Buckley v. Valeo,* 424 U.S. 1 (1976). Later in this Introduction, I argue that democratic self-government can be achieved only through a political process that is deliberative in a way that allowing unlimited expenditure in political campaigns, particularly for political advertising on television, subverts. In a

forthcoming article entitled "Television and Democracy," I argue that the *Buckley* decision should therefore be reconsidered, as inconsistent with the best understanding of what American democracy is.

13. See, e.g., Jürgen Habermas, "Reconciliation through the Public Use of Reason: Remarks on John Rawls' Political Liberalism," *Journal of Philosophy*, vol. 92 (March 1995), p. 109.

14. John Kenneth Galbraith, *The Age of Uncertainty* (Houghton Mifflin, 1977), chap. 12.

15. Learned Hand, *The Bill of Rights* (Harvard University Press, 1958), p. 73.

16. See *Law's Empire*, and "Equality, Democracy, and Constitution: We the People in Court," *Alberta Law Review*, vol. 28 (1990), p. 324.

17. See Robert Putnam, *Making Democracy Work: Civic Traditions in Modern Italy* (Princeton University Press, 1993).

18. The argument of the next few paragraphs is a summary of a longer argument in an article not reprinted in this collection: "Equality, Democracy, and Constitution: We the People in Court."

19. See my article "What Is Equality? Part 3: The Place of Liberty." *Iowa Law Review*, vol. 73 (1987), pp. 1–54.

20. See my article "Liberal Community," *California Law Review*, vol. 77 (1990), p. 479.

21. See *Law's Empire*, chap. 6.

22. See *Texas v. Johnson*.

23. See Lawrence G. Sager, "Fair Measure: The Legal Status of Underenforced Constitutional Norms," *Harvard Law Review*, vol. 91 (1978), p. 1212, and Christopher L. Eisgruber and Lawrence G. Sager, "Why the Religious Freedom Restoration Act Is Unconstitutional," *N.Y.U. Law Review*, vol. 69 (1994).

24. See my book *Life's Dominion: An Argument about Abortion and Euthanasia* (Knopf, 1993).

25. See "What Is Equality?" Parts 1 and 2, in *Philosophy and Public Affairs* (1981).

26. See Frank Michelman, "On Protecting the Poor through the Fourteenth Amendment," *Harvard Law Review*, vol. 83 (1969).

27. H. L. A. Hart, *The Concept of Law*, "Postscript" to the 1994 edition (Oxford University Press, 1994).

28. See *Law's Empire*.

Part I Introduction

1. *Compassion in Dying v. State of Washington*, 49 F. 3rd 586 (1995).

2. *Adarand Constructors, Inc. v. Pena*, 115 S. Ct. 2097 (1995).

1. *Roe in Danger*

1. It held that abortions could not be made criminal in the first three months of pregnancy and could be made criminal before the fetus became viable only when necessary to protect the health of the mother.

2. For a general discussion of the character and effect of the controversy, see Jane Maslow Cohen, "Comparison-Shopping in the Marketplace of Rights," *Yale Law Journal,* vol. 98 (1989), p. 1235.

3. Of the seven justices in the majority in *Roe v. Wade,* only three remain: Blackmun, who wrote the opinion, Brennan, and Marshall. Justice Stevens, who joined the Court later, has indicated his full support for the decision. The two *Roe* dissenters, Justice Rehnquist, who is now Chief Justice, and Justice White, have recently repeated their view that it is unsound, and Justice Scalia has often expressed himself as skeptical of rights with no "textual" basis. Justice O'Connor dissented in two later cases in which anti-abortion groups unsuccessfully sought to limit *Roe*'s force, but she has not suggested that the decision should be reversed. She and Justice Kennedy, Reagan's final appointee, hold the balance of power.

4. Some states have already adopted strong anti-abortion laws to take effect after any weakening of *Roe v. Wade* by the Supreme Court, and several others have declared their intention of doing so. Even if the Court does not reverse that case outright, but either weakens the rights it guaranteed or accepts Missouri's constraints on abortion as consistent with those rights, a rash of new state legislation, once again testing the boundaries of the Court's willingness to retreat, is expected. Only a clear reaffirmation of the basic *Roe v. Wade* principles could remove the issue from the political front burner.

5. Erwin Chemerinsky, "Rationalizing the Abortion Debate: Legal Rhetoric and the Abortion Controversy," *Buffalo Law Review,* vol. 31 (1982), p. 106.

6. Of course I do not mean to suggest that fetuses are no more important or sacred than corporations. As I insist later, the moral significance of a fetus should be clear and justifies whatever state regulation of abortion is consistent with constitutional rights. My point is only that no state is free to deny or substantially curtail rights the Constitution does establish by recognizing rights, or right bearers, that it does not. John Hart Ely pointed out, in an influential early attack on *Roe v. Wade,* that even though dogs are not persons under the equal protection clause, a state can stop demonstrators from killing dogs without violating the demonstrators' First Amendment rights (Ely, "The Wages of Crying Wolf: A Comment on *Roe v. Wade," Yale Law Journal,* vol. 92 [1973], p. 920). But, as Laurence Tribe pointed out, no one has to kill animals to exercise his right of free speech, though a pregnant woman does need to abort her fetus to regain control over her part in procreation. See Tribe, *American Constitutional Law,* 2d ed. (Foundation Press, 1987), p. 1349.

7. These scholars argue that for that reason anti-abortion laws are unconstitutional even if a fetus is considered a person, and they would certainly reject my much stronger claim that in that event many laws permitting abortion would be unconstitutional. The legal arguments rely on a famous and influential article about the morality of abortion by Judith Jarvis Thomson ("A Defense of Abortion," *Philosophy and Public Affairs,* vol. 1, no. 1 [Fall 1971). Thomson does not argue that every pregnant woman has a right to an abortion, even if a fetus is a person, but only argues that some do, and she recognizes that a woman who voluntarily risks pregnancy may not have such a right. The legal arguments applying Thomson's views to constitutional law are best and most persuasively presented in Donald Regan, "Rewriting *Roe v. Wade,*" *Michigan Law Review,* vol. 77 (1979), p. 1569.

8. In the article cited in the preceding note, Donald Regan questions the analogy between abortion and infanticide on the ground that parents have the option of arranging an adoption for their child. But that is not inevitably true: infants from poor minority families, in particular, may not be able to find adoptive homes, and their parents, of course, are not permitted to kill them or abandon them in circumstances that will inevitably lead to their death even when they can in fact make no other arrangement.

9. In oral argument Fried said that the Fourteenth Amendment does not "take any position" on the question whether a fetus "is not merely potential life but actual human life." That is true, as I said earlier. But it does not follow that the amendment takes no view on the different question I distinguished, which is whether the fetus is a *constitutional* person, that is, a person within the meaning of the requirement that a state accord every person equal protection. The Constitution, properly interpreted, must take a position on *that* point, because defining the range of its key concepts is part of what interpreting the Constitution is. And Fried's position is defensible only if, on the best interpretation, a fetus is not a constitutional person.

10. See "Brief of 281 American Historians as Amici Curiae Supporting Appellees" in *Webster v. Reproductive Health Services.* It is worth noticing that the historian cited in the government's brief to support the claim that anti-abortion laws are traditional in America, James Mohr, is one of the signers of this brief.

11. For an account and defense of this view, see Michael Tooley, "Abortion and Infanticide," *Philosophy and Public Affairs,* vol. 2, no. 1 (Fall 1972). The view has important implications, of course, for the end of life as well as the beginning. See my monograph *Philosophical Issues in Senile Dementia,* published by the Office of Technology Assessment, U.S. Congress (U.S. Government Printing Office, 1987).

12. See, for example, *Skinner v. Oklahoma,* 316 U.S. 535 (1942), *Griswold v. Connecticut,* 381 U.S. 479 (1965), *Eisenstadt v. Baird,* 405 U.S. 438 (1972).

See also *Carey v. Population Services International*, 431 U.S. 678 (1977). In *Griswold v. Connecticut*, the Court held that no state could forbid married people the use of contraceptives. It expanded *Eisenstadt v. Baird* to include unmarried people as well, and in *Carey v. Population Services International* it held that a state could not prohibit the sale of contraceptives even to teenagers.

13. Many lawyers believe that an equally or even more powerful argument for the result in *Roe v. Wade* can be based not on the due process clause and the privacy precedents, but on the equal protection clause I mentioned earlier. They argue that anti-abortion laws should be considered suspect under that clause because such laws cause very great disadvantage to women, in some circumstances destroying their opportunity to lead lives routinely available to men. Legislatures are still dominated by men, many of whom believe unmarried pregnant women deserve punishment rather than sympathy, and few of whom could fully appreciate the misery of their situation even if they wished to do so. For a particularly effective account of this argument, and of the special impact of abortion law on women, see Sylvia A. Law, "Rethinking Sex and the Constitution," *University of Pennsylvania Law Review*, vol. 132 (1984), p. 955.

14. *Griswold v. Connecticut* and the other contraception cases figured prominently in the 1987 debates over the unsuccessful nomination of Robert Bork to the Supreme Court. Bork had written that these cases should be overruled, and the enormous unpopularity of that suggestion helped persuade public opinion to oppose his nomination.

15. See the article by Donald Regan cited in note 7 above.

16. The Court recently upheld a statute that made acts of sodomy a crime (*Bowers v. Hardwick*, 106 S. Ct. 2841 [1986]). Justice White's opinion for the Court said that the fact that homosexual acts may take place in the privacy of the home was irrelevant, and that the contraception cases were not about private acts in that sense but "were interpreted . . . to confer a fundamental individual right to decide whether or not to beget or bear a child," and hence were irrelevant to the question of homosexual sodomy.

17. Justice White, in *Bowers v. Hardwick*. See the preceding note. White dissented in *Griswold v. Connecticut* as well as in *Roe v. Wade*. The acting solicitor general's brief in *Webster v. Reproductive Health Services* quoted these remarks.

18. The brief filed by then acting Solicitor General Fried in *Thornburgh v. American College of Obstetricians and Gynecologists*, 416 U.S. 747 (1986).

19. Fried, in the brief cited in note 18.

20. The historians' brief described in note 10 above argues that these statutes were motivated by concern for the safety of women, for doctors, and for the birth rate of nonimmigrants, which would not be permissible justifications for anti-abortion laws now.

21. The importance of resemblance, and of understanding the Court's concern with viability in that light, is skillfully analyzed by Nancy Rhoden in "Trimesters and Technology: Revamping *Roe v. Wade*," *Yale Law Journal*, vol. 95 (1986), p. 639.

22. Cases in which a threat to the mother's life or the fetus's development is noticed only after viability require different constitutional treatment, as the Court noticed in *Roe v. Wade*.

23. Ninety percent of abortions are performed during the first trimester of pregnancy, only 1 percent after twenty weeks, and only 0.01 percent in the third trimester. See "Brief of the American Medical Association (and several other medical groups) as Amici Curiae in Support of Appellees."

24. For an account of the courts' traditional role in making principle administrable as a matter of strategy, see Lawrence G. Sager, "State Courts and the Strategic Space between Norms and Rules of Constitutional Law," *Texas Law Review*, vol. 63 (1985), p. 959.

25. One hundred and forty United States senators and congressmen filed an amicus brief in *Webster v. Reproductive Health Services* arguing that respect for law would be weakened if *Roe v. Wade* were overruled.

26. See Gary B. Gertler, "Brain Birth: A Proposal for Defining When a Fetus Is Entitled to Human Life Status," *Southern California Law Review*, vol. 59 (1986), p. 1061.

27. See Brief for the Appellees in *Webster v. Reproductive Health Services*, p. 48.

28. *Maher v. Roe*, 432 U.S. 464 (1977).

29. *Poelker v. Doe*, 432 U.S. 519 (1977).

2. Verdict Postponed

1. In her concurring opinion, Justice O'Connor noticed the broad definition of "public facility," and suggested that some applications of the provision—against private hospitals leasing state-owned equipment or state land, for example—might perhaps be unconstitutional in spite of the Court's decision in *Webster*. She voted to sustain the statute against general constitutional challenge because she thought that "straightforward" applications of the statute to abortions performed in ordinary state hospitals were permissible under previous decisions. Her qualifying remarks are important, because her vote was necessary to sustain the provision.

2. Justice O'Connor is now the key figure whose votes and opinions are likely to determine future abortion cases. Careful observers have thought that in her concurring opinion in this case she seemed less opposed to guaranteeing women substantial rights to an abortion than she has on other occasions. Even in earlier opinions, however, she seemed not to object to the idea that states may not place "undue" burdens on abortions, and that regulations amounting

to total prohibition of early abortions except to save the mother's life might well be "undue." That might help to explain Justice Scalia's biting and condescending criticism of her concurring opinion. He ridiculed her for saying that the state has an "interest in potential life when viability is possible," a phrase he said was "irrational" because, since viability means that life is possible, the possibility of viability means the possibility of a possibility, which is absurd. O'Connor's linguistic sense was sounder than Scalia's. In the medical and legal literature, "viable" means having reached the stage of physical development, in particular of lung capacity, that makes survival possible. So it makes perfect sense to say that viability is possible, rather than certain, when it is uncertain whether a fetus is only twenty weeks or as much as four weeks older.

3. Justice Blackmun made the same point, in careful detail, in his dissent.
4. Justice Stevens, in dissent, criticized Rehnquist's interpretation.
5. Rehnquist's opinion is certainly consistent with that interpretation. His group lacked the necessary votes to overrule *Roe v. Wade* altogether, in this case because O'Connor made it plain that she would not vote that way now. If they had joined with Scalia, the headlines might have reported that the Court had decided, five to four, not to overrule *Roe*. On the other hand, if they had argued as O'Connor wished, that the Missouri statute is constitutional because it is perfectly consistent with *Roe* and other past decisions, that deference to *Roe* might have seemed to confirm its place in constitutional jurisprudence. So the Rehnquist group in fact did the most they could have done to damage *Roe* on this occasion by claiming that the Court, just in upholding the Missouri statute, had undermined the principles behind that precedent though not its actual ruling.
6. See Anthony Lewis's column, *New York Times* (July 6, 1989).
7. In a dissenting opinion in an earlier case Justice White also said that "a woman's ability to choose an abortion is a 'liberty,'" but not so "fundamental" a liberty as to justify "anything more than the most minimal judicial scrutiny." His opinion in *Griswold v. Connecticut* should also be taken into account. My statement in a note to Chapter 1 of this book that White had dissented in that case was wrong. I should rather have said that he did not join in the reasoning of the main opinion in that case, which recognized a general right to privacy, but concurred in the result because he thought Connecticut's prohibition on the use of contraceptives by married couples was not rationally related to the only objective the state had claimed: discouraging extramarital sex. Though he said that the state's interest must be "compelling" to justify limiting rights connected with family and childbearing, he left open the possibility that he might have accepted the statute if Connecticut had been in a position to claim that it was acting out of a conviction that contraception was itself immoral. In *Bowers v. Hardwick,* White wrote the Court's opinion

upholding a statute making homosexual sodomy criminal on moral grounds. He said the state was entitled to enforce its dominant morality.

8. Of course women do have a constitutional right to an abortion necessary to save their lives. But Rehnquist offered no reason why they do, and it is hard to see what reason he could offer that is consistent with his general approach to constitutional interpretation. There is nothing in the text of the Fourteenth Amendment or, so far as I know, in the legislative history of its enactment, to suggest that the framers believed the due process clause would prevent states from choosing to save a fetus rather than its mother, as many Americans believe they should, if a majority of its citizens approved and voted for that choice. The fact that, historically, anti-abortion statutes made that exception is no evidence the framers thought the due process clause required them to do so.

9. Indeed, that description of a state's interest would also justify prohibition of the most popular and safest forms of contraception, which act as abortifacients, and of common techniques of in vitro fertilization, in which several ova are fertilized and most later discarded, though it seems likely that if Rehnquist and his colleagues do adopt that description they will try to avoid those politically damaging consequences.

10. That view is, in effect, the position contemplated by Justice O'Connor in earlier opinions. See note 2 above. Several considerations would support defining a state's interest in this restricted way. Almost everyone would agree, for example, that preventing pain or suffering to the fetus would be a proper state goal, and that goal becomes pertinent only late in the development of the fetal nervous system, roughly at the same time as viability. See Gary B. Gertler, "Brain Birth: A Proposal for Defining When a Fetus Is Entitled to Human Life Status," *Southern California Law Review,* vol. 59 (1986), p. 1061. And most people would agree that it is proper for a state to worry that widespread abortion of late-stage fetuses might make its citizens more callous about killing and suffering in general. (I discuss this view of a state's interest in potential life in Chapter 1 of this book.) It is very implausible that early abortion, which can be hard to distinguish from contraception, has anything near the brutalizing impact that routine abortion of fully formed fetuses, who are indistinguishable from infants, does.

11. See, for example, *City of Akron v. Akron Center for Reproductive Health,* 462 U.S. 416 (1982), in which the Court, six to three, struck down a mandatory twenty-four-hour waiting period, and *Thornburgh v. American College of Obstetricians and Gynecologists,* 416 U.S. 747 (1986), in which, five to four, it invalidated a Pennsylvania law requiring doctors to inform patients of the risks of abortion and about public funds available for childbirth and child care.

12. It is significant that the opinion did not repeat the question-begging claims which some of the Rehnquist group had made in the past, and which were urged in both the Missouri and the Bush administration briefs, that the

Constitution contains no doctrine of privacy at all, and that the right the Court had recognized in *Roe v. Wade* was wholly invented. Instead, Rehnquist offered only two criticisms of *Roe*. I have already discussed the first: the undefended and unclarified assertion that a sufficient state interest in pregnancy arises before viability. The second was a series of bizarre complaints about constitutional style: Rehnquist said that the key concepts of the *Roe* structure—trimesters and viability—are not found in the Constitution, that the structure is too rigid and produces fine distinctions, and that it has turned the courts into medical review boards.

He made no effort to compare *Roe* with other important constitutional decisions in these respects, and Blackmun had no difficulty identifying, in his dissent, example after example of unquestioned constitutional doctrine that uses concepts not taken from the Constitution's text—how could doctrine interpret and formulate the Constitution's abstract language if it only repeated that language?—and that is set out in crisp rules allowing citizens and officials to apply it with confidence in nearly all cases but nevertheless requires fine distinctions in hard ones. A less rigid decision in *Roe*, declaring that abortion must not be prohibited except when it would be reasonable for the state to do so given the competing interests, for example, would have exacerbated rather than helped protect judges from narrow discriminations, and really would have turned courts into medical boards.

13. *Hodgson v. Minnesota*. The circuit court held, *en banc,* that the requirement to notify both parents was constitutional only if the state adopted a procedure allowing a judge to exempt a teenager from this requirement when it would be in her best interests to do so. Minnesota is appealing from that qualification.

14. *Turnock v. Ragsdale.*

15. See Chapter 1 and my book *Law's Empire* (Harvard University Press, 1986), chap. 10.

16. See *New York Times*, 1 (July 5, 1989).

17. Insisting that controversial issues of moral principle be decided in ordinary politics is likely to have other antidemocratic consequences as well. Moral issues are particularly likely to produce a legislative paralysis that only the courts, immune to the pressures of special interest minorities, can break, for example. Before *Griswold v. Connecticut*, in which the Supreme Court held that anticontraception laws were unconstitutional, it would have been extremely difficult for the legislature of the states in which contraception was illegal to change the law.

But even if that decision were now overruled, it would be inconceivable that many states would even contemplate prohibition again. The Court's decision plainly brought the law more into accord with majority will than the electoral process could, and the same may well be true in the case of abortion. The great majority of states prohibited abortion in varying degrees before *Roe v. Wade*, but not even the anti-abortion groups expect that they would all return to the same level of prohibition even if *Roe* were wholly overturned. So in retrospect the court may have broken a democratic logjam in 1973, a logjam caused by minority conviction and the apathy of middle-class voters who knew how to get an abortion if they needed one anyway.

18. Almost every European country has accepted the European Convention of Human Rights: The European Court in Strasbourg which interprets the convention has on many occasions directed sovereign nations to repeal or change decisions of their own parliaments. Two thirds of Europe has enacted the convention into its domestic laws, giving its own judges similar power, and there is now a lively campaign to incorporate the convention even in Britain, which has been committed to the majoritarian conception, and to the principle of unlimited parliamentary supremacy, since the last century. Many democracies in the rest of the world, including new and developing nations, are moving in the same direction, away from majoritarianism toward stronger institutions of judicial review interpreting abstract constitutional guarantees as matters of principle. In 1988 the Canadian Supreme Court, for example, held that the Canadian law limiting abortion was invalid because it violated the rights of women under the Canadian Charter of Rights and Freedoms.

3. What the Constitution Says

1. Justice Benjamin Cardozo in *Palko v. Connecticut*, 302 U.S. 319, 325 (1937).
2. Justice John Paul Stevens, "The Bill of Rights: A Century of Progress," *U. Chi. L. Rev.*, vol. 59 (1992), pp. 13, 20.
3. See, for example, Learned Hand, *The Bill of Rights* (Harvard University Press, 1958).
4. See John Hart Ely, *Democracy and Distrust: A Theory of Judicial Review* (Harvard University Press, 1980).
5. See Ronald Dworkin, *A Matter of Principle,* chap. 2 (Harvard University Press, 1985); Ronald Dworkin, *Law's Empire,* chap. 10 (Harvard University Press, 1986); and Ronald Dworkin, "Equality, Democracy, and the Constitution: We the People in Court," *Alberta L. Rev.,* vol. 28 (1990), p. 28.
6. See Robert H. Bork, *The Tempting of America: The Political Seduction of the Law* (Free Press, 1990) (especially chaps. 7, 8, and 13). See also Chapter 14 of this book for my review of Bork's book.
7. 478 U.S. 186 (1986).
8. Id. at 193–194.
9. Richard A. Posner, "Legal Reasoning from the Top Down and from the Bottom Up: The Question of Unenumerated Constitutional Rights," *U. Chi. L. Rev.,* vol. 59 (1992), pp. 433, 437–438.
10. Id. at 435.

11. Id. at 439–440. Posner objects to my claim that Bork has no coherent constitutional philosophy, that Bork has theories of particular clauses, but not of the Constitution as a whole. But Bork does not, as Posner says he does, distrust general theory. On the contrary, Bork claims a perfectly general, comprehensive, constitutional theory. He claims that all of the Constitution, not just particular clauses, are exhausted by the intentions of the framers, and he argues for that global theory by appealing to a single, global theory of democracy and a single, global account of what law, by its very nature, is like. Bork does not have a coherent constitutional philosophy, as I argue in Chapter 14. But that is not because he does not claim one.

12. Posner, *U. Chi. L. Rev.* vol. 59, 444–445 (cited in note 9).

13. Dworkin, *Law's Empire* (cited in note 5). See particularly id. at 65–68.

14. Posner, *U. Chi. L. Rev.,* vol. 59, at 446 (cited in note 9).

15. Id. at 449.

16. Id. at 447. Posner takes this phrase—which gives new meaning to the old realist thesis that the law is only what the judge had for breakfast—from Holmes. I should say that though I understand Posner's hagiographic admiration for that jurist, I do not share it. Holmes wrote like a dream. His personal conversion from the view that the First Amendment must be limited to a Blackstonian condemnation of prior restraint to the radically different view that it must be understood as a much more abstract and general principle was an epochal event in American constitutional history. But most of his gorgeous epigrams were the vivid skins of only very lazy thoughts, and his philosophical pretensions, almost entirely in the service of an unsophisticated, deeply cynical form of skepticism, were embarrassing—as I believe the metaphysical observations Posner includes in his own new collection of Holmes's writings demonstrate. See Richard A. Posner, Introduction, in Richard A. Posner, ed. *The Essential Holmes* (University of Chicago Press, 1992), pp. xvii–xx.

17. I discuss Posner's own recommendations in note 22.

18. See Chapter 15.

19. See Ronald Dworkin, "Pragmatism, Right Answers, and True Banality," in Michael Brint, ed., *Pragmatism and Law* (1992). See Posner, *U. Chi. L. Rev.,* vol. 59, at 447 (cited in note 9).

20. I discuss integrity at considerable length in *Law's Empire* at chap. 7 (cited in note 5).

21. I believe that Professor Fried unwittingly demonstrated this incoherence in defending the position in his recent book. See Charles Fried, *Order and Law: Arguing the Reagan Revolution—A Firsthand Account* (Simon and Schuster, 1991), and my review of it in Chapter 6 of this book, which originally appeared in *The New York Review of Books* in July 1991. See also Fried's letter to the editor and my letter in reply, *The New York Review of Books* (Aug. 15, 1991).

22. Posner describes my account of integrity-based constitutional reasoning as "holistic" and "top-down." He says it is "too ambitious, too risky, too contentious." Posner, *U. Chi. L. Rev.*, vol. 59, at 446 (cited in note 9). He says that when judges are called upon to interpret the great abstract moral clauses of the Constitution they should react as their "conscience" demands: they should cite the abstract moral language of these clauses to strike down only what they instinctively find "terribly unjust." Id. at 447. He would not require a judge to provide much, if anything, by way of a principled explanation of how or why he believes a law unjust, or to aim at consistency of principle even himself, from one day to the next, let alone with decisions other judges have made on other days. His views, as always, are striking and powerful. But how can he think that advice less "risky," or less likely to produce "contentious" decisions, than the more familiar advice that judges should at least do their best, as their time and talents allow, to discipline their initial reactions by accepting those responsibilities?

Is Posner right, at least, that his proposals are less "ambitious" because less "holistic"? He says judges should declare statutes unconstitutional, on moral grounds, only when there is a "compelling practical case" for doing so. Id. at 447. The word "practical" is a familiar obscuring device in pragmatist philosophy: it is meant somehow to suggest, with no further argument, that moral decisions can be based not on "reason" but on more hard-headed–sounding "experience" in the shape of obvious social needs. But Posner's extended discussion of *Griswold* shows that Connecticut's ban on contraceptives was not impractical but unjust. That will be true in almost every case in which a Posnerian judge's "can't helps" are in play: his decision will engage his moral convictions, not his practical good sense. Posner insists, however, that his moral convictions are discrete "instincts," not the product of some comprehensive theory of the entire Constitution. But the distinction is mysterious in this context, because any judge's opinions about whether a ban on contraception is profoundly unjust, or maximum-hours legislation deeply unfair, or affirmative action an insult to the very idea of equal citizenship, will reflect and be drawn from much more general opinions and attitudes that will also fix his reactions to other legislation he tests "viscerally" against other clauses, at least if he is acting in moral good faith on any of these occasions. If any judge's immediate reaction really was one off—if it really was just a response to one set of facts with no implications for others—it would not be a response of conscience at all, but only a whim or a tic.

So Posner's contrast between clause-by-clause and holistic adjudication seems wildly overdrawn. He uses the reason-passion vocabulary of eighteenth-century philosophical psychology. But he has in mind not an epistemological distinction between different mental faculties judges might use, but a contrast between two views of judicial responsibility. He rejects integrity, which insists that judges do the best they can to exhibit a principled basis for their decisions, in favor of a different standard that encourages them to keep that basis dark. I do not claim, in the discussion of abortion that follows, that integrity produces only one plausible view, or that it can end controversy. But I shall claim, at several points, that integrity rules out some accommodations that politics or weariness or even laziness might recommend, accommodations I fear Posner's unbuttoned license would guarantee.

23. See Chapter 1 of this book.

24. This book has since been published as *Life's Dominion: An Essay on Abortion, Euthanasia, and Individual Freedom* (Knopf, 1993).

25. 410 U.S. 113, 163 (1973).

26. Id. at 162–164.

27. These scholars argue that for that reason anti-abortion laws are unconstitutional even if a fetus is considered a person, and they would certainly reject my much stronger claim that in that event many laws permitting abortion would be unconstitutional. The legal arguments rely on a famous and influential article about the morality of abortion by Judith Jarvis Thomson: "A Defense of Abortion," *Phil. & Pub. Aff.*, vol. 1 (1971), p. 47. The legal arguments applying Thomson's views to constitutional law are best and most persuasively presented in Donald H. Regan, "Rewriting *Roe v. Wade,*" *Mich. L. Rev.*, vol. 77 (1979), p. 1569. Thomson argues not that every pregnant woman has a right to an abortion, even if a fetus is a person, but only that some do, and she recognizes that a woman who voluntarily risks pregnancy may not have such a right. In any case, her arguments assume that a pregnant woman has no more moral obligations to a fetus she is carrying, even if that fetus is a person with rights and therefore her son or daughter, than anyone has to a stranger—to a famous violinist a woman might find herself connected to for nine months because he needs the use of her kidneys for that period in order to live, for example.

28. In the article cited in the preceding note, p. 1597, Regan questions the analogy between abortion and infanticide on the ground that parents have the option of arranging an adoption for their child. But that is not inevitably true: minority infants, in particular, may not be able to find adoptive homes, and their parents are not permitted to kill them, or abandon them in circumstances that will inevitably lead to their death, whenever they can in fact make no alternative arrangement.

29. It is a separate question whether a state would violate the Eighth Amendment if it punished feticide with the death penalty. Though Illinois does use the death penalty, the statute making the killing of a fetus murder rules out that penalty for that crime. Homicide of an Unborn Child, Ill. Rev. Stat., chap. 38, P 9–1.2(d) (1989).

30. Abortion Law of 1975, id. at chap. 38, P 81–21(1).

31. Id.
32. Posner, *U. Chi. L. Rev.,* vol. 59, at 444 (cited in note 9).
33. Id.
34. Id.
35. 410 U.S. at 173 (Rehnquist dissenting).
36. Catholic doctrine, it is true, now holds that a fetus is endowed with an eternal soul at conception, and has interests for that reason. (Earlier in its history the Church held that God ensouled a fetus at some point after conception: at forty days for a male and eighty for a female, and that abortion before that point, though wrong because it violated the intrinsic value of God's creation, was not murder. Laurence H. Tribe, *Abortion: The Clash of Absolutes* [Norton, 1990], p. 31.) That argument offers a counterexample to my claim that nothing can have interests without a brain, though not to my more general claim that nothing can have interests without some form of consciousness, because I assume that a soul, which can suffer, is itself a special form of consciousness. If someone accepts this argument, then he does have a reason for insisting that a fetus (or more accurately the soul it contains) has an interest in continuing to live. But states are not entitled to act on reasons of theological dogma.
37. See Clifford Grobstein, *Science and the Unborn: Choosing Human Futures* (Basic Books, 1988): "To provide a safe margin against intrusion into possible primitive sentience, the cortical maturation beginning at about thirty weeks is a reasonable landmark until more precise information becomes available. Therefore, since we should use extreme caution in respecting and protecting possible sentience, a provisional boundary at about twenty-six weeks should provide safety against reasonable concerns. This time is coincident with the present definition of viability" (p. 130).
38. *McRae v. Califano,* 491 F. Supp. 630, 727–728 (E. D. N.Y.), rev'd as *Harris v. McRae,* 448 U.S. 297 (1980).
39. Kristin Luker, *Abortion and the Politics of Motherhood* (University of California Press, 1984), chap. 8.
40. *Webster v. Reproductive Health Services,* 492 U.S. 490 (1989).
41. Professor Tribe, for example, says that "if constitutional law is as constitutional law does, then after Webster, Roe is not what it once was." Tribe, *Abortion,* at 24 (cited in note 36).
42. See Michael de Courcy Hinds, "Appeals Court Upholds Limits for Abortions," *New York Times,* A1 (Oct. 22, 1991), discussing *Planned Parenthood v. Casey,* 947 F. 2d 682 (3d Cir. 1991), cert granted in part by 60 U.S.L.W. 3388 (1992), and in part by 60 U.S.L.W. 3446 (1992). In fact the majority opinion in *Casey* assumed the distinction between responsibility and conformity I defend in the text, and interpreted Justice O'Connor's "undue burden" test in *Webster,* 492 U.S. at 529–531 (O'Connor concurring), to presuppose that distinction as well.

43. See, for example, Sheryl McCarthy, "Climactic Battle Is at Hand," *Newsday*, 5 (Jan. 22, 1992); "Washington Brief," *Natl. L.J.*, 5 (Feb. 3, 1992).

44. In *Casey*, the Third Circuit, claiming to follow Justice O'Connor, proposed that the pertinent test should be whether the regulation imposed an "undue burden" on a woman's right to have an abortion if after reflection she wished one. 947 F. 2d at 695–697, 706–707.

45. Of course government sometimes forces people to do what they think wrong—to pay taxes that will be used to fight a war they think immoral, for example. But in such cases government justifies coercion by appealing to the rights and interests of other people, not to an intrinsic value those who are coerced believe requires the opposite decision.

46. See Ronald Dworkin, *Foundations of a Liberal Equality* (University of Utah Press, 1990), p. 1.

47. *United States v. Seeger*, 380 U.S. 163, 166 (1965).

48. Kent Greenawalt, "Religion as a Concept in Constitutional Law," *Cal. L. Rev.*, vol. 72 (1984), p. 753; George Freeman III, "The Misguided Search for the Constitutional Definition of 'Religion,'" *Georgetown L.J.*, vol. 71 (1983), p. 1519.

49. John Rawls, for example, distinguishes his own and other theories of justice from what he calls comprehensive religious or ethical schemes; political theories of justice, he says, presuppose no opinion about what is objectively important. In particular, they presuppose no opinion about if or why or in what way it is intrinsically important that human life continue or prosper, though of course political theories of justice are compatible with a great variety of such opinions. See John Rawls, "Justice as Fairness, Political not Metaphysical," *Phil. & Pub. Aff.*, vol. 14 (1985), p. 223.

50. See Dworkin, *Foundations of a Liberal Equality* (cited in note 46).

51. *McRae*, 491 F. Supp. at 690–702. I develop this point at length in *Life's Dominion*.

52. I do not mean that no stronger constitutional right of personal autonomy can be defended as flowing from the best interpretation of the Constitution as a whole. Indeed, I think a significantly stronger right can be. But I shall not defend any principle broader than the more limited one just described, because that principle is strong enough to ground a right of privacy understood to include a right to procreative autonomy.

53. 381 U.S. 479 (1965).

54. Id. at 500 (Harlan concurring) (referring to his dissent in *Poe v. Ullman*, 367 U.S. 497, 539–545 [1961]).

55. *Eisenstadt v. Baird*, 405 U.S. 438, 453 (1972) (emphasis in original).

56. See, for example, Robert H. Bork, "Neutral Principles and Some First Amendment Problems," *Ind. L.J.*, vol. 47 (1971), pp. 1, 7–10.

57. Nomination of Robert H. Bork to be Associate Justice of the Supreme Court

of the United States, Hearings before the Senate Committee on the Judiciary, 100th Cong, 1st Sess., 250 (Sept. 16, 1987). See Ethan Bonner, *Battle for Justice* (Norton, 1989), pp. 221–222, 260.

58. See Greenawalt, *Cal. L. Rev.*, vol. 72, p. 753 (cited in note 48); Freeman, *Georgetown L.J.*, vol. 71, p. 1519 (cited in note 48).

59. We can regard the Supreme Court's decision in *Smith v. Employment Division*, 494 U.S. 872 (1990), as an example of that kind of case, whether or not we agree with the decision.

60. 380 U.S. 163. The Court in *Seeger* construed a statute rather than the Constitution. But since the Court's decision contradicted the evident statutory purpose, commentators have assumed that the Court meant to imply that the statute was constitutional only if so construed.

In a recent book, Peter Wenz argues for a ground of distinction between religious and secular opinions that is different from the two possible distinctions I mention here (which he calls "epistemological"). He accepts the traditional view, that the argument over abortion is about whether a fetus is a person, but insists that the question whether an early fetus is a person is a religious one because it cannot be decided "entirely" on the basis of "methods of argumentation that are integral to our way of life." Peter Wenz, *Abortion Rights as Religious Freedom* (Temple University Press, 1992), p. 131. I agree with the conclusion he reaches: that the abortion debate is primarily a religious one governed by the First Amendment. But his test is not acceptable, because government must make and impose decisions on a wide variety of moral issues about which people disagree profoundly, and which cannot be decided on empirical grounds or by appeal to any convictions shared by everyone or by methods that are in any other way "integral" to any collective way of life.

61. Id. at 165–166.

62. See "Draft Declaration on the Church's Relations with Non-Christians," in *Council Daybook* (Vatican II, 3d Sess., 1965), p. 282, quoted and cited in *Seeger*, 380 U.S. at 181–182 and n. 4.

63. See the text accompanying notes 49–51.

64. *Gillette v. United States,* 401 U.S. 437.

65. Id. at 455 (footnotes omitted). The Court also endorsed, as on a careful view supporting the distinction between universal and selective opposition, the government's claim that opposition to a particular war necessarily involves judgment that is "political and particular" and "based on the same political, sociological, and economic factors that the government necessarily considered" in deciding whether to wage war. Id. at 458 (citing government's brief).

66. Posner, *U. Chi. L. Rev.*, vol. 59, at 444 (cited in note 9).

67. Id. at 443.

68. Such laws do raise other issues about intrinsic value, and in some extremely

unusual circumstances might violate a form of the principle of privacy more powerful than the weak form I described and defended.

69. I should mention a complexity. I have been arguing that many women's decisions about abortion reflect convictions, which may well be inarticulate, about whether abortion or childbirth would best respect what they believe intrinsically valuable about human life. That is not necessarily true of all women who want abortions, however, and the free exercise claim might therefore not be available, as a matter of principle, for everyone. But states could not devise appropriate and practicable tests for discriminating among women in that way, and in any case prohibition would be the establishment of an essentially religious position, even in cases when it worked to outlaw abortion for someone whose grounds were not religious in any sense.

70. Posner, *U. Chi. L. Rev.*, vol. 59, at 441 (cited in note 9).

71. See Grobstein, *Science and the Unborn* at 54–55 (cited in note 37).

72. *Facts in Brief: Abortion in the United States* (Alan Guttmacher Institute, 1991). See also Stanley K. Henshaw, "Characteristics of U.S. Women Having Abortions, 1982–83," in Stanley K. Henshaw and Jennifer Van Vort, ed., *Abortion Services in the United States: Each State and Metropolitan Area, 1984–85* (Alan Guttmacher Institute, 1988), p. 23.

73. See note 37.

74. The U.S. Bureau of the Census reports that 10 percent of the 1,559,100 abortions performed in 1987 occurred at thirteen or more weeks gestational age. U.S. Department of Commerce, Economics and Statistics Administration, Bureau of the Census, *The Statistical Abstract of the United States* (111th ed., 1991), p. 71. Since about 0.01 percent of all abortions are performed after twenty-four weeks (see note 72 and accompanying text), it can be inferred that about 9.99 percent of the abortions performed in 1987 occurred in the second trimester.

75. The RU 486 pill may in any case defuse the public controversy by reducing the need for abortion clinics that act as magnets for protesters, as in Wichita.

4. Roe Was Saved

1. In an advertisement published in the *New York Times* the day after the decision was announced, Planned Parenthood Federation of America said that "the decision in [*Casey*] threatens to put every woman back where she was nineteen years ago before Roe v. Wade ended back-alley horrors." The advertisement was intended to solicit support for the Freedom of Choice Act now before Congress, which remains urgent and important, particularly since the decision in *Casey* was only five to four. But it is wrong to suggest that a twenty-four-hour mandatory waiting period before an abortion is equivalent to forbidding abortion altogether.

2. Linda Greenhouse of the *New York Times* pointed out that, though all these four justices joined each of the two partially dissenting opinions, the opinions are actually, in important ways, inconsistent with one another. See *New York Times*, A1, A15 (June 30, 1992).

3. See "Center-Right Coalition Asserts Itself," *Washington Post* (June 30, 1992). In his partial dissent, Scalia referred bitterly to *Lee v. Weisman,* a recent decision in which O'Connor, Kennedy, and Souter joined with Blackmun and Stevens to rule that prayers at school graduation ceremonies violate the First Amendment's separation of church and state.

4. Statutes plainly inconsistent with *Roe* (and with the majority's five to four decision in *Casey,* have been enacted by the legislatures of Louisiana, Utah, and Guam, and these statutes are now under review in lower federal courts.

5. Since Rehnquist and Scalia also voted to uphold the sections of the Pennsylvania act that the three-justice group approved, the Court as a whole approved them, and the majority so held, in spite of partial dissents by Blackmun and Stevens declaring some of them unconstitutional. Since Blackmun and Stevens also voted to strike down the spousal notification requirement, that was also the decision of the Court, in spite of the votes of Rehnquist and Scalia to uphold that requirement.

6. They rejected, however, what they called the rigid trimester scheme that Blackmun had set out in *Roe* to enforce that central holding, and they also, in upholding most of the Pennsylvania restrictions, overruled certain Supreme Court decisions following *Roe* which struck down similar restrictions.

7. The joint opinion quoted Justice John Harlan's 1961 opinion in *Poe v. Ullman,* which the Court later adopted in *Griswold* when it declared prohibitions on contraception unconstitutional. Harlan insisted that "liberty" within the meaning of the due process clause is not a series of isolated, historically selected freedoms, but "a rational continuum which . . . recognizes, what a reasonable and sensitive judgment must, that certain interests require particularly careful scrutiny of the state needs asserted to justify their abridgment." See 367 U.S. 497, 543.

8. For a further explanation of the character and force of this argument, and of its bearing on the state's interest in regulating abortion discussed in later paragraphs, see Chapter 3.

9. The three justices added an important and moving declaration to their argument on this point, explaining why states must show more concern for the position of a pregnant woman than that of the potential father. "It is an inescapable biological fact," they said, "that state regulation with respect to the child a woman is carrying will have a far greater impact on the mother's liberty than the father's." They added the warning that though a state may acknowledge a father's interest in pregnancy as well, it "may not give to a man the kind of dominion over his wife that parents exercise over their children,"

and therefore may not give him the role that they may properly give the parents of teenage women.

10. I describe the arguments in favor of that different accommodation in Chapter 3.

11. It should be noticed, however, that Justice Brennan's opinion for the Court in one of the contraception cases, *Eisenstadt v. Baird*, 405 U.S. 438 (1972), declared that the right of privacy extends to a woman's decision whether to "bear" as well as to "beget" children.

12. See Chapter 6.

13. Justice Stevens, in his separate opinion, noted that of the fifteen justices who have considered the question, eleven have endorsed such a right, and that the only four who have rejected it happen to be on the Court now.

5. Do We Have a Right to Die?

1. In fact five justices—Justice O'Connor and the four dissenters—did declare that people have that right. But one of the dissenters, Justice Brennan, has retired, and it is not known whether Justice Souter, who took his place, agrees.

2. On July 1, 1990, the New York state legislature enacted a law, the "health care proxy bill," that provides for such delegation. Governor Mario Cuomo said that the *Cruzan* decision helped to break a logjam on the bill. See *New York Times* (July 2, 1990).

3. The well-publicized case of Janet Adkins, who killed herself using Dr. Jack Kevorkian's suicide machine in the back of his Volkswagen van, suggests the moral complexity of suicide provoked by illness, and the degree to which Americans are divided about the issues raised by such suicide. Adkins was fifty-three and in the relatively early stages of Alzheimer's disease. Her mental capacity had begun to diminish—she found tennis scoring and the foreign languages she used to speak too difficult, for example, though she had lost little physical capacity, and had recently beaten her thirty-three-year-old son at tennis. She was still alert and intelligent, and had retained her sense of humor. But she wanted to die before the irreversible disease worsened; the life she would soon lead, she said, "is not the way I wanted it at all." She telephoned Kevorkian, whom she had seen on television discussing his device. They met in Michigan, chosen because assisting suicide is not a crime there, in a motel room where he taped a forty-minute conversation which recorded her competence and her wish to die. Two days later he inserted a needle into her vein as she lay in the back of his van, and told her which button to push for a lethal injection. Michigan prosecutors charged Kevorkian with murder, but the judge acquitted him after listening to the tape.

The case raises serious moral issues that the *Cruzan* case does not. Janet

Adkins apparently had several years of meaningful life left, and Kevorkian's examination may not have been long or substantial enough to rule out the possibility that she was in a temporary depression from which she might recover while still competent. It is of interest that about half of the 250 doctors who wrote in response to a critical article in a medical journal approved of what Kevorkian did, while the rest disapproved.

4. See Chapter 1.

5. I do not mean to deny that animal life might have intrinsic importance, too.

6. I do not mean that many people often reflect on their lives as a whole, or live according to some overall theory about what makes their lives good or bad. Most people define living well in much more concrete terms: living well means having a good job, a successful family life, warm friendships, and time and money for recreation or travel, for example. But I believe that people take pride as well as pleasure in these concrete achievements and experiences, and have a sense of failure as well as displeasure when a job goes wrong or a friendship sours. Very few of them, perhaps, except those for whom religion is important, self-consciously think of their lives as an opportunity that they may either waste or make into something worthwhile. But most people's attitudes toward successes and failures do seem to presuppose that view of life's importance. Most of us think it is important that the lives of other people, as well as our own, be worthwhile: we think it is a central role of government to encourage people to make something of their lives rather than just survive, and to provide some of the institutions, including the schools, necessary for them to do so. These assumptions are premises of liberal education, and also of the limited paternalism involved in stopping people from using drugs or wasting their lives in other ways, and in trying to prevent or discourage people who are depressed or despondent from killing themselves when they could in fact lead lives worth living.

That human life has intrinsic value in this sense—that it is important that a life go well once it has begun—obviously has important though complex implications for the abortion issue. In Chapter 3 of this book, and in *Life's Dominion: An Essay on Abortion, Euthanasia, and Individual Freedom* (Knopf, 1993), I explored these implications. I argued that the idea that life has intrinsic value in the sense I described does explain many of our attitudes about abortion, including the opinion many people have that abortion even in an early stage poses moral problems. It does not follow that abortion is always wrong; indeed, it sometimes follows that abortion is morally recommended or required. I argued, moreover, that understanding our moral notions about abortion as flowing from respect for the inherent value of life reinforces the Supreme Court decision in *Roe v. Wade* that the state has no business coercing pregnant women to take a particular view about what the principle of respect for the inherent value of life requires.

6. Gag Rule and Affirmative Action

1. *McCleskey v. Zant,* 59 U.S.L.W. 3782.
2. *Arizona v. Fulminante,* 59 U.S.L.W. 4235.
3. *McCleskey v. Kemp,* 481 U.S. 279. Although blacks who murder whites are much more likely to be sentenced to death in Georgia than blacks who murder other blacks, or than whites who murder anyone, the court declared this irrelevant in deciding whether race played any role in a Georgia court's decision to execute a black defendant convicted of murdering a white victim.
4. *Rust v. Sullivan,* 59 U.S.L.W. 4451.
5. See Chapter 14 and also Lawrence Sager, "Back to Bork," in *The New York Review of Books* (October 25, 1990).
6. Fried emphasizes the role played in the *Griswold* decision by Justice Harlan's 1961 dissent in *Poe v. Ullman,* which supported a right to privacy. *Order and Law: Arguing the Reagan Revolution* (Simon and Schuster, 1991). Fried was Harlan's law clerk in that year, and presumably worked on that dissent.
7. He repeats a bad argument that he made to the Supreme Court: that the *Griswold* case, at least, only concerned whether the police should have the power to break into bedrooms to search for contraceptives. Only one of the several majority opinions in *Griswold* mentioned that reason, and cases after *Griswold,* which Fried does not suggest were wrong, decided, for example, that the states could not forbid the sale of contraceptives in drugstores, a prohibition that could certainly have been enforced without midnight raids on marital bedrooms. In any case, since Fried aims to display the moral principles that underlie the Reagan revolution, he must distinguish contraception from abortion in some deeper way: if the *Griswold* decision was a correct and important protection of liberty, but *Roe v. Wade* an unlawful imposition of naked power, then the difference between the two must lie in something more important than the dubious claim that prohibitions on contraception might tempt the police to search bedrooms.
8. Fried nowhere explains why, if that is so, states are not entitled to forbid the use of the safest and most popular contraceptive pills now in use, which are abortifacients, that is, pills that act by aborting just-conceived fetuses.
9. I do not mean that states would be required to follow that rule. See my discussion in Chapter 1.
10. See my article "The *Bakke* Decision: Did It Decide Anything?" *The New York Review of Books* (Aug. 17, 1978); Letters (Sept. 28, 1978).
11. 448 U.S. 448.
12. Nor is it defensible for the Court to have reached that result by overturning a longstanding interpretation of a congressional statute, which Congress itself could have reversed at any time in the last twenty years. Several congressmen, including Senator Danforth of Missouri and eight other Republican senators,

have already introduced measures to restore the *Griggs* rule. But Bush can veto any such measure, which means that the Court and enough congressmen to sustain a veto are now in a position, on this extremely important matter, to repeal an established congressional decision that the Court acknowledges is within the power of Congress to have taken.

13. 448 U.S. 469.
14. The scholars' statement appears in the *Yale Law Journal*, vol. 98, p. 1711, and Fried's reply in the *Yale Law Journal*, vol. 99, p. 155. The scholars replied to Fried's reply in the *Yale Law Journal*, vol. 99, p. 163.
15. Fried's extravagant claims about the scope of these decisions may well be overstated. They seem inconsistent with the Court's later decision—Justice Brennan's last substantive opinion—in a case in which Fried submitted a brief, but which was decided after he returned to Harvard, and presumably too late to be mentioned in his book. In *Metro Broadcasting Inc. v. FCC*, 110 S.C. 2997, the Court held that Congress could constitutionally adopt programs designed to increase minority ownership of broadcast stations without demonstrating that the lack of minority programming was the result of specific past discrimination rather than just social factors. The Court's opinion emphasized the peculiar role of the national Congress in implementing the Fourteenth Amendment but, as Fried has recognized in a later article, the decision could not be right if, as he says *Croson* established, the Constitution forbids any official affirmative action except subject to the conditions he described.
16. *Constitution*, Spring/Summer (1991), p. 73.

Part II Introduction

1. Chapter 8 discusses a hate speech case then pending in the Supreme Court. The Court declared the statute at the center of that case, which singled out racially motivated crimes for special punishment, unconstitutional because it limited its coverage to crimes motivated by certain specified opinions. See *R.A.V. v. St. Paul, Minnesota*, 112 S. Ct. 2538 (1991).

7. The Press on Trial

1. *The Juror and the General* (Morrow, 1986).
2. Uri Dan, *Against All Odds: The Inside Story of General Ariel Sharon's History-Making Libel Suit* (Simon and Schuster, 1987), pp. 105–109. Sharon claimed that *Time* was guilty of a "blood libel," which suggests an attack not only on him personally but on the Jewish people as a whole.
3. Adler reports none of the details of this settlement attempt, saying only that it was *Time* that "turned away" from it, which is contradicted by Dan's account.

4. Contrary to Uri Dan's claim that *Time*'s version "bore no resemblance to the text that Sharon had accepted so reluctantly," it differed in substance from that text only in stating that Sharon was now satisfied, on the basis of statements *Time*'s employees had made in the course of discovery, that the magazine had not meant to suggest that he had encouraged, condoned, or anticipated the massacres. It is unclear why *Time* asked for that addition—its journalistic integrity did not depend on Sharon's opinions about its motives— and it should have been ready to drop or qualify the addition in negotiation, and might have done so. In any case, if Sharon had cared only about the accuracy of *Time*'s statements about him, and not about punishing *Time*, he would not have barred further settlement discussion in the way Dan reports.

5. Duncan testified, at the trial, that *he* had made no attempt to investigate Halevy's sources, after the lawsuit began, because "a very big investigation" had been launched by *Time*'s lawyers. It hardly follows that no one at *Time* tried to check the story in any way before the suit began (Sharon's first suit, in Israel, was begun less than two weeks after the article was published) or that *Time* would have defended its story in court if its lawyers' investigation had shown that story to be false. In his letter to *The New Yorker*, Henry Grunwald, *Time*'s editor in chief, denied that it had made no investigation, and observed that Adler made no effort to interview the magazine or its lawyers about its efforts to check the story. (In her coda, she says that her book is based on trial attendance and transcripts and "does not purport to contain interviews," which are not part of the "genre of trial reporting." That hardly explains why she did not try to check, in the most natural way, a serious charge on which much of her argument is based and which could not have been sustained on the trial records alone.) She should at least have said what *Time* or its lawyers might have done, but did not do, to satisfy themselves that the story, as they now presented it, was true.

6. I agree with Adler that the conventions for reporting information gathered from confidential sources (e.g., "*Time* has learned . . .") often pitch these reports at too confident a level. It would be more careful of the truth to develop different conventions: "*Time* has been told . . ." for example.

7. Rodney Smolla, *Suing the Press: Libel, the Media, and Power* (Oxford University Press, 1987).

8. Bob Brewin and Sydney Shaw, *Vietnam on Trial: Westmoreland vs. CBS* (Atheneum, 1987). Brewin covered the trial for *The Village Voice*.

9. Dave Richard Palmer, *Readings in Current Military History* (United States Military Academy, 1969), p. 102.

10. For a fuller account of CBS's evidence and discoveries than Adler provides, see "The Strategy of Deception in the Vietnam War," *Philadelphia Inquirer Magazine* (Oct. 27, 1985), by David Zucchino, an *Inquirer* reporter who covered the trial day by day, and *Vietnam on Trial*, the Brewin and Shaw book

cited in note 8. Smolla, in the book cited in note 7, says that even after the trial reasonable people could have disagreed about whether the views of Westmoreland and his many powerful supporters or those of CBS and its mainly more junior military witnesses were closer to the truth. This moderate view hardly supports Adler's claim that the CBS position has been proved false.

11. For a good discussion of the complexity of any argument about what those who made the Constitution intended, see H. Jefferson Powell, "The Original Understanding of Original Intent," *Harvard Law Review,* vol. 98 (1985), p. 885.

12. She has in mind Justice Byron White's attempt, in a case after *New York Times,* to describe the state of mind of "reckless disregard" in more detail. He said: "There must be sufficient evidence to permit the conclusion that the defendant in fact entertained serious doubts as to the truth of his publication." (*St. Amant v. Thompson,* 390 U.S. 727 [1967] at p. 731.) Adler suggests (though she seems to retract this in the coda) that White meant, by "serious doubt," that anyone who is aware of arguments against what he publishes, or knows that he might be wrong in what he says, is guilty of reckless disregard, and she says that it cannot have been the intention of the framers to discourage good-faith doubt of that kind and to protect only those who publish in absolute and dogmatic certainty. But of course (as White's opinion makes plain) the serious doubt he had in mind is not the normal, commendable, scholarly sense of fallibility, but the very different attitude of someone who thinks that the evidence against what he says is about as strong as the evidence for it, but publishes anyway in disregard of the contrary evidence.

13. The Court had earlier decided that the First Amendment is made applicable to the states as well as the federal government by the Fourteenth Amendment.

14. 441 U.S. 153 (1979).

15. Adler says that if the jury had found for either Westmoreland or Sharon, the "higher courts would simply find that within the category 'public official' there exists a smaller category, 'high military officer,' which must meet an even more formidable burden of proof [than that imposed by the *New York Times* test], or perhaps be precluded from suing for libel at all." She cites no authority or any other reason for predicting any such ruling, and there is nothing in recent Supreme Court opinions to justify that prediction. Judge Sofaer, ruling on *Time*'s motion for summary judgment, explicitly rejected the idea that high military officers face a special burden of proof. Judge Leval said there was no authority for that idea, though he said CBS could argue the point at the end of the trial.

16. See his opinion in *Dun & Bradstreet v. Greenmoss Builders,* 105 S. Ct. 2939 (1985).

17. See *Gertz v. Robert Welch, Inc.,* 418 U.S. 323 (1974), and cases cited and discussed therein.

8. Why Must Speech Be Free?

1. 376 U.S. 254 (1964).
2. In a striking decision on April 15, 1992, Judge Shirley Fingerhood, of the New York State Supreme Court in Manhattan, refused to enforce a British libel judgment against a New York–based news service, on the ground that enforcing a foreign judgment rendered under libel law that lacks the protections of the First Amendment would decrease press freedom here. If the decision is upheld, it will substantially increase the freedom of American publications that are distributed abroad.
3. *Masses Publishing Company v. Pattern,* 244 F. 535 (1917).
4. *Abrams v. United States,* 250 U.S. 616 (1919).
5. *Whitney v. California,* 274 U.S. 357 (1927).
6. 315 U.S. 568 (1942).
7. Brennan, however, spoke for only six justices. Three others, Black, Douglas, and Goldberg, voted to make the protection of the press against libel suits by public officials absolute: they would not have allowed an official to sue even if he could prove actual malice.
8. See an important pair of articles by the Harvard philosopher Thomas Scanlon. In the first, "A Theory of Freedom of Expression," *Philosophy and Public Affairs,* vol. 1 (1972), p. 204, he developed a Kantian argument for the constitutive justification. In the second, "Freedom of Expression and Categories of Expression," *University of Pittsburgh Law Review,* vol. 40 (1979), p. 519, partly in criticism of the first article, he emphasized the complex character of any adequate account of the right to free speech, in which constitutive and instrumental factors must both figure.
9. Lewis describes the passage in Brandeis's opinion that begins in this way as the most profound statement ever made about the premises of the First Amendment.
10. For a more general discussion of the way in which different kinds of justification overlap in explaining abstract constitutional rights, see Chapter 3.
11. Robert Bork, "Neutral Principles and Some First Amendment Problems," *Indiana Law Journal,* vol. 47 (1971). In the Senate hearings considering his nomination to the Supreme Court, Bork said he had abandoned this view.
12. See *United States v. Associated Press,* 52 F. Supp. 362, 372 (1943).
13. Lewis points out that this remark reflected the opinions of Alexander Meiklejohn, a political scientist who had long been a passionate defender of the view, which merges aspects of the instrumental and constitutive justification, that censorship of political opinion is unjustified because citizens are entitled to as much information as possible in order to fulfill their responsibilities to govern themselves. Meiklejohn was unwilling to extend this responsibility to other aspects of citizens' lives, but he took a broad view of what was pertinent to

politics. He insisted, for example, that censorship of pornography deprived people of information and insights they needed properly to vote. See his "The First Amendment Is an Absolute," 1961 *Supreme Court Review*, p. 245.

14. *New York Times v. United States,* 403 U.S. 713 (1971).

15. 395 U.S. 444 (1969).

16. *Collin v. Smith,* 578 F. 2d 1197 (1968). The Supreme Court refused to stay the Seventh Circuit's decision. 436 U.S. 953 (1978).

17. For a discussion of the *Viktora* case, and its bearing on university regulation of similar speech, see "Justices Weigh Ban on Voicing Hate," by Linda Greenhouse, *New York Times,* B19 (Dec. 5, 1991), and "Hate-Crime Law Is Focus of Case on Free Speech," *New York Times,* A1 (Dec. 1, 1991).

18. See Stanley Fish, "There's No Such Thing as Free Speech and It's a Good Thing, Too," in *Debating PC,* ed. Paul Berman (Dell, 1992). Fish claims to consider and reject the argument that freedom of speech is the greater value to which other values must yield. But he construes that argument as the preposterous claim that the point of speaking is just speaking for its own sake. He confuses people's reasons for speaking, which are of course to promote some other purpose, with the reasons government might have for protecting their right to speak, which may include constitutive as well as instrumental reasons.

19. See Chapter 9.

20. For a recent survey of the scientific evidence, confirming that no causal link has been established between pornography and crimes of sexual violence, see Marcia Pally's report *Sense and Censorship: The Vanity of Bonfires* (1991), published by Americans for Constitutional Freedom and the Freedom to Read Foundation.

21. For example, the serial killer Ted Bundy, before his execution, said that pornography had led him into sexual violence and then to serial killing. Experts who had examined him, and people close to him including his own lawyer, dismissed that claim, and a specialist described it as rationalization based on false beliefs. The Bundy case, and other examples of highly dubious claims by both criminals and victims that pornography was responsible for crimes, are discussed in Marcia Pally's *Sense and Censorship,* pp. 159, 164.

22. The federal bill is limited to material that may be prosecuted as obscene under the latest rules adopted by the Supreme Court. But those rules allow juries to apply their local community standards in judging what is obscene, and publishers would be reluctant to distribute a video even in areas where local standards do not regard it as obscene, for fear that a criminal watching it there will rape a victim in some other part of the country where juries might take a very different view.

23. Feminists for Free Expression, a group which includes Betty Friedan, Susan Jacoby, Nora Ephron, Judith Krug, and Nadine Strossen, among others,

insists that there is no agreement or feminist code as to what images are distasteful or even sexist and that women do not need protection from explicit sexual materials. See Nat Hentoff, "Pornography War among Feminists," *Washington Post*, A23 (April 4, 1992).

24. *Butler v. Her Majesty the Queen*, decided Feb. 27, 1992.

25. I discuss in Chapter 9 the argument that pornography can be banned because it demeans women.

26. See Harry Kalven, "The Metaphysics of the Law of Obscenity," 1960 *Supreme Court Review*, p. 1. I do not mean to rule out (or to endorse) a rather different instrumental justification that has been suggested for permitting pornography: that pornography may be therapeutic for some people.

27. See *Jacobellis v. Ohio*, 378 U.S. 184, 197 (1964).

28. *Roth v. United States*, 354 U.S. 476 (1957).

29. *Paris Adult Theater I v. Slater*, 413 U.S. 49 (1973).

30. See David Richards, "Free Speech and Obscenity Law: Toward a Moral Theory of the First Amendment," *University of Pennsylvania Law Review*, vol. 123 (1974), p. 45.

31. 111 U.S. 1759 (1991).

32. The statute had never been interpreted to forbid mention of abortion before. After *Rust v. Sullivan* was decided, Congress passed another statute denying that its earlier act had that consequence. But Bush vetoed that further statute. So *Rust v. Sullivan* legitimates an odd method of legislating contrary to the majority will of Congress, a method that may have a future. The administration reinterprets some standing legislation in a bizarre way, the conservative-dominated Supreme Court affirms that reinterpretation as "not clearly wrong," and the President uses his veto power to sustain the Court's decision.

33. "Administration Partly Lifts Abortion 'Gag Rule,'" *Washington Post*, 1 (March 21, 1992).

34. *Rosenbloom v. Metromedia*, 403 U.S. 29 (1971).

35. *Curtis Publishing Company v. Butts*, 388 U.S. 130 (1967).

36. *Gertz v. Robert Welch, Inc.*, 418 U.S. 323 (1974).

37. See Chapter 7.

38. *Herbert v. Lando*, 441 U.S. 153 (1979).

39. Versions of the programs I describe in the text have been proposed, for example, by Professor Mark Franklin of the Stanford Law School, the Annenberg Washington Program, Professor David Anderson of the Texas Law School, and Pierre Leval, the federal judge who presided over the Westmoreland libel trial. For a summary of the details of the various proposals, see chap. 4 of *The Fourth Estate and the Constitution* (University of California Press, 1991), by Lucas A. Powe, Jr., a professor of law and of government at the University of Texas.

40. The constitutionality of requiring a paper to report a verdict against it may be doubtful. In *Miami Herald v. Tornillo*, 418 U.S. 241 (1974), the Supreme Court held that a Florida right-of-reply statute was unconstitutional. But both Brennan and Rehnquist said, in that case, that it might be constitutional to order a newspaper to report a judicial verdict of falsity against it.

41. Judges would have the power to dismiss any damage suit before the real trial begins if they found that the plaintiff has no chance of satisfying the *Sullivan* test. (Lewis suggests that Judge Leval should have dismissed General West-moreland's suit against CBS on that ground.) Judges would presumably be more likely to exercise that power to dismiss, and so save the press the expense and harassment of a long trial, if the plaintiff had the alternative of suing for a judicial declaration of falsehood.

9. Pornography and Hate

1. Isaiah Berlin, *Four Essays on Liberty* (Oxford University Press, 1968), p. 1vi.
2. MacKinnon explained that "if a woman is subjected, why should it matter that the work has other value?" See her article "Pornography, Civil Rights, and Speech," in *Harvard Civil Rights–Civil Liberties Law Review*, vol. 28 (1993), p. 21.
3. See my article "Do We Have a Right to Pornography?" reprinted as chap. 17 in my book *A Matter of Principle* (Harvard University Press, 1985).
4. *American Booksellers Association, Inc. et al. v. William H. Hudnut, III, Mayor, City of Indianapolis, et al.*, 598 F. Supp. 1316 (S.D. Ind. 1984).
5. 771 F. 2d 323 (U.S. Court of Appeals, Seventh Circuit).
6. That court, in a confused passage, said that it nevertheless accepted "the premises of this legislation," which included the claims about a causal connec-tion with sexual violence. But it seemed to mean that it was accepting the rather different causal claim considered in the next paragraph, about subordi-nation. In any case, it said that it accepted those premises only for the sake of argument, since it thought it had no authority to reject decisions of the city of Indianapolis based on its interpretation of empirical evidence.
7. See the *Daily Telegraph*, Dec. 23, 1990. Of course further studies might contradict this assumption. But it seems very unlikely that pornography will be found to stimulate physical violence to the overall extent that nonporno-graphic depictions of violence, which are much more pervasive in our media and culture, do.
8. See MacKinnon's article cited in note 2.
9. Frank Michelman, Conceptions of Democracy in American Constitutional Argument: The Case of Pornography Regulation, *Tennessee Law Review*, vol. 56, no. 291 (1989), pp. 303–304.

10. MacKinnon's Words

1. Catharine MacKinnon, "Pornography, Civil Rights, and Speech," reprinted in Catherine Itzin, ed., *Pornography: Women, Violence, and Civil Liberties, A Radical View* (Oxford University Press, 1992), p. 456. (Quotations are from pp. 461–463.)

2. *American Booksellers Ass'n v. Hudnut*, 771 F. 2d 323 (1985), aff'd 475 U.S. 1001 (1986). In a decision that MacKinnon discusses at length, a Canadian court upheld a similar Canadian statute as consistent with that nation's Charter of Rights and Freedoms. I discuss that decision in Chapter 8.

3. See Chapter 9.

4. Among the prestigious studies denying the causal link MacKinnon claims are the 1970 report of the National Commission on Obscenity and Pornography, appointed by Lyndon Johnson to consider the issue, the 1979 report of the Williams Commission in Britain, and a recent year-long British study which concluded that "the evidence does not point to pornography as a cause of deviant sexual orientation in offenders. Rather it seems to be used as part of that deviant sexual orientation." MacKinnon and other feminists cite the voluminous two-volume report of the infamous Meese Commission, which was appointed by Reagan to contradict the findings of the earlier Johnson-appointed group and was headed by people who had made a career of opposing pornography. The Meese Commission duly declared that although the scientific evidence was inconclusive, it believed that pornography (vast tracts of which were faithfully reprinted in its report) did indeed cause crime. But the scientists on whose work the report relied protested, immediately after its publication, that the commission had misunderstood and misused their work. (For a thorough analysis of all these and other studies, see Marcia Pally, *Sense and Censorship: The Vanity of Bonfires* [Americans for Constitutional Freedom, 1991].) MacKinnon also appeals to legal authority: she says, citing the Seventh Circuit opinion holding her antipornography statute unconstitutional, that "not even courts equivocate over pornography's carnage anymore." But this is disingenuous: that opinion assumed that pornography is a significant cause of sexual crime only for the sake of the argument it made, and it cited, among other material, the Williams Commission report as support for the court's own denial of any such demonstrated causal connection.

5. In "Pornography, Civil Rights, and Speech," MacKinnon said, "It does not make sense to assume that pornography has no role in rape simply because little about its use or effects distinguishes convicted rapists from other men, when we know that a lot of those other men *do* rape women; they just never get caught" (p. 475).

6. "Turning Rape Into Pornography: Postmodern Genocide," *Ms.*, 28 (July/Aug. 1993).
7. George Kennan, "The Balkan Crisis: 1913 and 1993," *The New York Review of Books* (July 15, 1993).
8. Itzin, ed., *Pornography: Women, Violence, and Civil Liberties*, p. 359. At one point MacKinnon offers a surprisingly timid formulation of her causal thesis: she says that there is no evidence that pornography does no harm. The same negative claim can be made, of course, about any genre of literature. Ted Bundy, the serial murderer who said he had read pornography since his youth, and whom feminists often cite for that remark, also said that he had studied Dostoevsky's *Crime and Punishment*. Even MacKinnon's weak statement is controversial, moreover. Some psychologists have argued that pornography, by providing a harmless outlet for violent tendencies, may actually reduce the amount of such crime. See Patricia Gillian, "Therapeutic Uses of Obscenity," and other articles reprinted and cited in *Censorship and Obscenity*, ed. Rajeev Dhavan and Christie Davies (Rowman and Littlefield, 1978). And it is at least relevant that nations with the most permissive laws about pornography are among those with the least sexual crime (see Marjorie Heins, *Sex, Sin, and Blasphemy* [New Press, 1993], p. 152), though of course that fact might be explained in other ways.
9. MacKinnon's frequent rhetorical use of "you" and "your," embracing all female readers, invites every woman to see herself as a victim of the appalling sexual crimes and abuses she describes, and reinforces an implicit suggestion that women are, in pertinent ways, all alike: all passive, innocent, and subjugated.
10. Reprinted in Itzin, ed., *Pornography: Women, Violence, and Civil Liberties*, pp. 483–484.
11. See Frank I. Michelman, "Conceptions of Democracy in American Constitutional Argument: The Case of Pornography Regulation," *Tennessee Law Review*, vol. 56, no. 2 (1989), pp. 303–304.
12. Not all feminists agree that pornography contributes to the economic or social subordination of women. Linda Williams, for example, in the Fall 1993 issue of the *Threepenny Review,* claims that the very fact that today a variety of different pornographies are now on the scene in mass market videos is good for feminism, and that to return to the time of repressing pornographic sexual representations would mean the resurgence of at least some elements of an underground tradition of misogyny.
13. See Barbara Presley Noble, "New Reminders on Harassment," *New York Times,* 25 (Aug. 15, 1993).
14. *Beauharnais v. Illinois,* 343 U.S. 250 (1952), abandoned in *New York Times v. Sullivan,* 376 U.S. 254 (1964) at 268–269.

15. See *Smith v. Collins*, 439 U.S. 916 (1978).

11. Why Academic Freedom?

1. I mean interpreting the social institution of academic freedom, not just identifying how far the law (including, in America, the Constitution) defines and protects that social institution, though the former is pertinent to the latter. There is, so far as I know, no law against the donor of an academic chair reserving the right to name its holders; but that would violate academic freedom. Nor is academic freedom the same as wise academic policy. It might be silly for a university English Department to turn itself entirely over to a trendy new form of criticism. But it would be a violation of academic freedom for the legislature to forbid this.
2. See Chapters 8, 9 and 10.
3. For a description of ethical individualism (though not under that name) see my *Foundations of Liberal Equality* (University of Utah Press, 1990).
4. *Rust v. Sullivan*, 111 U.S. 1759 (1991).
5. For an explanation of the idea of "moral harm," see my essay, "Principle, Policy, Procedure," in *A Matter of Principle* (Harvard University Press, 1985).
6. See my book *Life's Dominion: An Argument about Abortion, Euthanasia, and Individual Freedom* (Knopf, 1993).
7. A lower court in California recently invalidated the Stanford code as violating a state statute forbidding universities to impose stricter speech regulations than governments could impose. See "Court Overturns Stanford University Code Barring Bigoted Speech," *New York Times,* B8 (March 1, 1995).
8. People do have a right not to suffer from discrimination, which is different from ridicule or offense. They have a right not to be denied employment just out of prejudice against blacks or women or creationists or people of no imagination or very bad taste, for example.

12. Bork: The Senate's Responsibility

1. The idea of an *institutional* intention is deeply ambiguous, for example, and political judgment is required to decide which of the different meanings it might have is appropriate to constitutional adjudication. (See my book, *Law's Empire* [Harvard University Press, 1986], chap. 9.) And the original intention theory appears to be self-defeating, because there is persuasive historical evidence that the framers intended that their own interpretations of the abstract language they wrote should not be regarded as decisive in court. See H. Jefferson Powell, "The Original Understanding of Original Intent," *Harvard Law Review*, vol. 98 (1985), p. 885.

2. See Bork, "Neutral Principle and Some First Amendment Problems," *Indiana Law Journal,* vol. 47 (1971), pp. 12–15.
3. See Raoul Berger, *Government by Judiciary: The Transformation of the Fourteenth Amendment* (Harvard University Press, 1977), pp. 118–119.
4. See Bork's concurring opinion in *Ollman v. Evans,* 750 F. 2d 970 (1984).
5. For more general discussions of the same point in different contexts, see my *Taking Rights Seriously* (Harvard University Press, 1977), chap. 5, *A Matter of Principle* (Harvard University Press, 1986), chap. 2, and *Law's Empire,* chap. 9.
6. See, for example, *Craig v. Boren,* 429 U.S. 190 (1976).
7. I might have used many other areas of constitutional law to illustrate the point I have been making about the idea of original intention. In the 1971 article mentioned in note 2, for example, Bork offered a theory about the original intention behind the First Amendment's guaranty of freedom of speech. He said that the framers intended to limit constitutional protection to politically valuable speech, and that the First Amendment therefore does not prevent legislators from banning scientific works they disagree with or censoring novels they find unattractive. He recently announced that he long ago abandoned that view for the somewhat shaky reason that scientific works and novels may relate to politics (most of them do not). But he still apparently believes that the First Amendment has no application either to pornography or to what he regards as advocacy of revolution, on the ground that neither has any political value in his eyes.

   He offers no justification, however, for attributing to the framers the relatively narrow principle that only political ideas deserve protection. No doubt they focused on political censorship, which was one of the evils they had fought a revolution against. But since Milton's *Areopagitica,* at least, it had been widely supposed that political speech must not be censored for a more general and abstract reason that applies to other forms and occasions of speech as well: that truth will emerge only after unrestrained investigation and communication. (A tract in favor of free speech published in 1800 argued that "there is no natural right more perfect or absolute, than that of investigating every subject which concerns us.") So once again the choice of which principle to attribute to the framers will be decisive. If we concentrate on their special concern about political speech, Bork's formulation seems more appropriate. If we look instead to the philosophical antecedents of that special concern, it does not. We need an argument to justify the choice, not a flat declaration that one formulation does and the other does not capture the original intention.
8. He does so in a lecture to the University of San Diego School of Law on November 18, 1985, reprinted in the *San Diego Law Review,* vol. 23, no. 4 (1986), p. 823. Bork attempted to reply, in that lecture, to an argument by Dean Paul Brest of the Stanford Law School which was apparently similar to

the argument I have made here. Bork does not supply a reference to Brest's argument.

9. In an earlier article (*The New York Review of Books*, Nov. 8, 1984) I contrasted Bork's methods, as exhibited in the *Dronenburg* case, with the methods more traditional lawyers would have used.

10. Bork, "Neutral Principles," p. 10.

11. Bork, "Civil Rights—A Challenge," *The New Republic*, 19 (Aug. 31, 1963).

12. Bork, *Tradition and Morality in Constitutional Law*, The Francis Boyer Lectures, published by the American Enterprise Institute for Public Policy Research in 1984.

13. Bork did not, however, read Devlin very carefully. Devlin thinks the majority has a right to enforce its moral views only in unusual circumstances, when unorthodox behavior would actually threaten cultural continuity, and he does not think that his views would support making private homosexual acts between consenting adults criminal. See Patrick Devlin, *The Enforcement of Morals* (Oxford University Press, 1965).

13. What Bork's Defeat Meant

1. Nixon's nominations of Clement F. Haynsworth and G. Harold Carswell, and Johnson's promotion of Abe Fortas to the office of Chief Justice, were all rejected, but in each case the announced reasons were doubts about the candidate's ethical or intellectual qualifications. Thirty-three Democrats did vote against Reagan's nomination of William Rehnquist, then an associate justice, to succeed Warren Burger as Chief Justice. But most of them felt it necessary to justify their votes on grounds of character—charges had been made that Rehnquist had not acted properly as a trustee in a family matter, and the deed to his vacation house contained an (invalid) racially restrictive covenant. Antonin Scalia, a very conservative law professor whom Reagan had appointed to the same circuit court on which Bork sat, and against whom no charges of personal fault had been brought, was confirmed as associate justice in Rehnquist's place with not a single vote against him.

2. The Peck advertisement made four claims about Bork's record. It said that he "defended poll taxes and literacy tests," which suggests that he approved these devices for keeping people from voting; in fact Bork argued only that the Constitution did not make the devices unconstitutional. It said he opposed the civil rights laws (as he did, in 1963) but failed to add that he has changed his mind since. It said he thinks that free speech does not apply to literature, art, and music; without adding that, though he took that position without qualification in 1971, he recently said that freedom of speech does hold for the arts because, as he had not recognized then, the arts have a bearing on politics. It said, finally, that he "doesn't believe the Constitution protects your rights to

privacy," which is true, and, on the evidence of the hearings, the single most convincing charge the advertisement made.

3. Though he had argued for years that the equal protection clause of the Fourteenth Amendment gives special protection against discrimination only to racial and ethnic minorities, for example, so that the Supreme Court was wrong in supposing that it provided the same kind of protection to women, he offered the committee a very different view. He had also condemned the Supreme Court's holdings, in a long line of cases whose reasoning can be traced back to Oliver Wendell Holmes's famous dissents, that speech advocating violence is protected by the First Amendment, so long as the danger that it would actually incite violence is not clear and immediate. Over two days he seemed at first to withdraw his objection to the Court's view, and then to reassert it again. Some shifts were more subtle: he had said that the Court's opinion in *Griswold v. Connecticut,* forbidding states to outlaw contraceptives, could not be supported by any proper argument, and was therefore itself "unconstitutional." In the hearings he said he meant only to criticize the reasoning the Court had actually used in deciding the case, and had no opinion about whether a better argument for the Court's decision could now be found.

4. The *Wall Street Journal,* for example, in a series of editorials that amazed conservative as well as liberal lawyers, accused Bork's opponents of a "bloody campaign of distortion" and proposed that Reagan reappoint Bork, even after his defeat, during the next congressional recess (which would have ensured that Reagan could make no lasting appointment to the Supreme Court at all). The *Journal* also suggested that Bork's impending defeat caused a stock market fall, advised Reagan not to appoint any southern judges to the Court in order to punish the southern Democrats who had voted against him, and finally warned that the "victors" in the fight against him would "pay" for their victory. The *Journal*'s editorials were only the most conspicuously berserk of the articles and speeches and opinions published everywhere on the right.

5. In fact the jurisprudential part of Bork's claims is only a device for reporting conclusions reached in some other, more political way, because the idea of the framers' original intent is itself malleable and political decisions are necessary to justify describing that intent in any one way rather than another with respect to any particular issue. See Chapter 12.

6. 106 S. Ct. 2841 (1986).

7. The difference I am describing is important throughout constitutional law. Everyone now agrees, for example, that the Supreme Court made the right decision when it struck down school segregation in its 1954 *Brown* decision. But it matters very much whether that decision is treated as a sound act of judicial discretion, creating a new constitutional right for black schoolchildren out of admirable motives of sympathy or moral outrage, or as identifying,

within the Constitution conceived as a system of principle, a special principle condemning unfair discrimination against any group. Someone who treats the *Brown* decision as an act of discretion may not feel the same degree of compassion when he considers discrimination against women or the elderly. But someone who thinks *Brown* identified a general constitutional principle will be bound to explain, whatever he feels about those other groups, why that principle does not protect them as well.

8. *Neuschafer v. Whitley,* 816 F. 2d 1390 (1987).
9. *United States v. Leon,* dissenting opinion, 746 F. 2d 1488 (1983).
10. See *Spanger v. Pasadena,* 611 F. 2d 1239 (1979); *TOPIC v. Circle Realty,* 532 F. 2d 1273 (1976); and *AFSCME v. State of Washington,* 770 F. 2d 1401 (1985). In *TOPIC,* Kennedy dismissed a suit against real estate agents who "steer" home buyers to areas where their own race is dominant on the ground that the group bringing the suit were not actual buyers but only couples pretending they were in order to discover which agents engaged in that practice. The Supreme Court overruled his decision in a later case in which Judge Powell wrote the decision.
11. See *Beller v. Middendorf,* 632 F. 2d 788 (1980).
12. *U.S. v. Penn,* 647 F. 2d 876 (1980).
13. *Pierce v. Society of Sisters,* 268 U.S. 510 (1925).
14. *Chada v. U.S.,* 634 F. 2d 408 (1980).

14. Bork's Own Postmortem

1. See Chapters 12 and 13.
2. Robert H. Bork, *The Tempting of America: The Political Seduction of the Law* (Macmillan, 1990). All parenthetical page references appearing in the text and notes are to this book.
3. It is worth noting, either in support or in explanation of Bork's conspiracy theory, that nearly 40 percent of American law professors signed a petition opposing his confirmation. Kenneth B. Noble, "Bork Panel Ends Hearings," *New York Times,* B9 (Oct. 1, 1987).
4. Although Bork says he is against moral relativism (perhaps because the irresponsible view that liberals are moral relativists has become a shibboleth of the right), I know of no academic lawyer who is more firmly committed to relativism than Bork himself. See generally Robert H. Bork, "Neutral Principles and Some First Amendment Problems," *Ind. L.J.,* vol. 47 (1971), p. 1.
5. The parallel views have also been largely rejected in general jurisprudence and in other fields where the character of interpretation is debated. Few philosophers of law, in any legal culture, argue that a statute is only what its drafters intended, and few literary critics insist that a novel means only what its author meant.

6. See generally Ronald Dworkin, *Taking Rights Seriously* (Harvard University Press, 1977), and Ronald Dworkin, *Law's Empire* (Harvard University Press, 1986), for previous discussions. See also Paul Brest, "The Fundamental Rights Controversy: The Essential Contradictions of Normative Constitutional Scholarship," *Yale L.J.*, vol. 90 (1981), p. 1063.

7. See Dworkin, *Taking Rights Seriously* at 133, 226–229 (cited in note 6). The draftsmen deliberately chose a general formulation—"equal protection" shall not be denied to "any person"—rather than limiting the clause's application to black equality or racial equality. The language itself, read alone, does not suggest the various limitations that Bork places on it; rather, it leaves room for evolving conceptions of what equal protection means.

8. See generally Dworkin, *Law's Empire* (cited in note 6).

9. "The role of a judge committed to the philosophy of original understanding," he says, "is not to 'choose a level of abstraction.' Rather, it is to find the meaning of a text—a process which includes finding its degree of generality, which is part of its meaning" (p. 145). This is an opaque advice. The problem a judge "committed" to original understanding has is not deciding what an abstract provision says—it says something as abstract as the words it uses— but deciding what impact it has in concrete cases. He is trying to establish the Constitution's meaning in that sense, and it is no help to tell him that he must first discover its meaning.

10. Perhaps Bork senses that this discussion in effect confesses the emptiness of the original understanding doctrine. For there is much whistling in the dark in the discussion's neighborhood. "The precise congruence of individual decisions with what the ratifiers intended can never be known," he writes, "but it can be estimated whether, across a body of decisions, judges have in general vindicated the principle given into their hands" (p. 163). Of course that can be estimated. But different judges with different "minor premises" will estimate it differently because the premise will determine what each counts as vindication. "Of at least equal importance," Bork continues, "the attempt to adhere to the principles actually laid down in the historic Constitution will mean that entire ranges of problems and issues are placed off-limits for judges . . . That abstinence has the inestimable value of preserving democracy in those areas of life that the Founders intended to leave to the people's self-government" (p. 163). But the set of issues any judge regards as placed off limits is fixed by: (1) the judge's view about how best to capture the distinction between principle and application in determining what "the founders intended," which will depend on that judge's interpretive schema; and (2) what the judge considers the appropriate "minor premises" in applying the principle to concrete cases. For example, it is difficult to think of any political controversy that someone armed with the appropriate interpretive schema and set of minor premises would not regard as a matter of equality, and therefore brought within the

Constitution by the Fourteenth Amendment. Of course, the Constitution, properly interpreted, did designate many controversies as political rather than constitutional. But this conclusion results from choosing the appropriate interpretive schema, justified by the most attractive foundational interpretation of our constitutional democracy, not by virtue of any consequence of the concept of original understanding itself.
11. 109 S. Ct. 706 (1989).

15. The Thomas Nomination

1. See Thomas, "Why Black Americans Should Look to Conservative Policies," The Heritage Lectures, no. 8.
2. It is worth noting, however, that Professor Macedo has criticized almost every other opinion Thomas and other conservative lawyers hold. Macedo denies that fetuses have natural rights that entitle states to prohibit abortion from the moment of conception, for example, though he does think that some compromise should be struck about abortion that allows prohibition before the third trimester. In a recent book, *The New Right and the Constitution*, he sharply attacked Bork and other new-right lawyers for their moral cynicism, and for their hypocritical use of the original intention method of constitutional interpretation.
3. Chief Justice Rehnquist and Justice White dissented from the original decision in *Roe v. Wade*, and have in different ways continued to display their opposition. Justice Scalia dissented in the recent case of *Webster v. Reproductive Health Services*, which limited the right of abortion in various ways but stopped short of repealing *Roe* altogether, for the sole purpose of declaring his view that *Roe* should be repealed as soon as possible. Justice Blackmun wrote the decision in *Roe*, and has often stated his continued defense of that decision. Justices Stevens, O'Connor, Kennedy, and Souter have either written or joined in opinions from which general positions about abortion may be inferred.
4. See Chapter 14 and also Lawrence Sager's review of Bork's book *The Tempting of America: The Official Seduction of the Law* in *The New York Review of Books*, (Oct. 25, 1990).
5. Of course that problem does not arise if we accept a more extreme version of the framers' intention view: that judges should never recognize any concrete constitutional right they do not believe the framers themselves would have recognized as implied by their abstract clauses. But no one could be confirmed who really held that view, because that view entails that major landmark decisions of the Court, including many Thomas announced he supported, such as *Brown v. Board of Education* and *Griswold v. Connecticut*, were

wrong because the framers did not intend to outlaw racial segregation or to recognize a right to use contraceptives.

6. "Notes on Original Intent," submitted by Judge Thomas to the Judiciary Committee.

7. See Thomas, "The Higher Law Background of the Privileges and Immunities Clause of the Fourteenth Amendment," *Harvard Journal of Law and Public Policy,* vol. 12 (1989).

8. See my article "'Natural Law' Revisited," *University of Florida Law Review,* vol. 34 (1982), p. 165.

9. In fact many people who hold this view in substance would not describe it as appealing to "natural law," which is a term more often used by the view's detractors, perhaps because of the term's historical associations with religion. They prefer to say simply that judges must take people's moral rights into account in deciding how to interpret the abstract clauses of the Constitution. But the substance of their view is the view I describe in the text.

10. See note 6, above, pp. 63, 64.

11. Remarks of Clarence Thomas at California State University, San Bernadino, April 25, 1988.

12. See Chapter 6.

13. I try to describe what the constraint of integrity means in practice in my book, *Law's Empire* (Harvard University Press, 1986).

17. Learned Hand

1. James Bradley Thayer, "The Origin and Scope of the American Doctrine of Constitutional Law," *Harvard Law Review,* vol. 7, no. 3 (Oct. 25, 1893), p. 129.

2. Hand did, however, say that there were good arguments why a community might entrust the protection of free speech to judges even though, in his view, our Constitution does not.

3. Gunther suggests that Hand's treatment of *Brown* in his Holmes Lectures was the result of pressure by Frankfurter. Hand thought that if the Court's decision could be seen to rest on the assumption that the Fourteenth Amendment in its own terms allows no racial distinction whatever, the decision would be defensible, because it would not then have been the result of the Supreme Court's substituting its judgment for the legislatures' about whether discrimination was particularly offensive or unwise in the specific case of education. Frankfurter pressed Hand not to take that view of the decision, however, because Frankfurter did not think it would be wise for the Court soon to invalidate laws prohibiting interracial marriage, as it would have to do if it really had decided that all racial distinctions were unconstitutional. But Hand had his own reasons for rejecting that view of what the Court had decided in

Brown, and they were persuasive. Chief Justice Warren's opinion for the Court deployed elaborate sociological argument to explain why, at least in contemporary circumstances, separate educational facilities for blacks were inherently unequal, an explanation that would not have been necessary, as Hand pointed out in his lectures, had the Court intended a blanket invalidation of all racial distinction.

4. For Thayer's influence, see Harlan B. Phillips, *Felix Frankfurter Reminisces* (Reynal and Co., 1960), pp. 299–300. I should point out that Frankfurter and Holmes served on the Supreme Court, where the pressure on a judge to respond to deeply felt injustice is strong, and Hand did not. But even so it is striking that Hand's version of judicial restraint was so much more austere than their version. We cannot explain that austerity simply by pointing to the bad conservative decisions the Supreme Court was making when his judicial career began, because we can think these decisions wrong for two different kinds of reasons. The justices who held that maximum hour laws were unconstitutional argued in two steps: first, that the due process clause obliges judges to declare unconstitutional any infringement of an individual liberty so basic that it is essential to a free society, and, second, that freedom of employers and employees to enter into any contract they might think in their best interests is such a liberty.

We might say, as Hand insisted, that the first step in this argument is wrong: that judges do not have legitimate power to declare infringements of fundamental freedoms unconstitutional. But we might also say that this first step was right and the second was wrong, because the right of employers to engage people to work burdensome hours is not among the fundamental liberties essential to a free community. It is now generally agreed, after all, that freedom of contract is not a basic liberty: governments regularly restrict the power of contract not only to protect economically vulnerable citizens from bad bargains they might be forced to accept, but also to protect the community from the effects of contracts with injurious social or economic consequences, including, for example, contracts that restrain trade and competition.

Nor does history show that the Supreme Court makes mistakes about which liberties are fundamental so often that it would be better to deny it the power to make such judgments altogether. In fact, the most serious mistakes the Supreme Court has made, over its history, have been not in striking down laws it ought to have upheld, but in upholding laws it ought to have struck down. Most lawyers now agree that the court made a grave mistake, in 1896, in sanctioning Jim Crow legal arrangements under the "separate but equal" formula of *Plessy v. Ferguson.* Nor have the Court's mistakes in upholding bad laws been confined to racial matters. Lewis Powell, a conservative justice, said after his resignation that the most serious mistake he had made was in supplying the crucial fifth vote in the 1986 *Bowers v. Hardwick* case, which upheld laws making adult, consensual homosexual acts a crime.

5. Philippa Strum, *Louis D. Brandeis: Justice for the People* (Harvard University Press, 1984), p. 361.

6. Learned Hand, *The Bill of Rights* (Harvard University Press, 1958), pp. 75–76.

7. Learned Hand, *The Spirit of Liberty* (Knopf, 1952), p. 190.

8. Thayer, "The Origin and Scope of the American Doctrine of Constitutional Law."

9. Learned Hand, *The Bill of Rights*, pp. 73–74.

10. See chap. 5 of my book *Life's Dominion* (Knopf, 1993) and my "Equality, Democracy, and the Constitution: We the People in Court," *Alberta Law Review*, vol. 28, no. 2 (1990), p. 324.

11. See Christopher L. Eisgruber, "Is the Supreme Court an Educative Institution?" *New York University Law Review*, vol. 67, no. 5 (1992), p. 961.

Sources

Chapter 1
Originally published as "The Great Abortion Case" in *The New York Review of Books,* June 29, 1989.

Chapter 2
Originally published as "The Future of Abortion" in *The New York Review of Books,* September 28, 1989.

Chapter 3
Originally published as "Unenumerated Rights: Whether and How *Roe* Should be Overruled" in *University of Chicago Law Review,* vol. 59 (1992).

Chapter 4
Originally published as "The Center Holds!" in *The New York Review of Books,* August 13, 1992, p. 29.

Chapter 5
Originally published as "The Right to Death" in *The New York Review of Books,* January 31, 1991. Addendum originally published as "When Is It Right to Die," *New York Times,* May 17, 1994.

Chapter 6
Originally published as "The Reagan Revolution and the Supreme Court" in *The New York Review of Books,* July 18, 1991.

Chapter 7
Originally published in *The New York Review of Books,* February 26, 1987.

Chapter 8
Originally published as "The Coming Battles over Free Speech" in *The New York Review of Books*, June 11, 1992.

Chapter 9
Originally published as "Liberty and Pornography" in *The New York Review of Books*, August 15, 1991. Addendum originally published as "The Unbearable Cost of Liberty" in *Index on Censorship*, vol. 24, no. 3 (May/June 1995), p. 43.

Chapter 10
Originally published as "Women and Pornography" in *The New York Review of Books*, October 21, 1993. Addendum originally published as a letter to the editor, *The New York Review of Books*, March 3, 1994.

Chapter 11
To be published as "We Need a New Interpretation of Academic Freedom" in Louis Menand, ed., *Academic Freedom and Its Future* (Chicago: University of Chicago Press, 1996).

Chapter 12
Originally published as "The Bork Nomination" in *The New York Review of Books*, August 13, 1987.

Chapter 13
Originally published as "From Bork to Kennedy" in *The New York Review of Books*, December 17, 1987.

Chapter 14
Originally published as "Bork's Jurisprudence" in *University of Chicago Law Review*, vol. 57 (1990).

Chapter 15
Originally published as "Justice for Clarence Thomas" in *The New York Review of Books*, November 7, 1991.

Chapter 16
Originally published as "One Year Later, the Debate Goes On" in *The New York Times Book Review*, October 25, 1992.

Chapter 17
Originally published as "Mr. Liberty" in *The New York Review of Books*, August 11, 1994.

Index

Abortion, 1, 43, 83–116, 149, 162; arguments about, 83–92, 310, 345; and Catholicism, 363n36; conservative views of, 44, 309, 315; and contraception, 50–51, 55, 126, 153, 357n10, 358n17; and feminist movement, 227; information about, 147–148, 208–209, 251, 357n11; and intrinsic value of life, 120, 145, 369n6; and mandatory waiting period, 122–123; and natural rights, 318; parental consent to, 118, 358n13; polls on, 44; right to, 5, 12, 36, 78, 79, 126, 357n8, 362n27, 386n2; and the states, 48–49, 54–55, 57–68, 84, 87, 88, 89, 92, 96, 112–113, 120, 121–122, 123, 126, 140, 147, 153, 154, 308, 311, 352nn4, 6, 358nn12, 17, 367n9; statistics on, 355n23, 366n74; technology and, 116, 154; and viability, 57, 66, 113, 115, 117, 124, 127, 355nn21, 22, 356n2, 358n12, 363n37; vs. adoption, 353n8, 362n28. See also Right: to choose; Right: to life; Right: to privacy; *Roe v. Wade; Webster v. Missouri Reproductive Services*
Abortion clinics, 44, 122, 366n75
Abortion Control Act (Pennsylvania), 118
Abrams case, 197, 200, 202

Academic freedom, 166, 244–260; and decency, 254, 255–256, 260; and equality, 254; ethical role of, 250; and free speech, 247–248, 250; and insensitivity, 244, 256, 257–258; and intentional *vs.* negligent insult, 255, 256; and legislatures, 246–247, 380n1a; and professors, 251–252, 257, 260; relativist challenge to, 246
The Accused (film), 206
Adams, John Quincy, 318
Adams, Sam, 178, 184, 185
Adarand Constructors, Inc. v. Pena, 43
Adler, Renata, 167, 194, 371n3, 372nn5, 6, 373nn12, 15; *Reckless Disregard,* 168–186, 190, 191, 192
Affirmative action, 1, 31, 43, 157–161, 350n11; and judges, 12, 37, 74, 81, 361n22; and natural rights, 318; opposition to, 3, 307–308, 315, 317, 326; and quotas, 294–295, 299–300; and set-aside programs, 157–158, 159, 160, 317; and Supreme Court, 83, 267; views of blacks on, 325
Althans, Ewald, 224
American Bar Association, 279, 331
American Enterprise Institute, 274
American Medical Association, 45, 56, 62
American Nazi party, 221
Angelou, Maya, 327

393

81, 89, 104, 105, 110, 119, 125, 126, 127, 149, 300, 308, 309, 314, 317, 334, 337, 350n10, 354n13, 357n8, 388n4; equal protection clause of, 7, 8, 9–10, 11, 12, 13, 14, 47–48, 72, 73, 78, 79, 110, 111, 125, 127, 149, 153, 158, 159, 230, 234, 241, 267, 268, 270, 271, 274, 280, 294, 295, 296–297, 299, 300, 309, 314, 315, 337, 350n10, 354n13, 383n3, 385n7; and First Amendment, 73, 105, 234, 373n13; framers of, 9, 10; interpretation of, 150
Framers of U.S. Constitution, 8–10, 80, 286, 315, 343, 350n11, 373n12, 386n5; and abortion, 357n8; and capital punishment, 300–301; and First Amendment, 187, 199, 381n7; legal intentions of, 292, 380n1b; linguistic intentions of, 285, 291. *See also* Original intention theory
Frankfurter, Felix, 335, 340, 341, 342, 387n3, 388n4
Franklin, Benjamin, 342
Fraser, Elizabeth, 231
Freedom, 19; of choice, 64, 93, 114, 115, 117, 119, 121, 152, 366n1; and civil rights, 274; and constitutionalism, 21–26; of contract, 388n4; cost of, 226; economic, 109; of expression, 206, 231–232; positive *vs.* negative, 21, 215–216, 217, 218, 220, 221; of the press, 72, 73, 165, 168, 170, 173, 177, 187, 188, 189, 191–192, 195, 198, 199, 211, 374n2. *See also* Academic freedom; Free speech
Freedom of Choice Act, 366n1
Freedoms, personal, 12–13, 41, 42, 49, 64, 95, 119, 313
Free speech, 1, 2, 3, 21, 25, 32, 58, 148, 195–213, 215, 337, 338; and academic freedom, 247–248, 250, 259; and democracy, 165–166, 221; and equality, 166, 234, 235, 236, 239, 241; in Germany, 223–224; and government money, 148, 208; in Great Britain, 16; history of, 196–197, 227; limitation of, 188, 189, 208, 218, 236, 259, 338–339, 360n16, 381n7; negative liberty

of, 218; and prior restraint, 197, 198, 199, 360n16; and racism, 199, 204, 205, 227; right of, 7, 8, 72, 73, 78, 89, 165, 196–197, 232, 352n6, 375n18; and sexism, 199, 204, 205, 256, 257, 260; theory of, 18; two kinds of justification of, 201–209, 374nn8, 13. *See also* First Amendment; Pornography
Fried, Charles, 45, 48, 50, 51, 59, 149–162, 353n9, 360n21; *Order and Law: Arguing the Reagan Revolution,* 148, 150–162, 370nn6, 7, 8, 371nn14, 15
Friedman, Milton, 109
Fuller, Lon, 316
Furet, François, 71

Gag rule. *See* Abortion: information about
Galbraith, John Kenneth, 22
Gattozzi, Bernard, 184–185, 186
Gemayel, Bashir, 167, 173, 174
Gender discrimination, 78, 79, 127, 156, 234, 257, 272, 274, 285, 295, 299, 300
Germany, 20, 23, 223–224
Gertz case, 211
Gideon v. Wainwright, 198
Gillette case, 108
Ginsburg, Douglas H., 276, 284
Ginsburg, Ruth Bader, 6
Goldberg, Arthur, 189, 374n7
Gould, Milton, 167
Government: detached *vs.* derivative claims of, 84–87, 94; and free speech, 200, 202, 203, 208; by judiciary, 41; legitimate concerns of, 95–98, 113–114, 138; power of, 188, 364n45, 365n65; and taxes, 109
Grassley, Charles, 314
Great Britain: constitution of, 16–17; electoral system in, 27
Greenhouse, Linda, 367n2
Grey, Thomas, 288
Griggs v. Duke Power Co., 155, 156, 157, 160, 371n12
Griswold, Erwin, 161
Griswold v. Connecticut, 50, 81, 124, 320, 354n12, 361n22, 367n7, 370nn6, 7, 386n5; Robert Bork on, 103, 281, 282, 285, 354n14, 383n3;